MILITARY HISTORY SUPREMO

ESSAYS IN HONOUR OF DAVID HORNER AM FASSA

MILITARY HISTORY SUPREMO

ESSAYS IN HONOUR OF DAVID HORNER AM FASSA

EDITED BY JOAN BEAUMONT AND GARTH PRATTEN

ANU PRESS

ANU PRESS

Published by ANU Press
The Australian National University
Canberra ACT 2600, Australia
Email: anupress@anu.edu.au

Available to download for free at press.anu.edu.au

ISBN (print): 9781760466831
ISBN (online): 9781760466848

WorldCat (print): 1506273050
WorldCat (online): 1506274586

DOI: 10.22459/MHS.2025

This title is published under a Creative Commons Attribution-NonCommercial-NoDerivatives 4.0 International (CC BY-NC-ND 4.0) licence.

The full licence terms are available at creativecommons.org/licenses/by-nc-nd/4.0/legalcode

Cover design and layout by ANU Press. Cover photograph: Professor David Horner. Courtesy of David Horner.

This book is published under the aegis of the Asia-Pacific Security Studies editorial board of ANU Press.

This edition © 2025 ANU Press

Contents

List of illustrations	vii
List of contributors	ix
Acknowledgements	xv
Foreword Robert J O'Neill	xvii
Introduction Joan Beaumont and Garth Pratten	1

Part I: David Horner as soldier, scholar and colleague

1. Understanding the 'mechanism of war': the making of a soldier–scholar — 15
   Garth Pratten
2. Living the legacy: David Horner and Official History in Australia — 47
   Craig Stockings

Part II: Strategy and high command

3. The psychology of strategic decision-making: Ambon 1941–42 — 65
   Joan Beaumont
4. Why Australia has gone to war: some reflections on the nineteenth century — 87
   Jean Bou
5. History frames policy: David Horner and the future of Australia's defence — 105
   Hugh White

Part III: Command and commanders

6. A 'Crisis of Command' in Bengal, 1849–50: a Hornerian analysis — 127
   Peter Stanley

7. Filling the gap: Lieutenant General Sir Harold 'Hooky' Walker KCB, KCMG, DSO: a study in command   151
Chris Roberts

Part IV: Coalition warfare

8. The four pillars of human interoperability for multinational military integration: the Australian experience   187
Steven Paget

9. 'Everybody doing their thing': coalition warfare in southern Afghanistan, 2006–10   217
Rhys Crawley and Garth Pratten

Part V: Intelligence

10. Codebreaking in the Asia-Pacific War: struggle and triumph, May 1942 to December 1944   251
Richard Frank

11. David Horner, intelligence history and Venona   269
John Blaxland

Part VI: Changing environments

12. The history of the Australian Defence Force and space   291
Tristan Moss

13. Soldiers as peacekeepers, peacekeepers as soldiers: the Australian experience   313
Peter Londey

14. Disappointing the dragon: an Australian strategy and a fourth armed service for the grey zone   339
Bob Breen

Part VII: Epilogue

15. Australia's war dead: government policy, military practice and the Vietnam War   365
Kate Ariotti

Appendix 1: David Horner: professional career   387

Appendix 2: David Horner: publications   391

List of illustrations

Maps

Map 3.1: The Japanese offensive in Southeast Asia, December 1941 – March 1942	71
Map 6.1: British India in Napier's time	132
Map 7.1: Ottoman counterattacks at Anzac, 27 April 1915	159
Map 7.2: The August Offensive feints at Anzac, 6–7 August 1915	162
Map 7.3: Gough and Walker's attack options at Pozières, 20 July 1916	168
Map 7.4: Operations beyond Pozières, 18–21 August 1916	169
Map 7.5: First Australian Division operations against Boursies, Demicourt and Hermies, 8–9 April 1917	172
Map 9.1: ISAF expansion, 2003–06	220
Map 9.2: Regional Command South, 2006–10	223

Figures

Figure 6.1: Sir Charles Napier depicted in a characteristically heroic pose by the Calcutta artist Colesworthey Grant	129
Figure 6.2: A sharp satire on the relationship between political and military authority	146
Figure 6.3: A cartoon created after Napier's departure from India and shortly before his death, parodying Napier's tendency to pathos	148
Figure 9.1: ISAF Regional Command strengths, 2006–10	225
Figure 9.2: ISAF and RC South commanders, 2006–10	231
Figure 11.1: Allied intelligence organisation in the South-West Pacific Area, May 1943	271

Images

Image 1: David Horner, aged 17, in his Prince Alfred College uniform, Adelaide, 1965 — 177

Image 2: Lieutenant David Horner after joining the 3rd Battalion, the Royal Australian Regiment, 1970 — 178

Image 3: Lieutenant David Horner with his Platoon Sergeant Brian Payne, Nui Dat, South Vietnam, 1971 — 179

Image 4: A very lean Lieutenant David Horner showing the effects of the extensive patrolling that characterised his deployment, South Vietnam, 1971 — 180

Image 5: Lieutenant Colonel David Horner describing the battle for Finschhafen during a Joint Services Staff College (JSSC) tour, Papua New Guinea, 1989 — 180

Image 6: Dr David Horner filming an interview for the documentary *Kokoda: The Bloody Track*, Canberra, 1992 — 181

Image 7: Professor David Horner with the Governor-General, Quentin Bryce, after being made a Member of the Order of Australia for 'service to higher education in the area of Australian military history and heritage as a researcher, author and academic', Canberra, 2009 — 182

Image 8: Professor David Horner speaking at the launch of Volume I of the Official History of Australian Peacekeeping, Humanitarian and Post–Cold War Operations, Australian War Memorial, Canberra, 2013 — 183

List of contributors

Kate Ariotti is an Australian Research Council DECRA Senior Research Fellow in the School of Historical and Philosophical Inquiry at the University of Queensland. She is working on a history of the Australian war corpse and has published on the treatment of Australian war dead, as well as the experiences of Australian prisoners of war and the ways in which Australians have remembered and commemorated wars. Her first book, *Captive Anzacs: Australian POWs of the Ottomans during the First World War* (2018), was shortlisted for the inaugural Les Carlyon Literary Prize. Before commencing her position at the University of Queensland in 2022, Kate worked in the Military History section of the Australian War Memorial and as a Senior Lecturer in the School of Humanities and Social Sciences at the University of Newcastle. She is the series editor of the Australian Army Historical Collection.

Joan Beaumont is Professor Emerita in the Strategic and Defence Studies Centre at The Australian National University. She has published extensively on Australia in the two world wars and the Great Depression, including the multiple award-winning *Broken Nation: Australians in the Great War* (2013). Her 1988 study of Gull Force, the Australian force committed to Ambon in 1941, was republished in revised form by NewSouth Publishing in 2025.

John Blaxland is Director of the North America Liaison Office and Professor of International Security and Intelligence Studies at the Strategic and Defence Studies Centre at The Australian National University. A former Army officer, his publications include *Revealing Secrets: An Unofficial History of Australian Signals Intelligence and the Advent of Cyber* (2023); *The US–Thai Alliance and Asian International Relations* (2021); *Niche Wars: Australia in Afghanistan and Iraq, 2001–2014* (2020); *In From the Cold: Reflections on Australia's Korean War* (2020); *The Secret Cold War: The Official History of ASIO, 1975–1989*, vol. III of The Official History of ASIO (with Rhys Crawley, 2016); *The Protest Years: The Official History of ASIO, 1963–1975,* vol. II of The Official History of ASIO (2015); *The Australian Army from Whitlam to Howard* (2014); and *Strategic Cousins: Australian and Canadian Expeditionary Forces and the British and American Empires* (2006).

Jean Bou is an honorary senior lecturer at the Strategic and Defence Studies Centre at The Australian National University. He has written or edited 10 books on aspects of Australian military history. He first worked with David Horner on the second edition of the history of the Royal Australian Regiment, *Duty First: A History of the Royal Australian Regiment* (2008), and subsequently became a member of the team for the Official History of Australian Peacekeeping, Humanitarian and Post–Cold War Operations, writing large portions of Volume IV of that series, *The Limits of Peacekeeping* (2019).

Bob Breen graduated from Duntroon in 1973 and transferred to the Army Reserve in 1990. By this time, he had published his first Australian military history book. He published several more before completing his PhD at The Australian National University in 2006 and joining the team writing the Official History of Australian Peacekeeping, Humanitarian and Post–Cold War Operations, contributing to Volume IV and authoring Volume V, *The Good Neighbour: Australian Peace Support Operations in the Pacific Islands, 1980–2006* (2016). After his retirement in December 2022, Deakin University appointed him as an Honorary Professor at the Centre for Future Defence and National Security, Australian War College.

Rhys Crawley is a senior lecturer at the UNSW Canberra, and an author of the Official History of Australian Operations in Iraq and Afghanistan. He serves on the editorial advisory board of the *Australian Army Journal*, having previously worked at the Australian War Memorial and The Australian National University. His books include *The Long Search for Peace: Observer Missions and Beyond, 1947–2006* (with Peter Londey and David Horner, 2019); *Gallipoli: New Perspectives on the Mediterranean Expeditionary Force, 1915–16* (edited with Michael LoCicero, 2019); *Intelligence and the Function of Government* (edited with Daniel Baldino, 2018); *The Secret Cold War: The Official History of ASIO, 1975–1989*, vol. III of The Official History of ASIO (with John Blaxland, 2016); and *Climax at Gallipoli: The Failure of the August Offensive* (2014).

Richard Frank is an internationally recognised leading authority on the Asia-Pacific War. He published his first book *Guadalcanal: The Definitive Account of the Landmark Battle* in 1990. His second work, *Downfall: The*

End of the Imperial Japanese Empire (1999), has been called one of the six best books in English about the Second World War. Both Random House books won awards and became main selections of the History Book Club. In 2007, he completed *MacArthur* as part of the Palgrave Great Generals series. In addition to his numerous appearances on television and radio, he was a consultant for the epic HBO miniseries, *The Pacific*. Richard Frank serves on the Board of Presidential Counselors of the National World War II Museum in New Orleans, US, and has served for a term as head of that body. The first volume of his trilogy on the Asia-Pacific War 1937–45, *Tower of Skulls: A History of The Asia-Pacific War, July 1937 – May 1942*, published in March 2020, was a finalist for the Gilder Lehrman Prize for Military History 2021.

Peter Londey holds a PhD from Monash University on politics at Delphi in the fourth century BCE, but his career has been split between teaching in Classics, especially ancient Greek history, and a long period as a senior historian at the Australian War Memorial. Peter Londey curated the Memorial's first two major exhibitions on peacekeeping and wrote the first book-length history of Australian peacekeeping, *Other People's Wars* (2004). As a member of the team writing the Official History of Australian Peacekeeping, Humanitarian and Post–Cold War Operations, he was the lead author of Volume I, *The Long Search for Peace: Observer Missions and Beyond, 1947–2006* (with Rhys Crawley and David Horner, 2020). He is now attached to the School of History at The Australian National University.

Tristan Moss is a senior lecturer in history at UNSW Canberra. He is the author of *Guarding the Periphery: The Australian Army in Papua New Guinea, 1951–75* (2017); he also co-edited *Beyond Combat: Australian Military Activity Away from the Battlefields* (2018) and *Fighting Australia's Cold War: The Nexus of Strategy and Operations in a Multipolar Asia, 1945–1965* (2021). Tristan Moss previously worked at the Australian Command and Staff College, on the Official History of Peacekeeping, Humanitarian and Post–Cold War Operations, and on the Official History of Australian Operations in Afghanistan, Iraq and East Timor at the Australian War Memorial.

Steven Paget is Senior Development Lead, Research and Knowledge Exchange at Anglia Ruskin University Peterborough in the UK. Previously, he was Military Programmes Director at the University of Lincoln; and Reader in International Security and War Studies and the University of Portsmouth's Director of Air and Space Power Education at Royal Air Force

College Cranwell. His research focuses on the dynamics of multinational military cooperation, with a focus on the relationship between the armed forces of Australia, the United Kingdom and the United States. He is the author of *The Dynamics of Coalition Naval Warfare: The Special Relationship at Sea* (2017) and editor of *Allies in Air Power: A History of Multinational Air Operations* (2020).

Garth Pratten is a member of the Strategic and Defence Studies Centre at The Australian National University and series editor of the Australian Army Campaigns Series. A historian by training, he has previously worked for the Australian Army's Training Command and the Australian War Memorial. He also taught in the Department of War Studies at the Royal Military Academy Sandhurst. Among his research interests are the experience of command and the conduct of military operations. He was a member of the team that, under the leadership of David Horner, produced the Official History of Australian Peacekeeping, Humanitarian and Post–Cold War Operations.

Chris Roberts AM CSC saw operational service in South Vietnam with the 3rd Special Air Service Squadron. More senior appointments included, Commanding Officer, Special Air Service Regiment; Commander of the Special Forces; Director General, Corporate Planning—Army; and Commander, Northern Command. Following his Army career, he held executive appointments with the Multiplex Group. Chris Roberts is the author of *Chinese Strategy and the Spratly Islands Dispute* (1996), and the highly acclaimed *The Landing at Anzac, 1915* (2015). He co-authored *Anzacs on the Western Front* (2018) and *The Artillery at Anzac: Adaptation, Innovation and Education* (2021), and has contributed chapters to books on strategy and the Great War.

Peter Stanley recently retired as Research Professor at the UNSW Canberra. A longstanding specialist in Australian military social history, he was Principal Historian at the Australian War Memorial, where he worked from 1980 to 2007. He has published 50 books, including *Bad Characters: Sex, Crime, Mutiny, Murder and the Australian Imperial Force* (2010), which jointly won the Prime Minister's Prize for Australian History in 2011. While at UNSW Canberra from 2013 to 2023, Peter returned to the military history of British India, the subject of his 1993 Australian National University PhD thesis, writing *Die in Battle, Do Not Despair: The Indians on Gallipoli, 1915* (2015); *'Terriers' in India: British Territorials, 1914–19* (2023); *Hul! Hul!: The Suppression of the Santal Rebellion, Bengal, 1855*; and

John Company's Armies: The Military Forces of British India 1824–57 (2022). His most recent book is *Beyond the Broken Years: Australian Military History in 1000 Books* (2024).

Craig Stockings is Head of School, Humanities and Social Sciences, UNSW Canberra, and Official Historian of Australian Operations in Iraq, Afghanistan and East Timor. Craig is a graduate of both the Australian Defence Force Academy and the Royal Military College, Duntroon. He has published a wide range of scholarly articles, book chapters and books in the field, most notably: *Bardia: Myth, Reality and the Heirs of Anzac* (2009); *Swastika over the Acropolis: Re-interpreting the Nazi Invasion of Greece in World War II*, History of Warfare, vol. 92 (with Associate Professor Eleanor Hancock, 2009); *Letters from the Veldt: The Imperial Advance to Pretoria Through the Eyes of Edward Hutton and His Brigade of Colonials* (2020) and *Britannia's Shield: Lieutenant-General Sir Edward Hutton and Late Victorian Imperial Defence* (2018). The first volume of the Official History series, *Born of Fire and Ash: Australian Operations in Response to the East Timor Crisis of 1999–2000,* was published in late 2022.

Hugh White is Professor Emeritus of Strategic Studies at The Australian National University in Canberra. He spent much of his career in the Australian Government, including as Chief of Staff to Defence Minister Kim Beazley, International Relations Adviser to Prime Minister Bob Hawke and Deputy Secretary for Strategy in the Department of Defence. Hugh White was the founding Director of the Australian Strategic Policy Institute and head of The Australian National University's Strategic and Defence Studies Centre. He was the principal author of the 2000 Defence White Paper. His major publications include three Quarterly Essays: *Power Shift: Australia's Future Between Washington and Beijing* (2010), *Without America: Australia in the New Asia* (2017) and *Sleepwalk to War: Australia's Unthinking Alliance with America* (2022). He has also written two books: *The China Choice: Why America Should Share Power* (2012), and *How to Defend Australia* (2019).

Acknowledgements

Any collection of essays involves many people. Our thanks go, first, to the scholars who contributed to this volume. Their eagerness to pay tribute to David Horner's intellectual, professional and personal impact on their own lives made this book possible. We are particularly grateful to Professor Emeritus RJ (Bob) O'Neill for so willingly and early providing a foreword. We regret that he did not live to see the volume in print.

The Strategic and Defence Studies Centre at The Australian National University provided the essential intellectual environment and financial support for the editing of the manuscript. This volume adds to a tradition of honouring its senior academics in this way.

We also thank Pauline Kerr and Frank Bongiorno (in their capacities as ANU Press editorial board members) for their encouragement and advice during the approval stages for the manuscript. The (anonymous) readers supplied detailed and helpful comments. Glenine Hamlyn was the careful and patient editor, and Karina Pelling of CartoGIS, ANU, supplied the excellent maps.

As ever, we acknowledge, too, the tolerance, interest and support of our families along the long journey: Carol Holmes and Alexander Pratten; and Diana Beaumont, Caroline Beaumont and Julia Rhyder. They are as glad as we are to see that we have reached the end!

Joan Beaumont and Garth Pratten

Foreword

Robert J O'Neill

David Horner's quiet successes in his professional career since the 1960s make it well worth careful study, especially by other historians of war, be they in their early or late careers. I am very grateful to Professors Joan Beaumont and Garth Pratten for their invitation to join in this celebration of David Horner's professional successes. It is not only the motivation and hard work that Horner has inspired in many others, but also his readiness to join with other historians, to further strengthen our understanding of the nature of the world in which we live, with its lack of regulation and control, and its capacity for sudden eruptions into very costly conflicts. We are very fortunate to have a scholar of Horner's quality to help us survive the vicissitudes of national and international life.

One of the most enjoyable aspects of getting to know David Horner has been discovering his capacity for intelligent, understanding and sympathetic comments on the experiences of others. Throughout his career, from the time I first came to know him through assessing his student essays in the 1960s to the present day, he has shown a high capacity for understanding others and putting life into what could be routine word portraits. My colleague in the History Department at Duntroon in the late 1960s, Alec Hill, shared this opinion with me. We could recognise that David was someone special in the field of the History of War, and we used to get together to share the enjoyment of teaching him, learning much from our student as a result.

David established a high reputation as a student in his first years at Duntroon in the late 1960s. This was a good time for his own development because the Royal Military College was going through a major academic transformation, resulting in its development into a body of university status, the Faculty of Military Studies of the University of New South Wales. The academic development of the Australian Army in the 1970s opened up choices and career possibilities that had not existed in the earlier years of the College's existence. Without setting out to become a professional historian, David Horner was able to take advantage of a much wider field of choice than most of his predecessors.

One of his early interests was the constant competition for control between the senior officers of the major national headquarters in New Guinea during the Second World War. He began his investigation of the outcomes of these dramas with the celebrated struggle over command and strategy in 1942–43 between the generals MacArthur and Blamey. Having gained the necessary financial support for work on a master's degree, David began his research in 1976. Alec Hill and I were asked to be his supervisors. We soon noted David's capacity for choosing the key questions on which to work before trying to unravel the complex chains of cause and effect that told the real story of the development of allied strategy from 1942 onwards.

David Horner, at the age of 30, had developed into an excellent historian. He had a master's degree and was well qualified to work on the key issues of our time. He returned from a year of war service as a platoon commander in Vietnam in 1971. There, as a young lieutenant, he had walked the soft, silent trails of the jungle at night, learning to conquer fear and distraction, and to recognise rocks and logs from enemy soldiers crouching in the darkness waiting to attack unwary passers-by.

While the conflict was raging between pro-war and anti-war audiences over Australian and American policy in Vietnam, Horner had moved back into the still-hidden depths of what Australians did during the Second World War, focusing on the disputes and differences between General Douglas MacArthur and the Australian commanders in New Guinea in that time. Having secured the necessary financial support through scholarships, he embarked on the preparation of his first major book, *Crisis of Command: Australian Generalship and the Japanese Threat, 1941–1943*.

Crisis of Command was a highly successful book and is still a major text on the development of strategy during the Second World War. Horner moved across to The Australian National University while completing *Crisis of Command* during the late 1970s. By that stage, I had moved from teaching at the Royal Military College to The Australian National University, becoming head of the Strategic and Defence Studies Centre, working with colleagues such as Tom Millar, Bruce Miller, Hedley Bull and Peter Hastings. David fitted well into this team, working on the roles of individual Australian soldiers in past wars, and helping me and others at the Centre develop some new strategic ideas for use in Australia's defence planning. These ideas were published by the University of Queensland Press as *Australian Defence Policy for the 1980s,* edited by David Horner and myself. Horner quickly learned the elements of editorship through this and another project on which we worked together, *New Directions in Strategic Thinking,* which resulted in another book, published by George Allen and Unwin in 1981.

In the following year, I moved to London to become director of the International Institute for Strategic Studies. Horner remained in Canberra, and our individual research projects diverged. However, we retained one close working link—the chairmanship of the Armed Services Working Party of the Australian Dictionary of Biography. I had accepted an invitation from the General Editor, Professor Douglas Pike, to serve on the working party in the 1970s, and soon I found myself chairperson of that body. I remained chairperson of the Armed Services Working Party into the 1990s. David Horner fully took on this role around 1996. Horner, by that point in his career, had gone on to higher things. He was commissioned to prepare the Official Histories of Australian peacekeeping operations. The histories comprised a six-volume series focusing on Africa and the Middle East in the 1980s and early 1990s. Horner then moved on to become an official historian for the Australian Security Intelligence Organisation, a broad challenge that he carried off very successfully, winning the Prime Minister's Literary Award for history in 2015. On the way to these successes, he wrote other books, such as *Strategic Command: General Sir John Wilton and Australia's Asian Wars* (Oxford University Press, 2005), a biographical study of General Sir John Wilton, Australia's senior soldier during the Vietnam War.

David Horner has been the author or editor of 32 books and major articles, many of which have won him awards, including a Fellowship of the Academy of the Social Sciences in Australia. He has also been appointed a Member of the Order of Australia. Hence, it is with very great pleasure and high regard that his working friends offer him the tributes made in this volume. David Horner has consistently produced excellent histories that give the reader deep insights into Australia's record at war over the past 50 years.

The late Robert J O'Neill

Introduction

Joan Beaumont and Garth Pratten

Our title for this volume is taken from David Horner's 2000 biography of long-serving Secretary of the Department of Defence, Sir Frederick Shedden, *Defence Supremo*.[1] The Cambridge Dictionary defines 'supremo' as 'the person in charge of an organization or who is considered to have the most skill and authority in a particular type of activity'.[2] It is an apt characterisation for Horner. While he was not literally 'in charge' of Australian military history as a discipline or profession, Horner is one of Australia's leading practitioners and advocates of it. His knowledge and experience command significant authority, his approach is widely emulated, and few who undertake any serious research in the field can do so without consulting Horner. He served for 25 years in the Australian Regular Army, including an operational deployment to South Vietnam, and his scholarship is underpinned by deep and authentic knowledge of the requirements and challenges of employing military force. In terms of the sheer scale of his publications—running to 19 sole-authored books, 19 co-authored and edited volumes and over 100 articles, chapters, reports and reference work entries—Horner has few peers in the Australian historical profession.

Horner is best known for his work on higher-level command: its theory, practice, and influence on events and organisations from the Boer War to the Iraq wars. His reputation in this field was established with his earliest sole-authored books *Crisis of Command: Australian Generalship and the Japanese Threat, 1941–1943* (1978) and *High Command: Australia and Allied Strategy*

---

1 David Horner, *Defence Supremo: Sir Frederick Shedden and the Making of Australian Defence Policy* (Sydney: Allen & Unwin, 2000).
2 *Cambridge Dictionary* (online ed.), Cambridge University Press & Assessment, 2004, dictionary.cambridge.org/dictionary/english/supremo.

1939–1945 (1982), which remain definitive works.³ Indeed, *High Command* has often been described as the 'missing volume' of the Australian Official History of the Second World War. Horner's four biographies—*General Vasey's War* (1992), *Blamey* (1998), *Defence Supremo* (2000) and *Strategic Command* (2005)—continued to examine high-level decision-makers, and focus on the nexus between personality, leadership, and strategy and operations.⁴ Horner's expertise in the subject was recognised with a recall to duty in the Army in 2003 to conduct a study of Australian command and control in the Iraq War. This resulted in a classified monograph, *Australian Strategic Command in the Iraq War, 2002–2003*.⁵

However, Horner has not confined himself to examining command. As his extensive publishing record shows, he has roamed across a wide range of topics within the field of military history (detailed in the bibliography in Appendix 2). He has produced organisational histories of the Special Air Service Regiment, the Royal Australian Regiment, the Royal Regiment of Australian Artillery and the Australian Defence Force (ADF). He has also written introductions for re-print editions of the Australian Official History of the Second World War and employed the insights from his historical scholarship to examine various issues of military theory, defence policy, strategy and organisation.⁶ Reflecting an interest in advancing the discipline, to which we will return presently, Horner has periodically paused to reflect on the state of the field and his place within it, in essays such as

---

3   David Horner, *Crisis of Command: Australian Generalship and the Japanese Threat, 1941–1943* (Canberra: Australian National University Press, 1978); *High Command: Australia and Allied Strategy 1939–1945* (Sydney: Allen & Unwin, 1982)—in later editions the subtitle was changed to *Australia's Struggle for an Independent War Strategy*.
4   David Horner, *General Vasey's War* (Melbourne: Melbourne University Press, 1992); *Blamey: The Commander-in-Chief* (Sydney: Allen & Unwin, 1998); *Strategic Command: General Sir John Wilton and Australia's Asian Wars* (Melbourne: Oxford University Press, 2005).
5   David Horner, email to editors, 2 March 2024; David Horner and Leanne Rees, *Australian Strategic Command in the Iraq War, 2002–2003* (Canberra: Department of Defence, 2003).
6   David Horner, *SAS—Phantoms of the Jungle: A History of the Australian Special Air Service* (Sydney: Allen & Unwin, 1989)—expanded and republished in 2002 as *SAS—Phantoms of War: A History of the Australia Special Air Service* (Sydney: Allen & Unwin, 2002); David Horner, ed., *Duty First: The Royal Australian Regiment in War and Peace* (Sydney: Allen & Unwin, 1990)—expanded and republished in 2008 as *Duty First: A History of the Royal Australian Regiment* (Sydney: Allen & Unwin, 2008); *The Gunners: A History of Australian Artillery* (Sydney: Allen & Unwin, 1995); *Making the Australian Defence Force* (Melbourne: Oxford University Press, 2001); 'Introduction', in Gavin Long, *To Benghazi* (Sydney: William Collins, 1986), xvii–xxi; 'Introduction', in Gavin Long, *Greece, Crete and Syria* (Sydney: William Collins, 1986), xv–xxi.

'Military History in Australia' (1987), 'Writing History in the Australian Army' (1994), 'Australian Military Biographies' (1998) and 'Researching History at SDSC' (2016).[7]

This historiographical introspection did not imply an 'ivory tower' approach to history. Throughout his career, Horner has successfully bridged the various communities of Australian military history. His training and experience as an army officer alerted him to the utility of history for professional military education and drove him to write in a clear and accessible manner. Thirteen articles in ADF periodicals, 12 appearances at Chief of Army history conferences and membership of multiple advisory bodies, including the Honours and Awards Appeals Tribunal and the Army Battle Honours Committee, all speak to his role as one of the ADF's principal military history advocates and advisers. Horner has also used his plain-speaking approach to history to educate an audience outside of the academy and the military. Works specifically aimed at a wider audience feature in his career bibliography, among them *When the War Came to Australia* (1992), *The Second World War: The Pacific* (2002) and *Australia's Military History for Dummies* (2010).[8] Beyond this, he has regularly featured as a consultant and on-screen talent for documentary series, and in more recent years he has derived great pleasure from delivering historical lectures on cruise ships.

Horner's concern to promote understanding and informed discussion beyond academia is evident in his introduction to *Australia's Military History for Dummies*:

> [F]or the average Australian the details of their military history can be daunting … This book is a 'one-stop shop' for military history. If you don't know much about Australian military history, this is the place to start … I have focused on the how and the why. You might not always agree with my conclusions, but they will at least provide a starting point for debate.[9]

---

7   David Horner, 'Military History in Australia', in *Australians on War and Peace*, edited by Hugh Smith, 9–14 (Canberra: Australian Defence Studies Centre, 1987); 'Writing History in the Australian Army', *Australian Journal of Politics and History* 40, no. 1 (1994): 72–79; 'Australian Military Biographies', in *Ranging Shots: New Directions in Australian Military History*, edited by Carl Bridge (London: Sir Robert Menzies Centre for Australian Studies, University of London, 1998), 81–92; 'Researching History at SDSC', in *A National Asset: 50 years of the Strategic and Defence Studies Centre*, edited by Desmond Ball and Andrew Carr (Canberra: ANU Press, 2016), 121–36, doi.org/10.22459/NA.08.2016.
8   David Horner and Joanna Penglase, *When the War Came to Australia: Memories of the Second World War* (Sydney: Allen & Unwin, 1992); David Horner, *The Second World War (1): The Pacific* (Oxford: Osprey, 2002); *Australia's Military History for Dummies* (Milton: Wiley, 2010).
9   Horner, *Australia's Military History for Dummies*, 1, 2.

In the same work, Horner also explains one of the other defining preoccupations of his research career:

> I'm enthralled by Australian military history because in the most dramatic and exciting manner it tells the story for who we are as Australians. There is nothing like the stress of battle to bring out the true character of a person, just as there is nothing like a war for survival to test the mettle of a nation.[10]

Apart from its focus on military and security matters, Horner's career as a historian has been defined by an unwavering dedication to Australia's national narrative as a subject worthy of its own dedicated analysis. On the first page of *High Command*, he frames his work as part of a broader narrative of Australian political independence. The book, he writes, 'describes Australia's struggle for an independent war strategy'.[11] In the edited collection *The Commanders: Australian Military Leadership in the Twentieth Century* (1984), which followed soon after, he asked whether there was a distinctly Australian style of command.[12] And if we leap forward through Horner's career to the Official History of Australian Peacekeeping, Humanitarian and Post–Cold War Operations, which he conceived, co-authored and edited between 2004 and 2020, we see a continuing commitment to telling Australian stories and analysing the decisions and actions of Australians. A pair of soldiers, among missions of thousands of troops, are accorded equal attention to larger deployments.[13]

In the military history communities of the United Kingdom and the United States, Horner's focus on Australia might be seen as niche or provincial, but his work is by no means parochial. It seems as if he has internalised the guidance of the official historian of Australia's role in the First World War, Charles Bean: 'The historian will endeavour to observe a due proportion, and to present the part played by Australia in its true relation to the vast

---

10 Horner, *Australia's Military History for Dummies*, 1.
11 David Horner, *High Command: Australia's Struggle for an Independent War Strategy, 1939–1945* (Sydney: Allen & Unwin, 1992), 1.
12 David Horner, ed., *The Commanders: Australian Military Leadership in the Twentieth Century* (Sydney: Allen & Unwin, 1984), 1.
13 For example, the fourth volume of the series, *The Limits of Peacekeeping*, deals with the large ADF deployments to Somalia and Rwanda but also includes chapters dealing with much smaller Australian Federal Police missions in Mozambique and Haiti, and to the pairs of Australian Army officers deployed to Guatemala, Eritrea and Sierra Leone (Jean Bou, Bob Breen, David Horner, Garth Pratten and Miesje de Vogel, *The Limits of Peacekeeping: Australian Missions in Africa and the Americas, 1992–2005* [Melbourne: Cambridge University Press, 2019]).

events and mighty issues which were its setting'.¹⁴ Thus, although Horner is an unashamed Australianist, he is not nationalist, unlike much of the popular genre of Australian military history. He is always international in his approach. His work invokes some of the great international scholars in the field—Basil Liddell Hart, JFC Fuller and Archibald Wavell in *Crisis of Command*, Samuel Huntington in *High Command*, Gary Sheffield and Eliot Cohen in *The War Game*—and he has emphasised international context over exceptionalism.¹⁵ His scholarship of Australian peacekeeping and intelligence of necessity positions Australia in the global context of multinational diplomacy and military cooperation. How Australia has contributed, for good and bad, within coalitions led by the United Kingdom and the United States has been a key theme of his work, and his meticulous research has extended to the archives of those nations. Indeed, while he was researching one of his earliest projects, Horner first met one of the editors of this *festschrift* standing in a queue at the Public Record Office of the United Kingdom (now The National Archives).

Horner's focus on Australia has not precluded world-leading historical projects. His contribution to the field of official history is particularly notable. Here, he carried on the legacy of academic standards being applied to this genre, as bequeathed to him by official historians of the two preceding series, RJ (Bob) O'Neill (Australia in the Korean War 1950–1953) and Peter Edwards (Australia's Involvement in Southeast Asian Conflicts 1948–1975). The six volumes of the Official History of Australian Peacekeeping, Humanitarian and Post–Cold War Operations, spanning 62 years and multiple missions, have not been replicated by any other nation, including those to whom peace-support operations are at the core of their national military identity. The Official History of the Australian Security Intelligence Organisation (ASIO), which Horner also led and contributed to, was similarly an international exemplar. While not the first authorised history to lift the veil on the publicity-shy world of intelligence—two of Britain's three major intelligence agencies published histories in 2009 and 2010—the ASIO Official History is thus far the only one comprising multiple volumes,

---

14   CEW Bean, *The Story of Anzac: From the Outbreak of the War to the End of the First Phase of the Gallipoli Campaign, May 4, 1915* (Sydney: Angus & Robertson Limited, 1941), xlv.
15   Horner, *Crisis of Command*, xviii, xxi–xxii; *High Command*, 437; *The War Game: Australian War Leadership from Gallipoli to Iraq* (Sydney: Allen & Unwin 2022), 3–4.

published in 2014, 2015 and 2016.[16] His own volume in the series, *The Spy Catchers: The Official History of ASIO 1949–1963*, was awarded both the St Ermin's Hotel Intelligence Book of the Year Award in 2015—one of the most prestigious awards in the field of intelligence history, despite its idiosyncratic title—and the Australian Prime Minister's Prize for Australian History in the same year.

The claim that Horner is a supremo of Australian military history rests not only in this prodigious scholarship but also in his role in establishing and developing this field as a subject of serious academic study in Australia. To be sure, Horner was not the first Australian soldier to write history, nor was he the first historian to carry military subjects into the Australian academy. He was preceded by trailblazers like Ken Inglis at The Australian National University (ANU), who began writing about the origins and influence of the 'Anzac tradition' in the mid-1960s; Lloyd Robson (University of Melbourne) who produced his groundbreaking statistical history of the origins of the First Australian Imperial Force (AIF) not long after; and Bill Gammage (again at ANU), who was researching the PhD that would become *The Broken Years* at the same time that Horner was training to become an army officer at the Royal Military College Duntroon.[17] However, Horner became part of a vanguard launched by the Faculty of Military Studies at Duntroon, which advanced the study of strategy, operations and command as a 'legitimate area for academic study in Australia' and aspired to stimulate further study in these areas.[18]

Horner soon realised that developing an academic discipline, 'one that didn't exist before', was a task that could not be done alone.[19] His contribution to the discipline thus extended to include the roles of generous colleague, thoughtful mentor and meticulous editor of others' work. Over the years, his academic colleagues came to rely upon his ready sharing of his encyclopedic knowledge, and his generosity in reviewing and commenting

---

16   Christopher Andrews, *The Defence of the Realm: The Authorized History of MI5* (London: Allen Lane, 2009); Keith Jeffrey, *MI6: The History of the Secret Intelligence Service, 1909–1949* (London: Bloomsbury, 2010). Britian's third major intelligence agency, the Government Code and Cipher School (GCHQ), published its authorised history in 2020: John Ferris, *Behind the Enigma: The Authorised History of GCHQ: Britain's Secret Cyber-Intelligence Agency* (London: Bloomsbury, 2020).
17   KS Inglis, 'The Anzac Tradition', *Meanjin Quarterly* 24, no. 1 (1965): 25–44; LL Robson, *The First A.I.F.: A Study of Its Recruitment 1914–1918* (Melbourne: Melbourne University Press, 1970); Bill Gammage, 'The Broken Years: A study of the diaries and letters of Australian soldiers in the Great War', (PhD thesis, The Australian National University, 1970).
18   Horner, *The Commanders*, 5–6.
19   David Horner, interview with Garth Pratten, 12 March 2023.

on works in progress. His doctoral students, too, were the beneficiaries of his unparalleled mastery of the field, as well as his disarmingly pragmatic attitude towards the discipline required for writing ('Write all morning, take hour's walk for lunch, write all afternoon!'). Researchers beyond the academy meanwhile benefited immensely from Horner's editorial input, which enabled many promising, if indigestible, manuscripts to reach publishable form. Other historians followed Horner's path from military service to academic scholarship and yet more owed their later careers to the employment opportunities he created. Never one to appropriate the work of his assistants without attribution, Horner ensured that all members of the Official History teams that he led had the chance to write their own chapters or sections. If they faltered, he modelled how to complete the task. Beyond this, Horner recruited teams of contributors to write collaborative projects that shaped the field, such as *The Commanders* (1984) and *Duty First* (1990).

The breadth of Horner's influence is reflected in the diversity of authors contributing to this volume. They span a number of categories, though the boundaries are porous. Authors include army officers whom Horner initially met during his military service and later nurtured academically, often with roles in the Official Histories teams (John Blaxland, Bob Breen and Chris Roberts); colleagues within the academy, not only from the Strategic and Defence Studies Centre at ANU (Joan Beaumont, Jean Bou, Garth Pratten), but also more widely (Peter Stanley, Richard Frank, Peter Londey); policymakers who transitioned from the public service into academic careers (Hugh White); and, finally, the younger generations of historians of war whom he mentored and influenced (Kate Ariotti, Rhys Crawley, Tristan Moss, Steve Paget and, again, Jean Bou and Garth Pratten).

This diversity among the authors, alas, does not extend to gender equality. This should not reflect negatively on Horner. He has consistently striven to include female scholars in his research projects. However, military history of the kind Horner favours—strategy, command, operations, force structure and intelligence—has been largely the preserve of men. When women have ventured into the wider genre of the history of Australia at war—and they have done so in large numbers in the decades spanned by Horner's career—they have focused largely on the social and cultural dimensions of war: its impact on constructions of gender and sexuality, its role in changing gender relationships and employment patterns, the employment of women in the defence forces and, more recently, the memory and commemoration of war. Kate Ariotti's chapter, which concludes this volume, attests to the fact that Horner's legacy is apparent even across the divide. But the editors of this volume found it difficult to secure any further contributions by women. One positive reason was that several female scholars whom Horner employed over the years have made their contributions in other domains where their historical expertise remains relevant—such as the Australian War Memorial, the Australian Army History Unit, the Sea Power Centre–Australia and other parts of the Australian Public Service.[20] This transmission of knowledge across professional worlds is fitting, given Horner's own commitment to research that makes an impact and is accessible to publics beyond the academy.

This volume is, to use the classic term, a *festschrift*; that is, a book intended to honour a respected academic, with research essays in his or her field of expertise written by colleagues or former students. Authors pay tribute to Horner's legacy by engaging with his scholarly findings, applying his conclusions to new case studies and contexts, reflecting and expanding on the subjects and methodologies he employed, and pushing the boundaries of the military history he played such a role in founding. Of course, given the range of Horner's publications, it has not been possible to offer a response to all his scholarly contributions. As is the custom with *festschrifts*, authors have contributed research essays in their own fields of expertise while paying attention to the influence of Horner on the evolution of their own scholarship and engaging with key themes of Horner's own works.

First, we reflect on the practice of writing about Australian military history and the role within this historiography of the soldier–scholar, of which Horner has been an exemplar. This relationship between military service and military history in Australian historiography, and Horner's motivations in pursuing these parallel and ultimately converging careers, is explored particularly by Garth Pratten. Horner's signal achievements as an official historian are then examined by his successor, Craig Stockings. The series for which Stockings is responsible—Iraq, Afghanistan and East Timor—shares similarities with, and differences from, the series edited by Horner, but one key element of consistency is Horner's 'guiding hand'. The challenges and frustrations of the official historian, and the pitfalls of the tradition to which Horner made such a contribution—he successfully initiated the process that secured political approval for the later Official Histories—are here explored

---

20 Among these women are Nicola Baker, Miesje de Vogel, Rosalind Hearder and Kerry Neale.

by the scholar who has inherited the Horner legacy. His insights into the practice of writing this genre of military history stand as important historical sources in themselves.

The second aspect of Horner's scholarship with which authors engage is his analysis of strategic planning and policy at the highest level: national government, federal cabinet and defence leadership. This theme shapes our next section. Joan Beaumont studies a topic well canvassed in Horner's works, Australian strategy in 1941–42, but ventures into terrain that Horner's empiricism tended to eschew: the psychology of decision-making. While Horner has conceded the role of emotion and personality in decision-making in times of crisis, Beaumont argues that we can only fully understand the flawed strategy that saw battalion-sized forces sent to the islands to Australia's north if we move beyond the documentary record. She applies to Australian decision-making in times of crisis the analysis offered by the Nobel prize–winning behavioural psychologist, Daniel Kahneman. Jean Bou then examines the question that lies at the heart of much of Horner's research: Why has Australia so often gone to war? Whereas Horner has been most concerned with 'the war game' in the twentieth century, Bou considers the wars of the nineteenth century and the problems these highlight in its traditional conventions of periodisation and conceptualisation. Engaging with our theme of the practice of historians, Bou argues that Australian military history can be reconceptualised if we explore the cultural and societal attitudes informing Australian decision-making and pay more attention to the intersection between the proximate and the contextual. It is highly dangerous, he argues, to separate out the frontier wars, which are often conceived of as something confined to the early nineteenth century, from over a century of rolling warfare. Hugh White then returns us to the present and future—by arguing that Horner's work on Australia's strategic alliances of the past should act as a corrective to contemporary strategic planning, which continues to be based on a deep faith in the alliance with the United States. Horner, White argues, shows that alliances have historically depended upon an alignment of interests and objectives between allies, an alignment that Australians can no longer presume.

Our third theme is another one that is core to Horner's oeuvre: command and military biography. Peter Stanley acknowledges his debt to the Horner-esque approach in a study of the charismatic but contentious Sir Charles Napier, Commander-in-Chief in India, 1849 to 1851. He demonstrates how, in this very different historical period and context, we can readily employ Horner's themes, notably the relationship between military command and civilian authorities, and the importance of personality in the exercise of command. Like Joan Beaumont, he affirms the judgement of the eminent British historian, Basil Liddell Hart, that military history should comprise 'a study of the psychological reactions of the commanders, with merely a background of events to throw their thoughts, impressions and decisions into relief'.[21] Chris Roberts then shifts our focus to the First World War and a commander to whom Horner, for all his scholarship on command and commanders, paid relatively little attention: Major General Sir Harold 'Hooky' Walker. Roberts questions this oversight, arguing that Walker was more than a stop-gap commander as Australian senior officers acquired command experience. His conclusions align with Horner's elsewhere: namely, that the effectiveness of a fighting force (in this case the 1st Australian Division) was attributable to its leader's moral courage, sound judgement, common sense in standing up to his superiors and ability to command the respect of the men he led.

Australian strategy and command across the past century and a half have always required effective integration with multinational partners, another theme that features in much of Horner's work. In Part IV, Steven Paget builds on Horner's foundations by considering Australia's approach to enhancing procedural and human interoperability with multinational armed forces. Drawing on historical examples, Paget explores this theme through a focus on four pillars of interoperability: experience, education, personnel exchanges and exercises. Garth Pratten and Rhys Crawley, meanwhile, consider the challenges of coalition command in southern Afghanistan from 2006 to 2010. Compensating for the lack of access to the documentary record so important to Horner's classic works, these authors use senior army officers' interviews, declassified records and a growing body of secondary literature to argue that national policy agendas and the lack of a campaign mindset bedevilled progress until 2009, when revisions in command organisation and certain key personalities were able to unite multiple provincial-level fights into a regional campaign.

Like coalition warfare, intelligence threads its way through many of Horner's projects, culminating in the Official History of ASIO, which he oversaw. The chapter authored by Richard Frank in Part V complements Horner's histories of the Second World War, the earliest of which were written as

---

21 Basil Liddell Hart, *Thoughts on War* (London: Faber & Faber, 1944), 219. Horner's *Crisis of Command* quotes this very phrase, arguing that 'the heart of the military problem is the personality of the commander' (xvi). Horner reiterated this insight in his introduction to *The Commanders*, 1.

INTRODUCTION

the full implications of codebreaking for Allied victory over Germany and Japan were only just becoming apparent. Frank examines the all-important maritime component of the Asia-Pacific war and, specifically, the duel between the Allied radio intelligence organisation and the Imperial Navy's radio methods. John Blaxland, one of Horner's collaborators in the Official History of ASIO, then engages with Horner's scholarship on the 'Five Eyes' partnership of the Anglophone countries, the United States, the United Kingdom, Canada, New Zealand and Australia. Paying tribute to Horner's exemplary use of documentary evidence, Blaxland considers the enduring legacies of the Venona decrypts (a counterintelligence program begun in the Second World War aimed at decrypting messages transmitted by the intelligence agencies of the Soviet Union) for Australia's national intelligence arrangement and international security networks today.

As Blaxland attests, influential scholarship inspires others to venture into new fields or unexplored issues. In Part VI, Tristan Moss builds on Horner's work on the ADF and defence policy during the Cold War by examining how the Australian defence establishment conceptualised and used space. Although space developed as a new area of interest for militaries around the world from the 1950s on, the question of how the ADF thought about and prepared to use space has been studied only tangentially until this time. Peter Londey follows with a reflection on the theme of peacekeeping, which, while core to Australia's military history since 1945, is likely to pose new challenges in future deployments. Do soldiers make good peacekeepers, given the many civilian tasks involved and the blurred lines between the political and military? In the many deployments Australian military peacekeepers have shown—which the Official Histories edited by Horner so ably document— the Australian military has displayed necessary flexibility, but Londey asks whether this will remain the case in the future. Bob Breen, then, returns us to the subject already explored by Hugh White, contemporary Australian and Chinese security, by grappling with another question that has acquired salience in recent years: the growth of the grey zone, the mainly non-military domain in which states use techniques below the threshold of war to coerce other states. Breen draws on revelations from David Horner's histories of Australian strategy and higher command before and during the Pacific War 1942–45, and the development of Australian intelligence services and the Special Air Service Regiment, to suggest that Australia has some history that should not be repeated. Given the nature of the contemporary threat, Breen argues that Australia needs a sovereign grey zone strategy that does not depend on American or British promises, or urgent investments in conventional military power, but rather employs ingenuity and favours unique Australian organisations and operational concepts.

The final chapter acknowledges the degree to which the historiography of Australia's wars has diversified in the years of Horner's scholarship to incorporate, first, the social and cultural history of war and, second, with the extraordinary boom in war memory and commemoration since the 1980s, the loss that is war's inevitable price. Kate Ariotti examines Australian policy towards the dead of Vietnam with an archival rigour that models Horner's and pays tribute to the legacy he has left for the next generation of scholars by documenting the framework of government policy and military practice in which studies of war's social and cultural impact are necessarily embedded. Fittingly, her thoughtful study of human loss in the Vietnam War brings this collection of essays back full circle to the very conflict that shaped the experience and intellectual world of the remarkable scholar honoured in this volume, David Horner.

Part I: David Horner as soldier, scholar and colleague

1
Understanding the 'mechanism of war': the making of a soldier–scholar

Garth Pratten

David Horner merits his reputation as a pre-eminent scholar of Australian military history not simply because of his remarkable publication record and the breadth of his research, but also because of his role in establishing it as a viable academic discipline, including by mentoring emerging scholars. In my case, Horner seemed, at first, a stern and almost unapproachable figure—a perception that perhaps says more about me than him—but this impression was transformed when I joined the team he was assembling to write the Official History of Australian Peacekeeping, Humanitarian and Post–Cold War Operations. With Horner's encouragement, I found the energy and commitment to finish my doctoral thesis on battalion command in the Second World War and prepare it for publication. Within the Official History team, Horner provided a model of leadership: thoughtful, humble, generous and constructive in his critique. He was not necessarily easy to get to know, but you quickly realised that he knew, and was committed to, his job and had your back as a member of his team.

Horner spent 25 years as a professional soldier before becoming a full-time academic, and it is easy to draw analogies between the style of leadership expected of a military officer—professionally distanced but engaged—and that which I experienced in the Official History team. This reflection raises the question of how Horner's military experience shaped his scholarship. I have heard him described by colleagues as a 'soldier–scholar'—an apposite descriptor, but one that needs elaboration. A soldier–scholar is more than someone who has served in the military and writes a book. The individual to whom it is applied must have experienced a sustained period of service in the military, allowing them to intuitively understand its form and functions while demonstrating a similarly prolonged engagement with their scholarship, beyond the requirements of military career progression. Ideally, their service and scholarship should be symbiotic with the latter, serving to improve their personal capacity as a soldier or develop institutional knowledge and capability.

Thus, while there are many Australians with some degree of military service who have published or pursued careers in academia, far fewer can truly be described as soldier–scholars. Horner is one. Yet, while small in number, soldier–scholars laid the foundations of an academic school of Australian military history, informed by, but diverging from, the tradition established by the Official Histories of the two world wars.

Soldier–scholars and early Australian military history

Australian military historiography is often portrayed as beginning with Charles Bean's *Official History of Australia in the War of 1914–1918*.[1] The sheer scale of this series, and the subsequent reverence attached to it, has, however, obscured earlier efforts to record and disseminate Australia's military history. Some of the features that have dominated Australian military historiography were established in the era before Bean, and it was also in this era that a tradition of soldiers, or former soldiers, adopting the guise of historians was established. At least five Australian veterans produced historical accounts of the South African War, most of them histories of individual contingents.[2] These foreshadowed a much larger body of work

---

1   See, for example, Joan Beaumont, 'Australian Military Historiography', *War & Society* 42, no. 1 (February 2023): 100, doi.org/10.1080/07292473.2023.2150485.
2   William Henderson, *The NSW Contingents to South Africa from October 1899 to March 1900* (Sydney: Turner & Henderson, 1900); Richard Charles Lewis, *On the Veldt: A Plain Narrative of Field Service in South Africa* (Hobart: Walch, 1902); WT Reay, *Australians in War: With the Australian Regiment: From Melbourne to Bloemfontein* (Melbourne: AH Massina, 1900); Robert Scot Skirving, *Our Army in South Africa* (Sydney: Angus & Robertson, 1901); Arthur John Newman Tremearne, *Some Austral-African Notes and Anecdotes* (London: John Bale Sons & Danielson Limited, 1913).

in the form of the unit and formation histories that followed Australia's involvement in the First World War. Twenty-six were published between the end of the war and 1921, the year of the release of Bean's first volume, and another 29 would follow before Bean's series was completed in 1941. All but four were written by former soldiers. The remainder were penned by two unit chaplains, a nurse and a grieving father.[3] Although varied in content, scope and quality, these histories are notable for establishing both a narrative tradition and a generic form. Although most were produced by those with the requisite 'education and initiative' as well as 'a modicum of leisure', and often guided by editorial committees, it would be misleading to broadly characterise their authors as soldier–scholars.[4] Nonetheless, the First World War unit histories are one of the largest, if not the largest, collections of Australian military historiography authored by former soldiers.

All the authors of the First World War Official History, with the exception of Bean, had some form of military experience, although it varied in extent and capacity. Seaforth McKenzie served as a military lawyer and spent the war in administrative roles in Rabaul.[5] Frederic Cutlack and Henry Gullet, although both journalists, began the war in the British and Australian artillery respectively, and the former was later attached to the Australian Imperial Force (AIF) as a divisional intelligence officer. Both finished the war as official correspondents, having been plucked from their operational roles by Bean.[6]

Arthur Jose was the best qualified of Bean's authors and the closest to the archetype of a soldier–scholar. He was already a well-published historian on Australian subjects before the war. Bean described him 'as one of the greatest of Australian living authors—and the greatest Australian historian', and from 1915 he had worked inside the Navy Office compiling a classified history of Royal Australian Navy (RAN) operations in the Pacific, as well as

---

3   Calculated from Jean P Fielding and Robert J O'Neill, *A Select Bibliography of Australian Military History 1891–1939* (Canberra: The Australian National University, 1978), 223–36; and 'First World War Nominal Roll', Australian War Memorial, www.awm.gov.au/advanced-search/people?roll=First%20 World%20War%20Nominal%20Roll.
4   Paul Skrebels, '"Hand me down the book, Mum": Australian First World War Military Unit Histories and Their Readers', *The International Journal of the Book* 9, no. 1 (2012): 54–55, doi.org/10.18848/ 1447-9516/CGP/v09i01/57860.
5   Ronald McNicoll, 'Seaforth Simpson MacKenzie, 1883–1955', *Australian Dictionary of Biography*, vol. 10 (online ed., 2006), adb.anu.edu.au/biography/mackenzie-seaforth-simpson-7390.
6   AJ Sweeting, 'Frederic Morley Cutlack, 1886–1967', *Australian Dictionary of Biography*, vol. 8 (online ed., 2006), adb.anu.edu.au/biography/cutlack-frederic-morley-5859; AJ Hill, 'Sir Henry Somer (Harry) Gullett (1878–1940), *Australian Dictionary of Biography*, vol. 9 (online ed., 2006), adb.anu.edu. au/biography/gullett-sir-henry-somer-harry-448.

a variety of intelligence reports on the Pacific and East Asia.[7] Jose's military service, however, did not align neatly with his subject matter. He was a citizen forces intelligence officer attached to the RAN, had not gone to sea, and his wartime service was in an office in Melbourne. The Naval Board, seeking to censor Jose's Official History volume, called his authority into question:

> [T]he Naval Board feel they cannot give official recognition to the opinions which are based on insufficient knowledge of the facts, and are produced by a gentleman who, by training and experience, is perhaps not properly qualified to form sound judgement.[8]

Despite these criticisms, Jose's history is regarded as both reliable and scholarly, and his account of the campaign in the Pacific was commended by Admiral George Patey, Commander of His Majesty's Australian Fleet until September 1916.[9] However, while Jose continued to write history in the interwar period, he never returned to naval or military subjects.[10]

Two decades later, men with active service experience and tertiary qualifications were well represented in the team assembled under Gavin Long to write the official history of the Second World War. Dudley McCarthy, David Dexter, Barton Maughan and George Odgers had all seen operational service with the Army; both Dexter and Maughan were decorated.[11] Allan Walker had been a senior AIF medical officer for much of the war.[12] John Herington had served as a Catalina pilot in Coastal Command and had barely escaped an aircraft crash before transferring to the Royal Australian Air Force (RAAF) Historical Records Section.[13] Others in Long's team had served in supporting capacities: Douglas Gillison and G. Hermon Gill were

---

7   Bean to Macandie, 19 November 1919, cited in Stephen Ellis, 'The Censorship of the Official Naval History of Australia in the Great War', *Historical Studies* 20, no. 80 (1983): 370, doi.org/10.1080/10314618308682934.
8   Hardy to Smith, 11 October 1921, cited in Ellis, 'Censorship', 375.
9   'Jose, Arthur Wilberforce' in *The Oxford Companion to Australian Military History*, 2nd ed., edited by Peter Dennis, Jeffrey Grey, Ewan Morris, Robin Prior and Jean Bou (Melbourne: Oxford University Press, 2008), 296, doi.org/10.1093/acref/9780195517842.001.0001; Ellis, 'Censorship', 380.
10 Ross Lamont, 'Arthur Wilberforce Jose (1863–1934)', *Australian Dictionary of Biography*, vol. 9 (online ed., 2006), adb.anu.edu.au/biography/jose-arthur-wilberforce-6885.
11 Service dossiers, National Archives of Australia (NAA): McCarthy, Dudley, NAA: B2458, 27900; Dexter, David St Alban, NAA: VX38890; Maughan, David Wilfrid Barton, NAA: B883, NX21195; H Veitch, 'The Last Keeper of the Flame', *Sydney Morning Herald*, 31 March 2008.
12 'Walker, Allan Seymour', in *The Oxford Companion to Australian Military History*, edited by Dennis, et al., 562, doi.org/10.1093/acref/9780195517842.001.0001.
13 WR Clark, 'John Herington (1916–1967)', *Australian Dictionary of Biography*, vol. 14 (online ed., 2006), adb.anu.edu.au/biography/herington-john-10491.

public relations officers in the RAAF and the RAN, respectively, and Gill ended the war as head of the RAN's historical records section.[14] All but Gill were university-educated.

However, unlike in the United States, where the production of the Second World War service histories provided impetus to what Ronald H Spector described as the 'serious study of military history', with former official historians moving into academia, Long's team had little direct or ongoing influence on the development of the field in Australia.[15] Aside from Long, only two Official History authors remained active in the field of military history after the publication of their volumes. McCarthy's subsequent contribution was limited. After a distinguished diplomatic career, he returned to history in later life and published the first biography of Charles Bean.[16] Odgers's contribution was more substantial. He joined the reserve component of the RAAF after the Second World War, was deployed to Korea, Malaya and Vietnam, and finally retired in 1981 as the Director of Historical Studies and Information in the Department of Defence. Although primarily a journalist, Odgers published multiple military histories, most of them 'aimed at a popular readership' but 'without sacrificing either detail or rigour'.[17]

The impetus for establishing Australian military history as an academic discipline or subfield thus lay elsewhere. Several individuals who could be considered soldier–scholars laid the foundations of a tradition that would, in turn, shape and focus the interests of several Army officers, including Horner. Among the Army's most notable postwar soldier–scholars was Eustace Keogh, a driver in the First World War, a staff officer in the Second, and a civil engineer and surveyor in the years in between. Keogh's final posting of the Second World War was to the Directorate of Military Training, an organisation to which he returned as a civilian after demobilisation. Responsible for the production of training publications, Keogh inaugurated the *Australian Army Journal* as a means of professional

---

14 'Gill, (George) Hermon' and 'Gillison, Douglas Napier', in *The Oxford Companion to Australian Military History*, edited by Dennis, et al., 235–36.
15 Ronald H Spector, 'Military History and the Academic World', *Army History* 19 (Summer 1991): 3, 4.
16 'McCarthy, Dudley' in *The Oxford Companion to Australian Military History*, edited by Dennis, et al., 334; Dudley McCarthy, *Gallipoli to the Somme: The Story of C.E.W. Bean*, (Sydney: John Ferguson, 1983).
17 'Odgers, George', in *The Oxford Companion to Australian Military History*, edited by Dennis, et al., 400; Veitch, 'The Last Keeper of the Flame'.

development for Army officers. He hoped the journal would provide 'the basis of an Australian military literature … equal in diversity and dignity [to] the military literature of other countries'.[18]

As Jeff Grey noted in an exploration of Keogh's career and influence, he was a 'firm advocate of the importance of history to the education and development of Army officers'.[19] Between 1954 and 1965, he wrote six works to assist officers in preparing for the history component of the exams then required for promotion.[20] Although relying principally on secondary sources, they nonetheless represent a sustained body of work with an analytical purpose. In an *Australian Army Journal* article advising officers on the study of military history, Keogh urged officers to develop a critical, systematic approach because 'our history is full of great military myths most of which we thoughtlessly accept at their face value'.[21] This was a theme he continued in his preface to *The South West Pacific, 1941–45*:

> In analysing a campaign with the object of deducing useful lessons in the conduct of war, criticism of the actions of individuals is inescapable. If the conclusions are just, the person concerned can have no cause for complaint, for all who accept high office in the service of the State thereby submit themselves to the judgment of history.[22]

Keogh's writings reflected a mood among many senior leaders of the mid-century Army that officers needed to be better educated to guarantee that the military profession both kept pace with its civilian equivalents and remained an attractive career option, and to ensure that it was better equipped to confront the political, strategic and operational challenges of the period. This prompted the broadening of the curriculum of the Royal Military College (RMC)—dominated by science and mathematics—to include a liberal arts stream and a pathway for commissioned officers to graduate with a degree. This was a fraught and prolonged process, that

---

18 Jeffrey Grey, 'A Military Intellectual: Colonel E. G. Keogh' in *The Shadow Men: The Leaders Who Shaped the Australian Army from the Veldt to Vietnam*, edited by Craig Stockings and John Connor (Sydney: NewSouth Publishing, 2017), 104.
19 Grey, 'A Military Intellectual', 107.
20 Eustace Graham Keogh, *Shenandoah, 1861–62* (1954); *Suez to Aleppo* (1954); *The River in the Desert* (1955); *Middle East, 1939–43* (1959); *Malaya, 1941–42* (1962) (all Melbourne: Directorate of Military Training); Eustace Graham Keogh, *South West Pacific, 1941–45* (Melbourne: Grayflower Productions, 1965).
21 Eustace Graham Keogh, 'The Study of Military History', *Australian Army Journal* 188 (January 1965): 11.
22 Keogh, *South West Pacific*, x.

is well documented elsewhere, but one of its effects was the creation of a small history department at RMC.[23] It became the engine room of the development of Australian military history as a field of academic study, with several soldier–scholars playing prominent roles. It would be fundamental to shaping the early scholarship of Horner.

The first of these men was Alec Hill. A graduate of both Sydney and Oxford universities, Hill was a schoolteacher when he joined the Second AIF in 1940. He served as company commander during the Siege of Tobruk, a staff officer in Headquarters 9th Division at El Alamein, and as Brigade Major of the 20th Brigade in the Western Desert, New Guinea and Borneo. After the death of the original author of the Official History volume on the 9th Division's operations in the Western Desert, Hill was among those considered to replace him but was passed over for Maughan.[24] Following demobilisation, Hill returned to schoolteaching, but, in January 1966, he joined the staff of RMC as a lecturer in history and remained there until his retirement in 1979. Hill's influence was twofold. Not only did he teach history to a generation of staff cadets, from among whom several historians emerged who made notable contributions to the field. He was also at the vanguard of a genre of scholarly command biography—his *Chauvel of the Light Horse* was published in 1978—that, as one observer sardonically noted, challenged the 'then unfashionable notion that generals were at least as important as privates in winning battles'.[25]

Joining the RMC history department 18 months after Hill was one of the college's own graduates, whom a later history would describe as a 'model' soldier–scholar, Robert ('Bob') O'Neill.[26] After graduating from Duntroon in 1958, undertaking signals training and regimental service, and completing an engineering degree at the University of Melbourne, he took up a Rhodes Scholarship at Oxford in 1961. There, he completed a PhD on the relationship between the Nazi Party and the German Army in the 1930s. The contacts O'Neill made during his time in the United Kingdom set him up well for an academic career, but he returned to Australia in 1966 to resume his military service. An operational tour of South Vietnam as the Intelligence Officer of the 5th Battalion, the

---

23 See Darren Moore, *Duntroon: The Royal Military College of Australia 1911–2001* (Canberra: Royal Military College of Australia, 2001), 256–87.
24 Long to Morshead, 31 May 1954, Australian War Memorial: AWM93, 50/2/23/402.
25 Jeffrey Grey, 'Alec Jeffrey Hill AM, MBE, ED', *Australian Army Journal* 5, no. 3 (2008): 220–21.
26 Christopher David Coulthard-Clark, *Duntroon: The Royal Military College of Australia* (Sydney: Allen & Unwin, 1986), 205.

Royal Australian Regiment (RAR) followed.[27] O'Neill's first book, based on his doctoral thesis, was published while he was away.[28] At the conclusion of his deployment, he was seconded to Duntroon as a senior lecturer in history, where his arrival, the college's annual report noted, was 'particularly welcome in this period of establishing History as an important discipline in … the academic courses'.[29] Another three books followed in quick succession, along with several articles.[30] O'Neill's classroom would seem to have been the venue for the free exchange of ideas. A glimpse inside is provided by a note in his preface to *General Giap: Politician and Strategist*:

> A special mention is deserved by the final year history classes at Duntroon, Canberra, in 1967 and 1968 for their part in the discussion out of which many of the ideas in this book have grown.[31]

With the establishment of the Faculty of Military Studies at RMC in April 1968, a professor of history was required, and this brought another soldier–scholar to the college. Leonard Turner was born and educated in South Africa; he abandoned his doctoral studies in history to enlist in the British Army, with which he served throughout the Second World War. After the war, Turner was part of the team that produced the South African Official History; he authored two volumes and co-authored a third. In 1956, he left South Africa to pursue an academic career in Australia, which ultimately led to his appointment at RMC. While at Duntroon, Turner modelled an eclectic military scholarship ranging from Napoleon and the American Civil War to the First World War and gained a reputation for what one colleague described as 'tightly organised analyses of complex situations'.[32]

Turner headed the RMC history department until 1979, overseeing an increase in teaching staff from four to seven. Reflecting the independent status and academic aspirations of the Faculty of Military Studies, not all teaching staff had military experience, and not all specialised in Australian

---

27 David M Horner, 'The Evolution of Australian Official War Histories', in *War Strategy and History: Essays in Honour of Professor Robert O'Neill*, edited by Daniel Marston and Tamara Leahy (Canberra: ANU Press, 2016), 76–77, doi.org/10.22459/WSH.05.2016.

28 Robert J O'Neill, *The German Army and the Nazi Party, 1933–1939* (London: Cassell, 1966).

29 *Report on the Royal Military College of Australia* [hereafter *RMC Annual Report*] for the period 11 February 1967 to 26 January 1968 (Canberra: Commonwealth Government Printer, 1968),14.

30 Three titles by Robert J O'Neill: *Vietnam Task* (Melbourne: Cassell Australia, 1966); *Indo China Tragedy 1945/54* (London: Warnes, 1968); *General Giap: Politician and Strategist* (Melbourne: Cassell Australia, 1969).

31 O'Neill, *General Giap*, xi.

32 Peter Dennis, 'Leonard Charles Frederick Turner (1914–1984)', *Australian Dictionary of Biography*, vol. 18 (online ed., 2012), adb.anu.edu.au/biography/turner-leonard-charles-frederick--15565.

military matters. Most, however, embraced operations, strategy, or defence and security policy as part of their research interests. Among their number were several notable individuals—John McCarthy, John Robertson, Roger Thompson and Peter Dennis—who would continue to shape the development of military history as an academic discipline in Australia, an endeavour in which they would subsequently be joined by David Horner.[33]

'Jack Horner will surely be Duntroon's pride': the origins of a soldier–scholar

The interests that would define Horner's career were evident early, shaped by his home and school. During the Second World War, Horner's father, Murray, served briefly with the RAAF before transferring to the Second AIF and training as an anti-aircraft gunner. He manned defences at Whyalla and Fort Largs in South Australia, and Port Moresby in Papua, and was undergoing retraining as a cavalry commando when hostilities ended in August 1945.[34] Murray returned to service in the Citizen Military Forces after the war and, as his son later recalled, brought his 'hobby' home much more frequently than his civilian profession.[35]

From 1961, Horner attended Prince Alfred College (PAC), a Methodist boys' school in central Adelaide. The school's motto *Fac fortia et patere*— 'do brave deeds and endure'—exhorted its students to become men of character and assume leadership roles in society.[36] In his editorial to the centenary edition of the school's journal, its President, Reverend Arthur Jackson, noted the 'long list of men' who had passed through the school, and had held high and respected places in the community, distinguishing themselves admirably in various walks of life.[37] Although Horner was not among the school's most academically accomplished students, he was still awarded two Commonwealth scholarships in his second-last year.[38]

---

33 Compiled from academic staff listings in RMC annual reports 1968–79.
34 Service dossier, Horner, Murray Percival, NAA: B883, SX18001.
35 David Horner, in an interview with the author, 22 March 2023.
36 See, for example: CJC Bennett, 'Editorial', *Prince Alfred College Chronicle* XVIII, no. 245 (April 1965): 3.
37 AM Jackson, 'Editorial', *Prince Alfred College Chronicle*, XVIII, no. 253 (April 1969): 4.
38 'Public Examinations 1963', *Prince Alfred College Chronicle* XVIII, no. 243 (April 1964): 18; 'Public Examinations', *Prince Alfred College Chronicle* XVIII, no. 245 (April 1965): 18; 'Public Examinations 1965', *Prince Alfred College Chronicle* XVIII, no. 247 (April 1966): 24.

The PAC was a broad-based school, and Horner was active in many extra-curricular pursuits, including as a prefect in his final year. His most defining pursuit was the school cadets. The late 1950s and early 1960s were the heyday of the voluntary cadet movement in Australia, and cadet units at Australian high schools, both public and independent, were common. The PAC cadet unit was among the strongest in South Australia, with 269 members in 1963.[39] Although the Australian Cadet Corps was evolving from a military to a youth development organisation, in the early 1960s it was still widely seen as a means of preparing boys for military service.[40] Its training syllabus was dominated by infantry skills and influenced by the type of warfare taking place in South-East Asia. At the 1965 annual camp, the PAC's second-year cadets 'were instructed in advanced infantry training' before undertaking 'a realistic two-day exercise, in which they had to defend an airstrip against Communist infiltrators'. The third-year cadets, of which Horner was one, conducted mobile exercises at the Army training area at Cultana where 'they learned a great deal about guerrilla fighting and living in the field for long periods. They slept in ponchos, and even cooked for themselves for a short time.'[41]

Aligning with PAC's ethos, the school's cadet unit aimed to prepare future military leaders. Lamenting poor attendance at the January 1966 cadet courses camp, the author of the cadet unit's article in the school journal pointedly observed:

> This indicates that too few boys are willing to accept responsibility on a voluntary basis. It is hoped that next year more boys will attend courses and take on leadership now, rather than when it is forced upon them by someone who has drawn a dated marble out of a barrel.[42]

Horner, however, did not shy from such responsibility and excelled in the cadet unit. He moved through the ranks and, in his final year at the school, was a cadet under officer, responsible for the command of a platoon of 30 of his peers and answering to the adult officer of cadets commanding the

---

39   'Cadet Notes', *Prince Alfred College Chronicle* XVIII, no. 247 (April 1965): 30.
40   For a discussion of the Australian Cadet Corps in this period, see Craig Stockings, 'The Torch and the Sword: A History of the Army Cadet Movement in Australia 1866–2004' (PhD thesis, University of New South Wales, 2006), 205–39.
41   'Cadets', *Prince Alfred College Chronicle* XVIII, no. 246 (October 1965): 13.
42   'Cadets', *Prince Alfred College Chronicle* XVIII, no. 247: 20.

company.⁴³ Horner was twice bestowed with the award for the most efficient cadet, and his platoon won the Platoon Cup in 1965.⁴⁴ This early aptitude for military leadership was recognised by his peers: a verse celebrating the activities, accomplishments and character of PAC's prefects observed that '"Jack" Horner will surely be Duntroon's pride'.⁴⁵

In these school years, we catch the first glimpses of Horner the soldier–scholar or, perhaps more appropriately then, the cadet-scholar. He contributed several short articles on military history to the school journal and even a faith-inspired short story in a Second World War setting.⁴⁶ His abilities were recognised by staff, and he was asked to write a short history of the PAC cadet unit. Foreshadowing his approach to future projects, Horner enlisted the help of a friend as a research assistant and got to work.⁴⁷ Originally envisaged as just a few pages, Horner's *Prince Alfred College Cadet Unit: Extracts from Unit History 1898–1964* ran to 24 pages and was published, with illustrations, by the school.⁴⁸ Horner presented a copy of the history to Brigadier Tim Cape, the reviewing officer for the PAC cadet unit's annual ceremonial parade in October 1964.⁴⁹ A decorated Second World War veteran and senior member of the Royal Australian Artillery fraternity, Cape would be part of a committee that would commission Horner to write a history of the regiment in 1991.⁵⁰

Horner entered the RMC – Duntroon, as a staff cadet in January 1966. He was one of six young men selected from South Australia for that intake and among the approximately 65 per cent with experience as a school cadet.⁵¹ Since its inception in 1911, Duntroon had combined military and academic subjects, although with a strong emphasis on science and

---

43 Details of contemporaneous cadet unit organisation can be found in Stockings, 'The Torch and the Sword', 208–09.
44 'Cadets', *Prince Alfred College Chronicle* XVIII, no. 243 (April 1964): 27; 'Cadet Notes', *Prince Alfred College Chronicle* XVIII, no. 247 (April 1965): 30; 'Cadets', *Prince Alfred College Chronicle* XVIII, no. 247 (April 1966): 20.
45 'Prefects' Palaver', *Prince Alfred College Chronicle* XVIII, no. 246 (October 1965): 20.
46 David M Horner, 'The Battle of Ngakyedauk', *Prince Alfred College Chronicle* XVIII, no. 241 (April 1963): 46–47; David Horner, 'Gordon Avenged: The Battle of Omduran' and 'The Strange Mechanic', *Prince Alfred College Chronicle* XVIII, no. 242 (October 1963): 32, 33.
47 Horner, interview.
48 David M Horner, *Prince Alfred College Cadet Unit: Extracts from Unit History 1898–1964* (Kent Town: Prince Alfred College, 1964).
49 'Cadet Notes', *Prince Alfred College Chronicle* XVIII no. 245 (April 1965): 30.
50 David M Horner, *The Gunners: A History of Australian Artillery* (Sydney: Allen & Unwin, 1995), xi–xii.
51 'Purely Personal', *Prince Alfred College Chronicle* XVIII, no. 247 (April 1966): 54; Stockings, 'The Torch and the Sword', 206.

mathematics, which were seen as critical for equipping officers to wield the increasing technical means of war. Horner was also encouraged to study science, but he refused to be discouraged from further pursuing his interest in history and thus became one of Duntroon's 'artists'.[52]

This resolve was vindicated in the years that followed. In his first year—Fourth Class—he earned the prize for the highest combined marks in the arts course, and, in his third year, the prize for government in the arts course.[53] His guidance report that year noted he was 'thoroughly aligned to his academic studies, in particular History'. Bob O'Neill described Horner's work in History II as 'outstanding' and highlighted a 'number of original papers' he wrote in addition to the requirements of the subject and that would likely be published in the *Army Journal*.[54] The first of these, 'The Military Lessons of the Seven Weeks War', was published in December 1968, followed by a second, 'The Defence of Sydney in 1820' in May 1969 and a third 'The Fall of Atlanta' in June 1969.[55] The introductory footnote to this latter article, seemingly derived from the submission letter accompanying it, illustrates that Horner was already developing distinct ideas about the methodology of military history:

> This is a critical account, and it relies heavily upon the details of Sherman's orders and correspondence with his subordinates. For this reason I have quoted liberally from the Official records. It is, I think, far more satisfactory method than the constant paraphrasing of the correspondence, with its subsequent loss of intimacy and urgency.[56]

Many of the themes that would subsequently become hallmarks of Horner's work are evident in his analysis of Sherman's conduct of the battle for Atlanta. Its focus is on command decision-making in the context of the broader campaign, including the relationship between political, military and economic objectives. We perhaps also glimpse a prototype of his analysis of other commanders—a measured critique of poor decision-making without a denial of the subjects' broader historical contribution.

---

52 Horner, interview.
53 'General Comments', RMC – Duntroon Archives: cadet guidance file 2461 (1966), Horner, DM; 'Prize Winners', *Journal of the Royal Military College of Australia* 45, no. 56 (December 1968): 61.
54 'General comments', 1968, Harris to Thomson, '2461 S/C DM Horner', n.d. [c. 1968], Army Museum Duntroon: cadet guidance file 2461, Horner, DM.
55 David M Horner, 'The Military Lessons of the Seven Weeks War', *Australian Army Journal* 235 (December 1968): 44–49; David Horner, 'The Fall of Atlanta', *Australian Army Journal* 241 (June 1969): 28–44; David Horner and GP Walsh, 'The Defence of Sydney in 1820', *Australian Army Journal* 240 (May 1969): 13–23.
56 Horner, 'The Fall of Atlanta', 28.

Horner's time at Duntroon coincided with a period of upheaval in which degree-accredited programs were introduced, not to universal approval, and a public scandal resulting from the bastardisation of the Fourth (junior) Class prompted a public enquiry.[57] The increased emphasis on academic activities, and the public questioning of RMC culture and practices, earned the ire of some Army officers, who felt the reshaping of the college failed to heed the particular needs of the Army.[58]

Given the heavily programmed existence of the staff cadets, to succeed at university-level study at RMC required a particular type of focus and discipline.[59] It is no wonder that Horner's second-year report described him as a 'serious, hard-working cadet who should learn to relax a little'.[60] Some of the tensions playing out within RMC about the archetype of a modern military officer can perhaps be glimpsed in Horner's third-year reporting. He finished top cadet in both his first and second years at RMC and second-top in his third, all years in which the emphasis in the RMC program was intended to be on academic subjects.[61] Yet Horner's third-year report questioned his 'devotion to his academic work' and blamed this for the slow development of leadership 'qualities': 'He is at times quiet and withdrawn, and while he tries hard to *encourage* and *assist* [my emphasis] Junior classes, is not positive or forceful enough with them.' The report noted a concern that Horner's 'motivation towards an Army career … [was] … not as strong as it should be' and urged a stronger focus on military subjects in 1969, which was just what the RMC program intended.[62]

Horner does, indeed, seem to have focused on his military subjects in 1969. Much of the training in RMC's final year was centred on counterinsurgency, which the Army referred to at the time as counter-revolutionary warfare.[63] This included a period of training at the Jungle Warfare Centre at Canungra. Horner's report on his time there noted his 'good knowledge of minor tactics' and, specifically, in the role of platoon commander, 'depth of knowledge,

---

57   The most fulsome account of the bastardisation scandal is provided in Moore, *Duntroon*, 367–85.
58   Scott Bennett, 'Changes in Academic Courses at the Royal Military College', *The Australian Quarterly* 41, no. 4 (December 1969): 53, doi.org/10.2307/20634323.
59   Bennett, 'Changes in Academic Courses', 54.
60   'General Comments', Army Museum Duntroon: cadet guidance file 2461 (1967), Horner, DM.
61   *RMC Annual Report 1966*, 49–50 and *1968*, 37–38; Moore, *Duntroon*, 276.
62   'General Comments', Army Museum Duntroon: cadet guidance file 2461 (1968), Horner, DM.
63   *RMC Annual Report 1969*, 7.

tenacity, and good command ability': 'one of the best during this period'.[64] However, his final report at RMC noted 'some excellent theoretical results' but cautioned that he lacked 'practical aptitude and man management ability' and would need 'close supervision'.[65]

Other parts of the Army had fewer concerns with the emerging soldier–scholar. When interviewed by corps directors for his assignment beyond RMC, Horner asked if it was possible to do a master's degree while serving in their corps. The most sympathetic, Horner recalled, was the Director of Infantry, Colonel David Thompson. This suited Horner just fine, as his assessment was that the Royal Australian Corps of Infantry was 'where things happened'. He later explained his reasoning: 'An infantry officer could have artillery in support, and tanks under command, but he was the one who 'runs the show'. Thompson ordained both Horner's immediate and long-term future, telling him: 'If you do your time in the trenches, then I will make sure you get an opportunity to do a masters degree.'[66]

'Time in the trenches': Horner as soldier

Horner was commissioned at RMC on the stroke of midnight, 10 December 1969. He was second in his class overall, the top staff cadet in the arts course, and the winner of several prizes for his performance in aspects of both the academic and military courses, including the CEW Bean Prize for History.[67] He was deemed to have passed the academic course at university standards and was awarded a Diploma of Military Studies with Merit (full degrees were not awarded until 1971).[68] Of note, the fourth-placed graduating officer in

---

64 Ivor Hodgkinson (CI Battle Wing JTC), report, 4 November 1969, Army Museum Duntroon: cadet guidance file 2461, Horner, DM. Lieutenant Colonel Ivor 'Blue' Hodgkinson served in Korea with 1 RAR, in Malaysia with 3 RAR during *Konfrontasi* and in Vietnam as second-in-command of 5 RAR for the last five months of its first deployment.
65 'Military', Army Museum Duntroon: cadet guidance file 2461 (1969), Horner, DM.
66 Horner, interview. Horner decided early that infantry was his first preference. Formally nominating his preference at the beginning of his last year, he explained his rationale: 'I decided on Infantry two years ago and I have found no reason to change': Horner to Townsend (CO CSC), 26 February 1969, Army Museum Duntroon: cadet guidance file 2461, Horner, DM.
67 'Prize Winners', *Journal of the Royal Military College of Australia* XLV, no. 56 (December 1968): 48. Horner was one of three Blamey Scholars (awarded for being top student in each of RMC's three academic programs) in the 1969 graduating class and was also awarded the following prizes: Top Graduate in the Arts Course, the Oswald Watt Essay Prize for the best essay dealing with military aviation, the CEW Bean Prize for History in the Arts Course, and Staff Duties, Training and Intelligence.
68 *RMC Annual Report 1969*, 34; *1971*, 3.

the arts course was New Zealander Christopher Pugsley, who would follow a similar path to Horner and became one of his country's leading soldier–scholar historians.[69]

After completing specialist infantry training at Ingleburn on Sydney's outskirts, Horner was allocated to 3 RAR, then based at Woodside in South Australia and preparing for its second operational tour in the Republic of (South) Vietnam. Horner was appointed commander of 11 Platoon, part of D Company, commanded by Major Keith Sticpewich. The son of one of six survivors of the Sandakan death marches, Sticpewich had already served one operational tour in Vietnam with the initial rotation of Australian Army Training Team Vietnam in 1962–63.[70] By the time Horner joined 3 RAR in mid-1970, Australia's commitment to South Vietnam had passed its peak and was declining in parallel with that of the United States. 3 RAR was originally scheduled to deploy in October 1970 but in May the government announced the reduction of the 1st Australian Task Force (1 ATF) from three infantry battalions to two and its departure was delayed until February of the following year.[71]

The war that Horner found in Vietnam was different to that encountered by his academic mentor O'Neill five years previously. In 1966, the newly formed 1 ATF focused on establishing security in its area of operations, the province of Phuoc Tuy. By 1971, Viet Cong (VC) Main Force elements had largely been ousted from the province and it was among the quietest in Vietnam. VC local forces remained active but avoided contact. Intelligence, however, indicated that VC Main Force and North Vietnamese Army (NVA) elements were operating across Phuoc Tuy's northern border in Long Khanh province. With the 'Vietnamisation' policy to facilitate the exit of the United States and its allies from the war, responsibility for the security of much of the province, particularly populated areas, had been assumed by South Vietnamese forces.[72]

---

69   *RMC Annual Report 1969*, 34. As of July 2023, Christopher Pugsley was the author of 13 books on New Zealand, British and American military history, including the official history of New Zealand's involvement in the Malayan Emergency and *Konfrontasi*. Like Horner, Puglsey completed a PhD and began publishing while still serving in the New Zealand Army. After retiring from the Army in 1988, he taught history at the University of New England and the War Studies Department of the Royal Military Academy Sandhurst.
70   Michael C English, *The Riflemen: The Unit History of 3RAR in Vietnam 1971* (Loftus: Australian Military History Publications, 1999), 28.
71   English, *The Riflemen*, 32.
72   A Ekins, *Fighting to the Finish: The Australian Army and the Vietnam War, 1968–1975* (Sydney: Allen & Unwin, 2012), 515–16, 525–26.

The approach of 1 ATF's commander, Brigadier Bruce MacDonald, was to pursue the VC Main Force and NVA elements in Phuoc Tuy's hinterland so they could not return to the province in strength and interfere with pacification operations. The drawdown of Australian forces, however, meant 1 ATF was ill-equipped for the task—its area of operations was too large for it to cope comfortably. MacDonald sought to compensate with extensive patrol operations, but the enemy remained elusive.[73] Horner later observed: 'We had a funny tour in which we would patrol for weeks and not find anything and then it's an NVA regiment that's turned up.'[74]

Having decided upon a career in the Regular Army, Horner expected to be 'around for a while' and was determined to 'do the job properly' in Vietnam. He later reflected that this led to quite a 'rigid' approach to command initially, but not one he regretted:

> I'd start off by calling the corporals, corporals and soldiers, privates ... I didn't really start by calling them by their first name ... Some people might have seen that as ... [me] ... thinking I was high and mighty ... but I don't regret doing that. It's a good way to start. I wasn't there to be their mate. I kept myself a bit separate from the soldiers.[75]

The challenge he confronted was striking a balance between commanding his platoon, building the confidence of his men, and keeping good order and discipline. With some veterans of earlier Vietnam deployments in his platoon, he felt a 'degree of nervousness' at the beginning, stemming from his own inexperience: '[T]his soldier's been to Vietnam, he must know how to do it.' Horner's response was to act as he had been trained, 'and that turned out to be appropriate'.[76]

Horner's introduction to the realities of operational service in Vietnam came quickly. On 28 February, 3 RAR commenced in-country training intended to allow the battalion to practice Vietnam-specific procedures, particularly operations with supporting arms. It was conducted in an area not far from the Australian base at Nui Dat assessed to be relatively free of

---

73   Ekins, *Fighting to the Finish*, 521–23.
74   Horner, interview.
75   Horner, interview.
76   Horner, interview.

1. UNDERSTANDING THE 'MECHANISM OF WAR'

enemy. 'The problem with that', Horner wryly observed, 'is nobody told the enemy.'[77] On 1 March all of 3 RAR's companies encountered the enemy or sign of them; nevertheless, the exercise continued.[78]

Just after 8 pm the next evening, D Company was attacked in its night harbour. Horner's 11 Platoon, on the north-west of the perimeter, was the first to sight enemy, just 25 metres distant. Claymore anti-personnel mines were fired, and the area was engaged with machine guns. Horner called for artillery illumination and ordered a sweep of the area. As the sweep was about to commence, Horner's men sighted more enemy and fired again. Simultaneously, 10 Platoon also observed the enemy and engaged. The enemy returned fire and a large explosion reverberated through the night. The commander of 10 Platoon, Lieutenant John Wheeler, was killed in the blast, later assessed to have been caused by a thrown explosive charge; another soldier was killed by automatic fire, and a further two were wounded. More artillery illumination was fired, and RAAF helicopter gunships strafed the main area of enemy movement. The contact continued sporadically through the night as the enemy probed D Company's position, signalling with whistle blasts and small flares. As dawn approached, movement outside the perimeter subsided and the enemy withdrew. 3 RAR's Commanding Officer (CO), Lieutenant Colonel Peter Scott, reflected on the effect of these early casualties: '[They] shook us all up particularly David because … [John Wheeler] … was a classmate at Duntroon.'[79] Horner has recalled events differently, in a manner akin to many junior officers through history, noting he 'was too busy doing … [his] … job as platoon commander' to be shaken up.[80]

The heavy emphasis on patrolling during 3 RAR's deployment meant that 22-year-old Horner and his platoon often operated on their own for days at a time. Horner continued to question himself—'Did we harbour in the right place?'; 'Did I push them too hard that day?'—but his confidence in his knowledge and judgement grew.[81] One of his soldiers described him as a 'tough-minded optimist' and was impressed by his training and attention

---

77 FP Scott, '3RAR Combat Operations After Action Report Op Phoi Hop', 2, AWM: AWM95, 7/3/72; Horner, interview.
78 English, *The Riflemen*, 52; Horner, interview.
79 Account compiled from KE Sticpewich 'Combat Incident After Action Report', 12 March 1971, 3 RAR operations log, 1 March 1971, AWM: AWM95, 7/3/71, 72; Horner, interview; Scott email to author, 23 June 2023. Horner's platoon medic, Corporal Allan Lowe, received a Mention in Despatches for treating one of 10 Platoon's wounded under fire and carrying him back to company headquarters, as well as retrieving the bodies of its two fatal casualties; English, *The Riflemen*, 55.
80 David Horner, email to author, 2 March 2024.
81 Horner, interview.

to detail: '[H]is ability to take control of very dangerous situations really stood out.'[82] One such occasion was when 11 Platoon was laid up in a night ambush position during Operation Briar Patch I in April 1971. Lights were seen moving on the other side of an open paddy field, and Horner reported this by radio to his company commander; Sticpewich determined artillery was required. But the artillery captain attached to Horner's platoon as a forward observer panicked and eventually called down fire on its own position. Sticpewich ordered Horner to take over from the observer. Recalling the incident, Horner said, 'So I sacked him [the observer] … I said, "I am making you a rifleman in my platoon and I'll do your job." … I picked up the artillery net and called in the fire.'[83]

The largest operation involving 3 RAR was codenamed 'Overlord' and commenced on 5 June 1971. Most of 1 ATF was committed with the aim of locating and destroying an NVA battalion believed to be operating in the vicinity of the Phuoc Tuy–Long Khanh border. On the third day of the operation, 3 RAR's 5 Platoon was pinned down under heavy fire while advancing on a bunker complex. Casualties quickly mounted. A troop of Centurion tanks from C Squadron of 1 Armoured Regiment, soon joined by a second, commenced to fight through the bunker system from the opposite side to come to 5 Platoon's aid. The bunker system, however, was larger than expected, and the tanks were embroiled in a vicious engagement. They rapidly exhausted their ammunition and were ordered to halt while a resupply was arranged. Scott ordered D Company—his designated reserve—forward to complete the assault through the bunker system in concert with the tanks.

There was no avoiding what potentially awaited the assault force. While the tanks were being resupplied, D Company searched the well-constructed bunkers already captured. When Horner went to speak with the commander of the tank troop his platoon was teamed with for the assault, he emerged from the turret with blood streaming from his face, which had been peppered with shrapnel from a rocket-propelled grenade explosion.[84] The commander of the tank troop was Lieutenant Bruce Cameron, whom Horner would later help to publish a history of tanks in Vietnam.[85]

---

82 W Thomas email to author, 23 June 2023.
83 Horner, interview; D Horner email to author, 2 March 2024.
84 Account of Overlord derived from: Ekins, *Fighting to the Finish*, 564–70; F Peter Scott, *Command in Vietnam: Reflections of a Commanding Officer* (McCrae: Slouch Hat Publications, 2007), 78–82; Ronald NL Hopkins, *Australian Armour: A History of the Royal Australian Armoured Corps 1927–1972* (Canberra: Australian War Memorial, 1978), 292–95; English, *The Riflemen*, 102–03; Horner, interview.
85 Horner interview, 2019.

The assault commenced at 3.15 pm. The two forward infantry platoons, the left of which was Horner's, advanced in line with the front of the tanks. One of Horner's soldiers struggled with his fear. Horner's response showed his leadership style—reasoned and pragmatic. He told the soldier to walk behind one of the tanks, saying, 'You'll be safe there'.[86] The undergrowth was thick; the infantry struggled to keep up with the tanks. There was no enemy response—they had likely assessed a major assault was imminent and withdrawn—but it still took two hours to clear the bunker complex. It was later found to include 47 bunkers, covering a full square kilometre, and to have been defended by NVA troops. Horner realised how fortunate D Company had been: 'What it taught me was the value of tanks in … close quarter battle. People say we shouldn't have tanks now. All I can say is that I was very glad to have the tanks along.'[87] As to Horner's performance, Scott recalled he 'led his platoon with skill that day'.[88]

'The longest question asked in Monash Hall': the emergence of a scholar

Unlike O'Neill, or several of his own contemporaries, such as Robert Hall, Michael O'Brien, Gary McKay and Bruce Cameron,[89] Horner did not go on to write specifically about either his own experience in Vietnam or that of his battalion. Horner's publishing while a cadet at RMC reflected an emerging interest in the higher levels of command, a curiosity further piqued by his seven months on active service: 'As an infantry platoon commander my main focus was on my job, and there was not much scope for comprehending the larger war.'[90] As Horner turned his mind again to scholarship, 'boys' own stories' were not 'quite what … [he] … wanted to do'. There were bigger questions to be answered, which directed his interest

---

86   David Horner, conversation with the author, 2019.
87   Horner, interview.
88   Peter Scott, email to author, 23 June 2023.
89   Robert A Hall, *Combat Battalion: The Eighth Battalion in Vietnam* (Sydney: Allen & Unwin, 2000); Michael J O'Brien, *Conscripts and Regulars: With the Seventh Battalion in Vietnam* (Sydney: Allen & Unwin, 1995); Gary J McKay, *In Good Company: One Man's War in Vietnam* (Sydney: Allen & Unwin, 1991); Bruce Cameron, *Canister! On! Fire!: Australian Tank Operations in Vietnam* (Newport: Big Sky Publishing, 2012).
90   David M Horner, 'David Horner 3rd Battalion, RAR 1971' in *Vietnam: Our War—Our Peace*, edited by John Moremon (Canberra: Department of Veterans' Affairs, 2006), 132–33.

to 'the whole mechanism of war rather than just the experience of war'.[91] It was this conviction that would guide his 18-year transition from Army officer to university academic.

In the decade after his active service in Vietnam, Horner completed the postgraduate qualifications that would provide the foundations for his authority as a scholar. While there was no specific institutional support for the postgraduate study of history within the Army, Horner leveraged arrangements stemming from the transition to degree-level education at RMC to complete a Master of Arts in History as a full-time student in the Faculty of Military Studies at RMC—the first student to do so.[92] After a period of regimental service in 1 RAR (Horner's full military biography appears in Appendix 1), he completed a PhD in the Department of International Relations at the ANU, although he was still studying history.[93]

Old mentors were close at hand. Horner's MA on the command crisis in Papua in 1942 was completed under the supervision of Alec Hill, who had seeded the topic years before by describing Lieutenant General Sidney Rowell's sacking, after the general's presentation at RMC in 1969.[94] Bob O'Neill, by that time Head of the Strategic and Defence Studies Centre (SDSC) at ANU, assisted Horner in having his MA thesis published as *Crisis of Command: Australian Generalship and the Japanese Threat*, then supervised his PhD research, in which Horner examined Australia and Allied strategy in the Pacific War. In the acknowledgments to his thesis, Horner noted:

---

91   Horner, interview.
92   The University of New South Wales did not accredit studies completed before the establishment of the Faculty of Military Studies, so officers who graduated from Duntroon between 1967 and 1970 did not receive degrees. The Army later implemented a program to allow these officers to complete degrees. Horner had completed an MA qualifying course in his own time, so he used the scheme to undertake his MA (David M Horner, 'Writing History in the Australian Army', *Australian Journal of Politics and History* 40, no. 1 (April 1994): 75–76, doi.org/10.1111/j.1467-8497.1994.tb00091.x). The Faculty of Military Studies commenced postgraduate programs in 1972 (*RMC Annual Report 1972*, 10).
93   The status of the Strategic and Defence Studies Centre (SDSC) within The Australian National University at this time meant it could not have its own PhD students; they were enrolled with the Department of International Relations. As Horner has recalled, however, '[I]n [a] practical sense they were part of SDSC' (David M Horner, 'Researching History at SDSC', in *A National Asset: 50 Years of the Strategic and Defence Studies Centre*, edited by Andrew Carr and Desmond Ball [Canberra: ANU Press, 2016], 124–25, doi.org/10.22459/na.08.2016.07).
94   Horner, interview.

> I have benefited greatly from [O'Neill's] wisdom and advice not only whilst undertaking this study, but over the years from the time when in 1967 he encouraged a young staff cadet, who had never previously studied history, to believe that he might be capable of undertaking post-graduate studies.[95]

Writing in 2016, Horner further reflected: 'It was probably due to his expert supervision I was awarded the Crawford Prize for the thesis.'[96]

However, not all in the broader military community were comfortable with a junior officer delving into the Army's past. One senior officer whom Horner approached during his MA research wrote to the Commandant of RMC, affronted that Horner was examining the performance of Australia's wartime commanders.[97] When *Crisis of Command* was published, the Army's Military Secretary—its chief of officer appointments and promotions—urged that Horner be reprimanded for publishing a book without permission. The Chief of the General Staff, Lieutenant General Don Dunstan, disagreed; Horner had forwarded him a copy of the book, which he had read and thought of great value to the Army.[98]

This latter incident reveals two of the key characteristics of Horner as soldier–scholar. The first was his desire to write something 'useful to the military'.[99] *Crisis of Command* opened not with immediate reference to the Second World War but to the challenges faced by contemporary defence chiefs in reorienting Australia's defence posture from a policy of forward to continental defence in the post-Vietnam period.[100] *High Command*, the published version of Horner's PhD, closed with a similar practical tone: 'Australia's experience in strategic decision-making in the Second World War has many lessons which are relevant to present and future security problems.'[101] The second characteristic was the reputation he built within the higher echelons of the Army through the production of 'useful' history, alongside several staff postings inside Army Headquarters that put his

---

95   David M Horner, 'Australia and Allied Strategy in the Pacific 1941–1946' (PhD thesis, The Australian National University, 1980), xvi.
96   Horner, 'Researching History at SDSC', 125.
97   Horner, 'Writing History in the Australian Army', 76.
98   Horner, interview.
99   Horner, interview.
100 David M Horner, *Crisis of Command: Australian Generalship and the Japanese Threat, 1941–1943* (Canberra: Australian National University Press, 1978), xv.
101 David M Horner, *High Command: Australia's Struggle for an Independent War Strategy, 1939–1945* (Canberra: Australian War Memorial; Sydney: George Allen & Unwin, 1982), 446, doi.org/10.4324/9781003120193.

analytical skills to work.[102] He would become a trusted insider and authority of first resort on historical matters—access and authority that would endure beyond his retirement from the Regular Army.

The 1983 yearbook of the Australian Command and Staff College observed of Major David Horner:

> David's view on grand strategy, strategy, tactics etc… were established early in the year. Although the Commandant didn't know all the visiting lecturers personally, David did … He was the only member of the course who could say that he had not only read the book but had 'written the book'. His record for the longest question asked in Monash Hall is expected to remain in the College statutes for a long time.[103]

Now in his thirties, Horner was a mid-career officer and an established historian with two well-regarded books, in addition to another two edited collections and several articles to his credit. Horner's success was built on a distinct discipline and work ethic. His postgraduate theses were produced in finite windows of time before he returned to the mainstream Army; the rest of his research and writing took place in addition to the day-to-day duties of his postings, although his superiors were often supportive and the work complementary.[104] Ron Huisken, who shared an office with Horner when they were both PhD scholars, recalled:

> It will surprise no one that David Horner was as serious, studious and systematic as a PhD candidate as he has been throughout his academic career … I recall marvelling at the permanent order of his desk—even though he was writing his thesis and the book version more or less simultaneously.[105]

This discipline accounts not only for Horner's prodigious output as a scholar but also his unashamedly empirical, narrative style. Reflecting on his method, Horner noted he 'figured out' 'a system' early. He embarked on his MA thesis with a thematic approach in mind, but he soon dismissed it due to its lack of efficiency: '[Y]ou end up covering stuff again and again.' He decided to 'tell the story as a narrative', building up the historical context in a 'top down' fashion, modelled on the approach of Gavin Long,

---

102 Horner, interview.
103 'David Horner', *Tookarook: The Command and Staff College Journal*, 1983: 2–3.
104 Horner, interview.
105 R Huisken, email to author, 14 June 2023.

that moved through the strategic to the operational to the tactical level, if required: 'And if you've got issues to bring out, and you must have issues, you bring them out as you go.' This approach was supported by systematic archival research characterised by a mantra familiar to Horner's students and colleagues: 'An hour in the archives, an hour in the office.' Material derived from different archival sources and series was arranged in hard copy in chronological order to produce the 'story in the file' from which the initial draft of the narrative was written. Gaps in that narrative would guide further research, which was either archival or utilised interviews. Interviews have formed another pillar of Horner's research.[106]

Horner's narrative approach has also been shaped by the practical motivations of his scholarship:

> I am also conscious that I should be writing for the general public. I'm not writing for academics. I'd rather have a short sentence than a long sentence, I'd rather write to make the thing clear to people perhaps almost in a didactic sense—that they can understand it.

One of his PhD examiners chastised: 'This will be a better book than a thesis, which is no doubt what the student intended.' To which Horner's response was: 'Right on!'[107] Horner would, thus, not disagree with Joan Beaumont's characterisation of the tradition of history to which he belongs as 'strongly empirical, theoretically unadventurous'.[108] At a time when the Israeli military historian Martin van Creveld was warning of a divorce between 'academics and the general public' because of the substitution of 'rigorous analysis for narrative', Horner was seeking to reconcile the two.[109] While Horner may have eschewed theoretical engagement, let alone abstraction, this should not be read as a lack of sophistication nor undermine the pioneering nature of his scholarship. *High Command* is an exemplar of these aspects of his work. Not only did it examine Australian political aspirations and strategic decision-making, it did so in the context of Allied policies and objectives, the available intelligence and the personalities involved. In so doing, it opened areas of enquiry, such as Australian civil–military relations, that still await exploration in depth.

---

106 Horner, interview.
107 Horner, interview.
108 Joan Beaumont, 'The State of Australian History of War', *Australian Historical Studies* 34, no. 121 (2003): 166, doi.org/10.1080/10314610308596243.
109 Martin van Creveld, 'Thoughts on Military History', *Journal of Contemporary History* 18, no. 4 (1983): 554.

While much of Horner's work up until the 1980s was solitary scholarship, a continuing motivation was to advance the academic consideration of Australia's military history. The immediate post-Vietnam era, Horner recalled, was not the most conducive period to do so. Some in the civilian academic community were ambivalent, others openly hostile: 'You were a warmonger if you studied military history.' Horner drew on the analogy of cancer to argue his case: although cancer was seen as a universally bad phenomenon, it was still systematically studied to build understanding. War should be no different.[110]

More fertile ground for nurturing the study of military history was the Faculty of Military Studies at RMC, to which Horner returned, once more, as a Visiting Military Fellow in 1985. It was a position he had advocated for through contacts inside Russell Offices and reminiscent of O'Neill's secondment to RMC in 1967.[111] Horner was involved in research supervision and teaching, and, once his role transferred to the newly opened Australian Defence Force Academy (ADFA) the following year, program design.

By 1985, the RMC history department had significant academic momentum. Planning was well underway for its transfer to ADFA. It had established the international journal *War and Society* in 1983. Two MAs and two PhDs had been completed since 1979, and another five PhDs were underway. The department's postgraduate students hailed from both military and civilian backgrounds. Among the former were Christopher Coulthard-Clark, John Mordike, Peter Pedersen, Bob Hall and Brett Lodge, and among the latter, Kevin Fewster, Jeffrey Grey and Andrew Ross. Eleanor Hancock, a former diplomat, also joined the department as a member of the teaching staff in 1983 and would go on to complete her PhD at ANU.[112] The most notable of this cohort was Grey, whose PhD Horner supervised alongside Peter Dennis. Like Horner, Grey would rise to become a great in the field, and one of Australia's most internationally influential military historians.

This period also saw the beginnings of Horner's relationship with two other contributors to this volume: a staff cadet named John Blaxland, whom he first taught at RMC, and a major named Bob Breen, who sought his

---

110 Horner, interview.
111 Horner, interview.
112 Compiled from RMC annual reports 1979–85; Moore, *Duntroon*, 286.

guidance on a manuscript on 1 RAR in Vietnam.[113] Both would become soldier–scholars in their own right and future collaborators. Horner later reflected on his role as a mentor: 'I was interested in developing an academic discipline … You can't just rely on one person.'[114]

'A critical underpinning': Horner and history in SDSC

The circumstances of Horner's final transition from soldier to full-time scholar suggest the challenges inherent in maintaining a career as both. While at ADFA, Horner decided it was time to leave the Army. It was a time of relative peace and stability in the last years of the Cold War; there were limited deployment opportunities, and his prolonged absence from the sharp end of the Army meant he would not command an infantry battalion.[115] Ironically, having built a reputation as a historian of higher command and its function in the mechanism of war, Horner would never command above company level.

Horner's last posting in the Regular Army was at the Joint Services Staff College (JSSC). It was a position with both teaching and research responsibilities created by the Commandant, Brigadier Steve Gower, who was also a former student of PAC and would later become Director of the Australian War Memorial. While at JSSC, Horner worked on histories of the RAR and the Special Air Service Regiment, both of which—further demonstrating the reputation he had established in the Army as a history scholar—were commissioned by their respective leadership. He also began looking for a civilian position in an academic department. It took three years, but in 1990 he resigned from the Australian Regular Army with the rank of lieutenant colonel and joined the staff of the SDSC at ANU as a research officer.[116]

Horner's move to SDSC set him on the path to establishing his pre-eminent position in Australian military history. However, both patience and persistence would be required. It was four years before he was able

---

113 Bob Breen, *First to Fight: Australian Diggers, N.Z. Kiwis and U.S. Paratroopers in Vietnam 1965–66* (Sydney: Allen & Unwin, 1988).
114 Horner, interview.
115 Horner, interview.
116 Horner, interview.

to transition to an academic position in SDSC. Then, in 1999, the adoption of a very strict definition of the Pacific and Asia focus of SDSC's parent academic unit saw his position defunded. The Australian defence organisation, however, retained a belief in the value of Horner's work and, at the instigation of the Chief of the Defence Force, Admiral Chris Barrie, funded a Chair in Australian Defence History. That position remains the only named chair in Australian military history ever created and was held by Horner from 1999 until 2014.[117]

Horner's time at SDSC brought about a diversification of his work. His historical interests expanded from a predominantly Second World War focus to encompass more recent conflicts, and he ranged beyond strategy, command and operations into broader issues of defence policy and organisation, intelligence, and force structure. Conscious of the Centre's contemporary policy focus, he sought to alternately publish history books and those dealing with more contemporary issues. By his own admission, he was not as successful as he hoped: of the 18 books he published between 1990 and 2005, 'only four were on current defence issues'. Not all his history publications 'fitted into the template of … history with a currently policy relevance', but he believed most did.[118] Nonetheless, Horner considered that history provided a 'crucial underpinning for research into contemporary issues' at SDSC.[119]

In addition to teaching, supervision and publishing, Horner remained active within the wider military and history communities. He acted as an adviser to the Army, the Department of Veterans' Affairs and the Australian War Memorial. As a member of the Army Reserve, he was head of the Land Warfare Studies Centre (1998–2002). He also served for extended periods on the Defence Honours and Awards Appeals Tribunal (2008–15) and the Army Battle Honours Committee (2007–22).

Most notably, Horner shaped several projects of national significance. He was Chair of the Armed Services Working Party of the *Australian Dictionary of Biography* (1994–2020), the founding editor of the Australian Army History Series, which has become the most sustained collection of

---

117 Horner, interview; Horner, 'Researching History at SDSC', 127–28. See also Paul Dibb, 'SDSC in the Nineties: A difficult transition', in *A National Asset: 50 Years of the Strategic and Defence Studies Centre*, edited by Andrew Carr and Desmond Ball (Canberra: ANU Press, 2016), 110–11, doi.org/10.22459/NA.08.2016.
118 Horner, 'Researching History at SDSC', 126–27.
119 Horner, 'Researching History at SDSC', 126–27, 135.

academic publishing on Australian military history, and the official historian of Australian Peacekeeping, Humanitarian and Post–Cold War Operations, and of ASIO. Horner's advocacy was instrumental in the commissioning of an official history of Australian operations in Timor-Leste, Iraq and Afghanistan. His reflections on this role once again highlight his dual commitment to producing history of national significance and upholding the standards of the discipline that he helped to build:

> The argument that I put, among others, was that the sorts of fighting that took place in Iraq and Afghanistan might have some similarity with what's going to happen in the future. Technicalities might change … but it will be much better if people have read a book about what happened in Iraq and Afghanistan than they do about what happened in the Napoleonic Wars if you want to have some appreciation of what it might be like to fight in a future war … We need to have military history that's based on good information, not just on what some journo happened to get by interviewing a few people.[120]

Delivering a lecture in honour of another renowned soldier–scholar, Britain's Sir Michael Howard, Hew Strachan observed how rarely he drew upon his service as junior officer in the Second World War during his academic career:

> [H]is reflections on his own service have been scattered and infrequent, and often his allusions to his own experience are indirect rather than direct … [A]lthough he has given us flashes and insights into the nature of front-line experience, he has not chosen to write about that experience in a sustained way. Instead his response to the war has been to contextualise it.[121]

These remarks could be applied without adaptation to Horner. He carries his own service lightly. He speaks infrequently of it, and most know little of his experiences in Vietnam. Horner's contribution to a Department of Veterans' Affairs' commemorative booklet featuring 44 individual 'Vietnam stories' is characteristic: it focuses on his scholarship rather than his personal experience.[122] The origins of this reticence can only be surmised. Humility, perhaps? Just one year in a long career? Or a recognition, in the light of years

---

120 Horner, interview.
121 Hew Strachan, 'Michael Howard and the dimensions of military history', *War in History* 27, no. 4 (2020): 539–40, doi.org/10.1177/0968344520915028.
122 Horner, 'David Horner 3rd Battalion, RAR 1971', 132–33.

of study, of his small part in a much larger drama: 'Whether a particular platoon commander does well or not doesn't decide the fate of the nation ... Whether we get the strategy and high command right does'?[123]

Horner admits that there are some aspects of active service—such as the 'shared bond' of 'a platoon in Vietnam [that] might spend up to thirty days on patrol'—that can only be truly understood by those who have experienced it. Further, he has listed several 'advantages' that his military service lent to his practice of military history: 'immense credibility', a well-developed understanding of the 'military system', meaning it did not need to be learned from scratch, and access to records unavailable to others.[124] While serving in the Army, Horner was aware of his privileged position, but he was unapologetic:

> While I was working on ... [*Phantoms of the Jungle*[125]] an academic colleague complained to me that it was not fair that I had been given access to classified material that was not available to civilian academic researchers. I told him that he too could get such access if he cared to join the Army and serve for twenty years.[126]

Nevertheless, Horner has been a gracious mentor to many emerging scholars without military service, or who have military experience but have not heard the crack-thump of rounds fired in anger.

What matters to Horner is not an individual's background but their willingness to master the whole 'technical business'—what Jeffrey Grey once described as 'know[ing] a corps from a company'[127]—and then have confidence in its application. Horner's academic inclusiveness is best epitomised by his unlikely friendship with Des Ball. As Head of SDSC, Ball facilitated Horner's transition to civilian academia but had protested against Australia's involvement in Vietnam. Horner described Ball as holding political views 'on the verge of communism'. The two, however, worked closely on multiple projects. Horner's esteem for Ball is encapsulated in a single, short observation: 'Des would follow the evidence.'[128]

---

123 Horner, interview.
124 Horner, interview.
125 David M Horner, *SAS: Phantoms of War: A History of the Australian Special Air Service* (Sydney: Allen & Unwin, 1989).
126 Horner, 'Writing History in the Australian Army', 76–77.
127 Jeffrey Grey, 'Writing About War and the Military in Australia', *Australian Historical Studies* 34, no. 122 (2003): 385, doi.org/10.1080/10314610308596261.
128 Horner, interview.

Although Horner has often contextualised his history in terms of contemporary defence priorities, he has never been either an instrumentalist —seeking to identify specific lessons learned—or a vociferous public advocate for particular positions on defence policy issues. Horner writes to inform rather than instruct. The authority of his voice is founded in robust scholarship. His conclusion to the first edition of *Phantoms of the Jungle* is illustrative:

> It is not the purpose of this book to argue a detailed case for the employment of special action forces and the efficacy of special forces operations. However, the history of the SAS in Australia indicates there has been little clear thinking in Canberra about the whole issue of special forces and special operations. The history of the SAS is one of a continuing search for an acceptable role within the Army which generally had little idea how to use the unique skills of the unit.[129]

In *The Gunners*, there is subdued advocacy advanced with a clear allusion to his own service:

> Despite many technological developments, there is still no substitute for artillery fire support. The gunners know this. Any infantryman who has been in battle also knows it. The gunners' greatest challenge is to ensure that this lesson does not have to be re-learned on the battlefield again at great cost of lives.[130]

However, this is about as far as he goes. Despite his experiences during Operation Overlord, Horner has never entered the frequent, and often vigorous, public debates about the place of armour in the Army's force structure.

Horner, nonetheless, has continued to write to inform the wider community and has at times been frustrated that this component of his work has not received sufficient recognition within academia.[131] He is no populist, however, and has no truck with nationalist metanarratives. Indeed, he fell afoul of elements of the media and some veterans due to statements at the 2012 Australian War Memorial History Conference, asserting that the Kokoda Track campaign lacked the strategic significance popularly attributed

---

129 Horner, *Phantoms of War*, 459.
130 David M Horner, *The Gunners: A History of Australian Artillery* (Sydney: Allen & Unwin, 1995), 523.
131 Horner, interview.

to it.[132] Likewise, there are no heroes or villains in Horner's narratives. The influence of personality on command has been a continuing theme of his work, but he has sometimes been criticised for not being forthright in his judgements of individuals. Perhaps this aspect of Horner's approach speaks to the essential humanity underlying his scholarship. Commanders, he has noted, are 'not just machines … they're people who bring to the task a certain background … and they have a certain personality'. The recognition that there are shades of grey, and that commanders have difficult choices to make between less-than-ideal options, may also reflect the insight of someone who has commanded men in combat.[133]

Conclusion

Horner is the epitome of the soldier–scholar. Although he began his working life as a soldier in 1966 and finally retired as a university professor in 2014, his is not a career of two halves. Rather, it should be seen as a single vocation with a shifting emphasis between the practical and the intellectual. Recalling Colonel David Thompson's enjoinder for Horner to do his 'time in the trenches', this chapter has shown that he did so in both fields of endeavour. Although he may not express it this way, the core running through his career is service: to the nation and to his discipline.

In a *festschrift*, it is customary to sum up the subject's contribution to their field. What is Horner's? An unparalleled body of literature examining the dynamics of Australian strategy and command, set in the context of the nation's geopolitical circumstances, stands beside supporting histories of Australian intelligence, operations, force structure, and organisation. Horner has also fostered historians—military and civilian alike—across several generations, as the varied authorship of this volume attests. Through these tandem achievements, Horner—following, leading and alongside others mentioned in this chapter—laid the foundations for a profession of military history in Australia. He is one of the chief proponents of a tradition of military historiography that could perhaps be called the 'Duntroon School': one firmly grounded in empiricism, that privileges policy, strategy,

---

132 See, for example, S Black, '"Truth" Hits Diggers', *Gold Coast Bulletin*, 22 October 2012, 11; I McPhedran, 'Criticism is over the Top', *Herald Sun*, 22 October 2012, 5; S Black, 'Fury at Kokoda Dismissal', *The Daily Telegraph*, 23 October 2012, 15; S Black, 'Proud Battlers did it for Nation', *Herald Sun*, 3 November 2012, 11.
133 Parts of this section reflect discussions with Professor John Blaxland, for which I thank him.

command, operations and tactics over the social history of war; one that has shunned nationalist interpretations but that, with close links to the armed forces, generally does not take issue with their values and ethos. Nonetheless, taking up Keogh's baton, it is an approach that does not resile from criticism when the archival record demands it.

Horner has long inspired his students and colleagues with his energy and discipline. Rhys Crawley recalls the beginnings of a research trip to the United States with him:

> [W]hen [on the flight over] all I managed was a few movies and a few more beers, David edited two book manuscripts. Jetlagged, but at risk of missing our connecting flight, he then proceeded to beat me—36 years his junior—in a foot race from one LAX terminal to another.[134]

As the work on this *festschrift* neared its end, Professor Emeritus David Horner AM remained busy continuing to sit on PhD advisory panels and finalising another manuscript. In the interview that helped inform this chapter he observed: 'I have been interested in this subject as a discipline, and as a hobby, all my life. I can't see myself just stopping.'[135] The introduction of one of his more recent books, *The War Game*, however, reveals his continuing motivation to be more than just the habit of a lifetime:

> This [strategy] might seem to be an esoteric matter, but if governments get the strategy wrong, the cost is borne by the soldiers on the battlefield, their families, that nation's treasury and its reputation.[136]

It is the reflection of not just half a century of study, but also personal witness to the costs of the battlefield.

---

134 Rhys Crawley, draft of Chapter 9 of this publication.
135 Horner, interview.
136 David M Horner, *The War Game: Australian War Leadership from Gallipoli to Iraq* (Sydney: Allen & Unwin, 2022), 6.

2

Living the legacy: David Horner and Official History in Australia

Craig Stockings

One of David Horner's signal achievements was his appointment as Australia's fifth official historian, which included his leadership and general editorship of the six volumes of the Official History of Australian Peacekeeping, Humanitarian and Post–Cold War Operations between 1947 and 2006.[1] During that time, at least 30,000 Australian peacekeepers took part in over 50 operations in more than two dozen theatres of conflict around the world, and a similar number of disaster-relief operations. Yet, Horner's connection to Official History in Australia goes deeper still. It was he, for example, who scoped, agitated for and successfully initiated a process that led to government approval for the Official History of Australian Operations in Iraq and Afghanistan, and of Australian Peacekeeping Operations in East Timor. The two projects have similarities and a great many differences, but one key consistent factor is David Horner's guiding hand.

---

1 These six volumes are as follows (all published by Cambridge University Press, Melbourne): vol. I: P Londey, R Crawley and DM Horner, *The Long Search for Peace: Observer Missions and Beyond, 1947–2006*, 2020; vol. II: DM Horner, *Australia and the New World Order: From Peacekeeping to Peace Enforcement, 1988–1991*, 2011; vol. III: DM Horner and J Connor, *The Good International Citizen: Australian Peacekeeping in Asia, Africa and Europe, 1991–1993*, 2014; vol. IV: J Bou, DM Horner, B Breen, G Pratten, and M de Vogel, *The Limits of Peacekeeping: Australian Missions in Africa and the Americas, 1992–2005*, 2019; vol. V: B Breen, *The Good Neighbour: Australian Peace Support Operations in the Pacific Islands, 1980–2006*, 2011; vol. VI: S Bullard, *In Their Time of Need: Australia's Overseas Emergency Relief Operations, 1918–2010*, 2017.

What follows is a brief discussion of the power and pitfalls of the tradition of modern Official History in Australia, with a focus on Horner's influence on both his Peacekeeping series and my own, and the challenges he faced as an official historian. The chapter will highlight the evolution of these challenges—and of the process of researching and writing Official History—from 2004 to 2021, and from one series to the next. The nature of the restrictions placed upon the contemporary official historian will be examined, along with the impediments placed in the way of, and the frustrations that invariably confront, that person. 'The role of Official Historian,' wrote Prime Minister Malcolm Turnbull, 'is one of great national significance in ensuing the production of authoritative, comprehensive and accurate accounts of Australia's military operations.'[2] What that meant to Horner, what it means now, and his position at the front edge of this tradition for more than two decades remain key elements in the history of this historian.

The Australian Official History tradition

The writing of Official History in Australia has a century-old tradition, from 1914 to 2014. It is an institution tied intimately to the Australian War Memorial (AWM), which has sponsored such work from its inception. Yet the projects themselves have always been commissioned by the government. As such, they are histories of, and for, all Australians. They are a detailed, chronological record of all services and theatres of conflict, and they constitute an invaluable resource for readers at all levels, from the scholar to the general public. They are, moreover, enduring national assets: comprehensive, authoritative, independent and accessible accounts of the Australian experience of war.

The last point is worth dwelling upon. Unlike similar projects across the Anglosphere, Australia's Official History tradition is unique in that these works are produced outside the system. That is, no public service department or agency controls the research or production of Australian Official History volumes. No one may direct the contents of the history or unduly attempt to influence the official historian—at least, not in theory, but more on that later. In this sense, Official Histories are 'official' only inasmuch as they are commissioned by the government as the national record of Australia's

---

2   Letter, Turnbull to Stockings (C15/109467), 27 January 2016, in possession of author.

involvement in particular conflicts. The official historians are granted access to closed period and security classified government records, yet the volumes contain their authors' own interpretations and judgements; they do not follow any official or government line. They are, in this sense, a record of government actions and decisions based on government sources. They are not government stories, however, or means by which certain narratives might be perpetuated at the expense of others. They are the product of historical investigations by independent researchers. The government pays the bill—it does not decide what is written. Official Histories are also a foundation and framework for future historians, and an accessible way for the public and the veteran community to gain insight into the operations and theatres under examination. This is particularly important today, given perceptions of a disconnection between the 'wars' under study and the wider Australian public. It is also important in light of what might be described as mismatches between the public narrative of events in East Timor, Iraq and Afghanistan, and the historical evidence at hand. Our outlook has been straightforward. We have not self-censored. We have included the good with the bad—frictions and mistakes are as valid a part of the historical record as unbridled successes. Achievements in spite of institutional shortcomings tend to enhance the legacy of those involved, not the reverse. We have written it as we have seen it, and as the evidence trail has indicated. These volumes, therefore, aim to be truthful, not necessarily triumphal.

Australian governments have, thus far, commissioned six separate series of official war histories over this period, one for each of the major conflicts, or areas of conflict, in which Australia has been involved. The inaugural Official History of Australia in the War of 1914–1918 is a 12-volume series covering Australia's involvement in the First World War. The series was edited by the first Official Historian, Charles Bean, who personally authored six of the volumes and the series was published between 1920 and 1942. The books, with their familiar covers, 'the colour of dried blood', in the words of one reviewer, set both the standard and the tradition. Following Bean, the Official History of Australia's involvement in the Second World War represents one of the longest and largest historical projects Australia has ever seen. The enterprise began in January 1943 with the appointment of Gavin Long as official historian and amounted to some 22 volumes, written by 14 authors, and was published by the AWM over a 25-year period between 1952 and 1977. The third Official History series was produced under the guiding hand of Professor Robert O'Neill, who was appointed the official historian for a Korean War series of two volumes published jointly by the AWM and the Australian Government Publishing Service in 1981 and 1985. Next, Professor Peter Edwards was appointed as the nation's fourth official historian in 1982 to produce a series on Australia's involvement in South-East Asian conflicts from 1948 to 1975. This nine-volume series deals with the Malayan Emergency (1948–60), the Indonesian-Malaysian Confrontation (1963–66) and the Vietnam War (1962–72). In keeping with the previous Official Histories, the series covers Australian combat operations by all three services, as well as the areas of strategy, diplomacy, home front politics and society, and medical matters.

More recently, and as previously noted, in 2004 Professor David Horner was commissioned to write a fifth Official History, this one relating to peacekeeping and post–Cold War operations. This Official History was undertaken as a joint project between the AWM and the ANU. At the same time, Horner was busy laying the groundwork for a decision that would be made 11 years later, in mid-2015, to proceed with a sixth series documenting Australian involvement in Iraq (2003–11), Afghanistan (2001–14), and East Timor (1999–2012). This is the origin of my own rather long title of Official Historian of Australian Operations in Iraq and Afghanistan, and Australian Peacekeeping Operations in East Timor. The current Official History team and I are responsible for a four-volume series dealing with the Middle East, and a separate two-volume series dealing with East Timor, all under the banner of the above title.

The national significance of Official History speaks for itself. Leaving aside the nation-changing experiences of the two world wars, even most recently, Australia's involvement in the Middle East has been complex and long-running. Well over 40,000 ADF and public service personnel served or supported these deployments over 13 years of operations. Sadly, 44 Australians died on active service in these theatres, and hundreds were wounded. The social and military effect of these conflicts globally, and within Australia, has been profound. Australia's involvement in East Timor from 1999 to 2000 was Australia's largest mission conducted under United Nations (UN) auspices, the largest overseas deployment since the Vietnam War and instrumental in Timor-Leste gaining its independence. Subsequent ADF deployments gave vital support to the fledgling nation.[3] As was the case for conflicts covered in all previous Official History series, taken in

---

3   C Stockings, *Born of Fire and Ash: Australian Operations in Response to the East Timor Crisis 1999–2000*, vol. I of The Official History of Peacekeeping Operations in East Timor (Sydney: UNSW Press, 2022).

total these operations constitute an important part of Australia's recent past, one that clearly needs to be chronicled in an analytical and authoritative manner.

To this end, and to underscore Horner's personal significance in the substance and tradition of Official History in Australia, I will not expend too many words on his own Peacekeeping series: the quality and impact of the series speaks for itself. Within this series, Horner authored Volume II, *Australia and the 'New World Order': From Peacekeeping to Peace Enforcement, 1988–1991*, covering peacekeeping missions that began between 1988 and 1991, including Namibia, Iran, Pakistan, Afghanistan and the Persian Gulf (including the first Gulf War). This volume was published in 2011. He further co-authored Volume III with Dr John Connor: *The Good International Citizen: Australian Peacekeeping in Asia, Africa and Europe, 1991–1993*, published in 2011, and contributed to the multi-authored Volume IV, *The Limits of Peacekeeping: Australian Missions in Africa and the Americas, 1992–2005*, published in 2019.

Horner and the sixth Official History series

Rather than focusing on this series, and closer to home—for me at least—I will concentrate on Horner's concurrent efforts to establish the sixth Official History series. Although talked about in a number of academic, public service and even political circles for some time, the real impetus for establishing an Official History of Australia's military operations in Iraq, Afghanistan and East Timor came primarily through Horner's efforts. When he was appointed as the Official Historian of Peacekeeping in 2004, Cabinet authorised the researching and writing of the history of all multinational and post–Cold War operations in which Australia has participated since 1947. This mandate, however, against Horner's efforts and advice, excluded recent operations in East Timor, Afghanistan and Iraq, as operations in these theatres were ongoing. When military commitments to East Timor temporarily concluded in 2006, Horner went back to the government and asked again for East Timor to be included in the Peacekeeping series. Again, he was refused.

Horner chose not to sit idly by as the wheels of government bureaucracy seemed so set against an Official History of operations in East Timor, for to do so risked not only wasting a great deal of time but would provide an opportunity for officialdom to continue to make the wrong decisions.

Instead, Horner began at what he considered to be the source of the problem—the Department of Foreign Affairs and Trade. Time and again, he was told there was little chance that the decision to exclude East Timor would be overturned. Nevertheless, he persisted. When Horner suggested that he might like to speak directly to the Minister, he was told that such an outreach would be not only inappropriate but impossible. Suddenly, Horner was aware that, if this was the advice, his best course of action would be to do the reverse. He indeed sought, and was granted, an audience with Alexander Downer. Much to the chagrin of those officials in attendance, the Minister promptly agreed with Horner in that, of course, East Timor ought to be covered. Yet, such directions were not immediately translated into action.

Even as progress on his Peacekeeping series continued, Horner never stopped advocating for the inclusion of ongoing operations to be taken within his, or a subsequent, Official History series. At every chance, including at the launch of the Peacekeeping volume in April 2011, Horner spoke of the 'national disgrace' in the ongoing failure to capture and publicise the history of these operations. At this point, his advocacy gained traction. Kevin Rudd, then Foreign Minister, gave his support, and in September 2011, the AWM commissioned Horner to draft a feasibility study into the possibility of writing a new Official History series capturing Australian involvement in Iraq and Afghanistan. This was completed by the following March and turned into a Cabinet submission. Three times this submission was put forth, containing options to either expand the Peacekeeping series to include East Timor and other operations up to 2006, or to raise a new series for Iraq and Afghanistan. The first submission was set aside with the fall of the Gillard government in 2013, the second was shelved when Kevin Rudd called an election, and the third was presented to the new coalition Prime Minister, Tony Abbott.

As Horner, and AWM staff and management, urged in their third submission, there were compelling reasons for a new Official History to capture the large-scale and ongoing operations in the Middle East. The proximity and sensitivities surrounding these operations, Horner argued, should not prevent this. On the contrary, a new series, written as close as possible to the events they were chronicling, would provide a public who was interested in these events, yet in many ways disconnected from them, with an authoritative account of Australian involvement.

There soon emerged an obvious spanner in the works. If the Peacekeeping Official History series traced ADF operations up to, and including, the liberation of Kuwait in 1991, and the series proposed in 2012 picked up the story of Afghanistan from 2001 and the second war with Iraq in 2003, what then of East Timor? The blunt answer was not, of course, that Horner or the AWM had failed to consider operations in this theatre from 1999 to 2012. Indeed, the expansion of the Peacekeeping series to include East Timor had been a submission in itself, wrapped up in broader 'omnibus' Cabinet submissions that had also called for a new Official History of Iraq and Afghanistan. Rather, at the time, political signals were such that it was pointless to press the issue. Nonetheless, as a decision that looked like approval for the Middle East series was looming, the extraordinary potential arose for two separate Official History series dealing with deployments before and after operations had began in East Timor but leaving these critical operations out in the cold. This awkward proposition, as Horner had long argued, could not be allowed to stand. At last, for reasons that remain unclear, his cries fell on fertile ground. By the direction of the 2015 Abbott government, what was originally proposed as a six-volume study of operations in the Middle East was extended to include a single-volume study of East Timor.[4]

My own initial contact with the sixth Official History series was, again, initiated by David. Not satisfied with having secured a new series after much trying, he now set about conducting informal interviews with people he might consider fit to run it. Such was the reasoning behind a long lunch at Boffins, University House, the spiritual heart of the ANU. As we ate, David slowly introduced me to the idea and gently suggested I apply for the upcoming position of official historian. He was careful to guide me down the path of what such a project might look like, what types of challenges might emerge and how they might be solved. His was the hand on my shoulder, guiding the Official Histories forward as he had been doing for so long. After my own appointment as official historian, charged by Prime Minister Turnbull to deliver the new series, I began work at the AWM in mid-March 2016. One of my very first decisions was to raise a personal advisory panel. Horner was the first to be asked and was the first to agree to the appointment.

---

4   Record of Cabinet decision, 14 April 2015, TA15/0169/CAB, in possession of author.

Writing the sixth Official History

Undoubtedly, each of the five Official Histories that have preceded my own has faced its own specific challenges and enjoyed its own individual advantages.[5] At the same time, however, the process of writing such histories has evolved. The first two series each dealt with single wars, although these were enormous conflagrations with multiple theatres of conflict. The third covered a single conflict and theatre. Professor Peter Edwards covered three separate conflicts: the Malayan Emergency, the Indonesian Confrontation and the Vietnam War. Horner's last official series, covering peacekeeping, and humanitarian and post–Cold War operations, took in more than 120 missions over a period of more than 90 years. In this context this series—the Official History of Australian Operations in Iraq and Afghanistan, and of Australian Peacekeeping Operations in East Timor—looks, in structural terms at least, something akin to the volume-set dealing with South-East Asian conflicts. We cover three 'conflicts': East Timor (Timor-Leste), Iraq and Afghanistan, over a similar timeframe. It is here, however, that similarities end. The effort to chronicle a wide range of ADF operations, both near and far from Australian shores from 1999 to 2014, marks an entirely new paradigm. This series is not, and could never be, a repeat of past experiences, updated in a new era. This is especially so in terms of the sensitivities and security considerations associated with the unprecedented impact of intelligence and intelligence agencies on tactical military operations. It is true also of the mechanics of research, and the broader environment under which my team has laboured. It is less so, of course, in terms of the tradition and philosophy behind past Australian Official Histories, which we seek to extend and enhance.

One key difference between this series and those that have gone before it is the type and level of governance imposed upon, and within, the project. In a stark reversal of the situation in which Horner's Peacekeeping series found itself, I have been well funded for this task, and the team has enjoyed a level of resourcing not available to past official historians. The obverse of deep government and AWM investment in the project is, however, an extremely tight timeline and reasonably rigid governance frameworks. My author

---

5 During RJ (Bob) O'Neill's tenure, for example, while the Australian Government maintained its tradition of granting independence to his work, it is understood that the Attorney-General's Department attempted to influence the series' treatment of the journalist and alleged traitor Wilfred Burchett.

teams initially had five years to complete their volumes—extended to six-and-a-half years in early 2018. This is a great deal less than has been available to any Official History project to date.

Another indication of the different circumstances the project has faced, labouring under considerable delivery expectations, may be the administrative structures that surround it. I am, perhaps, not as 'free' in terms of externally imposed governance as some of my predecessors. Yet, I do not see the administrative framework associated with this project as having been an imposition—indeed, I helped build it. This is a 'public service' project and needs to be managed as such. The very first committee established after my own Advisory Council was the Official History Records Access Steering Group, chaired conjointly by the Department of Defence and the Department of the Prime Minister and Cabinet (PM&C).[6] The purpose of this group was (and is) to act as a high-level coordination body between the project and select government departments, including PM&C, Foreign Affairs and Trade (DFAT), the National Archives of Australia, Defence and the Australian Federal Police (AFP). The committee was subsequently expanded to include representation from the ASIO, the Australian Secret Intelligence Service (ASIS), the Defence Intelligence Organisation (DIO), the Australian Geospatial-Intelligence Organisation (AGO), the Office of National Intelligence (ONI) and the Australian Signals Directorate (ASD). This steering committee helped identify the most appropriate methods by which necessary files and data were made available, and maintained protocols and pathways for project and external agency staff to work together.

Importantly, as with my more recent predecessors, my commission provided for controlled access to relevant government files and records, authorised under 'Special Access' conditions as set out in the *Archives Act 1983*, subject only to national security requirements and restrictions. As was the case for Horner's Peacekeeping series, though these volumes are themselves unclassified, they are based on a thorough study of the classified documentary records made available by the government for the operations covered. Material excluded from the Official History team and from publication, in whole or in part, is judged by relevant government departments and agencies to be potentially damaging to Australian national security or national interests. Those agencies that have chosen to restrict their cooperation and access have done so on these grounds. I do not

---

6   Co-chairmanship of this committee was subsequently altered to remove PM&C and to add the Department of Veterans' Affairs (DVA).

believe such omissions have altered the conclusions reached in the Official History volume in any fundamental manner. Similarly, during the process of 'clearing' these volumes for public release, each stakeholder department and agency has reviewed them and sought amendment where necessary, again on national security or national interests grounds. Some stakeholders have proven more invested than others in this regard, and the process has sometimes been difficult, as I will detail forthwith. Nonetheless, no changes have been wrought that threaten the overall truthfulness, credibility, legitimacy or integrity of the volumes.

The challenges of Official History

In terms of methodology and structure, Horner's work has served as a model for my own series. As was the case with Peacekeeping, the era when official military histories could be written almost exclusively from Defence records alone has long passed. Like the operations they describe and analyse, such volumes have required input from whole-of-government sources. To this end, this study is based not only on the official Defence records but on documents sourced from all the departments and agencies represented on the Official Records Access Steering Group. In some instances, this record is not as complete as might be hoped, given the speed of events and the challenges posed to archiving by the growth of electronic media. Nor was the available body of records for the early volumes of this series helped by the fact that the period 1999–2005 was in the middle of a transition from paper to electronic files within the Department of Defence. In any case, as applied to Horner's Peacekeeping series, such a record has been supplemented by extensive interviewing programs, vital for getting behind what sometimes appears as an artificial consensus of paperwork. To this body of material has been added a mountain of information from the UN and the North Atlantic Treaty Organization (NATO), as well as unclassified material sourced in Australia, Belgium, Canada, Indonesia, the Netherlands, New Zealand, Timor-Leste, the United Kingdom (UK) and the United States (US). Despite the whole-of-government reality of the operations covered in this series, and with due recognition of the vital context of the work of a great many government and non-government agencies in these theatres, its volumes must nonetheless—by necessity and mandate—centre themselves upon ADF operations. They are, therefore, neither social histories, political histories, nor the record of Australians who voluntarily, or at government behest, deployed to these regions. That said, such a study based a wide range of departmental and official sources would be very valuable indeed.

Beyond method and structure, it is not too much to suggest that David Horner's work left a more subtle imprint upon my own efforts. Such an influence is difficult to quantify and is perhaps more akin to an unspoken expectation. This itself represents what might be called the evolution in the purpose of Official Histories across the span of a century. Bean wrote, unapologetically and in line with the expectations of his era—and within the trauma of postwar Australia—for nationalistic and nation-building purposes. He wrote to construct a narrative about a country recently federated, and for veterans and their families to build a conceptual and chronological framework for their own raw experiences. Long followed this tradition, though less overtly, in the shadow of Bean's opus. Neither challenged the need for a 'good' story in a serious manner. Neither sought to ask pointed questions. To this end, both historians focused on story at the expense of meta-analysis and stayed away from controversy. They had no choice. National trauma and veteran sensibilities aside (and they could not, of course, be put aside), to engage with these issues in the context of the times would have been to lose respectability and, therefore, credibility. O'Neill moved expectations from such origins closer towards what might be recognised as a more modern analytical history. The narrative still prevails, but the evidence speaks more for itself and less for a nationalistic agenda. The scale, public impact and context of Korea made this possible in a manner not available to O'Neill's predecessors. This trend continued under Edwards. The shift, once more, was not just 'what' happened but 'why', and all the while more controversial issues were able to be tackled. This was, at least in part, made possible by social expectations, which allowed for more open critiques of national policy and decision-making without crossing a line that risked rejection by the public and veteran communities. Perhaps the unpopularity of Vietnam, and the social backlash that had followed it, edged the door further open.

The key point in the evolution of the Official History style was that by the time Horner wrote, the tradition he inherited was not the same as that which Long, O'Neill or Edwards had faced. Each, in turn, had shifted expectations. Horner ran with this. He wrote quite determinedly, without fear or favour. The point was to get to the historical 'truth', insofar as that was possible for a positivist and empirical researcher. Where things had gone well, David was very clear on their success and effectiveness. Where mistakes had been made, David described them. Where policy had fallen short, history recorded it. This, more than any other issue, was the imprint David left on me. History is history. Bad news and mistakes are just as valid a part of the historical record as are triumphs. The nature of Australian military commitments from 1999 to 2014 is such that this is—in my view—a key principle.

I recall another of the topics of conversation that fateful day in Boffins being the challenge of accessing records, particularly electronic records, from government departments and agencies. To this end, and subsequently, Horner shared his thoughts and advice. Valuable as these insights proved, it was soon apparent that the bureaucracy looked at events in East Timor, Iraq and Afghanistan with a whole new level of concern and sensitivity than it had with regard to the perceived 'benign' nature of peacekeeping. The relatively free hand his project was given to sift through the Department of Defence's electronic repositories was never going to be replicated for me—not that I knew it at the time. Far more appeared to be at stake for various parties—connected, I suspect, as closely to institutional reputation as to information security. With procedural and structural barriers in place, and the flow of records unacceptably slow from Defence as the largest 'customer' for the new series, events came to a head in 2017. The next result was an 18-month extension and the raising of a whole new Directorate within the department whose sole job was to catch and forward material to the project at an acceptable rate. In the end, flow rates were attained, but the personal mental toll had been heavy. At all points, there were few who were aware of the intricacies, structures, forces and personalities against and within which I struggled. One was David Horner. I regularly sought his advice. Where there were no answers, at the very least there was empathy. It helped.

As records began to flow into the project at a rapid rate, another key difficulty emerged, this one methodological. The challenge emerged in two parts, one practical and one psychological. The practical challenge might be described as the risk of drowning in a sea of infinite data. That is, all records created by Defence and government officials that in any way related to events in the three theatres under investigation exist in electronic forms. All email, texts, PowerPoint presentations, Word documents, spreadsheets and any other form of data presentation conceivable have been retained and are considered official records. While certainly not all such data is easily accessed or curated in a form that is easy to use, the point is that the *amount* of material open for historical purposes is enormous. What, then, is an empirical researcher to do? There is insufficient time and resources to examine even a fraction of this record. The more typical 'trawl' method or research, by which a scholar might try to collect a large proportion of available records for interrogation, is simply not possible in twenty-first-century Official History research. Rather, normative approaches had to be modified towards a much more targeted approach. Robust sets of filters needed to be built. To a far greater extent than in my own previous experience, specific sets of research questions need to be framed in advance of primary source work. That is, we seek targeted answers for specific questions, accepting that gaps will emerge as we progress and filling these in a similar manner when required. This has represented a challenging adjustment to the work habits of most of the team.

There is risk then, as well as opportunity, in the digital age of empirical historical methodologies. On the one hand, there is so much data available, and more will continue to become available as digital records management and interrogation systems improve. I see a future in which AI algorithms—robots—sit between a researcher and the sea of infinite records. Imagine writing book on Kokoda, for example, if every scrap of paper, every verbal briefing, every tangible item and artefact were available, rather than the merest fraction of the record currently preserved at the National Archives. How much richer might the historical product become? Yet, with so much source material available, would such a book ever be finished? Moreover, with the 'robot' between the researcher and the records, how much is lost by removing an ability to simply browse the stacks? Most historians will remember cases in which they were searching for a particular type of document, only to find that the one next to it—the one they did not know they needed—made everything fall into place? Will this serendipity be possible in the digital age? What danger accompanies the opportunities?

No less of a challenge were the psychological ramifications of infinite data. For me and most of the team, previous empirical research projects have involved working through a finite number of archival stacks. I feel I have been duly conscientious, for example, when I can place my hand on my heart and tell myself I have viewed the whole, or a goodly part, of the relevant record. I write history then from what I have seen. In truth, this sense of security has always been built on a falsehood. Intellectually, I am aware that the record that has entered various archives only ever represented less than a fraction of a per cent of that produced at the time. It has long ago been culled, collected and curated. I have only ever written history from the smallest sliver of data made available to me. Yet, I find solace in the fact that what lies outside of the archival record no longer exists or is no longer accessible. Now, however, the game has changed. I write a volume of Official History in full knowledge that not only have I examined a very small part of the available record, but that if I kept looking, the product would be incrementally 'better'. When and where to stop? Where is my solace now? To this question, all I can say is that mindsets have altered, and they have had to. We have deadlines and fiscal constraints. We need to stop when reasonable answers have been garnered to the research questions at hand. We need to be comfortable with what has *not* been done. This has not been an easy or comfortable transition. It is, however, how all future empirical research in the digital age will be framed.

Despite the difficulties of the digital age, the most difficult, traumatic, frustrating, mentally and emotionally draining aspect of producing the first volume of the Official History series, without question, had nothing to do with research or writing. Rather, the bureaucratic process of 'clearing' the volume on the East Timor crisis of 1999—my own volume—has been my greatest challenge. In all, it took three years of negotiation, confrontation, compromise, mediation and conciliation to have the volume approved for public publication.[7] As noted, due to the nature of sources used in its preparation, the draft volume was produced as a 'classified' document. It then entered a clearance process to ensure it contained no material inappropriate to release into the public domain. The difficulty here, however, was never about information security. It was, instead, about institutional 'comfort' at various levels. It was about content, not classification. A very large part of those three years of struggle were discussions, for example, about how much contextual and background material such a volume ought to contain. My view was that the amount of such material it contained needed to be such that a public reader could make contextual sense of the events of 1999. This included, for instance, a longer-term survey of Australia's policy position with regards the issue of East Timorese independence. This was not a view shared by all stakeholders.

Conclusion

However, in the end we got there: the volume was cleared and was published in 2022 as *Born of Fire and Ash: Australian Operations in Response to the East Timor Crisis of 1999–2000*. There were times when I did not think this

---

7   See press articles such as: 'This Official History of Australia's Role in the 1999 Timor-Leste Crisis Unpacks Our "Military Myths"', *Sydney Morning Herald*, 10 November 2019; 'This Official History of Australia's Role in the 1999 Timor-Leste Crisis Unpacks Our "Military Myths"', *ABC*, 9 February 2023; and 'Official History of Australia's Peacekeeping Efforts in East Timor Back on Track', *Sydney Morning Herald*, 25 January 2020.

would be the outcome. In those dark moments, more than once I reached out to David Horner to seek his counsel. He has been there. He had striven against his own clearance challenges with the Peacekeeping series. His was an opinion, and a set of experiences, that I respected. I felt this kinship acutely, especially in the midst of struggles that made the position of official historian feel like a lonely one. The messages from Horner were clear and consistent, and they buttressed my own lines of thought. This project was important, too important to take the easy path. I was writing not just for myself, but for the series, for researchers whom I oversaw, and for the tradition that has stood for more than a century. I could not sacrifice credibility for convenience. There were red lines that could not be crossed. In the end, I thought, it was better to produce no volumes than to produce works that failed to live up to their due. But let me not plant a seed of undeserved bravery or determination on my part. I have wavered, and I have vacillated. The words, thoughts and support of colleagues such as David Horner help ease the burden. We have one volume down and five to go. As I write, the second East Timor volume has entered its own clearance process. I hope and trust the passage will be easier this time. But, if not, as problems emerge, and where required, I would reach out once more.

Taken in total, Australian Official Histories are written for those hundreds of thousands of Australians who deployed to various theatres of conflict from 1914 to 2014, and for the hundreds of thousands more who supported them on a professional level back home, or emotionally. In more recent times, they have also been, and are being, written to shed light on the events at hand for the wider Australian community, who have sometimes had only a brief or passing connection to those events. The volumes are, further, written, one hopes, for the interest and education of generations not yet born. To this end, such series are always only a start, an important first brick in a foundation of future scholarship. Within this context, and certainly from the second half of the twentieth century onwards, no individual has had a greater impact on the tradition of Official History in Australia than David Horner. He was long a student of such works before becoming an official historian and author within his own series, and thereafter the architect for new series that followed. For myself, I have occasionally been asked if I feel the weight of tradition and of the legacy of Charles Bean. The answer is that yes, sometimes I do, but this is consistently offset by the hand of David Horner—a teacher, friend, mentor and guide.

Part II:
Strategy and high command

3

The psychology of strategic decision-making: Ambon 1941–42

Joan Beaumont

I first met David Horner in the Public Record Office (now The National Archives) in London. The Public Record Office had recently moved to Kew, and David and I were queuing to collect documents or order photocopies at an unnerving price that could only be charged in the pre-digital age. It was 1977, and we were both aspiring postdoctoral scholars in our late twenties. David told me of his forthcoming book, *Crisis of Command: Australian Generalship and the Japanese Threat*.[1] Little did I know that this would be the first of (at last count) 38 books he would go on to write, co-author and edit. *Crisis of Command* explored a theme that would infuse much of Horner's later work: how well did Australia's political and military leaders respond to threats to the nation's security?

The years 1941 to 1942 provide a classic case study of this issue, since, to quote Horner, this was the moment in Australian military history when the Australian high command was subject to 'the greatest stress'.[2] In the frantic three months after the outbreak of war with Japan, '[t]he strategic situation

---

1 David Horner, *Crisis of Command: Australian Generalship and the Japanese Threat, 1941–1943* (Canberra: Australian National University Press, 1978).
2 David Horner, 'Lieutenant-General Sir Vernon Sturdee: The Chief of the General Staff as Commander', in *The Commanders: Australian Military Leadership in the Twentieth Century*, edited by David M Horner (Sydney: George Allen & Unwin, 1984), 149.

deteriorated rapidly and the threat to Australia mounted daily'.[3] When judging how well Australia's military and political leaders responded to this crisis, Horner's conclusions were judicious and balanced—qualities that characterise all his work. While Australian Army leaders failed to anticipate the speed of the Japanese advance, Horner concludes that they could not be held accountable for the dire strategic situation confronting Australia. The deficiencies in the organisation of Army Headquarters for command, the lack of trained troops in Australia, the shortage of equipment and the dearth of young experienced leaders were undeniable, but '[p]ractically none of these shortcomings should be laid at the feet of the army leaders'.[4] Given the fiscal and industrial constraints on rearmament in the 1930s, and the agreement of the government of Robert Menzies to contribute the majority of Australian resources to the war in Europe and Malaya, the naval and air forces in Australia in the latter part of 1941 were 'almost non-existent'.[5] Hence, the options for defending Australia's immediate north against Japan were limited. Within the context of these constraints, Horner concludes that although Australia's military leaders made mistakes, 'and their conduct was not always as pure as it might have been, generally speaking Australia was well served by her generals in 1942'.[6] Specifically, he praises the Chief of the General Staff, Lieutenant General Vernon Sturdee, who brought to crisis management his sense of propriety, a recognition of the importance of sticking to the rules and 'his determination to face the disasters in a logical and calm manner'.[7]

There were, however, exceptions that might qualify this judgement. Among them was the decision by Sturdee in January 1942 to leave an Australian force consisting of the 2/21st Battalion and ancillary troops on the island of Ambon, even when its commanding officer insisted that it was doomed to fail and should be evacuated. Horner concedes that the deployment of Gull Force and its equally unfortunately named counterparts, Sparrow and Lark Forces, to Dutch Timor and New Britain respectively was ill-conceived: it was a 'token contribution to forward defence … merely grasping at straws'. Army Headquarters must be 'indicted for failing to assess realistically the chances of these garrisons'. Horner attributes the fate of these garrisons—

---

3   David Horner, *Defence Supremo: Sir Frederick Shedden and the Making of Australian Defence Policy* (Sydney: Allen & Unwin, 2000), 134.
4   Horner, 'Lieutenant-General Sir Vernon Sturdee', 154.
5   Horner, 'Lieutenant-General Sir Vernon Sturdee', 151.
6   Horner, *Crisis of Command*, 280.
7   Horner, 'Lieutenant-General Sir Vernon Sturdee', 154.

all of which were rapidly defeated in early 1942—to the fact that the army leaders found themselves caught between the cleft stick of Singapore and the defence of Australia. 'If Singapore held firm with a substantial naval force ready to strike at the Japanese, then there was little need to strengthen the garrisons in the islands.'[8]

This chapter does not seek to challenge this assessment but suggests that we need to understand more about the processes of decision-making concerning the islands strategy. Notably, three questions invite further exploration. First, why was the initial decision to support the Netherlands East Indies (NEI) taken with so little rational analysis of the possibility of successful defence? Second, why were Australian forces still sent to the NEI when it was clear, after the sinking of the Royal Navy's HMS *Prince of Wales* and HMS *Repulse* on 10 December 1941, that Singapore had no naval defences, and that the NEI might become the first line of defence? Finally, why, when the commander on the ground predicted disaster, were Australians left on Ambon to fight a hopeless cause rather than be withdrawn and concentrated elsewhere: perhaps in Malaya, northern Australia, or even the north coast of Papua, where the Japanese attacked in July 1942?

The answers to these questions lie partly in the documentary record of which Horner is such a master, but arguably we can only fully explain this 'penny packet' strategy if we delve into the psychology of decision-making. This is inherently perilous terrain for military historians, and one that has been neglected in Australian historiography. However, the decisions made in the crisis of 1941–42 were not always rational. Rather, they were shaped by emotions, intuitive preferences and biases of which the decision-makers themselves were possibly unaware. Horner acknowledges the importance of emotions: 'Men' he writes in *Crisis of Command*, 'are not automatons and their decisions are governed as much by emotion as logic.' These emotions, he continues, can be discerned in part by reading the commanders' personal correspondence, wherein is revealed 'elation and depression, suspicion and confidence, frustration and satisfaction, fortitude and trepidation'.[9]

However, this chapter argues that emotions are only one element in what might be called modes of cognition. In arguing thus, I draw on the analysis of decision-making by the late Nobel prize–winning Israeli-American behavioural psychologist Daniel Kahneman. In his critically acclaimed 2011

---

8   Horner, *Crisis of Command*, 36.
9   Horner, *Crisis of Command*, xviii.

bestseller, *Thinking, Fast and Slow*, Kahneman argues that the machinery of human cognition incorporates two modes of thought: 'System 1', which is fast, instinctive, automatic and emotional; and 'System 2', which is slower, more deliberative, and more logical, but arguably less persuasive.[10] The catastrophe of Ambon almost defies explanation unless we see it as an instance in which System 1 infused, even dominated, System 2 in the thinking of Australia's military leaders.

Kahneman's analysis is preferred here to the classic 1976 study of military incompetence by the experimental psychologist Norman Dixon, although this, too, provides useful insights.[11] Dixon's four key symptoms of military incompetence—wastage of manpower, overconfidence, underestimation of the enemy and the ignoring of intelligence reports—were, as we shall see, manifested by Australian military leaders in 1941–42. However, Dixon's ultimate conclusion, following his analysis of mostly British military disasters over the last century and half, is that military incompetence was not a function of stupidity but rather of the authoritarian personality of commanders and of the military systems that attracted these types. Some non-authoritarian generals might also have been hopelessly incompetent, but, Dixon asserts, 'one is hard put to it to find a great general or admiral who was not conforming, submissive to authority, punitive, sexually inhibited, over-controlled, ethnocentric, anti-intellectual, assailed by doubts as to his virility, anal-obsessive, superstitious, status-hungry, rigid, possessed of a "closed" mind, and saturated in discipline'.[12] This splendidly provocative conclusion has generated considerable debate over the years, but its utility in the case of our Ambon case study is limited.[13] With perhaps one exception, we lack the documentary evidence and oral history that might sustain claims about the personality types of key decision-makers and their propensity, if any, to authoritarianism. My analysis thus focuses on what we might learn from applying Kahneman's analysis of decision-making, and his concepts of System-1 and System-2 thinking, to the development of planning about the defence of Ambon, as revealed in the the archival record.

---

10   Daniel Kahneman, *Thinking, Fast and Slow* (New York: Farrar, Straus and Giroux, 2011).
11   Norman Dixon, *On the Psychology of Military Incompetence* (London: Jonathan Cape, 1976). For a useful review, see William Eckhardt, 'A Review Essay', *Peace Research: The Canadian Journal of Peace and Conflict Studies* 21, no. 1 (1989): 47–51.
12   Dixon, *On the Psychology*, 347–48.
13   In one critique of Dixon, Amos Perlmutter notes that since 1914, strategy is 'fusionist, both a political and military skill'. Military incompetence is, thus, 'no longer the sole property of generals but results from the combined efforts of inept strategists, in and out of uniform'. Amos Perlmutter, 'Military Incompetence and Failure: A Historical, Comparative and Analytical Evaluation', *Journal of Strategic Studies* 1, no. 2 (1978): 121–38, especially 121.

Kahneman's systems 1 and 2

It is not possible in this essay to do full justice to Kahneman's complex book, which distils not only his lifetime of research but also the findings of multiple other psychologists, including his close colleague, Amos Tversky. For our purposes, the key arguments concern System 1 and System 2—what Kahneman calls the 'fictitious characters' in decision-making processes. System 1 'operates automatically and quickly, with little or no effort and no sense of voluntary control'.[14] Continuously generating impressions, intuitions, intentions and biases, it maintains and updates a model of the individual's personal world, which represents what is normal.[15] Given the inherently confirmatory bias of System 1, people making decisions seek data that are likely to be compatible with the beliefs they currently hold. When they believe a conclusion is true, they are also 'very likely to believe arguments that appear to support it, even when these arguments are unsound'.[16] System 1, Kahneman further argues, also maintains a model of the personal world that is:

> constructed by associations that link ideas of circumstances, events, actions, and outcomes that co-occur with some regularity, either at the same time or within a relatively short interval. As these links are formed and strengthened, the pattern of associated ideas comes to represent the structure of events in your life, and it determines your interpretation of the present as well as your expectations of the future.[17]

System 2, in contrast, 'allocates attention to the effortful mental activities that demand it, including complex computations ... [Its] operations are often associated with the subjective experience of agency, choice and concentration'. It is the conscious reasoning self that 'has beliefs, makes choices and decides what to think about and what to do'.[18]

Generally, people believe that their decision-making is the domain of System 2—it is 'who we think we are'.[19] But, Kahneman argues, System 2 is slower, and this is not where 'the action is'. At the centre of the storm is

---

14 Kahneman, *Thinking, Fast and Slow*, 20.
15 Kahneman, *Thinking, Fast and Slow*, 71.
16 Kahneman, *Thinking, Fast and Slow*, 45.
17 Kahneman, *Thinking, Fast and Slow*, 71.
18 Kahneman, *Thinking, Fast and Slow*, 21.
19 Kahneman, *Thinking, Fast and Slow*, 415.

System 1, which 'effortlessly originat[es] the impression and feelings that are the main sources of the explicit beliefs and deliberate choices of System 2'.[20] To be sure, System 2 has some ability to change the way System 1 works, 'by programming the normally automatic functions of attention and memory'.[21] Indeed, one of its main functions is 'to monitor and control thoughts and action "suggested" by System 1, allowing some to be expressed directly in behaviour and suppressing or modifying others'.[22] But System 2, which demands effort and acts of self-control is a 'lazy controller'. Efforts of will and self-control are tiring, depleting and unpleasant.[23] Indeed, if a satisfactory answer to a hard question cannot be found quickly, System 1 slips into a mode of substitution, answering easier questions than the one asked.[24] Notably, in situations of uncertainty, System 1 bets on an answer, and these bets are guided by experience.[25]

Committing Gull Force to Ambon, 1941

We can see both modes of thinking at play throughout the decision-making processes shaping the strategy of defending the islands to the northwest of Australia, but System 1 became progressively more dominant as the strategic crisis deteriorated (See Map 3.1).[26] The initial decision to send forces to the NEI was made in February 1941 at a Singapore conference of British, Dutch and Australian representatives (with the Americans as observers). Here, Australian authorities agreed that instead of the 8th Division of the 2nd AIF being sent to the Middle East, where the other three Australian divisions were being deployed, it would be split between Malaya, Rabaul and Darwin. While Lark Force would be sent in March 1941 to Rabaul, Gull and Sparrow Forces were to be held in Darwin in readiness to go to Ambon and Dutch Timor in the event of war breaking out with Japan. The RAAF would also contribute units to the defence of the Ambon–Timor–Darwin triangle.[27]

---

20   Kahneman, *Thinking, Fast and Slow*, 21.
21   Kahneman, *Thinking, Fast and Slow*, 23.
22   Kahneman, *Thinking, Fast and Slow*, 44.
23   Kahneman, *Thinking, Fast and Slow*, 42.
24   Kahneman, *Thinking, Fast and Slow*, 25–26.
25   Kahneman, *Thinking, Fast and Slow*, 80–81.
26   The following analysis draws on my earlier research on Gull Force: Joan Beaumont, *Gull Force: Survival and Leadership in Captivity 1941–1945* (Sydney: George Allen & Unwin, 1988).
27   For details of negotiations between Australia and the Dutch, see Herman Bussemaker, 'Australian–Dutch Defence Cooperation, 1940–1941', *Journal of the Australian War Memorial* 29 (1996), www.awm.gov.au/articles/journal/j29/herman.

3. THE PSYCHOLOGY OF STRATEGIC DECISION-MAKING

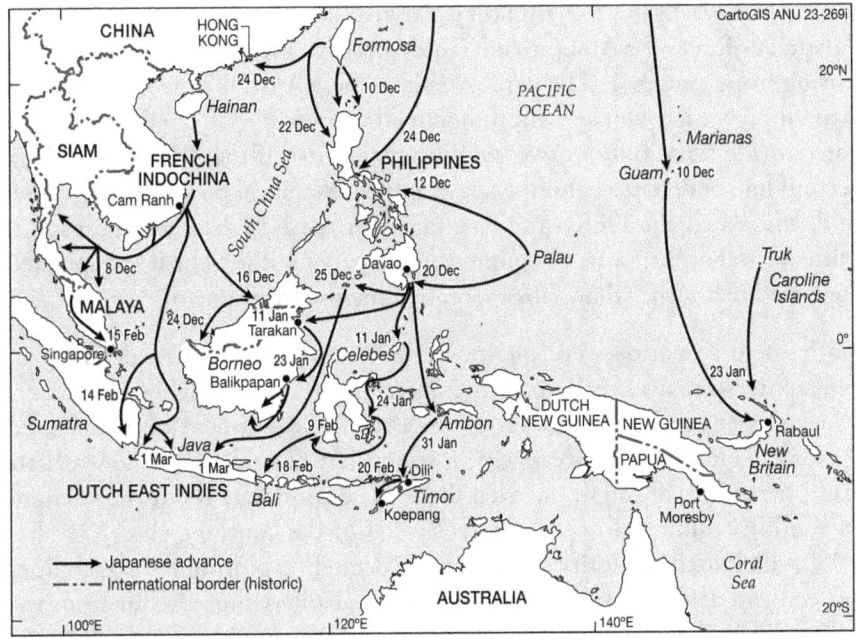

Map 3.1: The Japanese offensive in Southeast Asia, December 1941 – March 1942

This decision had elements of System-2 thinking: it was a seemingly rational adjustment of planning in the face of a changing and deteriorating strategic environment. Signals intercepts in early February 1941 suggested that the Japanese might have decided to push southward, even if this meant war with the British Empire. Moreover, Britain's capacity to provide the promised air and naval forces for the defence of Malaya and Singapore was clearly much reduced owing to the extension of the war to North Africa from late 1940 and the preoccupation of the Royal Navy with the Mediterranean and the Atlantic theatres after the fall of France. The support of the US, meanwhile, remained very ambiguous, unless it, too, were attacked by Japan. Given the geographical importance of the NEI as a barrier between Malaya and northern Australia, it was logical and rational to do everything possible to bolster the Dutch capacity to resist. The commitment to Timor and Ambon, which, like Rabaul, offered strategic airfields and harbours, was also a political gesture to the Dutch administration in the NEI. The Vichy French authorities in Indochina, after all, had succumbed to Japanese pressure.

Yet, if this was System-2 thinking, the decision to commit to providing Australian forces for Ambon and Timor was also imbued with impressions arising from System 1. The deployment of these Australian troops in single battalions, which violated the fundamental principle of concentration of force, made sense only in two circumstances: first, if the NEI were to be a second line of defence behind Malaya and British naval power at Singapore; and, second, if the Dutch military forces in the NEI had some prospect, with Australian support, of countering a Japanese onslaught if it happened that the NEI, rather than Singapore, became the front line of defence.

Both these scenarios were questionable by early 1941. The defences of Singapore were so weak that in January 1941, Prime Minister Robert Menzies went to London to lobby the British Government on the matter. As for the Dutch military capacity, it seems that Australian decision-makers had little data that might have led them to be confident about the strength of the NEI military forces in early 1941. On the contrary, since October 1939, the Dutch authorities had been desperately exploring the possibilities of securing defence supplies: modern tanks, artillery and aircraft from the UK and small arms ammunition from Australia, munitions that Australia was only partly able to provide because of its own tight supply situation.

The Australian decision to assume some responsibility for the defence of Ambon and Timor was, thus, anchored in assumptions, beliefs and impressions about the presumed superiority *and permanence* of imperial power. British and Dutch imperialism in the Asia-Pacific region was the normality that System-1 thinking was predisposed to maintain and update. Yes, there were gnawing doubts about the Singapore strategy, and little was known about Dutch colonial defences, but System 1's confirmatory bias served to seek information that was compatible with the beliefs the Australian leaders held. Predisposed to discount the Japanese on racial grounds—one of Dixon's four elements of military incompetence—Australian strategists slipped into the overconfident judgements that are typical of System-1 thinking. Horner is right to say that they were 'locked into reliance upon the Singapore strategy'.[28] However, the 'locking' arose partly from the systemic errors of System-1 thinking, which inhibited any exploration of a radically different paradigm to imperial defence.

---

28 Horner, *Crisis of Command*, 36.

Sending Gull Force to Ambon

The power of System-1 thinking became increasingly evident as Australian leaders failed to review the plans to deploy to the NEI in the months that followed the original February 1941 agreement—this, despite the Allied global strategic position deteriorating markedly throughout the year. The initial British successes against the Italians in North Africa were reversed after the intervention of the German Afrika Korps in February–March 1941. Disastrous losses, including many personnel of the Australian 6th Division, were suffered in Greece and Crete in April and May, and Japan extended its control over French Indochina. While Germany's attack on the Soviet Union on 22 June 1941 would ultimately be to the Allies' immense advantage, the Red Army's losses in the first months of Barbarossa were catastrophic. The British and American decision to support the Russians with munitions threatened to make resources for Singapore even scarcer. Furthermore, as 1941 progressed, British and American strategic priorities shifted away from the Pacific to the European war, with the 'Germany First' agreement in March 1941—whereby priority would be accorded to defeating Germany if war broke out with Japan—and the deployment of US warships to escort British convoys crossing the Atlantic.

To add to this, the feasibility of sending Australians to the NEI looked questionable on closer examination. In May and October 1941, the commander of the 23rd Brigade, ER Lind, and the commanders of Gull and Sparrow Forces conducted reconnaissance trips to Ambon and Timor. Their subsequent reports to Army Headquarters in Melbourne recommended that the forces would need Bren carriers and guns, and field or mountain artillery, since the Dutch artillery at Ambon at least seemed to be allocated to 'several alternative roles' (what these were was unstated). In July, Lind expressed his concerns directly to Sturdee; then, in October, he complained that the preparation by the Dutch authorities was 'far from satisfactory'. He felt:

> strongly that no part of our forces should be committed in either Timor or Ambon until the Dutch show by results that they attach as much importance to the well-being and safety of our troops as we ourselves do.

To send the forces without supporting artillery would be 'grossly unfair to the troops'.[29]

For all this, the decision to commit the battalion forces to support the NEI was not reviewed when war with Japan broke out. When the Japanese sank the *Prince of Wales* and *Repulse* on 10 December, any notion that the NEI could shelter behind a British naval shield at Singapore was shattered (as events would soon show—see Map 3.1). Gull and Sparrow Forces were nevertheless despatched without hesitation, their operational instructions being simply 'to strengthen the existing defences of the operational bases at Ambon and Koepang'.[30] While part of No. 13 RAAF squadron of Hudson bombers proceeded to Ambon, Gull Force left Darwin on 13–14 December, three days after the sinking of the British capital ships. The Australians joined about 2,600 Royal Netherlands East Indies Army (KNIL) troops, comprising several small and understrength companies of Indonesian troops, mainly officered by Dutchmen and supported by some coastal artillery.[31]

We have some insight into the decision-making processes of the Australian chiefs of staff at this critical time from the appreciations they prepared for the War Cabinet on 11 and 15 December 1941.[32] The former stated that the Japanese attack on Malaya three days earlier might well be a first step in the Japanese plan for a major attack on Australia. Moreover, this attack might take the form 'of a direct move on Australia via the islands to the north and north-east', including Rabaul, Port Moresby and New Caledonia. Hence, the chiefs recommended that these areas be held with a minimum of a brigade group with anti-aircraft and coastal defences. In addition, the forces needed to meet an invasion of Australia should be raised and trained (a recommendation Horner notes trenchantly that 'would have been an admirable aim a year earlier').[33]

However, in the second appreciation, the chiefs of staff modified their view, stating that Rabaul should be left with its current garrison of one battalion group, Lark Force. They realised that a battalion-sized force would be too small to resist an invasion successfully but argued that it was

---

29   Brigadier EF Lind, 'Reconnaissance Reports, Timor and Ambon, 6–12 Oct 41', Australian War Memorial (AWM) 54, 573/6/4.
30   'AHQ Operation Instruction no. 15, 6 December 1941', AWM 54, 573/6/3.
31   Lionel Wigmore, *The Japanese Thrust, Australia in the War of 1939–1945*, vol. IV, series 1—Army (Canberra: Australian War Memorial, 1957), 421.
32   For details see David Horner, *High Command: Australia and Allied Strategy, 1939–1945* (Canberra: Australian War Memorial and Sydney: George Allen & Unwin, 1982), 142–43.
33   Horner, *High Command*, 142.

essential 'to maintain a forward air observation line as long as possible and to make the enemy fight for this line rather than abandon it at the first threat'.[34] The inherent contradiction in this approach—leave the force too small but expect it to resist invasion—smacked of System-1 shortcuts or heuristics. The idea that the forces on Rabaul should be withdrawn and concentrated with other forces, as System-2 thinking might have suggested, was ruled out: first, because this operation was thought to be hazardous; and, second, because 'it must also be borne in mind the psychological effect which a voluntary withdrawal would have on the minds of the Dutch in N.E.I.'[35] The latter argument concerning the political importance of the island commitments had been influential in earlier decision-making and thus continued to shape thinking, even though it seems that at no stage in 1941—or for that matter, early 1942—was it ever subject to any serious System-2 type analysis or calculations substantiated by intelligence about morale in the NEI.

The refusal to evacuate Ambon

The logic that Lark Force was to remain on Rabaul, even though it had little chance of doing anything other than conducting a delaying action, would be applied also to Ambon and Timor. The problem for Sturdee and his Deputy Chief of Staff Sydney Rowell was that this logic was soon challenged by the commanding officer of Gull Force, Lieutenant Colonel Len Roach.[36] A First World War veteran and former militia officer, Roach was infuriated by Melbourne's lack of response to the earlier reconnaissance reports Lind had submitted. As Roach left Darwin on 13 December 1941, he wrote in a highly critical manner to WJR Scott, a staff officer at Army Headquarters, Melbourne, which had operational responsibility for Gull Force. Stressing the urgent need for additional troops and equipment, including anti-tank guns and field guns, Roach criticised the 'unpardonable stagnation' of the past seven months. This pointed to 'a policy of "wait and see" prevailing over reality and expediency'. He warned that '[i]f any of my excellent fellows do not arrive at their destination it will not be a case of "gallant sacrifice" but of murder due to sheer slackness and maladministration'.[37]

---

34 Horner, *High Command*, 143.
35 'Chiefs of Staff Appreciation—Defence of Australia and Adjacent Areas', 15 December 1941, National Archives of Australia (NAA): A2671 418/1941.
36 The account that follows, unless otherwise stated, draws on Wigmore, *The Japanese Thrust*, 420–24.
37 Roach to Scott, 13 December 1941, AWM 54 573/6/3.

Once on Ambon, Roach wrote again to Melbourne, on 17 December and on 23 December, reiterating the deficiencies in Gull Force's arms and equipment, and the 'imperative' need for guns and machine guns. Thanks to a clumsy system whereby Gull Force's lines of communications went through 7th Military District in Darwin even though the force was under direct operational control of Army Headquarters in Melbourne, some of Roach's messages took many days to be read. Increasingly frustrated, he signalled on 24 December that the combined army forces on Ambon were inadequate to hold vital localities for more than a day or two 'against determined attack from more than one direction simultaneously'. Even with the additional requested supplies, Gull Force's position would be 'precarious' if it lacked air and naval support.[38] The NEI forces, Roach reported three days later, had only five days of ammunition supply and proposed to vacate five forward posts in the event of simultaneous attack from two or three directions. '[A]dmittedly,' he conceded, 'they have not very favourable alternatives with their present strength.'[39]

On 26 December, Rowell replied: while Bren carriers would arrive on Ambon in the first week of January 1942, the additional units Roach requested were 'not repeat not available'. The task of Gull Force then was, 'in cooperation with local Dutch forces ... to put up the best defence possible with the resources you have at your disposal'. Roach replied on 29 December that all on Ambon were 'most eager [to] administer salutary punishment'. He felt 'confident enemy will waver before Australian fire and bayonets'. But it seems that Roach doubted his own heroic (System-1) rhetoric. Gull Force's intelligence officer, Captain Rod Gabriel, later recalled that when Rowell's message of 26 December arrived, Roach placed his hand over his metal badge of rank on his shoulder and said, 'This metal means nothing to me, but the lives of over 1100 men do'.[40] Then, on 1 January 1942, Roach wrote to Scott:

> I find it difficult to overcome a feeling of disgust, and more than a little concern at the way in which we have seemingly been 'dumped' at this outpost position, in the first place without any instructions whatever ... and in the second place with (so far) a flat refusal to consider any increase in fire power and the number of tps [troops], whilst the co-operation and assistance from the other two arms of the Service must be of very limited value indeed.

---

38 Gull Force to Army HQ, 24 December 1941, AWM 54 573/6/3.
39 Roach to AHQ Melbourne, Disposition Gull and NEI Forces, 27 December 1941, AWM PR 8/3/84.
40 Comment concerning Col. Roach provided by Gabriel to Joan Beaumont, February 1986.

Repeating his prediction that Gull Force would be able to hold out for two or three days against a large-scale attack from several directions, Roach asked:

> Is the intention to continue the policy of allowing small Forces, inadequately equipped for their task, to be spread over a vast area, so that they can be defeated in detail? I submit that it would be far preferable, if the striking power does not actually exist for offensive action whilst these outposts are held, to 'cut the loss' and concentrate all available Forces (including also American and Dutch) further South for a decisive engagement'.[41]

Roach admitted that he was speaking 'very frankly', but declared, 'I would feel very guilty if I did not do so, and many valuable lives were thus lost due to the fact that your HQ had not been made fully aware of the situation'. He asked that his letter be escalated to the Minister.

Soon, Japanese air attacks on Ambon began, with seven flying boats dropping 33 bombs at three points on the island on the night of 6 January. Air raids occurred almost daily thereafter. Roach signalled on 11 January that 'We are all completely in the dark … Prospects are gloomy'.[42] Then, two days later, he signalled Melbourne recommending the immediate evacuation of Gull Force. The support he had requested could not be expected, and if Ambon were to be attacked by combined enemy forces such as were then operating in the Menado area, the men of Gull Force could not hold out for more than a day. It would be a 'purposeless sacrifice of valuable manpower and arms' to leave them on Ambon.

Roach was not alone is this assessment. Several senior officers on Ambon advised Melbourne that they supported his views: the 2/21st battalion's second-in-command, Major Ian Macrae; the senior RAAF officer commanding Australian aircraft on the island, Wing Commander ED Scott; and the Area Combined Headquarters at Halong.[43] The latter sent a signal to Melbourne on 11 January pointing out that Japanese air bases were now established about 360 miles away and urgently requesting immediate reinforcement with fighters and dive bombers. Without these, only 'token

---

41 Roach to Scott, 1 January 1942, AWM 54 573/6/10.
42 ACH Halong to CWR Melbourne, A.12/11/1, 11 January 1942, AWM 54 573/6/10.
43 Macrae to Scott, 1 January 1942, ACH Halong to CWR Melbourne, 13 January 1942, AWM 54 573/6/10.

resistance [would be] possible with [the] present unsuitable aircraft', all of which would certainly be destroyed within a day's action by carrier-force enemy forces.[44]

However, despite the intelligence from all those on the ground, Gull Force was not evacuated. Instead, Army Headquarters ordered Roach to cease his messages at once and insisted that 'your staunch defence will have important effect ... in regard [to] future Australian Dutch cooperation'. Then, on 14 January, Roach was told by Rowell to return to Melbourne:

> It is apparent from messages received at Army Headquarters since your arrival, that you have not the necessary confidence in your ability to conduct a resolute defence of Ambon in co-operation with the local Dutch forces ... [You] have generally given the impression that you have accepted defeat as inevitable even before being attacked.[45]

Roach's place as commander of Gull Force could be taken by Scott, who had actually volunteered on 11 January to go to Ambon and lead Gull Force.

It might be argued that these decisions were justified on the rational grounds that Gull Force's presence at Ambon bought time for the defence of the Australian continent. Indeed, Scott said in a 1946 report:

> [Gull Force] did in fact hold up a complete Japanese Division with its transports and adequate Naval and Air support for at least two weeks and inflicted heavy loss upon the enemy ... [H]ad 'Gull Force' been withdrawn from AMBON before the Japanese attack, the Japanese Division with its Navy and Air Force support could have proceeded straight to Darwin ... I am unable to say whether this force would have been destroyed on arrival at Darwin during January/February 1942, but there can be said to be at least considerable doubt on this point.[46]

However, the documentary record for early 1942 provides no evidence that Army Headquarters gave any serious thought as to how long Gull Force might resist. Nor was any consideration given to the balance sheet of such a delaying action. By one later estimate, Japanese losses in occupying Ambon

---

44 Wigmore, *The Japanese Thrust*, 423.
45 Rowell to Roach, 14 January 1942, AWM 54 573/6/10.
46 Lt-Col. WJR Scott, 'Introduction', in Report on Ambon and Hainan, 8 May 1946, AWM 54 573/6/1A.

3. THE PSYCHOLOGY OF STRATEGIC DECISION-MAKING

were only 95 killed, 185 wounded and 1 minesweeper sunk.[47] Was this worth the loss of over a thousand Australian troops and the forfeiting of a strategic opportunity to deploy these men somewhere else? It seems that no one applied to these questions the kind of 'effortful' calculations that would be typical of System-2 thinking.

Similarly, it seems that no thought was given in mid-January 1942 to another System-2 calculation: namely, whether evacuation from Ambon was feasible. It might well have been impossible, given the shortage of shipping and the Japanese dominance in the air. But no one asked this. Instead, Melbourne addressed a substitute question: how could they silence the man whose predictions were so dire? It was an exemplar of System 1's substitution of an easier question for a harder one.

The dominance of System-1 heuristics—that is, the mental shortcuts that allow decisions to be made quickly without full consideration of their implications—was also manifest in the language Sturdee invoked to justify the retention of Gull Force on Ambon. We do not have a record of what he said to his Minister when seeking approval for Roach's recall. A draft memo prepared for this purpose was apparently not sent—a good thing given its tortured argument:

> The force provided, in co-operation with N.E.I. forces, is considered sufficient to retain the island against attempted occupation on a light scale. To provide sufficient forces to withstand a major attack is entirely beyond our means. Great value should accrue, however, if the enemy is denied the island except by the employment of overwhelming force.[48]

However, Sturdee said, when communicating his decision to General Archibald Wavell, the recently appointed supreme commander of the American–British–Dutch–Australian Command, that Roach was dismissed because he had made it clear since his arrival at Ambon that he had 'no spirit to conduct a resolute defence if attacked'. His latest messages indicated

---

47 National Defense College of Japan, *The Operations of the Navy in the Dutch East Indies and the Bay of Bengal*, trans. William Remmelink (Leiden: Leiden University Press, 2018), cited in 'Battle of Ambon', Wikipedia, en.wikipedia.org/wiki/Battle_of_Ambon.
48 Draft memo, Chief of the General Staff to Minister, January 1942, AWM 54 573/6/10.

a 'probable deterioration morale all troops Ambon [sic] which may be beyond power of new Australian commander to improve rapidly'.[49] Wavell responded in kind:

> So far as I can judge position at Ambon not critical and in any case I am opposed to handing out important objectives to enemy without making them fight for it. Quite appreciate feelings of lonely garrison but am sure Australians will put up a stout fight whatever happens. No doubt it is wise to change commander.[50]

Some weeks later, when writing his official despatch on the operations in South-East Asia, Wavell wrote:

> From the standpoint of higher strategy the situation [in early 1942] bore a distinct resemblance to that when we went to the assistance of Greece a year earlier. It might then have been more prudent to let Greece go and concentrate on holding Crete and our gains in Libya. It might possibly have been more prudent here to let the N.E.I. go and to concentrate on making Burma and Australia secure. But undue prudence has never yet won battles or campaigns or wars, and from the political point of view it would have been as unthinkable to abandon our stout-hearted Dutch allies without the utmost effort to help them as it would have been a year earlier to leave the gallant Greeks unsupported. Our assistance to Greece cost us Crete and placed us in great difficulties in the Mediterranean; our attempt to hold the N.E.I. has cost us Burma and has placed India and Ceylon in danger; but that in both instances we took the right, the only, decision, I have no doubt. Just as I still believe that our expedition to Greece was by no means the forlorn hope it may have appeared, so the Allied attempt to defend the N.E.I. might well have had a more fortunate issue. The principle of engaging the enemy as closely and as far forward as possible must be maintained at all costs and will in the end bring victory.[51]

This was an exemplar of System-1 thinking. The Allied failure in Greece was, by any standards, a comparison that had nothing to commend it, but Wavell reverted to it when justifying the strategy adopted in South-East Asia. This was more than an inept attempt at retrospective self-justification.

---

49 Sturdee to Wavell, 14 Jan. 1942, AWM 54 573/6/10. This was repeated to the Dutch commander of the KNIL, General Hein ter Poorten.
50 Wigmore, *The Japanese Thrust*, 424.
51 General Wavell's Despatch on Operations in South-West Pacific, 15 January – 25 February 1942, WO 10/2556, National Archives, London.

3. THE PSYCHOLOGY OF STRATEGIC DECISION-MAKING

In Kahneman's terms, Wavell manifested the pattern of associated ideas that represented the structure of events in his life and determined his interpretation of the present as well as his expectations of the future.

As for 'resolute defence', 'stout fight', 'lack of 'spirit' and 'lonely garrison': these were distancing clichés that spoke to System-1 assumptions about what were appropriate qualities for military personnel to display in time of war: honour, courage, determination and a willingness to die. Australian soldiers were meant to put up the best fight possible with whatever resources could be spared. Was this not what their forebears had done at Gallipoli and on the Western Front? Sturdee, for one, had served as engineer in highly exposed sites such as Steele's, Quinn's and Courtney's posts at Gallipoli at a time when it was clear that the Allies were not going to prevail in this campaign. He had won the Distinguished Service Order for his work in 1915 and 1916. Wavell, for his part, lost an eye and won the Military Cross in the Second Battle of Ypres in 1915.

Moreover, the codes of honour invoked by Sturdee and Wavell served, as the high diction of war commonly does, to ensure that a threatening situation was 'met by fight rather than flight'. As Dixon says, these codes do this:

> by making the social consequences of flight rather more unpleasant than the physical consequences of fight. Whereas the latter might lead to physical pain, mutilation and death, the former eventuates with greater certainty in personal guilt and public shame.[52]

The Australian authorities certainly shamed Roach. No officer at Army HQ met him on his return to Melbourne to ask what intelligence he might have about the Japanese. On 9 March 1942 he was discharged from the 2nd AIF and placed on the reserve of officers. In November 1943, Roach sought to have the operational order recalling him from Ambon on 14 January 1942 withdrawn, on the grounds that it was 'unjustifiable and casts an unwarranted reflection on my personal attributes and my methods of command'. The Adjutant-General, Major General CEM Lloyd, did Roach the courtesy of meeting him in early December 1943, but soon wrote that the Commander-in-Chief (General Thomas Blamey) considered it impossible to withdraw an order made by an authority that shortly after

---

52 Dixon, *On the Psychology*, 197. I owe the term 'high diction' to Paul Fussell, *The Great War and Modern Memory* (Oxford: Oxford University Press, 1977), esp. 21–22.

ceased to exist (presumably a reference to the dissolution of American–British–Dutch–Australian Command in February 1942). Nothing in the files, Roach was told, 'basically affects your military reputation'.[53]

The mystery of Scott

We are left with the mystery of why Scott volunteered to assume command of Gull Force on 11 January, a time when the Japanese had already occupied Kuala Lumpur and were only 320 kilometres from Singapore. It is a decision that seems to defy rational explanation.

Scott's earlier career was intriguing and complex.[54] He had a distinguished record of service in the First World War, serving in Gallipoli and France. Twice mentioned in dispatches, he was awarded the Distinguished Service Order for his work at Flers on 14 November 1916. Across the war years, he also suffered considerable injuries and ill health: malaria at Gallipoli in 1915; shell shock at Pozières in 1916; concussion when he fell from a horse in France in 1917; and debility in 1918.[55]

After the war ended, Scott was made responsible for arranging the shipping for the repatriation of the AIF from Britain in 1919, a role that he sees to have performed with distinction. On his return to Australia, Scott became an insurance broker but he continued to be active in military affairs, joining the militia, the loyalist and anti-communist King and Empire Alliance, and the clandestine counter-revolutionary group the Old Guard. Commonly Scott is thought to have been the model for Jack Callcott, a leading character in DH Lawrence's 1922 novel, *Kangaroo*. To add to the complexity, in the 1930s Scott also became an enthusiast for all things Japanese. He visited Japan in 1934, collaborated with Japanese consular officials and wrote articles for the *Sydney Morning Herald* praising Japanese industry and defending that country's foreign policy. His membership of the Australia–Japan Society, an organisation suspected by the Commonwealth Investigation Branch of espionage activity, proved a complication when in April 1935 Scott joined military intelligence: he was refused access to secret files.

---

53 This correspondence is found in AWM 54 573/6/10.
54 See Andrew Moore, *The Secret Army and the Premier: Conservative Paramilitary Organisations in New South Wales 1930–32* (Sydney: University of NSW Press, 1989) passim; Moore, 'Life Summary: William John Scott', *Australian Dictionary of Biography* (Canberra: The Australian National University, online edition), adb.anu.edu.au/lifesummary/scott-william-john-8373.
55 'Scott, WJR', B2455, NAA.

3. THE PSYCHOLOGY OF STRATEGIC DECISION-MAKING

After the outbreak of the Second World War, Scott was appointed in June 1940 to the General Staff in Melbourne. From February to May 1941, he commanded the guerrilla warfare training centre for independent companies at Wilsons Promontory. On his return to Army HQ, he assumed the role of liaison officer for Gull and Sparrow Forces.

Scott's offer to take over command from Roach was made in a personal and confidential handwritten note to the Director of Military Operations and Plans, which was attached as something of a postscript to an analysis of the aircraft available in the area of Gull Force. Writing at 2315 hours—perhaps not the optimal hour for System-2 thinking—Scott pondered the possible repercussions should Gull Force be the first objective chosen by the enemy:

> A stubborn resistance & a good fight even against overwhelming odds now, must stiffen resistance everywhere and clinch our association with the N.E.I. Not to mention the effect on the U.S.A. Withdrawal or a weak resistance will set the pace for future threats or worse, in the near Pacific Ocean area & Australia's itself. It could affect the action of A.I.F. troops in Malaya ... I am convinced that there is a political significance behind this which may well be worth consideration at least.

Hoping that his views would be taken 'as a very ernest [sic] opinion that much rests on this position in Ambon and not as an impertinence from a junior officer', he claimed that he would be 'proud indeed' to take over command of Gull Force immediately:

> I have no particular belief in my ability but I have a definite belief in my ability to inspire confidence in men and to lead them. I apologise for blowing my own trumpet in this way, but for the first time in my life I feel it perhaps justified.[56]

Unlike Wavell and Sturdee's decision-making, Scott's carried a high personal risk, and we can only assume that he was persuaded of the political and strategic value of the Ambon operation. He had made a note in the margins of an earlier message from Roach that predicted that Gull Force could not last for more than a day or two. 'Well worth it—what's the force there for?'[57] But, surely, Scott's judgement was also infused with the emotions and assumptions of System-1 thinking. He read Roach's protests not as rational—and as it happened, accurate—intelligence about the flaws of the

---

56   Scott to DMO&P, 11 January 1942, AWM 54 573/6/10.
57   Annotation on Roach telegram, Gull "G" & "I" matters, 24 December 1941, AWM 54 573/6/3.

island strategy but as the utterances of a man unfit to hold a position of command. Scott was, after all, a political soldier. In May 1921, he had stormed a socialist gathering at Sydney's Domain and four years later had taken instructions from Prime Minister Stanley Bruce to raise a force of 500 AIF veterans to assist police should plans to deport union leaders Tom Walsh and Jacob Johnson lead to union violence. As a senior member of the Old Guard, Scott also threatened to overthrow the New South Wales Labor government of Jack Lang. For Scott, then, the 'normal' world was one in which he thought politically.

There is every reason, too, to see Scott as identifying himself as a man of action. Did he find it demeaning to sit out the war in an office at headquarters? Did he think this was his last opportunity—he was already 53—to lead men in battle? His brother, Lieutenant Colonel (Alan) Humphrey Scott, had died while acting in command of the 56th Battalion at Polygon Wood in 1917.[58] Charles Bean concluded in his Official History of the AIF in 1917 (published in 1933) that had Humphrey survived, he would 'almost certainly have risen to brigade command'.[59] Perhaps Scott hankered to emulate his lost brother's success in command.

Possibly, too, given his experience with independent companies, Scott thought that Gull Force might retreat in the face of the Japanese attack and hold out in the more remote parts of Ambon (as the remnants of Sparrow Force and the 2/2 Independent Company did in Portuguese Timor). In 1954, Scott told the Official Historian, Lionel Wigmore, when asked to comment on a draft chapter on the Ambon campaign: 'You must remember that I was very well aware that I was taking on a job which held out no hope of survival.'[60] Whatever his motivation, it seems clear that Scott fell victim to System-1 heuristics and failed to take the time to process all the information available to him, and to weigh it up properly.

Scott also manifested the overconfidence typical of System-1 thinking. Kahneman warns that 'your intuitions will deliver predictions that are far too extreme and you will be inclined to put too much faith in them'.[61] When Scott arrived on Ambon on 16 January, he claimed that he was 'entirely satisfied' with the morale of Gull Force, and 'impressed' with Colonel Joseph

---

58 'Scott Alan Humphrey', B2455, NAA.
59 CEW Bean, *The A.I.F. in France, 1917*, vol. IV of The Official History of Australia in the War of 1914–1918, (Sydney: Angus & Robertson, 1933), 836n.
60 Scott to Wigmore, 15 June 1954, AWM 67 3/353.
61 Kahneman, *Thinking, Fast and Slow*, 194.

Kapitz commanding the Dutch forces.⁶² But the situation soon proved to be as dire as Roach predicted. As Japanese air raids increased from mid-January onwards, Allied aircraft were either destroyed or withdrawn. When, on 28 January, the few remaining serviceable Hudsons of No. 13 RAAF squadron were evacuated, Gull Force had no air support. On the night of 30 January, the Japanese attacked. Outnumbered and outgunned, the Dutch forces dissolved, the purported psychological value of the Australian presence proving, it seems, to have been of no use. Most of the Australians retreated, with some energetic defending actions, including on Mount Nona, to Eri, on the tip of the southern peninsula of the crab-shaped island. Three days later, with his troops lacking food, water and ammunition, and exposed to Japanese bombing and shelling, Scott surrendered. Meanwhile, across the bay, the detachment of Australian troops defending the Laha airfield were overwhelmed by a concentrated attack of enemy troops, dive bombers, fighter planes and artillery. Most were soon executed by the Japanese.

Scott then faced three-and-a-half years of humiliating captivity, a period in which he suffered a mental collapse, which might be attributed in part to the unresolved trauma of shellshock in the First World War. With considerable malice, he sought to allocate blame for his failure to others: first, the Dutch troops and Kapitz, of whom Scott wrote in his 1946 report:

> It is unfortunate that there is nothing to be said which could be regarded as bringing credit either to the one or the other. My unhappy experience with these people both at Ambon and Hainan leave [sic] me convinced that there is no one characteristic which an Australian or a Dutchman could find in common.⁶³

Scott's second target was Gull Force, the men he had thought he could lead but whom he now viewed as an undisciplined rabble. Faced with what he saw as poor behaviour within the POW camp on Ambon, Scott manifested behaviour that had some of the elements of Dixon's authoritarian personality. In March 1942, he threatened to hand over to the Japanese for punishment Australians who were guilty of stealing, refusing to obey orders or insolence to their officers. When later interned on Hainan, he carried out this threat—with the result that the men in the camp ultimately mutinied and took discipline into their own hands, while the Australian officers debated whether to declare Scott insane and assume responsibility

---

62 Cited in 'Wavell from Sturdee', 18 January 1942, AWM 54 573/6/10.
63 Scott, 'Introduction'.

for management of the camp themselves.[64] When the survivors of Ambon returned to Australia, it was not Scott but Roach they chose to lead them on Anzac Day marches.

Conclusion

Any attempt to analyse the cognitive processes behind military decision-making, as this essay has done, is necessarily speculative and subjective. For one thing, the documentary evidence tracing the processes by which Australian military leaders made decisions in 1941–42 is thin. Most of Australia's leaders in the Second World War, alas, did not keep self-reflective diaries as did the British Chief of the Imperial General Staff, Field Marshal Sir Alan Brooke. Moreover, no leader of the 1940s was ever subjected to psychological examination or interviewed by oral historians. We can only infer what might have been the assumptions and biases infusing their thinking. Nonetheless, perilous though it might be, the exploration of decision-making through the lens of later behavioural psychological theories of modes of cognition can only enrich the empiricism of military history. Understanding System-1 and System-2 thinking does not, of course, exonerate Australia's military leaders. Horner's judgement that Army leaders should be indicted for the island strategy still stands. But we can perhaps better appreciate how it was that these men persisted with a strategy that became increasingly irrational as the strategic situation changed in 1941–42 and that would, they ultimately knew, condemn thousands of Australians to death or captivity. Moreover, we can address the need, flagged by Horner, for military historians to acknowledge more fully the human element that shapes military decision-making in times of crisis.

---

64   See Beaumont, *Gull Force,* 96–97, 180–85.

4

Why Australia has gone to war: some reflections on the nineteenth century

Jean Bou

David Horner's prodigious scholarly output is remarkable. As proud as he undoubtedly is of this, and justly so, it is a source of gentle ribbing from those around him who, capable of less Herculean production, might light-heartedly enquire of him how many books he has written this last month! While he has ranged widely in his long career, David Horner's high reputation began with his studies on command and a large corpus of work examining Australia's Second World War, particularly in the Pacific theatre. However, the 'hook' for this chapter, as it were, is his most recent book, *The War Game*, and a less obvious example of his erudition, *Australian Military History for Dummies* (2010). In case this second book causes any aesthetes to sniff, there a few reasons for my choosing it. First, this book exemplifies David Horner's laudable willingness to write for a popular or general audience—an approach with which any of us who have had their work edited by David Horner will be familiar. Second, as Horner pointed out to anyone who listened when the ANU deemed *Dummies* a non-scholarly publication, producing such a book requires a good deal, perhaps a lifetime, of scholarship to underpin it, and to make it more than a collection of military history factoids and shallow summation. Finally, *Dummies* is, somewhat dismayingly, one of a very small number of monographs, along with Jeffrey Grey's *Military History of Australia*, written on the entirety of Australian military history.[1]

In fact, as far as this author can ascertain, David Horner's *Dummies* and Jeff Grey's *Military History* are the *only* monographs produced by any single scholarly author that have sought to appreciate the significant and weighty matter of all of Australia's military history. There are some edited collections, such as Michael McKernan and Margaret Browne's now rather aged *Australia: Two Centuries of War and Peace*,[2] and, of course, a larger number of books that grapple with a narrower timeframe or one of the multitudes of subfields.[3] However, Grey and Horner have been the only two solo authors to have examined, in quite different formats, the entirety of the topic in one volume. While this is a perplexing and curious situation, and one that should cause scholars of the topic to wonder why there are not more (surely there *should* be more), it matters to this author because of a growing interest in the question of why Australia goes to war.

It is a short and seemingly simple question, but, as with most things in history, the answers are not necessarily easy to come by. Certainly, a diligent and thoughtful historian can find comparatively easy, if not always satisfying, responses to any *particular* war that you care to choose: the proximate influences of threat, international affairs, international or imperial obligations, political motivations, domestic pressures, military strategy and the like, even if these responses are imperfect and debatable. David Horner has written much about these sorts of influences on given conflicts, and while the book is a wider consideration of Australian war leadership, *War Game* necessarily examines government decisions about going to war from 1914 to the early 2000s in this vein.

This sort of analysis is tremendously helpful, but a focus on political-military decision-making such as Horner's is indelibly linked to an examination of a particular war or other military commitment, including peacekeeping (which still involves a war, just someone else's). These proximate causes

---

1   Jeffrey Grey's *A Military History of Australia* (Cambridge: Cambridge University Press, 2008) went through three editions before his unexpected death, the last being published in 2008. doi.org/10.1017/CBO9780511481345.
2   Michael McKernan and Margaret Browne, *Australia: Two Centuries of War and Peace* (Canberra: Australian War Memorial and Sydney: George Allen & Unwin, 1988).
3   Such as Craig Stockings and John Connor, *Before the Anzac Dawn: A Military History of Australia to 1915* (Sydney: NewSouth, 2013).

matter very much because whatever arguments there may be about their relative importance, they have a direct influence on events. In trying to answer the broader question of why Australia goes to war, however, the explanatory power of proximate causes diminishes, perhaps rapidly. They become elements of a bigger picture, one that requires a view taken from further back. From this greater distance, one starts to wonder about patterns, or the lack of them, and other parts that, though painted less vividly, contribute to the whole. Hence the reason for invoking David's *Dummies* and Jeff Grey's *Military History*: it is because they are the biggest paintings in this peculiar gallery.

The broader question of why Australia goes to war requires more than setting out proximate causes. It requires more of that most mercurial but demanding historical consideration that might awkwardly be summed up as context. Context is made up of the less distinct influences of politics, economics, culture and society (and anything else judged relevant) that require attention, all the more so as changes over time have to be weighed up—the *long durée*. This, then, is the large picture that must be viewed from further back, to take in the setting and composition before stepping forward again to examine the details.

It should be added at this point that neither this chapter, which is advanced as a sort of 'think piece' to explore some developing ideas, nor the longer work that it hopefully foreshadows, is an attempt to unearth or develop a general theory of why Australia goes to war. If investigating proximate causes in isolation does not provide wholly fulfilling reasons why Australia went to any given war, it seems unlikely that the reverse will be true, either. Sweeping statements about culture, precedents, supposed habits, alliance entanglements or whatever the purported reasons may be are likely to only seem partly true as well, and even then, perhaps only true for a particular and possibly quite narrow period. Moreover, it also seems probable that sooner or later such broad ideas, despite the authority with which they are often stated, will start to look awkward or feeble when weighed against the proximate matters that motivated Australian governments at given moments. The point is to look at the broad, flowing course of history to appreciate the way that currents near and far have combined.

MILITARY HISTORY SUPREMO

Proximate and contextual: a case study

It feels somewhat redundant to point out that proximate and contextual matters combine in history—the historian's equivalent of 'Duh!'. But the twain do not always meet, as is perhaps best exemplified by the debates about Australia's commitment to the First World War.

As numerous historians, not least David Horner, have pointed out over the years, Australia made almost no decisions about becoming a belligerent in 1914. Lacking the legal power or institutional capabilities to make independent choices about foreign policy or war-making, the ailing government of Prime Minister Joseph Cook, which soon lost the coming general election, seems not even to have wondered if there was a way to not go to war. Britain was at war, and so was Australia.[4] Any student of the war looking for a plausible, verifiable or even historical argument about direct proximate causes in Australian decisions about whether go to war in 1914 is very much out of luck. Even our most esteemed historians, when they have written about this, struggle to eke out more than a few paragraphs about what the Cook government was doing.[5] Which is not to say that there is no historical debate about Australia joining the war: far from it, as anyone reading this chapter is likely to know. Indeed, despite this paucity of government deliberation in August 1914, or perhaps because of it, what lay behind Australia's entry into the war has been keenly debated for decades in books, scholarly journals, conferences, symposiums, press articles, television panels and undoubtedly many more places.

Without much evidence of an active Australian decision, beyond willing conformity to London's actions, the discussion about the country's entry into the war immediately becomes based on context. Usually, this soon turns to the ardour of Australia's commitment. Following the near compulsory invocation of Andrew Fisher's electioneering pledge of support to 'the last

---

4 David Horner, *The War Game, Australian War Leadership from Gallipoli to Iraq* (Sydney: Allen & Unwin, 2022), 20–21. Horner gives an outline of the essentials. Similar summaries abound. See, for example, Joan Beaumont, *Broken Nation: Australians in the Great War*, (Sydney: Allen & Unwin, 2013), 12–20.
5 See, for example, Beaumont, *Broken Nation*, 12–13; John Connor, Peter Stanley and Peter Yule, *The War at Home*, vol. 4 of The Centenary History of Australia and the Great War (Oxford: Oxford University Press, 2015), 85–86; Horner, *War Game*, 22–26.

man and last shilling',[6] the exposition often turns to matters like public and private expressions of loyalty to the empire, placing the Australian fleet at the Admiralty's disposal (in accordance with previous agreements and once the Australian coast seemed clear), the decision to send expeditionary forces first to Europe and then to seize German New Guinea, and, then, four years of doing the utmost to fight the war. Included in this is the bearing of huge casualties, the financial costs and the willingness to drive the country into profound division over conscription. From these actions, in which political-military thinking and decisions can be traced, and which were actions that the Australian Government had the power and means to pursue, plausible and often convincing arguments can be made about motivations, will and aims, particularly as the war progressed. The zeal of Australia's commitment is a fascinating question in its own right, and investigating it helps inform us about attitudes to the war. However, given the lack of evidence about that thinking in the fateful days of early August 1914, pondering it is something of a proxy for the question of why Australia went to war. The two matters were undoubtedly intertwined, but that does not mean they occupy the same part of the painting, to return to the analogy.

From there, explanatory models radiate outwards and, often, back a few decades as historians have sought other explanations as to why Australia fought and, vitally, fought the way it did. Hence, historians have variously claimed that imperial loyalty was the root cause,[7] or that Imperial Germany was a threat to Australia, either because it was militarist and malign in intent, an evil to be confronted or through its threat to the British Empire's place in the world, or perhaps some combination of these. Others dismiss this (sometimes harshly, in the view of one historian it is an 'imperial romance')[8] and have highlighted Australian anxieties about ascendant Japan. They claim that Australia, worried about the Pacific, acted the way it did to underwrite the insurance provided by Britain's naval protection. Leaving aside imperial sentiments, these interpretations tend to emphasise Australian

---

6   The original use of 'to the last man and last shilling' has been attributed to an unknown member of one of William Gladstone's cabinets. It was a known phrase by the mid-1880s. Hence, when Fisher uttered it in 1914, he was drawing on a well-known expression invested with meanings of imperial collective defence. Kevin S Inglis, *The Rehearsal: Australians at War in the Sudan, 1885* (Kevin Weldon & Associates, 1985), 62.
7   For example, Joan Beaumont, '"Unitedly We Have Fought": Imperial Loyalty and the Australian War Effort', *International Affairs* 90, no. 2 (2014): 397–412, doi.org/10.1111/1468-2346.12116.
8   Greg Lockhart, 'Effacing the Nation' in Peter Stanley, ed., 'Why did Australia Go to the Great War? Proceedings of a Symposium Held at the University of New South Wales, Canberra, 8 May 2018', ACSACS Occasional Paper Series 8 (Canberra: Australian Society for the Study of Armed Conflict and Society, 2019), 3, passim.

realism, in the international relations sense of the word, and self-interest. In other interpretations, however, anxiety about Japan enabled London to manipulate Australian politicians and officials into eliciting imperial commitments for the looming war, with or without the connivance of those local officials. Others have contended that the Australian Government was simply unthinking and abandoned its responsibilities to act in the national interest, or that the White Australia Policy and a desire for 'racial purity' was the essential element in Australia waging war the way it did.[9]

In these contentions, two broad interpretational schools can be identified. The first school holds that Australia was effectively an imperial patsy, doing what it did because it lacked the nous, sense of independence or institutional development to pursue its own course. According to the second school, Australia went into the war with its eyes at least fairly wide open and did so in order to pursue its own objectives. It is interesting that both are *nationalist* interpretations that find a place in, possibly competing, notions about Australia's relationship with the imperial centre. In the former, Australia should have been smarter and more independent-minded. In the latter, Australia was displaying flashes of these qualities, even if hesitantly and nascently, and the decisions about the war tend to be portrayed as early steps on the way to a more independent and assertive nation.[10] Both views have their merits, but they also have an air that rather than outlining what happened, some authors have perhaps been motivated by their view of what *ought* to have been going on.

Not surprisingly, the same broad ideas echo across time. Similar arguments are part of the debates about earlier military contributions to the Sudan and South Africa. They are implicit in the notion that before 1914, there was division in defence circles between 'Australianists' and 'imperialists'. This idea has also been revamped for later periods, with Washington and the American alliance being substituted for London and the empire. At its heart, the debate surrounding these two themes is one about Australia's independence from Britain. Was it achieved, or did we simply shift to an American benefactor? If it was achieved, when? And should it have occurred sooner? What characterised the attaining of that independence?

---

9 Concise versions of most of these threads are encapsulated by the various authors in Stanley, 'Why did Australia?'. See also Peter Cochrane, *Best We Forget: The War for White Australia, 1914–18* (Melbourne: Text Publishing Company, 2018).
10 It is tempting to ascribe these to radical and conservative political traditions, though I will resist the urge to do so here, as I am not yet convinced that this is appropriate.

4. WHY AUSTRALIA HAS GONE TO WAR

These two interpretational approaches are suggested with some hesitation. First, dichotomies are rarely a satisfactory explanatory model in history. The realities were usually much more complex, with many currents swirling about. Second, some historians would probably bristle at the way these ideas have been presented, and decry the oversimplification or lack of nuance. They may be right, and it is not unusual to try to blend or reconcile the ideas, but in this case, a degree of coarseness may help to draw out some essence from the discussion.

In all these interpretations there tends to be an emphasis on, or at least an assumption of, rationality and clarity. That historians impose rationality and casual links onto wild, unkempt events is an old, and justified, accusation of the craft. War is chaotic and demanding, scarcely less so off the battlefield than on it. People and their leaders, who all have their own 'baggage', form judgements, make decisions and carry out actions in an atmosphere in which things change rapidly. The information they have may be wrong or incomplete. They have limited control, and thoughts and actions may soon be tempered, modified or obviated by any number of developments. That Australian politicians and other officials were, to at least some extent, simply extemporising, or responding with passion rather than reason, is rarely given much thought, whether the example is the First World War or any other war.

This chapter offers no support for, or critique of, any of these ideas about why Australia chose to fight in the First World War. They all potentially have a place on the painting described, and in the longer work that this chapter foreshadows, but here is not the place to ascertain if they should be on the canvas, or where—space precludes, and my thinking about this specific topic is developing. It should, however, be promptly added that the historical 'truth' is not necessarily somewhere in the middle of them,[11] if for no other reason than that perhaps other things should be considered, too.[12]

I have focused on the debates about the First World War to highlight the ways in which the proximate and contextual factors, and interpretations about Australia's war-making decisions, can (but sometimes do not) interact.

---

11 A synthesis of sorts was attempted at the ADFA symposium cited above. After what had been a remarkably acrimonious day, it may have been an attempt to pour some oil on the troubled waters, but I, for one, did not find the synthesis very satisfying.
12 As someone who has written and thought about this period, I have formed some views previously, but in the spirit of a 'fresh take' about this subject I am doing my utmost to be open-minded.

Trying to develop a response to the question of why Australia goes to war by starting at 1914 is wrong-headed, however. Instead, we should start at the beginning.

War in nineteenth-century Australia

The historiography of war-making in nineteenth-century Australia is not particularly strong, and, in general, some commonly applied selections, periodisations and established interpretations may hinder and obscure rather than help.

The first matter concerns the place of Australia's frontier wars, which ran from soon after white settlement through to the first decades of the twentieth century. When writing his book, *The Australian Frontier Wars*, in 2002, John Connor contended that he was attempting to bring those wars 'into the mainstream of Australian military history'.[13] That process had started in the late 1960s with WEH Stanner's observations about the 'great Australian silence' and gradually intensified via Henry Reynolds's *The Other Side of the Frontier* (1982) and other works, so that by the 1990s, there was already a body of work by military and other historians acknowledging and seeking to understand frontier fighting. This momentum continued, and there is now a plethora of books and other sources that grapple with the frontier wars in one way or another, though whether it has yet 'reached the mainstream' of Australian military history must be open to some doubt. The mere fact that blood was still being spilled in the twentieth century, even if police and pastoralists had become the main conduit of violence rather than soldiers, should give pause to anyone thinking about Australia and its history of warfare. You are unlikely to find references to the events at Coniston in 1928, for example, in any examination of Australia's wars from that century.[14]

The SBS television series, *The Australian Wars*, gives a similar impression about the consideration of these conflicts, as it, along with a good portion of its interviewees, still seems to be out to establish that these frontier wars

---

13 John Connor, *The Australian Frontier Wars 1788–1838* (Sydney: UNSW Press, 2002), xii.
14 The last widely recognised event was the killings at Coniston in the Northern Territory in 1928. Bill Wilson and Justin O'Brien, '"To infuse universal terror": A Reappraisal of the Coniston Killings', *Aboriginal History Journal* 27 (2011), doi.org/10.22459/ah.27.2011.06.

happened.[15] This probably reflected a desire to widen the appreciation of the history to more 'popular' audiences, a need for which had been evidenced by, if nothing else, the Australian War Memorial's long-term but recently overcome resistance to the idea that it should do something to acknowledge frontier wars.[16] What it also possibly reflects is that Australia's frontier wars, while readily finding a place in discussions about white colonisation, may not be easily settling into Australia's history of warfare, at least not in the way that John Connor might have intended in 2002.

Certainly, modern military histories deal with frontier war in Australia as a matter of course, and any recent book, and indeed many that are now rather aged, will have a section or chapter that examines these conflicts.[17] These examinations tend to be limited, however. First, while the longevity of this series of wars is widely acknowledged, the examination of them tends to be summed up in a section based on the early nineteenth century. With that done, the author or editor moves onto other events, such as the New Zealand wars or the Sudan, or perhaps the uniformed citizen-soldiers of the late colonial period, and then onwards to the more familiar twentieth century with its big wars and big commitments. Second, this treatment tends to be rather 'stand-alone', in that the importance, severity and duration of frontier warfare is recognised, but little or no effort is made to consider *how* or *if* it fits into any longer-term explanation of Australia and its wars. The result is an apparent contrast with the treatment of the almost entirely expeditionary commitments that otherwise characterise the country's war-making. So, whatever earnestness is given to the topic,

---

15 *The Australian Wars*, Blackfella Films, SBS TV, 2022; For an example of his notion, see: H Norman and AM Payne, 'In the Australian Wars, Rachel Perkins Dispenses with the Myth Aboriginal People Didn't Fight Back', *The Conversation*, 21 September 2022, theconversation.com/in-the-australian-wars-rachel-perkins-dispenses-with-the-myth-aboriginal-people-didnt-fight-back-190967.

16 *The Australian Wars* seems to have been the straw that broke the camel's back, and the Australian War Memorial (AWM) is now, after decades of calls by a phalanx of historians and others, aiming to do something to correct this. As a former historian at the AWM, I recall staff there who, while acknowledging the events, felt that it was not the AWM's remit to address frontier wars. An internal paper on the topic also seems to have helped sway the AWM council's views in 2023. AWM Council 178, AWM Freedom of Information, Reference 2022-23-06, www.awm.gov.au/sites/default/files/2022-23-06.pdf.

17 See, for example, Richard Broome, 'The Struggle for Australia: Aboriginal–European Warfare, 1770–1930' in *Australia, Two Centuries of War and Peace*, edited by Michael McKernan and Margaret Browne (Sydney: Allen & Unwin, 1988); John Coates, *An Atlas of Australia's Wars* (Oxford: Oxford University Press, 2006) [text and cartographic material]; Jeffrey Grey, *Military History*, 28–40; Horner, *Dummies*, 39–55; Jonathan Richards, 'Frontier warfare in Australia', in Stockings and Connor, *Before the Anzac Dawn*, 21–38.

it can be conceived of as somewhat anomalous when compared to the clearer examples offered by identifiably uniformed military personnel in familiar military organisations, embarking and going off to fight overseas.

In fairness to the historians who have done this (of whom I am one, having done much the same when teaching survey courses on Australian military history), Australia's history of warfare, probably like that of most countries, is highly episodic. Military historians tend to focus, for obvious and fair reasons, on the war of their choice. They contemplate their chosen aspect in detail, which is the way the historians' world works. A perhaps unintended consequence, however, is that the periods between wars tend to become background, or the period in which certain things happened to help shape the character of the next war or the Australian response to it, in one way or another. The result is that in surveys of Australian wars, the wars are the 'highlights' and the periods in between are almost interludes. Important things might have happened in these interludes, but, often, the tracing of these is limited to the author's conception of what is most relevant to outline in relation to their central subject, which is usually their chosen war or, in a survey, the next war in the sequence. While the tendency might be minimised in books with a wider span, such as in Grey's *Military History* or Horner's *Dummies*, it is not entirely overcome.

Again, periodisation and its close cousin, conceptual boundaries, are old and oft-noted problems in history. Historians must start and stop somewhere; otherwise, every history would begin with tales of hominids knocking rocks together in Africa some millions of years ago. Context must be constrained and relevant to get to the point. Similarly, historians must necessarily break their examinations into manageable portions to research, conceptualise and write. Moreover, the audience also seeks reasonable boundaries, with the history divided up into digestible segments. Hence, historians carve up history along what seem reasonable temporal or conceptual fault lines, which, while they vary somewhat from historian to historian and source to source, tend to become habitual, well-worn and eventually criticised as near-arbitrary distortions that hinder.[18] Any student of Australia's wars could readily list the most likely divisions that could and have been applied. For this chapter, 1914 (or, perhaps, the 1915 Gallipoli landings) and Federation in 1901 would be the two most relevant ones.

---

18   See, for example, David Blackbourn, '"The Horologe of Time": Periodization in History', *Publications of the Modern Language Association of America* 127, no. 2 (March 2012): 301–07, doi.org/10.1632/pmla.2012.127.2.301.

4. WHY AUSTRALIA HAS GONE TO WAR

The problems that stem from periodisation and the episodic character of our history of warfare seem particularly evident when we consider the nineteenth century. This period, conventionally bookended by the arrival of the First Fleet in 1788 and Federation in 1901 (possibly making it a 'long' Australian nineteenth century, to draw on another tradition in periodisation), is replete with 'episodes' or 'periods' that tend to be assessed in relative isolation. The treatment of the frontier wars—examinations of which often petered out in the middle of the nineteenth century, although their actual end was closer to the middle of the twentieth—has already been mentioned. In addition, we have a degree of Australian colonial involvement in the New Zealand wars in the 1860s, New South Wales's Sudan contingent of 1885, the Second Anglo-Boer War of 1899–1902 and the small contingents sent to the Boxer Rebellion in 1900–01. The latter two point to the problems with periodisation because of the way that they straddle Federation in 1901.

Except for the significant contribution to the war in South Africa, these nineteenth-century military expeditions have attracted little historical attention, which is not surprising given they were relatively small and brief. It is sometimes suggested that they deserve more consideration, but there is no tsunami of scholarship on the horizon at present. Until the recent appearance of Craig Wilcox's book on Australians and the war, the New Zealand wars were given little consideration because, apart from one Victorian colonial warship, there was no 'commitment' as such.[19] Nevertheless, several thousand individual volunteers crossed the Tasman to fight, largely in return for promised parcels of land.[20] The latter three conflicts tend to be considered in isolation, with them generally viewed as expressions of 'imperial loyalty' or responding to 'the call of empire'—ideas that were neatly encapsulated in the old 'Soldiers of the Queen' gallery at the AWM.

It is useful to examine the historiography of one of these conflicts, the Sudan expedition of 1885, in more detail. As noted, there is not a large body of work that considers it. David Horner's *Dummies* covers it in a page of brief paragraphs, which perhaps reflects his stronger interest in events of the twentieth century and, probably, some confines of the format. In his

---

19 Craig Wilcox, *Australia's Tasman Wars: Colonial Australia and Conflict in New Zealand, 1800–1850* (Melbourne: Australian Scholarly Publishing, 2022).
20 A good summation is Damien Fenton, 'Australians in the New Zealand Wars', in Stockings and Connor, *Anzac Dawn*, 118–47. Drawing on various sources, Fenton suggests 2,500 or so such volunteers (139 and 319). See also Jeffrey Hopkins-Weisse, 'Australian Involvement in New Zealand's Wars of the 1840s and 1860s' (MPhil thesis, University of Queensland, 2004), 143.

Military History, Jeff Grey, on the other hand, describes it as a 'minor incident' but expends a few pages highlighting what it might tell us about colonial attitudes to the empire and war. Conversely, in McKernan and Browne's *Australia: Two Centuries*, the Sudan expedition does not garner even a complete sentence.[21] Craig Stockings and John Connor's *Before the Anzac Dawn: A Military History of Australia before 1915* includes a typically erudite chapter by Craig Wilcox that contrasts the expedition to Sudan with the commitments to South Africa at the turn of the century to chart the evolution and arguments about of the concept of imperial defence.[22]

Monographs offer little more. Michael Tyquin's book on the campaign is fundamentally a conventional military history that focuses on the formation, despatch and doings of the contingent without wondering too much what the deployment might tell us about the nation's wider history of warfare.[23] The provision of context is limited to what is necessary to sustain this. Peter Stanley's small edited collection, *But Little Glory*, contains a strong chapter by Chris Clark about the New South Wales offer and British acceptance of the contingent, providing a good outline of the proximate influences involved.[24] Ken Inglis's brief book, *The Rehearsal*, remains, nearly 40 years after its publication, the best on the subject, but while it examines much of the politics, debates and cultural response to the despatch of the contingent, it in many ways treats the matter as a precursor to Australia's response to the outbreak of the First World War, as the title suggests.[25]

There is nothing to be scorned in this modest literature. The expedition was small, brief, barely fired a shot and suffered no deaths in battle (the few unfortunates died of disease). The popular enthusiasm that accompanied its despatch had turned to indifference, almost embarrassment, by the time of its return, and the bigger wars that came later have easily eclipsed it. Its status as an 'episode' in the historiography is readily evident, with it often being examined in isolation, and, even then, there is a tendency in some

---

21 Horner, *Dummies*, 51; Grey, *Military History*, 48–50; Peter Stanley, '"Soldiers and fellow countrymen" in Colonial Australia', in *Australia: Two Centuries of War and Peace*, edited by Michael McKernan and Margaret Browne, 89.
22 Craig Wilcox, 'Australians in the Wars in Sudan and South Africa', in *Before the Anzac Dawn*, edited by Craig Stockings and John Connor (Sydney: NewSouth, 2013), 204–29.
23 Michael Tyquin, *Sudan: 1885* (Sydney: Big Sky Publishing, 2014).
24 Chris Coulthard-Clark, 'The Despatch of the Contingent', in *But Little Glory: The New South Wales Contingent to the Sudan*, edited by Peter Stanley (Canberra: Military Historical Society of Australia, 1985), 19–30.
25 Ken Inglis, *The Rehearsal: Australians at War in the Sudan 1885* (Adelaide: Rigby Publishers, 1985).

sources to downplay or dismiss its significance.²⁶ Those historians who have attributed more significance and sought to extract meaning from it have done so largely by using it as another case study to examine the relationship between Australia, or, in this case, one of its precursor colonies, and the imperial centre. In doing so, they have essentially followed the nationalist tradition outlined above and used it as a waypoint to examine the emergence, or otherwise, of an independent Australia.

Intriguingly, a similar approach is taken by another book that considers the Sudan expedition at some length: Henry Reynolds's 2016 book, *Unnecessary Wars*. Reynolds's book is particularly relevant to the question of why Australia has gone to war because it argues that the response to the Boer War shaped the nation's approach to war at the founding moment of Federation. His central argument is that the despatch of contingents to the Boer War in 1899–1902 created a 'habit' of uncritically and enthusiastically sending Australian contingents to fight alongside either Britain or, later, the US when Australia, in his view, should have been more circumspect, focused on its own development and generally more peaceful in its outlook.²⁷ *Unnecessary Wars* is an idiosyncratic work, and decidedly polemic. It has a noble intent and outlines some history very well, but the argument that sending contingents to the Boer War shaped so much that came after is not persuasive. Fundamentally, this is because Reynolds's interpretation amounts to a general theory of Australian war-making that pays little heed to the myriad proximate matters alluded to above in explaining a range of wars over a long period. Even when considering matters in the era it examines, its apparent unfamiliarity with a range of developments in Australian military affairs of the period, such as arguments about imperial defence, or the attempts by military personalities in New South Wales in the 1890s to raise contingents for imperial service, are ignored. This diminishes the book's impact. Thus, while it is interesting and thought-provoking, it is not generally convincing.

Moreover, in examining the events around the Sudan expedition (and the Boer War), *Unnecessary Wars* frequently becomes a paean to those who opposed sending the contingent, often radicals with a republican bent,²⁸

---

26 A PhD thesis by Alex Little, 'Negotiating Imperial Unity: Colonial Australian Contributions to British Wars, 1885–1902' (Australia Catholic University, 2023), considers the links between the Sudan, Boer War and Boxer Rebellion commitments. I thank one of his supervisors, Thomas Rogers, for this reference.
27 Henry Reynolds, *Unnecessary Wars* (Sydney: NewSouth, 2016), ix–15.
28 Reynolds, *Unnecessary Wars*, passim.

rather than an attempt to explain the forces that brought about the effort. Instead, these are largely scorned as subservient and unthinking. Analysing the opposition to the war is illuminating and vital to understanding, but it is only half the story about why there was a decision to join the war. Most important from the point of view of this chapter is that in all this, Reynolds examines Australian military adventures of the late colonial period by making them, once again, part of the history of Australia asserting independence (or, in Reynolds's view, failing to assert independence) from the empire.

This examination is intriguing because Reynolds has built a distinguished history career on his work on Australian frontier wars; he is virtually the father of the field. Yet, in looking at the late colonial period to establish that a belligerent 'habit' was formed, he, too, seemingly succumbed to the habits of periodisation, conceptualisation and nationalist argument that have characterised the history of Australia and its wars in the nineteenth century. In so doing, Reynolds, of all historians, has focused on the expeditionary wars of the period and elided Australian frontier warfare in *Unnecessary Wars*. This is perplexing, because in a previous book, *Forgotten War*, he contrasted the Sudan commitment with the frontier wars, although his main purpose in so doing was to highlight how the African commitment has been remembered and commemorated, and frontier bloodshed ignored.[29]

This leads to a key point of this chapter: why do historians, and anyone else with an interest, continue to do this? Why are the frontier wars still treated as something apart?[30] And, conversely, if this intellectual partition is broken down, what effect might it have on our appreciation of Australia's willingness to go to war?

This brings us back to proximate and contextual, sometimes long-running, influences in history. In considering the Sudan contingent, to continue with the example, it would be unwise to overlook the matters immediately surrounding the decision to despatch the force: the death of General Charles Gordon at the hands of the Mahdi's army at Khartoum (incidentally, something that David Horner wrote about while still at school);[31] the

---

29 Henry Reynolds, *Forgotten War* (Sydney: NewSouth, 2013), 194–227 and passim.
30 In fairness to Reynolds, he wondered something like this in *Forgotten War* but saw two disjointed narratives before explaining how joint commemoration might relink them with a goal to having the frontier conflicts brought into the national memory; see 228–56.
31 David M Horner ('D.M.H.'), 'Gordon Avenged: The Battle of Omdurman', *Prince Alfred Chronicle*, October 1963, 32.

empire-wide grief and indignation that it spawned; the hyped jingoistic atmosphere that resulted; and the desire among politicians and others to do something both symbolic and seemingly practical to help Britain in a 'moment of need'. However, another contextual, concurrent, matter in 1885 was the ongoing violent conquest of the Australian continent. It was occurring mostly on the fringes of white colonist expansion, as it always had, meaning that by then, most cases occurred in far north Queensland and western Queensland, and what is now the Northern Territory. However, it was certainly still occurring.[32] To not count this as a rolling, ongoing, if intermittent, war relies predominantly on arguments about definitions: it was carried out by 'police' forces or pastoralists, hence not by the accepted agents of war—'soldiers'; they were 'massacres' or instances of 'frontier violence' but not (possibly very one-sided) battles; there was no declaration of war, or some such arguments. These sorts of objections have frequently been raised in the decades since the 'great Australian silence' started being less mute, but they have largely been broken down by the bloody weight of evidence that continues to build up, and the realisation that if it did not seem like 'war' from the conqueror's side, it very likely did from the Indigenous side.

So, if we explicitly juxtapose the New South Wales Government's decision to send a contingent to the Sudan to aid Britain's imperial war there with the still ongoing, but by then nearly century-long, history of warfare occurring on the Australian continent, does it change the complexion of the 1885 African adventure? I think that it does. Rather than being a stand-alone, almost forgettable, episode, the Sudan commitment might highlight quite a different aspect of Australia's relationship to the empire. Its contemporaneousness with continuing frontier bloodshed points to the Sudan contingent being more than simply a case study or a moment in a nationalist debate, and suggests that Australians were also active, energetic and ardent *agents* of imperialism—that they were not simply going along for the imperial ride as the price or experience that led to attaining something else.

This realisation is significant because it prompts one to ponder an enduring centrality of conquest in Australia's history of making war. The frontier warfare that was still occurring in the 1880s, having been ongoing for

---

32   A quick look at the iterative *Colonial Frontier Massacres Map* produced by the project team at the University of Newcastle suggests there were more than two dozen massacres between 1880 and 1885, c21ch.newcastle.edu.au/colonialmassacres/map.php.

a century, and which was to continue for several more decades yet, was fundamentally about imperial conquest—about bloodily pushing aside the Indigenous people who lived on the continent, and the taking of the territory and its resources. This impulse to conquer was also the fundamental purpose of Britain's empire building, and, indeed, that of all other colonisers as well, and by the 1880s Australian governments were increasingly inclined to become involved. In seeking out themes or recurring approaches in the history of why Australia has gone to war, it is difficult to escape imperial conquest and subjugation, for they come up again and again, certainly in the nineteenth century and probably beyond. They suggest that, contrary to the way the matter has generally been treated, there may be an enduring link between frontier war in Australia and the growing willingness to despatch contingents to overseas wars in the late colonial–early Federation period, and that the purpose was more than fostering imperial defence or demonstrating loyalty.

Moreover, if the same lens is run over a series of other events, that large painting of Australia's history of going to war starts to look darker than hitherto. Regarding the wars already mentioned, it is worth noting that the New Zealand wars were triggered by the tendrils of white maritime colonisation that, in good part, stretched outwards from Sydney across the Tasman Sea.[33] Perhaps most obvious is Queensland's decision to annex southern New Guinea in 1883, which, together with 'blackbirding' and economic exploitation of islanders, has led some historians to argue that Australia also fought frontier conflicts in the Pacific.[34] What of attempts, initiated in the Australian colonies, not London, to create military units for imperial use in the 1890s, particularly in New South Wales? Or the British authorities' use of the light horse to supress the Egyptian Revolution of 1919? Or even the brief fantasies apparently entertained by some Australians in 1945 that once Australia had taken Borneo, it might become Australian-administered territory?[35] With more thought it probably would not be very difficult to add to this list. Not all of these were wars or events in which military forces were used, but they were acts that appear to be highly

---

33   Fenton, 'Australians', 119–20.
34   Craig Wilcox, 'Australia's Maritime Frontier Conflicts, 1802–1918', War Studies Seminar, Strategic and Defence Studies Centre, The Australian National University, 8 October 2018, sdsc.bellschool.anu.edu.au/news-events/podcasts/audio/6555/australias-maritime-frontier-conflicts-1802-1918 (site discontinued); Wilcox, *Australia's Tasman Wars*, 1–17.
35   Graeme Sligo, *The Backroom Boys: Alfred Conlon and Army's Directorate of Research and Civil Affairs, 1942–46* (Newport: Big Sky Publishing, 2013), 208–21.

relevant context, and it is possible that Australia's history of warfare in the period, apart from perhaps being knit together by frontier bloodletting in the nineteenth and twentieth centuries, starts to look less episodic.

Historians have often pointed to the imperial character of many wars that Australia has been involved in, but the notion that Australians may have been ardent and willing conquerors, at home and abroad, is not a strong theme in our history of war. The ugliness of colonial campaigning is acknowledged (although not always), but except for Australia's taking over New Guinea, the imperial impulse is mostly attributed to Britain, and Australia's participation tends to be rationalised or minimised, or simply not thoroughly thought through. The 'call of empire' or 'soldiers of the Queen' is used as a handy 'hook', with little contemplation of its implications.

This is not to assert that conquest and willing imperialism might have been the only motivation for Australia going to war in the nineteenth century. Appreciating nuance and the available evidence remains vital; other interpretations are far from extinguished, and it is still important to weigh up the proximate motivations. There is, for example, plenty of evidence of Australian ambivalence or discomfort about Britain's empire building in the period, and of Australian colonial and federal governments being wary of being drawn into the many 'small wars' that came with it.[36] Some of these wars drew conspicuous, if unsuccessful, opposition from parts of colonial society. Equally, however, these qualms were patently overcome from time to time and, as the above suggests, there were continuities that have been overlooked. A recent conference paper (2023) by Thomas Rogers, for example, has highlighted the way the Sudan contingent used language that had echoes of the language used to describe Indigenous peoples and actions against them in Australia.[37]

Conclusion

What this 'think piece' chapter suggests is that as soon as we begin to contemplate *why* Australia has gone to war, query some well-worn conventions and ask other questions about the nation's history of war,

---

36 See, for example, Wilcox, 'Australians in the Wars', passim.
37 Thomas Rogers, 'Avenging General Gordon? The 1885 NSW Contingent to Sudan as Punitive Expedition' (paper, Australian Historical Association Conference, Australian Catholic University, Melbourne, July 2023). Copy provided to author.

it becomes clear that some things require re-examination. This is nowhere more apparent than when contemplating the wars of the nineteenth century, which have largely been characterised as series of curious episodes with little to link them together, apart from imperial loyalty or kinship. Most troubling in this is the treatment of the frontier wars, which continues to be conceived of as something that is perhaps anomalous, certainly apart. This tendency to separate out well over a century of rolling warfare and, too often, tuck it away in the early 1800s is both regrettable and, probably, historically dangerous. It elides too much and, importantly, may well miscue our appreciation of both contemporaneous and subsequent events. The question of why Australia goes to war is important because it highlights motivations without diminishing actions. Focusing on the latter is important, but it emphasises the proximate influences. Appreciating motivations requires more than considering the proximate and leads to valuing the wider contextual influences—the currents of history that create the 'preconditions' for waging war. These motivations, importantly, are also an indication of what Australian governments and peoples thought they were trying to achieve by fighting. This is a profoundly political matter, in that politics is fundamentally about the way that a polity or community wants to exist and function, and how it would like to exist and function in the future.[38] Deciding to go to war is a clue to what Australians thought strongly enough about themselves and their place in the world that they were willing to fight for it.

---

38   I am influenced here by the discussion of politics and societies in David Graeber and David Wengrow, *The Dawn of Everything: A New History of Humanity* (London: Allen Lane, 2021), 78–87, 93–96.

5
History frames policy: David Horner and the future of Australia's defence

Hugh White

No one, I think, has studied the evolution of Australia's defence and strategic policy for longer than David Horner, nor with such singular dedication and focus. It is now nearly 55 years since his first book, *Crisis of Command: Australian Generalship and the Japanese Threat, 1941–1943*,[1] was published, and since then he has produced an astonishing number of historical and biographical works covering almost every aspect of the development of our approach to national defence. It is a corpus of work unmatched in the field, and no one seriously engaged in it can have failed to be instructed and profoundly influenced by his work. I first encountered Horner's writing at the very start of my own engagement with defence and strategic policy. The note on the flyleaf of my battered copy of his *High Command: Australia and Allied Strategy 1939–1945*[2] reads: 'Canberra, Summer, 1983'. It was only the second book I had ever read on the history of Australian strategic and defence policy, the first being Tom Millar's *Australia in Peace and War*.[3]

---

1 David Horner, *Crisis of Command: Australian Generalship and the Japanese Threat, 1941–1943* (Canberra: Australian National University Press, 1978).
2 David Horner, *High Command: Australia and Allied Strategy 1939–1945* (Canberra: Australian War Memorial and Sydney: George Allen & Unwin, 1982).
3 Thomas B Millar, *Australia in Peace and War: External Relations, 1788–1977* (Canberra: Australian National University Press, 1978), hdl.handle.net/1885/114800.

What struck me then and still impresses me today is the way Horner drew broad and powerful conclusions about the biggest and most enduring questions in Australian strategic policy—above all the interplay between the alliances on which we depended, and the unique Australian interests and objectives we sought to protect and promote—from a detailed study of the nuts and bolts of actual policy and command decisions, and the way they were made. The same approach—systematic, scrupulous, thorough, insightful and, in the best sense, scholarly—has characterised the whole of Horner's extraordinary body of work over those five decades.

That work provides an essential and substantial foundation for the work ahead as we try to reframe Australian defence and strategic policy to meet the unprecedented challenges ahead. It has become commonplace to say that Australia's strategic circumstances today are more dangerous than at any time since the Second World War. There are good reasons to think that this pessimistic assessment is correct—better reasons, perhaps, than many who offer the assessment understand. For the first time since the defeat of Japan in 1945, US domination of the Western Pacific is challenged by a formidable Asian maritime power. This imperils Australia because we have always depended for our security on the unchallenged primacy of our close allies over the vast waters that surround our continent.

New challenges

The naval power of the US has been the real guarantor of Australia's security since as long ago as 1904. That was when it took Britain's place as the Western Pacific's strongest naval power, as the Royal Navy's main fleet units were withdrawn from Asian stations to join the Grand Fleet then being assembled to meet the rising threat from the Imperial German Navy in the North Sea. Japan emerged as the only serious rival to the US in the Pacific after it destroyed the Russian fleet at Tsushima in 1905. Once Japan's challenge was decisively defeated in 1945, US maritime primacy in East Asia became unassailable, and after Nixon's meeting with Mao in 1972, US strategic supremacy in East Asia was effectively uncontested for four decades.

All that has now changed. China today seems determined to push the US out of the region and take its place, and it has the means to do so. China has developed air and naval forces that pose the first serious challenge to US naval supremacy since the Pacific War. Yet, China is a much more formidable rival than Japan could ever have been, because its economy is far bigger, relative to that of the US, than Japan's economy ever was. Indeed, on some measures, China's GDP is already bigger than that of the US. Moreover, its strategic energies are overwhelmingly focused on its US rival, whereas Japan's efforts were divided between its war in China and defeating the US. In addition, China has nuclear weapons, which allow it to carry a war to the US homeland in a way Japan never could.

There must, therefore, be real questions as to whether the US can defeat China's challenge. This uncertainty suggests that the comparison between our situation today and the late 1930s may, if anything, understate how serious things are. At no time since European settlement have either of our great and powerful friends faced such a formidable rival to their positions in Asia as the US faces today, and, thus, never before has the foundation of our security been so seriously challenged.

This does not mean that China today threatens Australia directly, the way Japan did in 1942. It is important to be clear about this. It is not, I think, credible to argue that China could pose a direct military threat to Australia in, say, the next three years, as a recent series of newspaper articles suggested.[4] To be more specific, a direct attack on Australia by Chinese forces within that kind of time frame would only be a serious prospect if Australia had started things by joining a military coalition—presumably led by the US—against China in a conflict over an issue like Taiwan. If we do not attack China, there is little danger that China will attack us over, say, the next decade or so.

However, this assumption seems less clear when we look further ahead. China's growing power and ambition may not yet threaten Australia directly, but its challenge to the strategic position of the US in Asia—a challenge not just to US strategic primacy, but to the maintenance of any substantial US strategic role in East Asia and the Western Pacific—threatens to overturn the foundations of regional order that have ensured our security from armed aggression by a major power for so long. If, as I have argued elsewhere,[5] China does succeed in pushing the US out of the region altogether, Australia will become, over time, more vulnerable to major power attack than we have ever been since European settlement. The primacy of US power, and,

---

4 'Australia faces the threat of war with China within four years, and we are not ready', *Sydney Morning Herald/The Age*, 7 March 2023, www.smh.com.au/politics/federal/red-alert-20230306-p5cpt8.html.
5 Hugh White, 'Without America: Australia in the New Asia', *Quarterly Essay* 68 (Collingwood: Black Inc., 2017).

specifically, its complete military predominance in the maritime domain, backed by its nuclear arsenal, has not only upheld but enforced a regional order that has effectively precluded major inter-state aggression, especially by maritime power projection. It has also underwritten US bilateral security commitments to Australia. Together, these factors have ensured that, in the face of US power, China has had no military capacity to attack Australia.

That will not be true in future. As the distribution of wealth and power tilts increasingly China's way, and, more specifically, as the maritime military balance in Asia shifts in China's favour, the willingness and capacity of the US to constrain China's capacity to use armed force directly against Australia will decline, and the risks that China will do so will correspondingly increase. Indeed, in terms of capability (as opposed to intention or motive), China will have a greater capacity to attack Australia than any power has ever had. So, in time, will India, and perhaps eventually, also, Indonesia. Whether any of these Asian great powers might ever have reason to attack Australia is, of course, a very different question. Great powers do not launch military operations without reason, but history shows they can do so for many different reasons, and the more powerful they are relative to a potential military target, the lower the threshold for resorting to force becomes. We can see this in the relatively careless way that the US has chosen to use force since the end of the Cold War. Nor is it easy to predict what issues and differences might arise between Australia and its regional major-power neighbours in future decades, when the international system may be working very differently from the way it does today. It is one thing to say that we can see no reason why China, India or Indonesia would use force against Australia today, even if they could. It is quite another to say with any confidence that they will not have such reasons in future, when their capacity to do so is greater.

Faltering steps

All this suggests that if Australia is to be serious about its defence over the decades ahead, it needs to start now to plan and build the forces it would need to defend itself independently from armed attack by a major Asian power in the decades ahead. This is a much more ambitious strategic objective than the one that guided Australia's defence policy after Forward Defence was abandoned in the early 1970s. The self-reliant Defence of Australia, which was the primary objective of the policy set out on the 1976 and 1987 Defence White Papers, only encompassed independent defence against the very low levels of attack that could credibly be mounted by Indonesian forces of that time—the so-called 'low level contingencies', with limited provision for expansion to meet more demanding scenarios after 10 years' warning. It has been clear since the 1994 Defence White Paper that China's rise would eventually transform Australia's strategic environment and require fundamental changes to the foundations of defence policy, to encompass much more ambitious objectives than these. The Howard government's 1998 Strategic Policy Review and 2000 Defence White Paper offered cautious progress towards these changes, but for almost a decade after the terrorist attacks of 2001 Australia's defence policy debates were sidetracked by the War on Terror, which was seen for a time, quite mistakenly, to constitute the country's primary strategic challenge in the new century.

Thus, it was not until the Rudd government's 2009 White Paper that Canberra first acknowledged that the time had now arrived to radically reframe Australia's defence policy in the light of China's rise. Since then, a succession of policy documents—the 2013 and 2016 White Papers, the 2020 Strategic Defence Update and the 2023 Defence Strategic Review and the 2024 National Defence Strategy—have attempted to do this. None have succeeded. Only the rhetoric has changed. The government now routinely warns that our strategic circumstances are more dangerous than at any time since the Second World War, but there has been no substantial shift in the substance of our defence policy in response. Our force plans—with one exception—have not materially altered, and defence spending commitments as a share of GDP remain broadly where they have been since 2000. More fundamentally, these successive efforts have failed, and indeed have hardly attempted, to develop a new set of force-planning concepts on which a new defence program and budget could be developed. The rigorous set of strategic objectives, operational plans and capability priorities that framed defence policy in the 'Defence of Australia' from the 1970s have yet to be replaced by a new set that matches the new circumstances. There is, thus, no robust basis on which to design a new force and justify the commitment of resources needed to build and sustain it.

Three decades after the strategic challenge of China's rise was first clearly identified, and a decade and a half after it was declared to be urgently upon us, Australia has still not found a credible defence policy response. Future historians will, I think, find this failure quite remarkable and will seek to explain it. They might find a key to the problem in the exception noted in the previous paragraph. The one genuinely new, and startlingly unexpected, change in defence policy over the past decade was the decision to acquire nuclear-powered submarines in partnership with the US and Britain under the AUKUS (Australia, UK and US) arrangement. What future historians will see as the peculiarity of this arrangement is that at a time when Australia's strategic imperative is so plainly, and, indeed, urgently, to reduce our military dependency on our US ally, AUKUS thrusts in the opposite direction. It deepens and tightens our strategic connection with the US in complex and powerful ways.

Under AUKUS, Australia is entrusting the future of one of our most important capabilities to Washington in a unique way. Of course, Australia sources much key military equipment and systems from the US, including F-18 and F-35 combat aircraft, but the arrangement for us to acquire nuclear-powered submarines is different. The US sells combat aircraft to many countries, including non-allies like Singapore, but it has only ever shared nuclear propulsion technology with Britain, and that was at the very height of the Cold War. Moreover, it has never sold complete nuclear-powered submarines to any other country as it proposes to sell Virginia-class boats to Australia.

Operating nuclear-powered submarines successfully and safely requires the mastery of a unique set of advanced technologies in which Australia has very little or no expertise. Australia will, therefore, depend on the US much more for day-to-day operational support of its nuclear-powered submarines than it does for other US-sourced platforms and systems. That will apply to both the Virginia-class boats that are planned to come into service with the Royal Australian Navy in the early 2030s, and the proposed UK-designed AUKUS submarines, which will incorporate key US technology. This support can only be assured in the decades ahead if the US remains actively engaged strategically in Asia and strongly committed to Australia's defence. That cannot be taken for granted.

But AUKUS raises deeper strategic questions as well, questions that go beyond the future of Australia's submarine force. There can be no doubt that Washington has only decided to take the exceptional step of sharing this technology on the expectation that Australia will remain completely and unconditionally committed to supporting the US diplomatically and militarily in Asia. If Australia fails to meet that expectation, the future of our submarine capability will be in very grave doubt, so Australia's commitment to AUKUS entails a clear assumption that it will provide the US with the support it expects for decades to come. That will be a critical and difficult issue. As strategic rivalry between the US and China escalates, the costs to Australia of supporting the US in that contest will rise, and if it leads to war between them, Australian support for the US would commit it to take part in an exceptionally serious conflict. Moreover, it cannot be taken for granted that Australia's strategic interests and objectives in Asia will remain aligned with those of the US, or, indeed, whether they are aligned today. Washington clearly aims to perpetuate US strategic primacy in Asia and preserve the unipolar regional order that is based on it. Australia, on the other hand, seems to seek a different objective: the evolution of a multipolar regional order in which the US plays a role alongside China and other regional powers. Nonetheless, AUKUS appears predicated on a clear expectation that Australia is committed to supporting US objectives rather than its own.

It is important to recognise what all this means. For the first time since the alliance was formalised in the ANZUS (Australia, New Zealand and United States Security) Treaty, Australia has now, through AUKUS, pre-committed itself to going to war against a major power in support of the US. Such pre-commitments have characterised US alliances in Europe and north-east Asia since the 1950s, but they are quite new for Australia under ANZUS. AUKUS thus signifies a qualitative shift in the nature of Australia's alliance with the US and offers a ready explanation for the failure of Australian defence policy to effectively address the challenges posed by the rise of China and other Asian great powers. Quite simply, the more threatening the strategic environment has become the more Australian policymakers have believed that there is no alternative but to rely on the US for protection, and the more willing they have become to commit to supporting the US in return, and the less seriously they have taken the need to build Australia's capacity to defend itself independently. Australia has thus chosen to depend more and more heavily on the US as both its power and its willingness to sustain a credible and substantial strategic role in Asia have waned. One cannot help but be reminded of our response to that earlier strategic crisis to which our leaders so often refer. By endorsing and supporting the United Kingdom's Singapore Strategy, we doubled down on an alliance relationship and shaped Australian capability to the associated strategy, despite serious questions as to its viability.

Alliance attitudes

How has this happened? One key factor is a change in attitudes to the US and the alliance that can be traced back some 25 years to the mid-1990s. Over that time, faith in the reliability of the US as a guarantor of Australia's security has grown to the point of now being, it seems, unquestionable among political leaders, senior policymakers and most influential commentators. This faith has almost eclipsed the prudent and, one might say, proper awareness of the natural limits of the alliance that had characterised earlier generations of the Australian foreign and defence policy establishment. The change can be traced in the way the alliance is described and the way its history is understood. Something of the new tone can be seen in an exchange between the prime minister and a journalist on the occasion of the launch of the Albanese government's Defence Strategic Review in April 2023:

> **Journalist:** What is your assessment of, in the decades ahead, the US's reliability as an ally, and whether there's any risk of isolationism growing in the decades ahead?
>
> **Prime Minister:** The US remains an important ally. It's a relationship between nations, it's a relationship between peoples and it's based upon our common values.[6]

That is all he said, and all—it seems—that he thought needed to be said. For him, the strength of the alliance was presumed to flow directly and automatically from those 'common values', as if a nation's interests and objectives are entirely determined by its values rather than by its circumstances and are thus thought to be immutable. This naturally gives rise to, and is in turn supported by, a distorted and highly sentimentalised account of the history of the alliance, which was perfectly encapsulated in the slogan coined to mark the centenary of the Battle of Hamel in 2018, '100 Years of Mateship'.[7] In the same spirit, the then prime minister, Scott Morrison, erased a lot of Australian history when, at the initial announcement of AUKUS, he described Australia's partnerships with both Britain and the US

---

6 Press conference, Canberra, 29 March 2023, www.pm.gov.au/media/press-conference-parliament-house-canberra-11.
7 'History of Mateship', Embassy of Australia, Washington DC, usa.embassy.gov.au/timelines-alliance.

as 'forever partnerships'.[8] Indeed, the enthusiasm with which, even before AUKUS, Australian political leaders on both sides embraced the idea that Britain might once again become—or more remarkably still, has never ceased to be—a key Australian ally, speaks volumes for the way in which Canberra's thinking about alliances has become detached from any real sense of either contemporary strategic circumstances or historical realities.

It would be interesting and instructive to explore the causes of this marked shift in attitudes towards our alliance with the US. Those causes might include, as well as the rise of China itself, John Howard's long prime ministership, the impact of the War on Terror and generational changes in attitude as those who experienced the Vietnam War and the Cold War give way to those who came of age politically in the 1990s, when the US seemed set to exercise global supremacy. However, at this moment it is perhaps more important to remind ourselves just how far today's idealised, sentimentalised view of the alliance diverges from the messy, complex, contested reality of how it actually worked in previous decades, and to draw from that understanding a more nuanced view of how it will work in future. In this endeavour, David Horner's work provides an essential guide.

Enduring questions

One of the great strengths of David Horner's work is the way in which, in many different ways and in a wide range of circumstances, he has illuminated the great question that has always been, and still remains, at the heart of our strategic and defence policy debates: how to balance priorities between supporting our allies and defending ourselves. The importance and persistence of this question for Australia arises from the acute dilemma posed by the fundamentals of our strategic circumstances in terms of space and distance. On the one hand, we feel that our sparsely populated country is too big for us to be able to defend ourselves, so we must depend on great allies to defend us, so our priority must be to support them in the hope that our support will help ensure that our allies have the strength and the willingness to come to our aid when we need them. On the other hand, our allies' homelands are far away, and we have never been able to take for granted that they would see a threat to us as a threat to them, and that

---

8   Andrew Tillett, 'PM Hails New Subs Deal as "Forever Partnership"', *Australian Financial Review*, 16 September 2021, www.afr.com/politics/federal/pm-hails-new-subs-deal-as-forever-partnership-20210 916-p58s3t.

they would be willing or able to respond as we would want, so we must give priority to defending ourselves. Therein lies the dilemma: we must depend on our allies, but we cannot depend on our allies; we cannot defend ourselves, but we must defend ourselves.

From the very start of his career as a historian, Horner has contributed to our efforts to understand and manage the dilemma by focusing with great clarity on how our alliances have actually worked in times of stress—times when the easy verbiage of alliance loyalty has fallen away, and both sides have had to make hard choices about precisely what real costs and risks they are willing and able to shoulder on behalf of their partners. *Crisis of Command* looked in detail at the workings of the alliance with the US under the stress of the faltering campaign against Japan in PNG in 1942–43. *High Command* expanded this analysis, covering both the UK and the US alliance across the whole of the Second World War. Many of Horner's subsequent works have explored the same issues in other settings: the biography of Shedden[9] explored the UK alliance as threats grew in the 1930s, the biography of Wilton[10] analysed our UK and US alliances in the early phases of the Cold War in Asia, and his Official History[11] studied their workings in the post–Cold War of the 1990s, to mention just a few.

The lesson to be drawn from all of this work is not that the US and Britain have been bad or faithless allies. Horner's work shows that both of our great and powerful friends have generally been good allies, and that, overall, these alliances have served Australia's interests well in their times. Indeed, Horner's work is a vital corrective to the tendency, so common in our debates on foreign policy, to see our alliances as either 'good' or 'bad' in themselves. It teaches instead that the right question to ask is whether, and how well, these alliances have worked to support our interests and objectives, and whether the support they have provided has justified the costs and risks they have imposed. What his work shows is that our alliances worked best when our allies' interests and objectives aligned most closely with ours, and that

---

9 David Horner, *Defence Supremo: Sir Frederick Shedden and the Making of Australian Defence Policy* (Sydney: Allen & Unwin, 2000).
10 David Horner, *Strategic Command: General Sir John Wilton and Australia's Asian Wars* (Melbourne: Oxford University Press, 2005).
11 David Horner, *Australia and the New World Order: From Peacekeeping to Peace Enforcement 1988–1991*, vol. II of The Official History of Australian Peacekeeping, Humanitarian and Post–Cold War Operations (Port Melbourne: Cambridge University Press, 2011).

they did not work at all well when (as with Britain in 1941–42, or the US in the later stages of the Pacific War) our interests and objectives diverged sharply from theirs.

This tells us something important about the nature of alliances—something amply demonstrated by the history of such relationships throughout the ages, but which we in Australia have found hard to absorb, and in consequence have had to repeatedly relearn. It is that no serious alliance—one that imposes real costs and risks on its members—is founded on anything resembling 'mateship': the links of shared history, culture, language, traditions and values that are so routinely invoked to assert the strength and durability of these relationships. The fact that we do genuinely share these links with our great and powerful has always made it easy—and still makes it easy today—to imagine that this is what the alliance is founded upon. That assumption is not seriously tested when interests and objectives do align, or when the costs and risks that alliance obligations impose on its members are low. But the more the interests and objectives of the allies are challenged and the higher the costs and risks involved in meeting such challenges, the clearer it becomes that the allies' willingness to shoulder those costs and risks on behalf of alliance partners depends almost entirely on how closely their priorities, interests and objectives align.

The key conclusion to draw—one that is seemingly obvious, but oddly elusive—is that the worth of alliances is not as fixed and enduring as the idea that they spring from shared history, values and so on implies, but varies with circumstances, as allies' interests and objectives change. This is crucial to understanding our current situation. It is often said that Australia has no choice but to maintain and even to deepen the alliance with the US as its rivalry with China grows. 'That choice was made a long time ago, if it ever truly existed,' as one commentator wrote.[12] However, Australia's choices about the alliance hitherto have been made in different times and circumstances. Our task today is to ask how well it will work for us in the new circumstances of today and in the decades ahead. That requires us to consider how well our interests and objectives align with those of the US now and in the future, and how the costs and risks of the alliance will mount. It also requires us to ask the same questions from Washington's perspective:

---

12   Philipp Ivanov, 'Australia's Delicate Dance with the United States and China', *The Interpreter*, 12 April 2023, www.lowyinstitute.org/the-interpreter/australia-s-delicate-dance-united-states-china (site discontinued).

how far will our interests and objectives align with theirs? We have to ask not just whether we should choose to stick by the US, but whether the US will choose to stick by us.

Rethinking objectives

Reassessing our alliance with the US requires us to delve more deeply into some issues that have for too long been taken for granted. What outcomes does Australia seek to the crisis of the Asian strategic order that is now underway, and what outcomes does the US seek? The answers are not clear. Starting with Australia, there are two trends or themes. The dominant one is that Australia simply wants to preserve the old status quo, the US-led order that emerged in the 1970s after the US opening to China. This objective has not been set out in these terms; instead, successive governments in Canberra have alluded to it by using expressions like the 'rules-based order'. Nonetheless, what they mean is clear: the perpetuation of US primacy. For a long time, even as China's power and ambition grew, it was widely assumed that this preferred outcome was not just possible but virtually guaranteed, because it was presumed that Washington was determined to maintain its primacy in Asia, and Beijing would not dare to seriously challenge it. That presumption has now been proved false, but the expectation that US primacy can and will be sustained remains strong.

The secondary theme in Australia's thinking about its objectives is the idea, set out by Foreign Minister Penny Wong, that it seeks a new multipolar regional order in which the US no longer dominates but continues to play a major role in maintaining what Wong calls a 'balance of power' in the region, ensuring that no one power—especially China—dominates. This is only a 'secondary' theme because, although Wong has explored it in a number of speeches both before and since becoming foreign minister,[13] she has failed to spell it out as a fully developed and authoritative statement of Australian policy, and it has not been articulated at all by the Prime Minister or other ministers. It is, however, the only objective that makes any real sense given the circumstances. The clearer it becomes that China will not

---

13   Hugh White, 'Hugh White on the Choice Facing Penny Wong', *The Interpreter*, 19 April 2023, www.themonthly.com.au/issue/2023/april/hugh-white/penny-wong-s-next-big-fight; www.lowyinstitute.org/the-interpreter/hugh-white-choice-facing-penny-wong.

be readily deterred from its challenge to US primacy, and the harder the US and its allies will have to push to defeat that challenge, the less sense it makes for Australia to remain fixated on that objective.

But what of the US: what are its objectives as it confronts China's challenge? Does it seek simply to perpetuate the old US-led status quo, or might it seek instead to build a new and different order that, in some way and to some extent, takes account of the new distribution of wealth and power in Asia by stepping back from primacy and adopting a balancing role instead? It seems clear that the Trump administration was committed to the first of these options.[14] At the time of its inauguration, there were some signs that the Biden Administration might take the second course, as advocated in 2019 by two figures who went on to senior roles in the Biden White House.[15] However, it has now become clear that there is no appetite in Washington for such moderation: even as Biden and his colleagues call for 'guardrails' to manage strategic competition, the Administration has given no indication that it is willing to concede any significant stepping back from the leadership role that the US had occupied in the Asian strategic order for so long. Where the second Trump Administration will land is something of a mystery, with the hawkish views of many of his senior appointees offset by the more complex attitudes of the president himself.

A hawkish Washington might sound like good news for Australia, and for Australia's US alliance—a Washington committed to the same primary objective as Canberra—but, alas, it is not as easy as that, for two reasons. First, because it is far from clear that Washington really is committed to that objective, especially under the Trump Administration. Despite the tough talk from both Democrats and Republicans about, in Biden's words, 'extreme competition' with China,[16] the reality is that the US has done very little so far to marshal the resources required to meet and defeat China's challenge in Asia. Its economic initiatives have failed to offset China's place as the region's, and much of the world's, most important economic partner. It has done nothing substantial to reverse the decisive shift in maritime military advantage in China's favour. And it has failed to translate the

---

14 'US Strategic Framework for the Indo-Pacific', trumpwhitehouse.archives.gov/wp-content/uploads/2021/01/IPS-Final-Declass.pdf.
15 Kurt M Campbell and Jake Sulllivan, 'Competition Without Catastrophe: How America Can Both Challenge and Coexist with China', *Foreign Affairs*, September/October (2019), www.foreignaffairs.com/articles/china/competition-with-china-without-catastrophe.
16 'Biden: China Should Expect "Extreme Competition" from US', *AP News*, 8 February 2021, apnews.com/article/joe-biden-xi-jinping-china-8f5158c12eed14e002bb1c094f3a048a.

deep unease felt by many countries—both China's neighbours and more distant partners—into wholehearted and unambiguous support for the US against China.

These failures are most dangerously evident in the dangers now building of the risk of a confrontation over Taiwan. Washington has moved a long way towards abandoning 'strategic ambiguity' in favour of a clear commitment to defend Taiwan from any Chinese attack, while at the same time it has become steadily clearer that it cannot do so successfully, and that the costs of such a war—win or lose—would be enormous.[17] As the chances dwindle that either side could win a decisive victory in a conventional conflict, the risks of swift escalation across the nuclear threshold grow. The combination of stronger talk and weaker capability is especially perilous because it must tempt the Chinese leadership to consider calling Washington's bluff. They may well wonder why, if the US is not willing to fight 'World War Three' over Ukraine—as Biden has often proclaimed[18]—it would be willing to do so over Taiwan. And if Beijing does decide to call Washington's bluff, whoever is then in the Oval Office will face a terrible choice: between backing down, which would destroy the strategic standing of the US in Asia, or launching into a war that it cannot win and that might well become the worst in US history—or indeed, in world history.

The harsh realities of great power geopolitics suggest that the US can only hope to deter and defeat China's challenge in Asia the same way it contained the Soviet Union—by convincing Beijing that it is willing to fight a full-scale nuclear war in order to do so—and there is no evidence that the US is willing to do that, or that it can convince Beijing that it is. Moreover, despite the tough talk of some of our political leaders,[19] there is no evidence

---

17 Many recent wargames have demonstrated the high costs and uncertain outcomes of a US–China war over Taiwan—for example, Mark F Cancia, Matthew Cancian and Eric Heginbotham, 'The First Battle of the Next War: Wargaming a Chinese Invasion of Taiwan', Centre for Strategic and International Studies, 9 January 2023, www.csis.org/analysis/first-battle-next-war-wargaming-chinese-invasion-taiwan; and Stacie Pettyjohn, Becca Wasser and Chris Dougherty, 'Dangerous Straits: Wargaming a Future Conflict over Taiwan', Center for a New American Security, 15 June 2022, www.cnas.org/publications/reports/dangerous-straits-wargaming-a-future-conflict-over-taiwans. It is notable that where these studies postulate eventual US victory, they do so on the basis of expectations that US resolve in the face of high costs and risks is equal to, or greater than, China's, which seems a questionable judgement.
18 Josh Wingrove, 'Biden Says He'd Fight World War III for NATO But Not for Ukraine', Bloomberg, 12 March 2022, www.bloomberg.com/news/articles/2022-03-11/biden-says-he-d-fight-world-war-iii-for-nato-but-not-for-ukraine#xj4y7vzkg.
19 Angus Thompson, '"Reality of Our Time": Dutton Warns Australians to Prepare for War', *The Sydney Morning Herald*, 25 April 2022, www.smh.com.au/politics/federal/reality-of-our-time-dutton-warns-australians-to-prepare-for-war-20220425-p5afuy.html.

that Australia is really prepared to support the US in a war on the scale of a US–China conflict. Public opinion is very mixed. While recent polling shows increased support for joining a US war against China, it also shows strong support for contrary views, including 77 per cent agreeing that 'Australia's alliance with the United States makes it more likely Australia will be drawn into a war in Asia that would not be in Australia's interests'.[20] Moreover, it is far from clear that those who support a military commitment have any idea what kind of war they believe we should join. Governments have done nothing to inform the public about these questions or explain why this is a war that would be worth fighting. Likewise, Australia has little capacity to contribute significantly to such a war, should it choose to join in. The ADF would be hard-pressed to deploy and sustain more than one submarine, one major warship, a squadron of F-18 E/F and some support forces, which would make no material difference to the operational outcomes of the conflict.

Thus, the US has little chance of achieving its objective of preserving US primacy, and Australia has little willingness or capacity to help it. What, then, will the US do instead? Canberra might hope that they would step back from primacy to the more modest, more achievable, less risky option of accepting a balancing role in a multipolar Asia—the kind of posture that Penny Wong has at times suggested. However, there is little interest in this option in the US. Even those in the US debate who have advocated some accommodation of Beijing's ambitions to play a larger regional role, or indeed to take the US's place as the regional hegemon,[21] tend to underestimate the scale of concessions that would be required to establish a stable balancing relationship with China. Most US policymakers and analysts simply refuse to countenance any serious accommodation at all—especially over the most sensitive issues like Taiwan. At the heart of this reluctance is a deep resistance to the idea of the US treating China as a co-equal great power, which is the essential precondition to any long-term, stable US–China relationship in Asia. The conclusion I have drawn from many years of conversations with Americans on this question is stark: if they cannot remain the region's primary power, Americans would rather withdraw strategically from Asia, then remain on the basis of a co-equal balancing relationship with China.

---

20   Lowy Institute Poll 2024, poll.lowyinstitute.org/charts/war-over-taiwan/.
21   See, for example, Lyle J Goldstein, *Meeting China Halfway: How to Defuse the Emerging US–China Rivalry* (Washington, DC: Georgetown University Press, 2015), doi.org/10.1353/book39628.

This analysis has grave implications for the future of the US–Australia alliance, and, therefore, for Australian defence policy. It suggests that there is a real risk of deep misalignment between Australian and US strategic objectives in Asia over the years ahead. The objective on which they might seem most readily to agree—that of preserving US primacy—is out of reach, and the more seriously the two allies pursue it, the more likely they are to find themselves in a devastating war they cannot win. Perhaps for that reason, Australia's support for this objective is very unsure. Penny Wong, at least, clearly has deep reservations, and so might her colleagues if they came to understand the costs and risks involved. If and when that objective proves unachievable, the US is likely to abandon any substantial strategic role in Asia, just as Britain did progressively over the decades after 1904, culminating in the final withdrawal 'east of Suez' completed in the early 1970s. It is important to remember, amid the revived talk of Britain as an Australian ally in the context of AUKUS, what happened then. The strategic connection with Britain, which had seemed so central to Australian policy and identity for so long—which indeed defined Australia's place in the world—ceased to carry any real significance for Australia's security, because Britain's priorities, interests and objectives no longer aligned with Australia's. It is a fond illusion to imagine that today's talk in London of a 'return to Asia' changes that, and to imagine that the same thing could not happen to our alliance with the US if and when the US follows Britain in deciding that the costs of sustaining active strategic engagement in Asia exceed the benefits, as it is quite likely to do over the next decade or two.

A new start

This brings us back to the question of how Australia's defence policy should respond to the circumstances we face in Asia today and over the decades to come. The foundation of any effective defence policy is a clear statement of strategic objectives—what tasks the ADF should be designed primarily to perform. As we have seen, successive defence policy documents over the past two decades have failed to define new strategic objectives that meet our new strategic circumstances. They have instead prevaricated between two broad alternatives. One is to adopt an upgraded version of the Forward Defence objectives of the 1950s and 1960s, in which the primary task of the ADF is to help support American forces in a war with a major-power adversary like China. The other is to adopt an upgraded version of the Defence of Australia objectives of the 1970s and 1980s, in which the primary task of the ADF is to defend Australia independently from the forces that a major Asian power like China could bring to bear against our territory.

These alternative strategic objectives reflect different overall geopolitical assessments and objectives. An upgraded Forward Defence posture aims to preserve the US-led regional order and prevent it being replaced by a new order dominated by Asian great powers. An upgraded Defence of Australia posture aims to prepare the country to survive in the eventuality of a post-US–Asian order, rather than preventing it. Since the 2009 White Paper, Australian defence policy has been paralysed by an inability to choose between these options. As we have seen, doubts about the durability of US regional leadership, which naturally incline policymakers towards the Defence of Australia option, have been more than balanced by the conviction that the power of the US in Asia must somehow survive and its support for Australia's security endure.

In an ideal world, of course, we might build forces that can achieve both strategic objectives, and successive governments have sometimes sought to excuse their failure to make a clear choice between them by claiming that this is what they are doing. It is an illusion, because while there is some overlap in the kinds of forces required, they dictate fundamentally different force priorities. To put it perhaps a little too simply, an upgraded Forward Defence posture means projecting armed force against a major Asian power, while an upgraded Defence of Australia posture means preventing a major Asian power projecting armed force against us. By failing to choose clearly between one or the other, we would ensure that we were unable to do either. What we need, as the Albanese government's 2023 Defence Strategic Review acknowledged, is a 'focused force' clearly prioritised to meet our primary strategic objectives. It just failed to say what those objectives should be.

This prevarication about geostrategic trajectories has been reinforced by a reluctance to accept the implications of choosing either of the alternative strategic objectives, because both carry huge price tags. To build and maintain the forces required to do either of them would require a major increase in defence spending and a radical transformation of the Australian Defence organisation. A few years ago, in *How to Defend Australia*, I estimated that it would cost between 3 and 3.5 per cent of GDP to defend Australia independently from attack by a major Asian power.[22] It would

---

22   Hugh White, *How to Defend Australia* (Melbourne: La Trobe University Press, 2019).

cost as much to build forces that could make any more than a purely token contribution to a US effort to sustain its primacy in Asia. By fudging which of these objectives the ADF is supposed to be able to achieve, successive governments have made it easier to conceal the reality that on current plans it will not come anywhere close to being able to do either.

My own view is that our focus should be on the Defence of Australia option. To be more precise, our primary strategic objective should be to defend Australia from the scale of attacks that a major Asian power like China or India could mount with the forces they could deploy and sustain in our approaches, without relying on the US. The choice has a simple two-part rationale. First, even a major effort on our part would, in practical terms, do little or nothing to increase the chances that the US will remain strategically engaged in Asia, so there is no overriding imperative to make that effort. If the US nonetheless remains actively strategically engaged in Asia, then we can probably continue to rely on it to ensure our defence from major-power attack, and we do not have an overriding imperative to expand capabilities. However, if the US withdraws from Asia, we will have no alternative but to defend ourselves if we are not to simply go defenceless. That is the circumstance in which Australia has an overriding imperative to expand our forces, and this is the objective on which that expansion should be focused.

This objective entails an overriding priority for operations to deny our maritime approaches to adversary air and maritime forces. I have argued elsewhere, in some detail, what that operational priority means for Australian force planning.[23] Very briefly, it means investment priority for maritime and air surveillance and strike, primarily using air- or space-based systems, with some priority for submarines to extend the range of maritime strike beyond the range of land-based air systems. Priority is also given to land strike against targets—primarily adversary bases—within extended aircraft range of the continent. Priority is not given to sea-control forces that include major surface combatants, or land forces suited to large-scale amphibious operations or continental maneouvre campaigns.

Such proposals necessarily raise complex and contentious issues, and generate intense debates at a number of levels—technical, tactical, operational and strategic. David Horner's work can make a material contribution to many of those debates. His extensive writings on the ways in which previous

---

23   White, *How to Defend Australia*.

5. HISTORY FRAMES POLICY

generations of defence decision-makers at all levels have grappled with similar questions is a major resource for us facing these issues today. This kind of contribution calls to mind the work of another very eminent military and strategic historian. Sir Michael Howard's *The Continental Commitment*, written in 1972, aimed to inform his country's momentous post–imperial defence policy debates by offering a superb—and superbly concise—account of the evolution of British defence policy from 1900 to 1970. His opening passage went like this:

> The student of defence policy who tries to educate his judgment by studying the manner in which that policy has developed since the beginning of this century [he wrote in 1972] will find himself traversing very familiar ground.

Howard then went on to describe that familiar ground in a long sentence of singular grace and force:

> The division of our attention between Europe and the rest of the world; the degree of commitment to and involvement in the politics of Europe; the obligations we retain to the small and dependent but distant states for whose security we are or were at one time responsible; the apportionment of resources between expensive armed forces; above all the identification and assessment of military threats, and the judgment as to how much of national resources can be spared to deal with them: all this still remains the stuff of British defence policy, as it did at the beginning of the century.[24]

Twenty years ago, in an idle moment, I took a stab at adapting Howard's sentence to Australia's circumstances, trying capture the continuities, the 'familiar ground', in Australian defence policy debates since 1900.

The division of our responsibilities between our immediate region and the rest of the world; the degree of our commitment to and involvement in the politics of Asia; the interests and obligations we retain to support our allies in distant theatres; the enduring responsibility for attending to the defence of our own continent; the apportionment of resources between expensive armed forces; above all, the identification and assessment of military threats, and the judgement as to how much national resources can be spared to deal with them: all this remains the stuff of Australian defence debate today, as it was at the time of Federation.

---

24 Michael Howard, *The Continental Commitment: The Dilemma of British Defence Policy in the Era of the Two World Wars* (London: Maurice Temple Smith Ltd, 1972), 9–10.

I thought that worked pretty well, and in some ways it still does, which is a testament to the strength of Howard's original formulation. Re-reading it now, however, there is a sense that something big is missing. Today, our defence policy debates must encompass something that we have not faced before—that big question about how far we should commit ourselves to supporting our allies in wars with a major power in Asia, and how far we should prepare ourselves to defend Australia from a major Asian power independently.

Australia will not begin to frame a credible response to these questions until we reach a sober, unsentimental, coolly realistic, evidence-based understanding of the underlying drivers of strategic change, the consequences for our allies and alliances, and the implications for the strategic objectives we should design our forces to achieve. David Horner's work provides a vital resource and foundation for all this.

Part III: Command and commanders

6

A 'Crisis of Command' in Bengal, 1849–50: a Hornerian analysis

Peter Stanley

I first encountered David Horner in 1981. I think I signed him in at the 'back desk' of the old administrative offices, soon after a pass system was imposed on an institution into which visitors had been free to simply find their own way. The Australian War Memorial (AWM) (which I had joined in 1980 as a junior clerk in its History and Publications section) had begun its engagement with the scholars of Australian military history who did so much to impel the field in the 1980s and 1990s. Horner was one of a generation of 'educated soldiers' whose career was to exemplify the value to the Army and the wider community of encouraging academic endeavour. Horner's PhD thesis—famously the 'missing' volume of the Second World War Official History, which traced the higher direction of Australia's war effort—deserved to be published. Allen & Unwin, soon to become one of the premier publishers in this burgeoning field, naturally saw the symbiotic value of developing what became a fruitful relationship with an ambitious cultural institution, awaking from the somnolence of decades and reviving what had been a backwater of Australian publishing. Accordingly, Horner's *High Command* was published in 1982 in association between the AWM and Allen & Unwin.[1] As a result, Horner, then a major, appeared in the corridor outside the office of the progenitor of the Memorial's renaissance,

---

1   David Horner, *High Command: Australia and Allied Strategy, 1939–1945* (Canberra: Australian War Memorial and Sydney: George Allen & Unwin, 1982).

Dr Michael McKernan. His staff (all four of us) became aware that here was a soldier and a scholar who exemplified the fresh insights that soldier–scholars could bring to the field we wanted to invigorate. Thereafter, Horner became a frequent contributor to AWM projects, such as its now defunct *Journal*, its annual history conferences and ultimately, as he grew in stature in the academic world, as official historian on two major series, both administered and partly funded by the AWM. The publication of *High Command* demonstrated that the AWM was using its resources and stature for good. All I did was sign him in at the back door.

'This extraordinary man': Charles James Napier

On a pleasantly warm day in January 1845, the East India Company's 2nd European Bengal Fusiliers were marching along a dusty track in Beloochistan, recently conquered and now part of British India. A sergeant described how its progress was interrupted by the arrival of an elderly man on horseback, a general, accompanied by a small retinue of staff officers.

The general was Sir Charles James Napier (1782–1853), dressed in his customary jockey cap and jackboots. With his hawknose, tiny spectacles and long, whispy beard, Napier presented a striking figure (Figure 6.1). He had the fusiliers form a hollow square about him and addressed them, in characteristic style:

> Second Europeans! I … have to say one or two things to you …
> I'm highly pleased with your appearance but I have one thing to say
> to you—talking in the ranks I will not allow. [2]

After a brief but demanding conversation with the fusiliers' officers, Napier galloped on. Soon after, he sat for the first photograph taken of a British general.[3] Napier then returned home after several years of active service in one of British India's most strenuous campaigns, and more of the acrimonious public controversy that dogged his career. He was to return to India in 1849, becoming Commander-in-Chief of its armies until a clash with the Governor-General, Dalhousie, prematurely ended his command and his career.

---

2 'Jot book' of Sergeant-Major George Carter, 2nd European Bengal Fusiliers 1839–61, British Library, MSS Eur. E. 262.
3 National Army Museum neg. N/PH 5261 acc. PA6204/3/84, taken by Surgeon John McCosh, probably at Ferozepore: Anon, *The Army in India 1850–1914: A Photographic Record* (London: National Army Museum/Hutchinson & Co, 1968), 166.

6. A 'CRISIS OF COMMAND' IN BENGAL, 1849–50

Figure 6.1: Sir Charles Napier depicted in a characteristically heroic pose by the Calcutta artist Colesworthey Grant
Source: Colesworthey Grant, *An Anglo-Indian Domestic Sketch*, 1849, and *Sketches of the Public Characters of Calcutta*, 185?.

MILITARY HISTORY SUPREMO

Sergeant-Major George Carter, who called Napier 'this extraordinary man', was not the only British soldier to notice Napier. He became one of the most notable, colourful figures in an army hardly devoid of characters. Napier became one of the foremost heroes of the Victorian army, celebrated in print and pottery, in the names of pubs, of towns in Australia, New Zealand and Canada; he was even accorded a statue in Trafalgar Square—one largely paid for through subscriptions from private soldiers. The statue's subject was at first recognised, then vaguely recalled and is now unknown. The Greater London Authority plans to replace Napier's statue with one more 'appropriate' to a post-imperial, post-industrial Britain.[4]

Ironically, Napier was arguably the one Victorian general whose philosophy would not automatically render him obnoxious to today's sensibilities. He sympathised with the reformist ideals of the Chartists and became the first general to mention private soldiers in despatches previously reserved for officers. His downfall as Commander-in-Chief could arguably be attributed to his sympathy for the plight of the Indian soldiers who formed the bulk of his army. Napier was, indeed, an extraordinary man.

Napier was also a complex, paradoxical, infuriatingly contradictory man. Though a lifelong, compulsive hero, he first commanded an army in battle at the age of 60 and fought only a handful of large actions. A man of unquestioned honour, he was responsible for one of the most cynical conquests in the expansion of the Victorian empire. Though a man who enjoyed comradeship and good company, he was an inveterate controversialist, repeatedly embarking on petty, complex and dogged feuds. Inspiring love among his subordinates, he provoked bitter animosity among his many antagonists. Of a distinguished Anglo-Irish Whig noble family, connected to Whig powerbrokers, he was named after the great Charles James Fox. Though poor for most of his life, and espousing unfashionably liberal and radical views at a time of social turmoil, he prospered under both Whigs and Tories. A man of vision and passion, a writer of romances, he resigned ostensibly after the Governor-General countermanded his mistaken direction over an obscure financial regulation. A hypochondriac,

---

4   Philip Johnston, 'Old statues given marching orders', *Daily Telegraph*, 20 October 2000. Twenty-five years on, however, Napier's statue, a Grade 2-listed monument, remains in place.

he endured immense physical suffering from severe wounds. He demanded obedience and loyalty from his subordinates but repeatedly pursued his own stubborn course, until, finally, obstinacy destroyed his career.[5]

Eccentric in dress, politics and behaviour, Charles Napier was certainly a curiosity, but he is of interest not only as an exception to more conventional officers. Napier commanded the Indian Army for just 18 months, yet he sought to challenge and change its military culture: if he had succeeded, tantalisingly, his reforms might have forestalled the 1857 mutiny and rebellion.

Napier justifies his position in this *festschrift* as an example of a study of command-in-context, which is the essence of David Horner's approach to the discipline of military history and to the understanding of the significance of command in it. This essay examines the career of Sir Charles James Napier, and especially the crisis of his truncated term as Commander-in-Chief in India, approaching it through the sorts of techniques and tools that Horner's work has exemplified. This episode prefigures and demonstrates a vital strand of David Horner's scholarship: the relationship between political and military authority. Napier's fall was precipitated by flaws in his psychology, but it operated within a command system both peculiar to British India and of more general relevance, in that the relationship between political and military command in India in 1849 was essentially identical to that which has obtained in Australia since 1901. It raises the perennial question: to what degree is command a function of both individual personality and of the system in which the commander operates?

---

5   Napier has been the subject of two waves of biographies. Many contemporaries idolised him, and he was accorded admiring biographies by contemporaries (often relatives), including William Napier Bruce's *Life of General Sir Charles Napier* (London: John Murray, 1885). In the twentieth century, Napier attracted several studies: Hugh Lambrick's *Sir Charles Napier and Scinde* (Oxford: Oxford University Press, 1952); and a biography entitled *Charles Napier, Friend and Fighter* by Rosamond Lawrence (née Napier) (London: John Murray, 1952). Between 1971 and 1995, Priscilla Napier published seven books on the Napier brothers, chronicling them as a phenomenon in British society and politics in the first half of the nineteenth century. Her focus, however, was on character rather than context, and as the series progressed, the volumes increasingly contained paraphrases of the abundant family papers rather than attempts to explain Charles's impact on the empire and army.

Map 6.1: British India in Napier's time

Before his sixties, Napier's life was one of heroic obscurity. Commissioned at 12 years of age, later a regimental infantry officer in the Peninsular war, he demonstrated a reckless courage that saw him wounded six times and captured. By 1814, he commanded the 102nd Foot (formerly the New South Wales Corps) in North America, commanding it with his characteristic combination of high expectation and charisma. He awarded flogging rarely and reluctantly (it was 'a punishment as terrible and disgusting as it is disgraceful'). Instead, he appealed to his men's 'high feeling of honour.'[6] As the senior officer in the British Ionian Islands in the 1830s, Napier

---

6   Charles Napier, *Remarks on Military Law and the Punishment of Flogging* (London: T and W Boone, 1837), 71.

showed his predilection towards argumentation.⁷ Liable to fall out with colleagues and superiors, he devoted immense energy to pursuing most vituperative feuds. In 1839, he became commander of the British Army's Northern District, where his sympathy for the aspirations of working-class reformers arguably deterred Chartists from rash actions. A Whig government rewarded him with an active command on the frontiers of the empire. He was summoned from the 'misery of smoke and tall chimneys' to an Indian battlefield, a transition that would make and, in due course, break him.⁸ Map 6.1 illustrates what British India looked like in Napier's time.

At almost 60, Napier held only modest, even depressing, hopes for his career. 'I shall never win a victory!' he gloomily assured a friend, 'I never expect to command ... in chief.' Relatively poor and notoriously frugal, he had a reasonable hope of making India pay but expected merely to retire to Cheltenham, already a resort of retired generals, to die at an optimistic 90, 'an old yellow wizened canting ill tempered son of a bitch'. He did not hope for 'Victories in the Punjaub', but he did want 'to try my hand with a good handful of soldiers ... if fate wills it'.⁹

'The tail of the Afghan storm': Napier in Scinde

As it happened, fate intervened. In the course of the disastrous British intervention in Afghanistan (1838–42), British India impinged increasingly on the province of Scinde, a desolate tract bisected by the Indus and lying between Persia, the Bombay presidency and the Sikh-ruled Punjaub, under feudal emirs. As British power penetrated north-western India, the Government of India signed successive treaties with the emirs to open the River Indus to steam navigation. In 1841, the rising Bombay officer James Outram became Political Agent for the province of Scinde and Beloochistan. Outram was one of the most effective of the 'politicals' (military officers seconded to advise on, and conduct dealings with, Indian states). A year

---

7   W David Wrigley, 'Dissension in the Ionian Islands: Colonel Charles James Napier and the Commissioners (1819–1833)', *Balkan Studies* 16, no. 2 (1975): 11–22, details the protracted quarrels inflaming Napier's tenure, which the author represents convincingly as 'calculated and selfish'.
8   Napier to Edward Davenport, 25 February 1841, Bromley Davenport Muniments, Rylands Library, Manchester.
9   Napier to Edward Davenport, 14 September 1841, Bromley Davenport Muniments, Rylands Library, Manchester.

later, Napier assumed command in the province. British perception of, and attitude towards, the emirs determined their actions in the province and forged, and then destroyed, the relationship between Outram and Napier.

Napier, suspicious and contemptuous of 'politicals' like Outram, at first lauded him, then (when he disagreed with Napier's policy) reviled him. Their feud, conducted in print and through the claims, insinuations and insults of supporters, poisoned the politics of British armies in India for a generation. Although Napier and, even more, his hero-worshipping younger brother William argued intemperately that Napier had been correct in both his analysis and his actions, a dispassionate assessment would favour Outram.[10] The emirs need not have been pushed into war: the bloody battles of the spring of 1843 need never have occurred.

On the face of it, the Outram–Napier controversy reflected conflicting and seemingly irreconcilable attitudes to British relations with frontier powers. Napier regarded British interests and principles as paramount, to be enforced without compromise. Outram believed that feudal past and imperial present could coexist, and he was prepared to work with the emirs to reach a compromise. Outram was 'attacked in the newspapers both by General William Napier and anonymous scribblers', in a Parliamentary report on the conquest of Scinde (in which he alleged that 'footnotes of surpassing bitterness' were appended to letters that had already been answered). William then turned the dense despatches into 'an exciting romance which he dignifies with the title of a history'.[11] The contest flowed in charge and countercharge, with officers, officials and newspaper contributors variously conscripted, or volunteering, to give testimonials to the rascality, incompetence or folly of the one and the virtue, success or wisdom of the other. The details are tedious and irrelevant. The significance of the feud is to demonstrate Napier's ineradicable confidence in his own judgement and his willingness to sacrifice anything—in this case the friendship of a man he admired and even loved—rather than consider that he might be mistaken. It also points to how the Napier brothers acted in concert, 'all clever but troublesome', as John Hobhouse noted, with William, as the Duke of Wellington said, 'the cleverest, but very perverse'.[12] Those involved

---

10 The description is that of Napier Bruce, *Life of General Sir Charles Napier*, v.
11 James Outram, *Conquest of Scinde: A Commentary* (London: W Blackwood, 1846), 7.
12 Lord Broughton (John Cam Hobhouse), *Recollections of a Long Life* (London: John Murray, 1911), vol. VI, 275–76. Hobhouse's memoir appeared in 1865, but his daughter, Lady Charlotte Dorchester, produced a later edition, including extracts from Hobhouse's diaries. Hobhouse became Lord Broughton in February 1851.

in ruling India came to detest the Napiers. Member of Parliament and sometime Chairman of the East India Company Sir James Hogg recorded his exasperation 'that this family is exempt from the rules applied in the rest of the world'.[13]

At the end of August 1842, Napier embarked from Bombay on the hazardous voyage to Kurrachee, then only a mud-brick village. Surviving a cholera outbreak aboard ship, Napier's luck held, at least until landing, when a rocket exploded prematurely, laying his calf open to the bone, adding to his scars. When he could walk, he stepped into what his brother described as 'the tail of the Affghan storm', though he exacerbated rather than stilled it.[14] The politics in which the drama of Scinde were played out were complex. On his own side, Napier had to deal simultaneously with his military and civil superiors in Bombay, an incompetent Governor-General (Lord Auckland) whom he despised, distant and divided British governments, a doubtful Court of Directors and public in Britain and, on the spot, officials opposed to his direct approach. He faced the 18 ruling families of the emirs of Scinde, each permeated by their own labyrinthine duplicities, animosities and alliances. Rather than comprehend and work with local rulers, he chose to disregard diplomacy or subtlety, and decided on conquest.

Napier's only period of sole command in the field occurred in the spring of 1843. He marched on the (unoccupied) desert fortress of Emaum Ghur, destroying it needlessly but spectacularly. His patron, Wellington, praised the march as a work of military genius. Closer observers were less impressed. The Bombay officer John Jacob described William Napier's exaggerated account of the supposed triumph as 'a shameful perversion'.[15] Napier then won two genuinely striking victories against the emirs' Baluch warriors. His methods in directing and leading his troops in battle offer clues to the kind of commander that he was. At Meeanee (17 February) he won what an admirer justifiably described as 'a brilliant victory'.[16] Indeed, his tiny (1,400-strong) army defeated a Baluch force of 20,000. A month later, he won a second victory, at Dubba (also known as Hyderabad; 24 March).

---

13   Hogg to Dalhousie, 7 June 1850, in Lee-William Warner, *The Life of the Marquis of Dalhousie* (London: Macmillan and Co. Ltd, 1904), 325.
14   William Napier, *The Conquest of Scinde, with Some Introductory Passages in the Life of Major General Sir Charles James Napier*, Part I (London: T & W Boone, 1845), 24.
15   Jacob's comments on Napier's *Conquest of Scinde*, 42, British Library, MSS. Eur. F. 209/96.
16   Lt Robert Fitzgerald to his father, Hyderabad, 19 February 1843, British Library, MSS. Eur. D. 1171/2.

In these actions, Napier shared the dangers of the front line and the hazards of campaigning at the height of Scinde's summer, but he added a new province to the Company's domains. (The pun attributed to Napier and published in *Punch*—'Peccavi' that is, 'I have sinned/Scinde'—was, in fact, written by a 16-year-old Catherine Winkworth, an error not yet fully corrected.[17])

These victories made Napier's reputation. His solicitude for his men, his most precious military asset, and, above all, his gallantry in battle, won admiration in India and at home. The contrast between Napier's vigorous and often personal command and the supine conduct of other Queen's generals in Afghanistan impressed popular opinion in Britain, despite the reservations of those who saw that Napier's eccentricity as ruler of the conquered province marked him as dangerous and unreliable.[18]

Scinde introduced Napier to the armies of British India (first, Bombay: each of the three presidencies of Bengal, Madras and Bombay maintained its own army), forming judgements that he acted upon for the rest of his career and underpinning his actions when Commander-in-Chief seven years later. Of the Bombay Army, he thought that even 'the general frame work of this army is bad'. His fellow officers were 'full of the superiority of Europeans', and Napier wondered whether and how his more numerous sepoys would fight. Captains and lieutenants commanded regiments, their seniors enticed to fill more lucrative staff and civil positions. However, while exercising the Poonah garrison in unaccustomed field-days, he noticed that their 'native' officers (as they called them) were 'the real officers ... steady, thoughtful, stern-looking men, very zealous and very military'. He worried that in Bombay as a whole, 'the military spirit seemed to have gone'.[19] His desire to reform the armies of India began with his first parades in India. The conclusions he formed then were to be a powerful factor in his final humiliation.

As military governor in Scinde, Napier cultivated a reputation (carefully crafted by his brother's reports published in Britain) as a robust civiliser, but in 1847, exhausted by arduous duty in a harsh climate, he at last returned home to ostensible retirement, though one marked by public controversy.

---

17   *Punch*, 18 May 1844; Box 0001.01, Napier Papers, Cheshire Military Museum, Chester.
18   While Queen's generals had often failed in Afghanistan, Company's generals, notably George Pollock and William Nott, had succeeded brilliantly; but Company officers were denied the prize of the highest commands in India.
19   William Napier, *Conquest of Scinde*, 174.

'A playful poke in the ribs': Napier and Dalhousie

The expansion of the Company's domains nevertheless continued. In 1845, the long-anticipated tension between it and the Sikhs, India's last independent power, exploded. Two hard-fought and costly wars brought the Sikh kingdom's capitulation. The second war, 1848–49, saw the disastrous battle of Chillianwallah (13 January 1849), when Hugh, Lord Gough, recklessly attacked a Sikh army, losing 2,400 casualties, only technically claiming a victory. The Irish Gough's reckless and costly 'Tipperary tactics', deplored by popular opinion, finally induced the British Government to decide on his replacement as Commander-in-Chief.[20] Wellington himself, (Commander-in-Chief in Britain) chose Napier, the most successful British general to serve in India, a reputation fostered by his brother's partisan writings. Wellington had urged Napier to accept return to India even before news of Chillianwallah. Following Chillianwallah, Wellington implored him again, with Napier melodramatically claiming that the octogenarian Duke declared, 'If you don't go, I must'.[21] Napier, always susceptible to the dramatic, responded to this risible proposition, affecting a reluctance overcome by duty. His Scinde reputation made the appointment popular, accepted even by those with whom he had fallen out (including the Company's Court of Directors). After a farewell dinner, at which he and they suppressed their mutual loathing, Napier sailed for India within days. Wellington reassured Dalhousie, the newly appointed Governor-General, that he would find in Napier 'everything you could wish for at the Head of an Army in the Field'. However, by the time Napier arrived early in May, the army was no longer 'in the field': Gough had defeated the Sikhs, but he was supplanted nevertheless.[22]

Disappointed that the war had ended, and at height of the hot weather of 1849, Napier travelled to the summer capital of Simla, there to stay with Dalhousie. The clash between the two—the fundamental impossibility of

---

20 'Tipperary tactics'—a reference to Gough's Irish origins current at the time—appears in virtually every account of his campaigns, such as the *Dictionary of National Biography*: en.wikisource.org/wiki/Dictionary_of_National_Biography,_1885-1900/Gough,_Hugh.
21 Charles Napier, *Defects, Civil and Military of the Indian Government* (London: Charles Westerton, 1853), 7.
22 Wellington to Dalhousie, 6 February 1849, Napier Papers, PRO30/64/8, National Archives (UK).

their working together—formed the core of the crisis of command that developed over the next two years. Hence, it is important to appreciate their characters.

The young politician James Andrew Broun-Ramsay, 1st Marquess of Dalhousie, himself the son of a Commander-in-Chief of India, was, at 36, the youngest governor-general ever appointed. Officially austere, obsessive as an administrator, Dalhousie was also informally (as a visiting officer observed) 'young-looking, fair, handsome, bright and witty'. For all his brilliance, however, Dalhousie remained a pedant and a worrier and, moreover, 'a hard and in many ways an unfeeling man', an administrator who embraced British India's appetite for the written record.[23] He brought profound change to British India, expanding its territories (and revenue) in the Punjab and Burma, introducing canals, railways and the electric telegraph, as well as expanding English education and strengthening impartial administration. Additionally, by enforcing the 'doctrine of lapse', which saw the Company subsume Indian states—including Oudh, the home of many of the Bengal Army's sepoys—he arguably exacerbated the stresses that contributed to their mutiny in 1857.

The young Tory governor-general and the old Whig general established an unlikely cordiality in their first months together, as they enjoyed Simla's temperate climate in the summer of 1849. Even then, the antipathy that was to end Napier's career became apparent. Aware of Napier's aversion to political officers, Dalhousie assured Napier that he 'would never see a political near him'. But he also frankly told Napier that influential members of the India interest in Britain had warned Dalhousie that Napier would try to usurp his power as governor-general. Dalhousie assured Napier that he was certain that Napier would 'do nothing of the kind', adding ('laughing') that if he did, 'I should take damn good care to prevent you!' He explained that the accompanying nudge was 'not the belly-go fister of a pugilist' but rather a 'playful poke in the ribs of a friend'.[24]

Napier assumed the arduous duties of the Commander-in-Chief. However, with war against the Sikhs over, his work was entirely administrative, and that severely constrained. The powers of the Commander-in-Chief in

---

23 Memoirs of Geoffrey Pearse, British Library, MSS Eur. E. 417/7, 17.
24 Dalhousie to Sir George Couper, 25 November 1853, in JGA Baird, ed., *Private Letters of the Marquess of Dalhousie* (Edinburgh; London: W Blackwood and Sons, 1910), 276. In Napier's version, Dalhousie is supposed to have replied that he 'would take damned good care I should not' (*Defects, Civil and Military*, 10). The tone, rather than the actual words, is significant.

India were analogous to those of his counterpart in Britain and equally circumscribed. A contemporary authority explained that 'as regards the organisation, the promotion, the discipline, the field movements, and the welfare of the army, he receives orders direct from the monarch'—that is, the Governor-General—but that his own powers, except in command in war, were limited.[25] Napier himself put it more colourfully: it was a 'low-bred, miserable, sneaking, toad-eating post'. He complained that he was unable to raise or even move units, had limited financial discretion, was trammelled by having to work through distant and sclerotic civilian bureaucracies and, though possessing limited patronage, unable to promote or demote as he would have liked.[26]

Napier was complaining about a limitation he had surely long known. As a contemporary explained the essential constitutional authority:

> Each presidency has its separate army, but the Governor-General is commander-in-chief of the whole; and he has authority to make peace or war, and to direct the military operations in any part of the country.[27]

Indeed, in the all-important table of precedence, the Commander-in-Chief ranked only twelfth (after governors, chief justices and bishops), but only if he was not a member of the Supreme Council (as Napier was not); otherwise, he ranked 11 places lower, after the Recorder of Prince of Wales's Island.[28] The Commander-in-Chief actually advised and recommended more than commanded.

'Quite a sensation': Napier as Commander-in-Chief

Already celebrated in India for his victories in Scinde, Napier impressed the army (and British opinion in India) with his idiosyncratic appearance and his flamboyant address. Though a stern disciplinarian, Napier dressed eccentrically and carelessly, reported to have been sworn in as Commander-

---

25 Henry Byerley Thomson, *The Military Forces and Institutions of Great Britain and Ireland* (London: Smith, Elder & Co., 1855), 50.
26 Napier, note, 3 September 1849; William Napier, *The Life and Opinions of General Sir Charles James Napier*, vol. IV (London: John Murray, 1857), 187.
27 *India Pictorial, Descriptive, and Historical* (London: Henry G. Bohn, 1854), 330.
28 Joachim Stocqueler, *The Oriental Interpreter and Treasury of East India Knowledge* (London: James Madden, 1848), 303.

in-Chief with his aiguillette on the wrong shoulder and his sword suspended on a bit of string.[29] Denied the chance to lead the Indian armies in war, Napier's mission became the reform of what he saw as fatal weaknesses in the armies' British officers especially. His 'remarks', issued weekly through the General Orders printed in every presidency and distributed to every unit, read out at successive parades in a dozen languages, ensured that his personality penetrated the entire force. His words were read but not always heeded or appreciated. Officers regarded his General Orders as 'most eccentric and original', saying they created 'quite a sensation'. The officers would 'watch ... for them with ... impatience and curiosity.'[30]

Within weeks of meeting him, Dalhousie predicted that Napier would soon 'astonish the Bengal army'; and, he added, 'much they need it'.[31] Napier believed that among the Indian armies' many defects, one of the most serious was 'a deficiency of discipline among the European officers'.[32] This he resolved to arrest, delivering homilies against duelling, gambling and excessive drinking. Napier, who had never fought a duel, gambled or been drunk, had long been appalled that British officers in India indulged in all three vices. Indian newspapers often reported scandalous examples. In 'the Ferozepore gambling case', the commanding officer of the 17th Bengal Native Infantry, 'a notorious gambler', cleaned out a young officer then challenged him to stake his future pay, and took that off him too. He won a staggering amount, but then lost Rs26,000 to an equally reckless fellow officer.[33] That officer was dismissed.

The largest single category of offences among officers in the general court martials in Napier's term were the seven (all of the Company) convicted of 'misconduct in money'.[34] His rants aroused the ire of many officers, who were not all gambling drunkards and who resented being abused as '*infamous ... CHEATS ... whose society is contamination*'. Abusing officers as 'champagne-

---

29   Col. Armine Mountain (Adjutant-General, Queen's troops) to General Sir George Brown, 24 May 1849, Brown Papers, MS 2846, f. 274, National Library of Scotland.
30   Osborn Wilkinson and Johnson Wilkinson, *The Memoirs of the Gemini Generals* (London: AD Innes, 1896), 211.
31   Dalhousie to Sir George Couper, 12 June 1849, in *Private Letters of the Marquess of Dalhousie*, edited by JGA Baird (Edinburgh: William Blackwood and Sons, 1911), 68.
32   'Extract of a Letter from General Sir J Napier to the Duke of Wellington, 15 June 1850', Parliamentary Papers, 1857 II, vol. 29, 103.
33   *Bengal Hurkaru* (Calcutta), 23 July 1849; Proceedings of a General Court Martial, Lahore 28 September 1849, Military Consultations, no. 252, 28 December 1849, National Archives of India.
34   John Mawson, ed., *Records of the Indian Command of General Sir Charles James Napier, G.C.B., Comprising All His General Orders, Remarks on Courts Martial, Etc. Etc.* (Calcutta: RC Le Page, 1853), analysing the 50 cases of officers (14 Queen's and 36 Company's) tried under Napier's tenure.

drinking swindlers' who fell into debt offended men who were virtually all heavily in debt.[35] They resented the 'brisk dose of Napier purge'.[36] His denunciation of their customary retreat to hill stations to evade the summer heat brought sarcastic comments in newspapers, largely sustained by military officers' subscriptions. *The Delhi Sketch Book* published a satirical verse:

> ... all leave to the hills
> Has been stopped, and one grills
> In the plains ...
> While all the time he [Napier] swears
> That public affairs
> Prevent him from doing, as he'd like to do, the same ...[37]

Though the scourge of what he considered ungentlemanly conduct, Napier was also seen as the soldiers' friend. As an officer made destitute after losing his belongings in the Ganges wrote, Napier was 'one ray of hope shining through this dark vista of sorrows'.[38] Napier accelerated his predecessors' reforms, making improvements, not just in weapons, equipment and dress, but in procedures and, crucially, in the construction or provision of comforts in barracks.[39] He waged a dogged bureaucratic war to get the ossified Military Board (virtually autonomous and responsible for, among many things, buildings) to construct new barracks or to improve existing ones by, for example, installing punkahs to cool rooms, providing married quarters and, in particular, giving soldiers larger, healthier bungalows. A particular obsession was reducing the excessive baggage trains that dogged Indian armies' movements, with even junior officers commonly using a dozen or more draught animals to carry belongings, comforts and even furniture. Napier was scandalised that his own entourage used up to 90 elephants, 400 camels and as many bullocks, and hundreds of labourers, with 50 men solely employed to carry glass doors for his tent. He reduced this to 30 elephants and 334 camels, though critics accused him of exaggeration— the glass doors required only 16 carriers.[40]

---

35 *General Orders*, (Bengal), 15 December 1850, National Archives of India.
36 John Kaye, 'Recent Military Memoirs', *Calcutta Review*, vol. XIV (1850): 273.
37 Cited in Raaja Bhasin, *Simla: The Summer Capital of British India* (New Delhi: Viking, 1992), 33.
38 Military Proceedings, vol. 1210, 1–15 February 1850, no. 32, detailing the case of Lt [name] Selby, HM 24th Foot, National Archives of India.
39 Sir Charles Napier's recommendations to the Government of India 1849–50, Dalhousie Papers, GD45/6/376, National Archives of Scotland.
40 Note, 7 November 1849, William Napier, *The Life and Opinions of General Sir Charles James Napier*, vol. IV (London: John Murray, 1857), 205–06; Col. Armine Mountain to General Sir George Brown, 4 January 1854, MS 1855 George Brown Papers, National Library of Scotland.

From the first, Napier expressed concern for the security of the Company's newly won domains. It was a common refrain among officers in India, although only Napier could send long, alarmist minutes to the Governor-General. Late in October 1849, he drafted papers expressing his fear that India lay threatened by external and internal foes. His army, he complained, was 'scattered here and there like a pepperbox', weak everywhere.[41] In a series of closely argued minutes, Napier decried the armies' dispositions. 'The whole country ... South of the Nerbudda [River] is unsafe and that to the North very little bit better' (making the whole of India potentially at risk). Nepal, increasingly the source of mercenaries, was, he claimed 'hostile and ready to strike'; as were Afghanistan and Burma. Kashmir, Hyderabad and other large 'country powers' were untrustworthy. Napier repeatedly warned of the threat from the Punjab, recently conquered, where the Sikhs awaited an opportunity to rise again. The Manja, the region around Amritsar, he regarded as the cradle of a 'third Sikh war' and urged that it be garrisoned more strongly. (Yet, in 1850 some 96,000 troops held the Punjab, almost a third of the entire army.[42]) Napier disdained local officials' advice, especially those he despised as 'politicals'. The biographer of the Punjab's chief 'political', John Lawrence, regarded Napier's assertions as 'exaggerated and ... often reckless and untrue'.[43]

Dalhousie rightly disagreed: not a single one of Napier's forebodings came to pass. Indeed, in 1857, the Punjab became a loyal bastion against rebellion. Napier urged Dalhousie to consolidate the army in several huge garrisons, in the Punjab, and (bizarrely) on the Brahmaputra, in the unhealthy north-east, where British troops were never stationed. Achieving this concentration anticipated the construction of strategic railways, the first of which opened in 1855 and which were completed over the next 50 years, a sign that Napier's strategic sense was not always bluster. Dalhousie wrote elaborately courteous minutes in reply, which Napier would ignore for months, only to then complain that he had been disregarded. Within six months of Napier's arrival, he and Dalhousie were at loggerheads, an impasse masked by the formality of their correspondence.

---

41   Minute, 29 November 1849, nos 114–17, Secret Consultations, 26 April 1850, Military Department, National Archives of India.
42   'The Military Occupation of the Punjab' [1836–56], Papers of Lt-Col Herbert Bruce, British Library, Add. MS 44001, vol. XII.
43   R Bosworth Smith, *Life of Lord Lawrence*, 2 vols (London: Smith, Elder & Co., 1883), vol. I, 340.

6. A 'CRISIS OF COMMAND' IN BENGAL, 1849-50

'The reprimand affair': protest and retribution

Napier's regard for the feeling of the Bengal Army's Native Infantry (its 74 regiments being the largest single component of his command) was to precipitate his downfall. His arrival coincided with a change in the Pay and Audit Regulations for the 'native' infantry stationed in the newly conquered Punjab. In essence, while it had been foreign territory, sepoys had been paid modest allowances to compensate them for more expensive provisions. With the Punjab's incorporation into British India, however, those allowances ceased. The justification, perfectly clear to the Bengal Army's all-powerful Military Auditor-General, was poorly explained to the sepoys who, having to buy lentils, flour, salt and ghee at higher prices, naturally felt aggrieved. The difference in pay between the 1845 and the 1849 Pay and Audit Regulations was a few pence per man per month; but married sepoys also had to support their families, living separately in the Ganges valley. Dalhousie seemed unaware of the import of the change and, when asked, he endorsed the auditors' logic.

From July 1849, regiment after regiment either refused to accept the reduction in pay or protested at it. Several broke into armed resistance. Napier, having faced a similar protest in the mid-1840s in Scinde and believing that a widespread sepoy mutiny was '*the* greatest danger' threatening the Company's hold on India, urged Dalhousie to act swiftly to meet what he saw as a conspiracy spreading within (Napier claimed) 30 regiments.[44] Already believing British tenure to be tenuous, its frontiers open to invasion and facing further Sikh rebellion, his awareness of the scarcity of European troops impelled him to act decisively.

As regiments received orders to march into the Punjab, intermittent unrest continued. Sepoys were sentenced to death, imprisonment and dismissal after outbreaks in several regiments. In February 1850, however, the men of the 66th Bengal Native Infantry, garrisoning the former Sikh fort of Govindghur (adjoining Amritsar, in the heart of the Manja) broke into armed unrest, forestalled only by a few officers' resolute actions and the fortuitous arrival of loyal cavalry. Napier promptly exceeded his authority, ordering the regiment to be disbanded, its sepoys replaced by Gurkhas from Nepal.

---

44   Charles Napier, *Defects, Civil and Military*, p. 12; p. 1.

When the crisis Napier had feared seemingly arose, Dalhousie was absent from Calcutta, recruiting his health at sea. The 'Supreme Government' lay in the hands of General Sir John Littler in Calcutta, the senior member of Dalhousie's Council, effectively a month distant by the swiftest dawks (posts). With Dalhousie absent and Littler (Napier reasoned) his military inferior, Napier took upon himself the responsibility for approving the local commander's restoration of the sepoys' allowances. While this may have seemed like capitulation, Napier saw it as pragmatic, convinced that once explained to Dalhousie and his Council, his action would be endorsed retrospectively.

While awed by the Bengal Army's sacred Pay and Audit Regulations, many officers did not believe the 'native' army to be on the brink of a widespread mutiny; and it did not come to pass. Dalhousie represented an argument over the monthly payment of a few pounds per regiment as a matter of principle, with Napier usurping the authority of his political superior. The controversy became the Indian Army's most serious crisis of command until Lord Kitchener and Lord Curzon fell out, 50 years later, over the respective power wielded by the Commander-in-Chief and the Viceroy; a contest that Kitchener won. In 1850, Napier's attempt to assume greater powers brought him down.

Justifying his reading of the regulations, Napier believed that he had saved British India from disaster. Dalhousie disagreed, rescinding Napier's order, a decision insultingly conveyed not by a personal letter, but in an officious minute over the signature of one of Napier's staff. For months both engaged in a dogged exchange of minutes and memorandums, asserting to their British superiors the rightness of their case, with William Napier orchestrating a campaign of lobbying, righteous justification and outright vilification. Charles Napier described the opposition he faced as 'a low underhand war against me ... waged by pitiful intriguers', a typical example of the invective the Napiers made their own.[45] Dalhousie, no novice in framing detailed argumentative despatches, demonstrated that he could match Napier's claims. Finally, Napier submitted a memorandum reiterating his version of events concluding that 'such are the shackles put upon my conduct ... I no longer feel safe, and shall resign'.[46]

---

45 Charles Napier, *Defects, Civil and Military*, 154–55.
46 Parliamentary Papers, House of Commons, 1854, vol. 47, Memorandum, 22 May 1850, 205–07, with Dalhousie's rejoinder at 208–17. The two exchanged further detailed memoranda, but the matter went to the Company, the President of the Board of Control and the Commander-in-Chief in Britain in the Military Proceedings submitted by Dalhousie.

Dalhousie prevailed. Napier overplayed his hand, gambling that the directors of the Company and the president of the Board of Control (the British minister) would prefer him to Dalhousie. Napier's many enemies within the Company and the 'India interest' in Parliament and beyond seized on this as an opportunity to be rid of a vexatious general, and Wellington, disillusioned with his protégé, advised the Queen to accept his resignation. The Duke immediately recorded his view that Napier 'had no right to act upon that opinion' (that mutiny threatened), that Dalhousie could not with propriety have acted otherwise, and recommended that Queen Victoria accept Napier's resignation.[47] The vindicated Court of Directors (conventionally signing as Dalhousie's 'affectionate friends') indicated 'our entire satisfaction'.[48]

Dalhousie did not show Napier the Duke of Wellington's minute: Napier had 'repudiated any private intercourse' with him. Though Dalhousie continued to treat Napier with 'public respect & private courtesy', the two communicated frostily through notes borne by aides-de-camp.[49] When he finally did read Wellington's letter tersely accepting his resignation, he said simply, 'Well that's short', only later lamenting 'with much agitation' that he had given up a yearly salary of 17,000 pounds because of 'that viper Dalhousie'.[50]

'The reprimand affair', as Napier called it, was not just a spat between a young Tory governor-general and an old Whig general.[51] Its roots lay deep in British constitutional history. 'Sir Charles Napier', a Company director's minute affirmed, 'has now in effect declared that he will not be bound by the constitution of the Government of India', an outcome neither the directors nor the British Government could countenance.[52] The primacy of civil over military authority remained one of the most cherished principles inherited from the British civil wars (Parliamentarians had executed King Charles I exactly 200 years before the Govindgurh outbreak) and the horror of military rule under Cromwell's interregnum had never abated. Figure 6.2 presents a satirical take on the relationship between civil and military rule.

---

47 Wellington's Memorandum, 30 July 1850, PP 1854, vol. 47, 254–56.
48 Military Despatch from the Court of Directors, 7 August 1850, PP 1854, vol. 47, 256–60.
49 Dalhousie to Hogg, 6 Nov 1850, Hogg Papers, British Library, MSS Eur. E. 342/13 Letters from Lord Dalhousie, 1850.
50 Records of conversations, Lt-Col Patrick Grant [Adjutant-General of the Bengal Army], 15 November 1853, and Dalhousie, 18 November 1853, Dalhousie Papers, GD45/6/339, National Archives of Scotland.
51 Napier to Lord Broughton [formerly Sir John Hobhouse, President of the Board of Control], 28 May 1851, British Library, Broughton Papers, F 213/19.
52 Lee-Warner, *Life of Dalhousie*, 336.

MILITARY HISTORY SUPREMO

Figure 6.2: A sharp satire on the relationship between political and military authority

Note: 'James Andrew' (Lord Dalhousie) is shown manipulating Napier's successor as Commander-in-Chief, Sir William Gomm, who is depicted literally as a puppet: '[a] very useful and ingenious contrivance' that 'when I pull the string ... does any thing I like'. Napier, in the living portrait at top right, is astonished.

Source: *The Delhi Sketch Book*, 1 August 1852.

'Poor Charlie Napier': judgement

On Napier's return to Britain early in 1851, political London ignored and reviled him. He did not bother to call upon East India House, of course, but when he attended a royal levée, 'the Queen scarcely looked at him' (as James Hogg maliciously told Dalhousie).[53] Characteristically, Napier devoted his last years to denouncing the *Defects, Civil and Military of the Indian Government*, while his brother produced four volumes of his exculpatory *Life and Opinions*.[54] Napier died in August 1853, supposedly having caught a 'chill' as a pallbearer at Wellington's funeral the previous November. In 1854, Dalhousie's parliamentary supporters published the correspondence as a Blue Book, including the Duke of Wellington's judgement.

John Lawrence feared that 'poor Charlie Napier' would 'probably make an ass of himself in his posthumous work'.[55] Napier, however, continued to arouse admiration and detestation. His standards became many Indian officers' benchmark. In 1854, an officer of Bombay irregulars described how he had marched 155 miles in four days in summer—'which I am sure poor old Charlie Napier could not have grumbled at'.[56] George Malleson, the author of the celebrated 'red pamphlet' of 1857, in which he claimed that Napier had foreseen, and might have forestalled, the mutiny, pointedly concealed his identity as 'One Who Has Served Under Sir Charles Napier'.[57] Within four years of his death, most of the Bengal Army's troops had broken into mutiny and rebellion. Posthumously, Napier again divided the Indian Army. His admirers claimed he had warned of the coming catastrophe, John Bruce Norton asking of Napier and Dalhousie 'which of the two was the most far-sighted'.[58]

---

53 Hogg to Dalhousie, 24 March 1851, British Library, Hogg Papers, MSS Eur. E. 243/1.
54 Charles Napier, *Defects, Civil and Military*; William Napier, *Life and Opinions*, vol. IV.
55 John Lawrence to F Courtney, 29 October 1853, in Bosworth Smith, *Life of Lord Lawrence*, vol. I, 419.
56 William Johnson, *Twelve Years of a Soldier's Life* (London: AD Innes & Co., 1897), 47.
57 'One Who Has Served Under Sir Charles Napier', in GB Malleson, *The Mutiny of the Bengal Army* (London: Bosworth and Harrison, 1857).
58 John Bruce Norton, *The Rebellion in India: How to Prevent Another* (London: Richardson Brothers, 1857), 27.

Conclusion

Figure 6.3: A cartoon created after Napier's departure from India and shortly before his death, parodying Napier's tendency to pathos

Note: Portrayed in the persona of Claude Melnotte, a character from Edward Bulwer-Lytton's popular melodrama *The Lady of Lyons*, Napier self-pityingly tells an aide, 'The Bengal Army ... will never know how deeply it was loved'. 'Be a man,' the aide counsels. '[T]hat false Dalhousie did not deserve thee.'

Source: *The Delhi Sketch Book*, 1 May 1853.

In his *Crisis of Command*, David Horner argued that 'the heart of the military problem is the personality of the commander'.[59] He quoted Basil Liddell Hart, who argued that military history should comprise 'a study of the psychological reactions of the commanders, with merely a background of events to throw their thoughts, impressions and decisions into relief'.[60] In that book, Horner demonstrated how significant personalities had been in the south-west Pacific in 1942. He quoted the German *Generalleutnant* Albert von Boguslawski (1834–1905), who saw in the study of generalship 'every human passion and excitement'.[61] The saga of Napier's fall bears out the centrality of human passion (see Figure 6.3 for a visual parody on Napier's tendency to pathos). It also raises the question of how Horner might have assessed him, had *Crisis of Command* been set in the Punjab in 1849 and not in Papua in 1942. In that, as Horner rightly asserts, 'command includes

---

59 David Horner, *Crisis of Command: Australian Generalship and the Japanese Threat, 1941–1943* (Canberra: Australian National University Press, 1978).
60 Basil Liddell Hart, *Thoughts on War* (London: Faber & Faber, 1944), 219. On re-reading Horner's *Crisis of Command*, I found that he quoted this very phrase, arguing that 'the heart of the military problem is the personality of the commander' (xvi). Horner reiterated this insight in his 'Introduction' to *The Commanders: Australian Military Leadership in the Twentieth Century* (Sydney: George Allen & Unwin, 1984), 1.
61 Horner, *Crisis of Command*, xv, quoting JCF Fuller, *Generalship, Its Diseases and their Cure* (London, 1933), 5.

administration and requires technical competence as well as the qualities of leadership', he might have judged Charles Napier's brief tenure in command a failure.[62]

Re-reading several of Horner's outstanding biographies—of George Vasey, Frederick Shedden, John Wilton and, above all, Thomas Blamey—demonstrates how the analysis of personality is an inescapable component in the evaluation of command or leadership in war. Having for a time researched Napier intensively, for nearly 20 years I abandoned further work because I considered that his behaviour was what Victorians called mad (what we might today regard as a personality disorder) and that his conduct was not susceptible to conventional historical analysis. The example of David Horner's studies in command persuaded me that while there may be aspects of Napier's personality that we can never fully explain, his actions (and especially the reactions of his antagonists and contemporaries) can be traced, analysed and assessed in the Hornerian tradition of command in context.[63]

---

62   David Horner, *Towards a Philosophy of Australian Command* (Canberra: Centre for Defence Command Leadership and Management Studies, 2002), 3.
63   I gratefully acknowledge the support of a fellowship awarded by the General DK Palit Trust, which allowed me to spend several weeks in New Delhi in 2003, consulting the military proceedings relating to Napier's term as Commander-in-Chief, in the National Archives of India.

7
Filling the gap: Lieutenant General Sir Harold 'Hooky' Walker KCB, KCMG, DSO: a study in command

Chris Roberts

I first met David Horner when we were cadets at the RMC – Duntroon. He was a newly arrived Fourth Class cadet, and I was in my third year. We both had a keen interest in military history. With the support of Alec Hill, our history lecturer, we formed The Bridges Society, an informal gathering of cadets to discuss topics of military history. I next saw him when he visited the Australian Army Staff College. When David mentioned that his first book, *Crisis of Command: Australian Generalship and the Japanese Threat, 1941–1943*,[1] was about to be published, he was asked to give an impromptu talk to the student body on it. With less than half an hour's notice, he gave a superb presentation that captured everyone's attention.

I followed Horner's career as an academic historian with interest. After he was appointed to write the history of the Special Air Service Regiment, and when I was the Director of Special Action Forces, I sought to guide him on a particular matter. He quite rightly replied that he would not be told what to write; indeed, this was not my intention. A friendly discussion over dinner resolved the issue, and Horner went on to publish his excellent *SAS:*

---

1   DM Horner, *Crisis of Command: Australian Generalship and the Japanese Threat, 1941–1943* (Canberra: Australian National University Press, 1978).

Phantoms of the Jungle.[2] Since then, he has influenced me in writing on the Great War through both the example provided in his many books and his sound personal advice.

I was delighted to be invited to contribute a chapter to this *festschrift*. Australia is deeply indebted to David Horner for profoundly raising the profile of our military history as an accepted academic discipline, for the prolific contribution he has made in recording many aspects of our nation's history, and through his guidance and encouragement to a growing number of younger Australian military historians. He has my deepest respect, and I offer this chapter as a small token of that respect.

During his highly productive career, Horner, a former infantry officer who served in Vietnam, wrote extensively on command in the Australian context. In *The Commanders,* he considered Australian command from the Great War to Vietnam, intending 'to analyse the performance of selected Australian senior commanders under the stress of action and policy making'. He said that up to that point, there had been 'few true analyses of the performance of senior Australian military commanders'.[3] Of the five commanders he chose to represent the Great War, one was a Royal Navy officer seconded to the RAN. Acknowledging that his choices 'might still be open to some comment', Horner suggested there was scope for a chapter on one or two of Australia's Great War divisional commanders. In listing them, he included Major General Ewen Sinclair-MacLagan, a British army officer who served in the AIF from 1914, but he failed to mention Major General Sir Harold 'Hooky' Walker, the British army officer who had commanded the 1st Australian Division for three years.[4] In his later work, *Strategy and Command: Issues in Australia's Twentieth-century Wars* (2022), Horner mentioned Walker in the chapter on the AIF's commanders, noting that he 'had served the AIF well, filling the gap until Australian commanders gained sufficient experience'.[5] While Horner's focus on largely Australian-born commanders is entirely understandable, the contribution of British Army officers serving with the AIF remains, on the whole, unexplored. Was Walker simply a gap-filler?

---

2   DM Horner, *SAS: Phantoms of the Jungle* (Sydney: Allen & Unwin, 1989).
3   David Horner, ed., *The Commanders: Australian Military Leadership in the Twentieth Century* (Sydney: Allen & Unwin, 1992), 1.
4   Horner, *The Commanders*, 3.
5   David Horner, *Strategy and Command: Issues in Australia's Twentieth-Century Wars* (Melbourne: Cambridge University Press, 2021), 64, doi.org/10.1017/9781009067041.

Contemporary comments suggest otherwise. During the final week of June 1918, officers drawn from every unit of the 1st Australian Division visited its headquarters to bid farewell to the divisional commander. The Australian Government had long been pushing for the senior commands of the AIF to be filled by Australians, and by early 1918 it was felt that there were sufficient capable candidates do so. On 30 June, Walker handed over to Major General William Glasgow. Colonel William McCann, formerly Commanding Officer of the 10th Battalion, recalled that:

> Walker was a great leader, always most solicitous for the welfare of the fighting troops ... He led our division through many hard-fought battles, and, when we heard of his transfer ... we felt that we were losing not only a great leader, but also a very dear and sincere friend.[6]

Lieutenant Colonel Ernest Herrod, commanding the 7th Battalion, considered Walker to be:

> [c]ool and courageous in action, possessing a military knowledge of the highest order ... [W]hile most exacting as to duties, [he] was, at all times very considerate to his troops, and was deeply respected by all ranks of his division ... [T]here can be no doubt as to the personal influence he exercised.'[7]

Many years later, Major Geoffrey Drake-Brockman of the 2nd Field Company remarked that Walker 'was admired by all of us'.[8] Yet, although he commanded an AIF division for longer than anyone else, and despite the high regard in which he was held, Walker is almost unknown in Australian military history. That his papers were lost at sea possibly explains why there is no biography of him. The overly nationalist narrative advanced in much Australian military history may offer another explanation. Nevertheless, Walker deserves attention as a key figure in the AIF.

Walker and the nature of command

Before considering Walker's performance, it is essential to understand the responsibilities of commanders and what attributes are expected of them. Command is the authority vested in a person to determine and

---

6   Quoted in Lieutenant-Colonel HG Viney, 'Sir H.B. (Hooky) Walker, K.C.B., K.C.M.G, D.S.O.', *Reveille* 7, 1 December 1934, 64.
7   Viney, 'Sir H.B. (Hooky) Walker'.
8   Geoffrey Drake-Brockman, *The Turning Wheel* (Perth: Paterson Brokensha Pty Ltd, 1960), 83.

direct the activities of a military unit or formation. It carries with it the responsibility for the sound administration and operational effectiveness of the organisation, and for the discipline, morale, and welfare of its members. These are achieved through the training of all ranks under the commander's direction and supervision. In battle, commanders are expected to have tactical acumen based on sound judgement, deep professional knowledge and good situational awareness. By their character, leadership and performance, they must gain the trust and confidence of their officers and men.

While command can be exercised successfully in different ways, certain attributes are considered essential. Horner addressed them in *Crisis of Command* and *The Commanders* by drawing on the views of former officers who had held command at various levels. Among the qualities he highlighted were robustness—the ability to stand the shocks of war—and courage, both physical and moral, of which Field Marshal Sir William Slim believed the latter to be pre-eminent.[9] That is, commanders must demonstrate a willingness to speak out and do what they consider right, particularly when their political and military masters desire a contrary course of action, regardless of the personal consequences. Horner stressed that the personal factor should never be overlooked, highlighting the importance of the commander's presence on the battlefield and personal contact with their troops.[10] In Horner's view, commanders cannot be remote from those they lead, but need to be seen by their soldiers frequently; they must go forward as far as possible to see the ground and conditions for themselves, discuss issues with their subordinates, and judge the needs and morale of their troops. Field Marshall Sir Archibald Wavell highlighted a genuine interest in humanity, and commonsense—the knowledge of what is possible and what is not, based on a sound grasp of the mechanics of war.[11] Major General JFC Fuller regarded brains as one of the three pillars of generalship.[12] By 'brains', Fuller means intellect—the faculty of rational and logical reasoning to objectively reach correct conclusions about what is achievable and not achievable in reality.

---

9   Field Marshall Sir William Slim, *Courage and Other Broadcasts* (London: Cassell and Company Ltd, 1957), 6.
10 Horner, *The Commanders*, 7 and *Crisis of Command*, xx.
11 General Sir Archibald Wavell, *Generals and Generalship* (New York: Macmillan Company, 1943), 10.
12 Major General JFC Fuller, *Generalship: Its Diseases and Their Cure* (Harrisburg: Military Service Publishing Co., 1936), 31–35.

In 1914, Walker had more active command experience than his Australian counterparts, even though he had not commanded above battalion level. After a year at Cambridge University, he was commissioned into the Duke of Cornwall's Light Infantry in 1884, and he saw active service during the Sudan War (1884–85), in Egypt (1885–86) and, later, on the north-west frontier of India (1897–98). During the South African War (1899–1902), he led the 4th Mounted Infantry, gaining a reputation for always applying maximum effort, for which he was twice mentioned in despatches and awarded the Distinguished Service Order. In 1908, he was promoted to the rank of Lieutenant Colonel to command the 1st Battalion, the Border Regiment. Promoted to the rank of Colonel in 1912, he served as a General Staff Officer, Grade 1, in India, and in December 1914 was appointed Brigadier General, General Staff—Chief of Staff (COS)—of the Australian and New Zealand Army Corps (ANZAC) under Lieutenant General William Birdwood.[13]

Walker preferred to work with the troops rather than undertake staff work. He had a chance to do so again at Gallipoli on 25 April 1915. The first of Birdwood's staff ashore at Anzac Cove, he was temporarily put in command of the New Zealand Infantry Brigade in lieu of its commander, who was ill, and led it through the first four days of fighting. On 30 April, following the death of Colonel Henry MacLaurin, he took charge of the 1st Australian Infantry Brigade. After Major General William Bridges was mortally wounded, Walker then took command of the 1st Australian Division on 15 May and stayed in this role until Major General James Legge arrived from Australia in late June, when he returned to the 1st Brigade. Colonels James McCay, John Monash and Harry Chauvel all objected to Legge's appointment, arguing it should have gone to one of them. Consequently, Legge was sent to Egypt to raise the 2nd Australian Division, and Walker returned to command of the 1st Division on 26 July, which he retained until 30 June 1918.[14]

With the possible exception of Monash, none of Walker's Australian counterparts appear to have taken as keen an interest in personally directing and supervising training, and improvements in tactical proficiency, as he

---

13 *The Quarterly Army List for the Quarter Ending 31st December 1918*, HMSO, London, 1919, 42; P Burness, 'In search of Hooky Walker' (unpublished manuscript, 2013), 3–4.
14 NZ Inf Bde WD, 25 April 1915, Australian War Memorial (AWM): AWM4 35/17/3; 1Bde WD (30 April 1915), AWM: AWM4 23/1/2 Part 1; Report on Operations 25/415-1/515, 1 Bde WD (April–May 1915), AWM: AWM4 23/1/4; 1 Div WD (15 May 1915), AWM: AWM4 1/42/4 Part 1; 1 Div WD (26 July 1915), AWM: AWM4 1/42/6; 1 Div WD (30 June 1918), AWM: AWM 1/42/5.

did. Regularly among the troops, he maintained high standards, quickly correcting deficiencies and what he regarded as substandard work, even returning training programs for revision that he deemed unsatisfactory. He took particular interest in officer training, dispensing both individual praise and areas for improvement, and giving lectures himself, often stressing the importance of administration—a matter that Wavell described as the real crux of generalship.[15]

All of this would have been familiar to those who had served under Walker in the 1st Border Regiment. As its commanding officer, he was regarded as:

> an outstanding soldier, who brought his Battalion [sic] to the highest state of efficiency ... His exercises were well thought out and instructive ... He never fussed, but kept his battalion on the tip of its shoes, eager, and active.[16]

Walker displayed this same verve and drive in action. Within a few days of assuming command of the 1st Brigade, its defences were reported as much improved.[17] Three days after replacing Bridges in command of the 1st Division, he issued instructions for essential improvements to the trenches and personally supervised defensive arrangements. Of particular concern were the unnecessary casualties incurred from shelling, and from men standing behind open loopholes, which made them vulnerable to enemy snipers. Effective remedies were quickly put in place.[18]

---

15   RG Casey, personal diary, April–June 1915, AWM: AWM38 3DRL 6673/170; 1 Div WD 9, 10, 11, 13, 15, 17, 19, 24, 27 March 1917, AWM: AWM4 1/42/26; Appendix VIII, 1 Div WD May 1917, AWM: AWM4 1/42/28; 1 Div WD 2, 4-9, 11–12, 18–30 June 1917, AWM: AWM4 1/42/29; GS Memo No. 27,1 Div WD July 1917, AWM: AWM4 1/42/30; GS Memo No. 29, Appendix XI, 1 Div WD August 1917, AWM: AWM4 1/42/31; First Div memo 7 March 1917 and appendix, Lecture: 'Discipline and Interior Economy', and First Div Memo 13 March 1917 and appendices, 1 Div Admin WD March 1917, AWM: AWM4 1/43/26; 1st Div Confidential letter dated 27 April 1917, 1 Div Admin WD April 1917, AWM: AWM4 1/43/27; 1 Div Admin WD 1, 2, 16, 20, 21, 22–27, 29 June 1917, AWM: AWM4 1/43/29; 1 Div Admin WD 11, 13, 18 July 1917, and Appendix 'D' 14 July 1917, 1 Div Admin WD July 1917, AWM: AWM4 1/43/30; Robert Stevenson, *To Win the Battle: The 1st Australian Division in the Great War, 1914–1918* (Cambridge: Cambridge University Press, 2013), 102–03; Wavell, *Generals and Generalship*, 2.
16   Stevenson, *To Win the Battle*, 95.
17   1 Bde WD 4 8, 13 May 1915, AWM: AWM4 23/1/5 Part 2.
18   Memo 18 May 1915, 1 Div WD May 1915, AWM: AWM4 1/42/4 Part 6; Op Memo No. 2, Op Memo No. 4,1st Div WD May 1915, AWM: AWM4 1/42/4 Part 11; 1 Div G61 and G115, 1 Div WD May 1915, AWM: AWM41/42/4 Part 9; 1 Div G156, 1 Div WD May 1915, AWM: AWM4 1/42/4 Part 10; 1 Div G377 and G670, 1 Div WD June 1915, AWM: AWM4 1/42/5 Part 3; Operation Memo No. 6, 1 Div WD June 1915, AWM: AWM4 1/42/5 Part 4; Memo No. Ig52 1 Div WD June 1915, AWM: AWM4 1/42/5 Part 7; Operational Memo No. 3 and attached Memo, 1 Bde WD June 1915, AWM: AWM4 23/1/7.

Lieutenant Richard Casey, Walker's aide-de-camp, recorded that from mid-May to late June 1915, Walker visited units in the front line every day, except for a week when he was ill. He discussed defence issues and preparations for sorties with his brigade and battalion commanders, and arrangements for new saps and tunnels with the engineers. He then oversaw the work to remedy any weaknesses he found.[19] Through his efforts, the operational efficiency of the 1st Division steadily improved, gaining Walker the trust and confidence of his men. Sergeant Cyril Lawrence of the 2nd Field Company remarked that Walker 'and the Australians have learned to know each other and, because he is not a funk or a dugout general, he is a favourite'.[20] According to Charles Bean, the Australians 'had become attached to Walker as a brave and considerate commander'.[21]

The Gallipoli campaign

Walker's judgement, tactical acumen and moral courage were prominent during the planning for the Gallipoli landings, and, again, on the evening of 25 April.[22] He was so opposed to the Gallipoli operation, considering 'the general prospect of success was so small that the attempt should not be undertaken', that Birdwood threatened to leave him behind.[23] On the evening of 25 April, the ANZAC landing not having achieved its objectives, both Bridges and Major General Sir Alexander Godley, commanding the New Zealand and Australian Division (NZ&A Division), urged Birdwood to order the immediate evacuation of the forces ashore. Walker protested vigorously to Bridges, to the point of insubordination, 'in terms that could have jeopardised his career'.[24]

---

19   Casey diary, April–June 1915; 1 Bde WD 8 and 13 May 1915, AWM: AWM4 23/1/5, Part 2.
20   Les Carlyon, *Gallipoli* (Sydney: MacMillan Pan Macmillan, 2004), 285–86.
21   CEW Bean, *The Story of Anzac from 4 May, 1915, to the Evacuation of the Gallipoli Peninsula*, vol. II of The Official History of Australia in the War of 1914–18 (Sydney: Angus & Robertson, 1924), 423.
22   Viney, 'Sir H.B. (Hooky) Walker', 12.
23   Viney, 'Sir H.B. (Hooky) Walker', 12; Robert Rhodes James, *Gallipoli* (Sydney: Angus & Robertson, 1965), 82, 242; CEW Bean, *The Story of Anzac from the Outbreak of War to the End of the First Phase of the Gallipoli Campaign, May 4, 1915*, vol. I of The Official History of Australia in the War of 1914–18, 6th edition (Sydney: Angus & Robertson Ltd, 1937), 230.
24   Bean, Official History, vol. I, 455; James, *Gallipoli*, 129; Christopher Pugsley, *The Anzac Experience: New Zealand, Australia and Empire in the First World War* (Auckland: Oratia, 2016), 88; Robert Stevenson, 'Crisis in Command: Senior Leadership in the 1st Australian Division at the Gallipoli Landings', in *Gallipoli: New Perspectives on the Mediterranean Expeditionary Force, 1915–1916*, edited by Rhys Crawley and Michael Locicero (Solihull: Helion & Company Ltd, 2018), 316.

A withdrawal on land in contact with the enemy is difficult enough; an evacuation by sea while in action, as the ANZAC was, would have courted disaster. As Walker realised, it amounted to pure folly. With units disorganised and a dysfunctional command structure, the inexperienced and inadequately trained force was facing a determined enemy in difficult and unfamiliar terrain. Furthermore, it was dark, and there were insufficient boats to complete the evacuation by dawn. Had it been attempted, it would have resulted in chaos and the loss of the majority of the force ashore.

This would not be the last time Walker opposed an operation he thought had little chance of success or did not justify the likely casualties. Nor would it be the last time that Walker's experience contrasted with the greenness of Bridges, who had never held a field command previously. Most of the other senior Australian commanders were as inexperienced as Bridges, which is why Walker, particularly in this early stage of the war, stood out among them.

During the heavy Ottoman counterattacks on 27 April (Map 7.1), Walker took control of the fighting on Russell's Top, reinforcing Lieutenant Colonel George Braund's 2nd Australian Infantry Battalion with troops from the Wellington Battalion. There he made an immediate and lasting impression on Second Lieutenant Herrod, who was manning the battalion's telephone. Returning from a reconnaissance, Walker took the phone and reported on the situation to 1st Division headquarters. Herrod recalled:

> [H]ad he been reading from a carefully prepared text book I doubt whether it could have been better stated. The wealth of information conveyed in proper sequence, the positive and negative made clear, the topography of the front, the enemy and our own troops, their numbers, disposition, and condition etc.—all this was rounded off by a few, but decisive words of appeal for water and food for our men ... The general left me with a brisk but cheery word of farewell, and took with him a lifelong admiration of at least one humble Anzac.[25]

---

25   Lieut-Colonel EE Herrod, '"Hooky" Walkers's Teachings', *Reveille* 6 (1 July,1933): 2; FW Taylor and TA Cusack, *Nulli Secundus: A History of the Second Battalion, A.I.F. 1914–1919*, John Burridge Reprint (1992), 81–82.

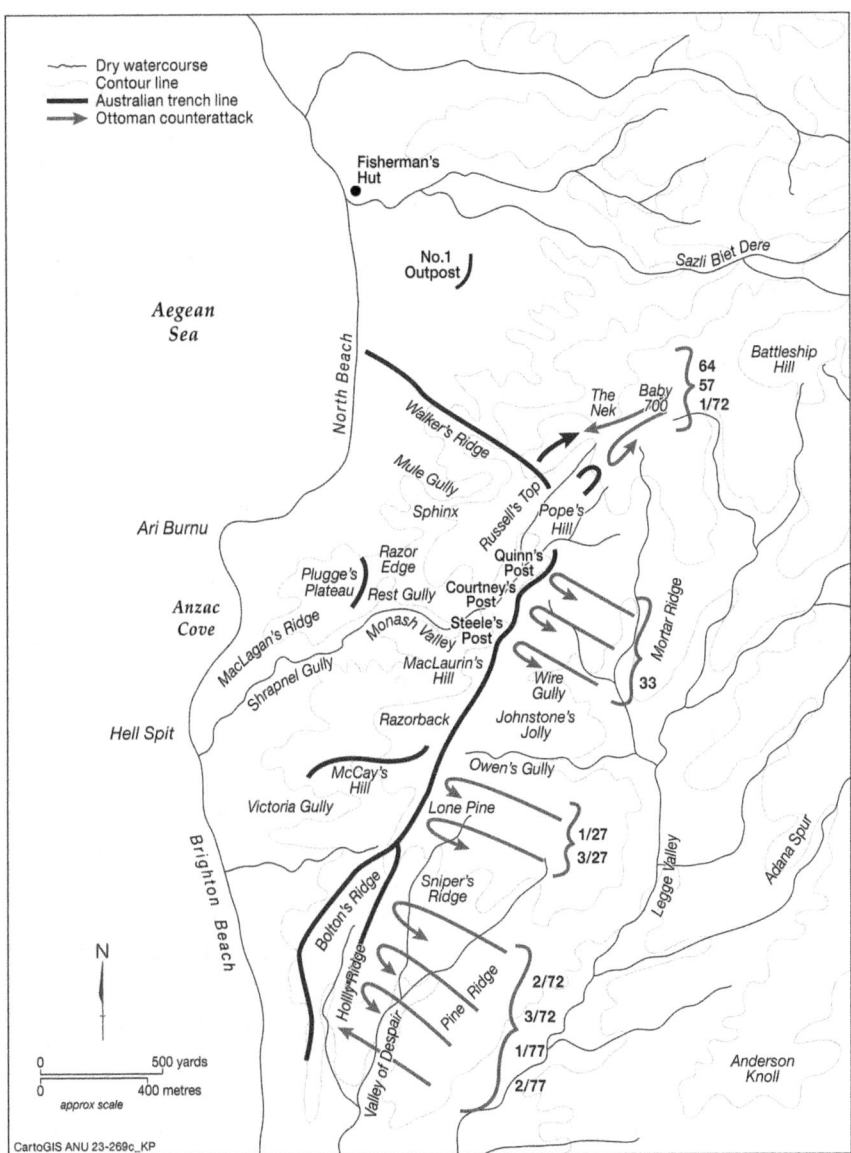

Map 7.1: Ottoman counterattacks at Anzac, 27 April 1915

Under Walker and Braund's leadership, a critical situation was stabilised on ANZAC's northern flank. Had the Ottomans been able to seize the length of Russell's Top, they would have pierced the ANZAC position, dominated Monash Valley at its heart and been able to fire into the rear of the ANZAC line clinging to the seaward slope of what was known as Second Ridge, 900 metres inland from Anzac Cove. The result would have been catastrophic.

Hoping to gain a better defensive line, on 30 April Birdwood planned a general advance by both the 1st Australian Division and the NZ&A Division to secure the dominating Baby 700 and the inland edge of Second Ridge. Now commanding the 1st Australian Brigade, Walker opposed it. Taking Bridges forward to reconnoitre the ground at the junction of the two divisions, he pointed out the obvious flaw in the plan, which called for adjoining brigades to attack on diverging axes, creating a gap between them almost from the outset. Also pointing out the weakened state of the division's brigades following the landing, he condemned the operation as too risky and convinced Bridges not to commit the division.[26] Walker's practical experience and common sense once more carried the day. Godley, on the other hand, agreed to attack. The NZ&A Division's assault on Baby 700 on 2 May was a debacle, incurring massive loss for no gain whatsoever.

On taking over the 1st Division, Walker again demonstrated his concern to prevent questionable attacks and consequent unnecessary casualties in the immediate aftermath of the failed Ottoman offensive on 19 May. When Birdwood suggested a local counterattack against the southern flank of Lone Pine, Walker opposed it, believing that the opportunity had passed.[27] He was right. Birdwood's proposal involved a long assault over a series of low spurs, necessitated a change of direction and would have been enfiladed throughout by the Ottoman defences further south. Moreover, the Ottomans had regrouped within their own lines and were laying down continuous and heavy shellfire. A minor, hastily arranged counterattack at Lone Pine would have achieved little, even if successful. That same day, Godley, on the other hand, agreed to a local counterattack at the opposite end of the line at the Nek. Launched over a much shorter distance and across level ground, it was shattered.

---

26   Bean, Official History, vol. I, 583; CEW Bean, *Two Men I Knew: William Bridges and Brudenell White, Founders of the AIF* (Sydney: Angus & Robertson, 1957), 69; Christopher Pugsley, *Gallipoli: The New Zealand Story* (Auckland: Libro International, 2014), 180; Carlyon, *Gallipoli*, 237.
27   CEW Bean, *The Story of Anzac from 4 May, 1915, to the Evacuation of the Gallipoli Peninsula*, vol. II of The Official History of Australian in the War of 1914–1918, (Sydney: Angus & Robertson, 1924), 163–64.

In July, Walker was briefed on the plan for the coming August Offensive from the Anzac beachhead, which would turn out to be the climax of the Gallipoli campaign. The main assault sought to capture the dominating Sari Bair range from Baby 700 to Hill 971 on the northern flank on the night 6–7 August (see Map 7.2). This was to be preceded by a series of feints on the southern flank intended to divert the Ottomans' attention and draw in their reserves. Birdwood allocated responsibility for the feints to the 1st Division. It was to strike the 400 Plateau, comprising Lone Pine and Johnston's Jolly, at 3 pm on 6 August, capture German Officers' Trench further north at midnight, and conduct minor feints south of Lone Pine. Birdwood waxed optimistically that the capture of the plateau, in particular, would attract all of the Ottoman reserves within the Anzac area.[28] Walker was less sanguine. In fact, he was decidedly unenthusiastic about the 1st Division's role.

Walker's first objection was that capturing the three objectives, all of them formidable, was beyond the division's strength. He also questioned the timings, venturing that attacking the 400 Plateau so early would enable the Ottomans to concentrate artillery fire on the ground captured, making its consolidation difficult. The weight of Ottoman reserves could well eject his men before the breakout to the north commenced, thereby nullifying the reason for the feint. Moreover, Walker thought, the different timings of the feints would alert the Ottomans to 'our tendency to extend our attack to the left'.[29]

Walker further believed that the attack on the 400 Plateau would be futile unless the dominating ground to the north had either been seized beforehand or was attacked simultaneously with the 1st Division's assault. He argued that if his division were to attack the three objectives, it should do so either at the same time as the assault on Baby 700, or that the assaults should be made progressively down Second Ridge, commencing with the attack on Baby 700.[30] That is, they should be launched on a broad front, starting from the high ground and progressing down the ridge to the low ground.

---

28   ANZAC Order no. 18, 2 August 1915, Table A, Instr for GOC Australian Division 4 August 1915, ANZAC WD August 1915, AWM: AWM4 1/25/5 Part 3; Appreciation for attack on Lone Pine, German Officer's Trench and Johnston's Jolly, AWM: AWM25 367/10 Part 1; Bean, *Official History*, vol. II, 452–60; *Two Men I Knew*, 103.
29   Considerations affecting First Australian Division, Note on proposed attack by 1st Aust Div, Note of the attack on Lone Pine, 1 Div WD August 1915, AWM: AWM4 1/42/7 Part 5; Bean, *Official History*, vol. II, 454, 496; *Two Men I Knew*, 102–04. Notes on proposed operations of Australian Division by GOC. Aust Div, ANZAC WD June 1915, Appendix 9, AWM: AWM4 1/25/3 Part 3.
30   Appreciation attack on Lone Pine, German Officers' Trench and Johnston's Jolly, AWM: AWM25 367/10 Part 1.

Once Baby 700 was taken, this would render the Chessboard untenable and thus weaken the Ottoman hold on German Officers' Trench, aiding his own attack on the feature. Confronted with progressive attacks on a wide frontage, the Ottoman reserves could have been dissipated, making it more difficult to respond to the greater threat higher up Sari Bair.

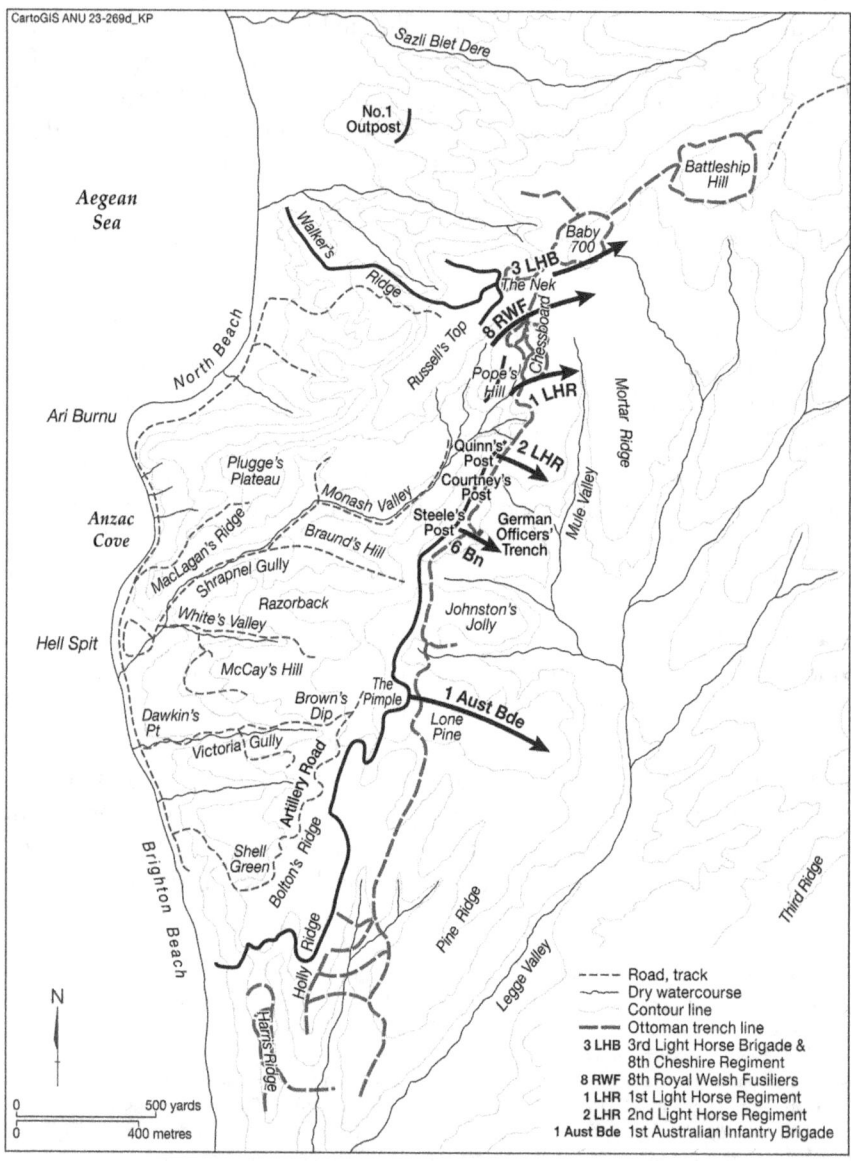

Map 7.2: The August Offensive feints at Anzac, 6–7 August 1915

Overall, Walker doubted that the feints would succeed, or that they were the best way to use the 1st Division. He suggested employing it, instead, as part of the actual breakout from ANZAC. Its mission would be the capture of the Chocolate and W Hills well beyond the northern flank, where it could set up outposts to assist the concurrent IX Corps landing at Suvla Bay.[31] This would secure the junction between IX Corps and ANZAC on high ground, and the entrance to the Anafarta Valley, both highly desirable outcomes. However, whether it could have been achieved with the troops available, given the trenches held by the 1st Division at Anzac would need to be taken over, was another issue. While the British 13th (Western) Division was earmarked to support the breakout, two brigades of this inexperienced formation may have been better employed in holding the 1st Division's position at Anzac.

In the event, the only concessions Walker wrung from Birdwood were dropping Johnston's Jolly as an objective, thereby confining his attack to Lone Pine and German Officers Trench, and delaying the Lone Pine assault until 5.30 pm.[32] With his concerns and recommendations largely overridden, Walker nonetheless did all he could to ensure success. Tunnels were pushed forward at Lone Pine and connected to form an underground trench, which would be opened up just before the assault. This reduced the length of the assault by 20 to 25 yards.[33] Walker also had the barbed wire in front of the Ottoman defences destroyed—achieved after four days of shelling. When the ANZAC fire plan to support the assault was issued, Colonel Talbot Hobbs, the 1st Division's Commander Royal Artillery, modified it to meet Walker's requirements. These changes included increasing the duration of the fire immediately before Zero Hour to 60 minutes and pounding the flanks and rear of Lone Pine to provide protection from enfilade fire during the assault, as well as disrupting Ottoman attempts to interfere with the

---

31   1 Div G54 29 July 1915, 1 Div WD August 1915, AWM: AWM4 1/42/7 Part 6; CEW Bean, Extract Book no. 5, 29, AWM: AWM38 3 DRL 1722 Item 5.
32   ANZAC Order no. 16, 3 August 1915, Note 'Dear Skeen', Note Ga 69 4.8.15, and Instr. for GOC Australian Division 4 August 1915, 1st Div WD August 1915, AWM: AWM4 1/42/7 Part 6.
33   1st Div G54, Considerations Affecting Forward Move of the First Australian Division, 1 Div WD August 1915, AWM: AWM4 1/42/7 Part 5; Bean, Official History, vol. II, Map 13.

consolidation of the position.[34] The careful planning and preparations paid off, with the 1st Brigade seizing Lone Pine with relatively little loss, although three days of brutal fighting involving heavy casualties were necessary to retain it.

German Officers' Trench was a different matter. The planning was largely entrusted to Brigadier General John Forsyth, commanding the 2nd Brigade, whose 6th Battalion was to make the attack. As at Lone Pine, tunnels had been driven forward and an underground line established close to the Ottoman line. Along it, 21 recesses were to be opened from which the infantry would attack. Additionally, mines were to be exploded in other tunnels over a 30-minute period beforehand to deter the Ottomans from occupying their front trenches. However, the assault was stopped dead. Walker ordered a second attack, which met the same result, and then a third. His actions were uncharacteristic for a commander with a proven concern for his men, and who always weighed up the merit of an operation against the likely loss.[35]

In mitigation, Birdwood's orders emphasised that the attack was to assist those to be undertaken further north at dawn, an aim the responsible officers should bear in mind. Walker, in turn, stressed the point to Forsyth during the operation. On learning that the northerly attacks had crumpled, Walker cancelled the third attack on German Officers' Trench. It seems that, in ordering the subsequent attacks, he sought to divert Ottoman attention away from the impending northern attacks that he deemed were essential in turning the enemy defences along Second Ridge. Colonel Brudenell White, Walker's Chief of Staff (COS), later admitted they had blundered in ordering the second attack and that both he and Walker had failed to ascertain the situation accurately, but that they learned to never again order a second attack after the first had failed.[36]

---

34 1st NZFA Bde WD 3–6 August 1915, AWM: AWM4 35/7/2; Appendix A to ANZAC Order no. 16 3 August 1915, NZ&A Div WD August 1915, AWM: AWM4 1/53/5 Part 3; 1st Div Artillery Operation Order no. 1, 3–8–15, 1 Div Operation Order no. 9 4 August 1915, 1st Div WD August 1915, AWM: AWM4 1/42/7 Part 7; 1st Div Artillery WD August 1915, AWM: AWM4 13/10/12 Part 1. Chris Roberts and Paul Stevens, *The Artillery at Anzac: Adaptation, Innovation and Education* (Newport: Big Sky Publishing, 2021), 135–40.
35 2 Bde Operation Order no. 1, 4 August 1915, 6th Bn WD August 1915, AWM: AWM4 23/23/4; 2 Bde KB742, KB 747, and KB 748, AWM: AWM25 367/10 Part 4; Bean, Official History, vol. II, 598–603.
36 2 Bde WD 7 August 1915, AWM: AWM4 23/2/6; 6 Bn War Diary, 7 August 1915, AWM: AWM4 23/23/4; 1 Div G805, G821, 2 Bde KB760, KB755. 1 Div G838, GG851, 1 Div WD August 1915, AWM: AWM4 1/42/7 Part 11; Letter, White to Bean, 21 May 1924, AWM: AWM38 3DRL 7953/4 Part 2.

The fact remains, however, that the planning and preparations for the attack were subpar. Launching it from the recesses rather than from the full length of the underground trench enabled the Ottomans to concentrate their fire on the exits as the attackers emerged. Inevitably, the recesses became congested with wounded, impeding those following. Had they surfaced from a fully opened underground trench, the attackers could have rushed forward on a broader front, giving them a better chance of success. Moreover, the mines had been dug too deep and were ineffectual, and the successive firing prior to Zero Hour simply alerted the Ottomans to the impending attack. White conceded that German Officers' Trench was not regarded as having 'anything approaching the importance of Lone Pine', and so arrangements 'were not as well made by Divisional headquarters'.[37] In not carefully reviewing the plans, Walker was clearly remiss and bears a large measure of blame for what occurred. It was his worst performance of the war.

Even so, Walker's pessimism about the feints were justified by events. Birdwood's hope that they would absorb all of the Ottoman reserves was unrealistic, not only because the objectives were too small for the purpose. Lone Pine and Sari Bair were sufficiently close that reserves reacting to the Lone Pine attack could be redirected swiftly to the greater threat at Sari Bair. In the event, Lone Pine drew in two Ottoman battalions, while the bulk of the reserves were sent to Sari Bair. Furthermore, the assault on Lone Pine, instead of diverting forces, did the opposite; it immediately prompted the Ottomans to transfer forces from the south to Anzac, some of whom arrived on Sari Bair early on 7 August, thwarting the New Zealanders' attempts to take Chunuk Bair.[38] Worse still, Lone Pine assumed a life of its own, soaking up one Australian battalion after another to retain ground of little tactical value. Ironically, it was one of only two minor successes of the August Offensive, which ended in total failure, leading to the evacuation in December.

---

37 Letter, White to Bean, 21 May 1924.
38 Mesut Uyar, *The Ottoman Army and the First World War* (Abingdon: Routledge, 2021), 185, 189–91, doi.org/10.4324/9781003033967; Harvey Broadbent, *Gallipoli: The Turkish Defence, The Story from Turkish Documents* (Melbourne: Miegunyah Press, 2015), 248–56; C Aspinall-Oglander, *May 1915 to the Evacuation*, vol. II of The Official History of the War, Military Operations, Gallipoli (London: William Heinemann Ltd, 1932), 181.

On the Western Front: 1916

Walker's time at Gallipoli with the 1st Division ended on 13 October when he was seriously wounded while—typically—visiting the front line.[39] Evacuated to Egypt, he did not return to the division until 14 March 1916 and found it had been split in half to help in form two new divisions, then filled with largely untrained reinforcements.[40] Arriving in France in late March, Walker characteristically ensured the division underwent a short period of intensive training before being deployed to the front line, and he continued issuing training instructions thereafter.[41] From mid-July, operational involvement in the great Anglo–French offensive on the Somme left the 1st Division little time for training and, by November, Walker considered it was 'suffer[ing] very much from inefficiencies', largely due to its junior officers' lack of training. Consequently, he prescribed specific measures to improve standards across the division, notably as regards officer training and the importance of administration.[42] There was to be no let-up in the coming year.

In late April 1916, the 1st Division entered the line on the Western Front near Armentieres to gain further experience. Walker's plain speaking when he considered the Division's interests threatened was once again evident. When Lieutenant General Richard Haking, GOC XI Corps, sought to employ the division in an attack near Fromelles in May, Walker 'refused to have anything to do with it', maintaining 'it would involve his troops in unnecessary casualties without any guarantee of success'.[43] The idea was dropped. In comparison, a little over three weeks after arriving in France, the newly raised 5th Australian Division, under the recently promoted Major General McCay, carried out the disastrous attack on Fromelles in July, shattering the division for no gain. That month, in far more dramatic

---

39 Birdwood Dairy 13 October 1915, AWM: AWM 3DRL 3376 Series 1, Wallet 1; Bean, *Official History*, vol. II, 828–29.
40 Jean Bou and Peter Dennis, *The Australian Imperial Force*, vol. 5 of The Centenary History of Australia and the Great War (Melbourne: Oxford University Press, 2016), 194; CEW Bean, *The Australian Imperial Force in France, 1916*, vol. III of The Official History of Australia in the War of 1914–18 (Sydney: Angus & Robertson, 1929), 42.
41 1 Div War Dairy 3–19 April 1916, AWM: AWM4 1/42/15; 1 Div Memo 3 April 1916, 1 Div WD April 1916; Memo Practical Use Trench Mortars in Defence, GS Memos no. 32, no, 39, no. 42, no. 44 and no. 46, typewritten page, 29 May 1916, 1 Div WD May 1916, AWM: AWM4 1/42/16 Part 1; and Note 16 June 1916, AWM: AWM26 25/11.
42 Notes Div Comd's Conf, GS Memo no. 78, 17 Nov 1916, 1 Div WD November 1916, AWM: AWM4 1/42/22.
43 Viney, 'Sir H.B. (Hooky) Walker', 64.

circumstances on the Somme, Walker opposed an officer more senior than Haking: General Hubert Gough, the controversial General Officer Commanding of the Reserve Army, soon to be renamed Fifth Army.

Arriving on the Somme on 18 July, Walker was peremptorily told by Gough: 'I want you to go into the line and attack Pozières tomorrow night.' Aware that Pozières crowned one of the highest parts of the Somme battlefield and had defied earlier British assaults, Walker vigorously protested there was insufficient time for him to reconnoitre the area and make the necessary preparations—indeed, his division was not yet fully concentrated in the area.[44] Gaining a postponement, he recorded in his diary that evening, 'Scrappy and contradictory orders from Reserve Army. Hope I shall not be rushed into an ill-prepared operation but feel I shall.'[45] In the meantime, he arranged to issue to all of his units three instructional circulars from Headquarters, British Expeditionary Force, that set out the tactical lessons and procedures learned in the three weeks since the offensive had begun.[46]

According to Walker, on 20 July, Gough directed him to attack Pozières from the south-west (Map 7.3). Once again, Walker demurred, telling Gough he wanted to attack from the south-east. The British 34th Division had twice been repulsed on a southwesterly approach, and Walker saw that his flank would be raked by enfilade fire there. Nevertheless, Gough continued to insist. Still reluctant to comply, Walker took Major Edward Beddington, a staff officer whom Gough trusted, forward to show him the ground and explain his plan. Seeing that Walker was right, Beddington recommended his plan to Gough, who finally relented.[47] The 1st Division would attack from the south-east. Walker recalled:

> If I had not fought most strenuously for my plan and insisted on a staff officer accompanying me and being shown my plan, we should have been compelled to undertake an operation which would have failed.[48]

---

44 Bean, *Official History*, vol. III, 468–69; Stevenson, *To Win the Battle*, 152; Meleah Hampton, *Attack on the Somme: 1st ANZAC Corps and the Battle of Pozières Ridge* (Solihull: Helion & Company Ltd, 2016), 31–32.
45 Letter, Walker to Bean, 13 August 1928, AWM: AWM 38 3DRL 7953/34 Part 1.
46 GS Memos no. 54, no. 55 and no. 56, Notes Div Conf 13 July, 1 Div WD July 1916, AWM: AWM4 1/42/18 Part 1.
47 Letter, Walker to Bean, 13 August 1928.
48 Letter, Walker to Bean, 13 August 1928.

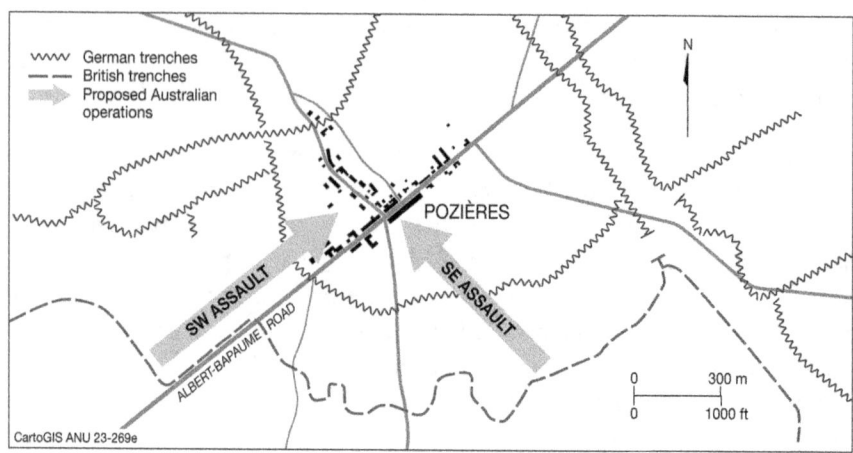

Map 7.3: Gough and Walker's attack options at Pozières, 20 July 1916

For his part, Gough disagreed with Walker's account, stating that 'the whole idea of the plan in my head was to make a flank attack, not a direct one'. He did not think that Walker had had much to do with the direction of the attack.[49] Interestingly, Walker wrote in his post-operation report that when he first saw Gough on 18 July, Gough had suggested alternative directions for the attack—either from the south-east or the south-west.[50] Whatever the facts were, there was clearly some sort of disagreement between Gough and Walker, as evidenced by Walker taking Beddington to reconnoitre with him.

Having secured additional British artillery support, Walker discussed his plan with his talented COS, Lieutenant Colonel Thomas Blamey, who drafted the orders for its execution and took care of the specifics Walker wanted. These included a direction that all ranks must be fully informed of the details of the attack—in particular, the locations to be reached at each stage and the actions to be taken on arrival. As Robert Stevenson writes:

> [In battle,] Walker expected his troops to do more than just obey orders and trudge behind the barrage, he expected them to understand his intent and encouraged initiative in his junior officers.[51]

An outstanding success resulted, with all objectives captured.

---

49 Letter, Edmonds to Bean, 16.ix.27, AWM: AWM38 3DRL 7953/34 Part 1.
50 1 Div Report 3 August 1916, 1 Div WD July 1916, AWM: AWM4 1/42/18 Part 2.
51 Robert Stevenson, *The War with Germany*, vol. 3 of The Centenary History of Australia and the Great War (Melbourne: Oxford University Press, 2015), 67.

7. FILLING THE GAP

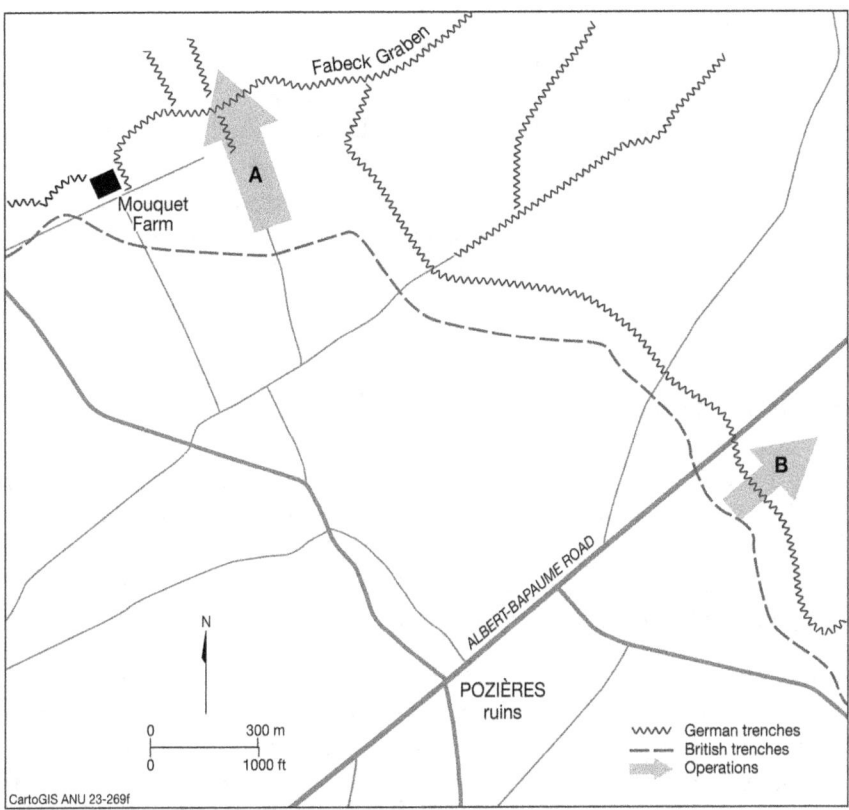

Map 7.4: Operations beyond Pozières, 18–21 August 1916

After three weeks' rest, the 1st Division returned to the maelstrom raging north and east of Pozières. Walker was advised the division would participate in a joint Reserve Army and Fourth Army operation on 18 August. The division was to assault in two directions: northwards in Operation A against Fabeck Graben trench, and in Operation B on the other flank, an attack to the north-east astride the Bapaume–Albert Road in conjunction with Fourth Army's attack (Map 7.4).

Walker shrewdly pointed out that Operation B constituted a portion of Fourth Army's operation and could occur simultaneously with it. However, Operation A, he maintained, was really a separate attack altogether, while the need to ascertain where the front line in the area ran raised doubts it could be carried out on 18 August. Walker proposed, instead, gaining a jumping-off position that day and postponing the main Operation A assault on the Fabeck Graben to 20 August.[52] In her study of Pozières, Meleah Hampton contends that Birdwood ignored Walker, who did 'not insist on having his suggestions and request followed'.[53] On the contrary, the I ANZAC order of 17 August shows that Birdwood accepted Walker's recommendations, setting objectives for a jumping-off position halfway to Fabeck Graben.[54] Along with Operation B, the resulting attack commenced on the 18th. Operation A was completed on the 21st, taking Fabeck Graben, but only a stretch abutting Mouquet Farm could be held against German counterattacks.[55]

Fading from history: 1917–18

From this point on, Walker fades from the histories of the AIF. He is rarely mentioned in the succeeding volumes of Bean's Official History, and little is known about him over the next 22 months, during which he commanded the 1st Division. Therefore, assessing his command becomes a matter of extrapolating from the division's performance in this period.

Walker's attention to training was still evident during this period. In early 1917, based on lessons from the Somme, the British Expeditionary Force developed new tactical doctrine centred around platoons and reorganised the infantry battalions to implement it.[56] With a focus that was not evident in the war diaries of the other four AIF divisions, Walker ensured that the changes were quickly adopted in the 1st Division. Within two days of its coming out of the front line, the new platoon organisation was in place, and extensive training and exercises in the new tactics began under his supervision.[57] By comparison, in the 4th Australian Division there appears to have been an unevenness in adopting the new organisation and a lack of intensity in training.[58] During 1917, the 1st Division trained longer and harder than in any other year of its history, spending a third of its time

---

52   I ANZAC S671, 1 Div S/16/815, 1Div WD August 1916, AWM: AWM4 1/42/19 Part 2.
53   Hampton, *Attack on the Somme*, 141.
54   I ANZAC Order no. 29, 17-8-1916, and Map *Ferme du Moquet* 1:5000, 1 Div WD August 1916, AWM: AWM4 1/42/19 Part 2.
55   Bean, Official History, vol. III, 785–800.
56   *SS135, SS143, SS144 and SS139/4,* Army Printing and Stationary Service, December 1916 and February 1917.
57   1 Div WD 8 March 1917; 1 Div GS Memos no. 7, no. 8, no 9, no. 11 and no. 13, Tactical Exercise 17 March 1917, 1 Div WD March 1917, AWM: AWM4 1/42/26.
58   Jeff Hatwell, *Brave Days: The Fourth Australian Division in the Great War* (Melbourne: Echo Books, 2021), 180–81; 4 Div WD March 1917, AWM: AWM4 1/4812.

7. FILLING THE GAP

doing so.⁵⁹ By mid-September, after four months of intensive training, the 1st Division was at its peak, both operationally and administratively.⁶⁰ Walker set the foundations, promulgating instructions and syllabi for both individual and collective training, competitions in skill at arms, and tactical exercises.⁶¹ He also took a keen interest in the preparation of its reinforcements undertaken by the 1st Training Group in England, regularly corresponding with the commanding officer on relevant issues, receiving bi-monthly reports from him, and sending officers from the division to observe its activities.⁶² In June 1918, the *Melbourne Herald* reported that it was 'largely due to [Walker] that the First is still the crack division of the Australian Army'.⁶³

Following its time on the Somme front during the winter of 1916–17, the 1st Division next saw action during the advance to the Hindenburg Line in April 1917. Here, Walker was tasked with capturing three fortified villages in front of the Hindenburg Line: Boursies in the north, Demicourt in the centre and the larger Hermies in the south, the key to the position on the ridge above the Canal du Nord. Walker employed innovative tactics, involving a diversion against Boursies and a surprise attack from two directions against Hermies, with the intent that after both had fallen, the Germans would withdraw from Demicourt, thereby negating the need to attack it (Map 7.5). The operation, which Gough praised as 'skilfully planned' was entirely successful.⁶⁴ Walker played little part in the bloody fighting at Second Bullecourt in May, his brigades being placed under the orders of the 2nd Australian Division. According to Lieutenant Colonel Horace Viney, one of Walker's Australian staff officers, he never forgave Gough for Bullecourt.⁶⁵ In recalling his time in Fifth Army, Walker thought Gough 'the very worst exhibition of Army commandship [sic]'.⁶⁶

---

59 Stevenson, *To Win the Battle*, 181–82.
60 1 Div WD 14–31 May 1917; 1 Div WD 1–30 June 1917; 1 Div WD 1–31 July 1917; 1 Div WD 1–31 August 1917; 1 Div WD 1–12 September 1917, AWM: AWM4 1/42/28–32 Part 1.
61 GS Memos no. 22, no. 23 and no. 25, 1 Div WD May 1917; Appendix I, Appendix II and Appendix III, 1 Div WD June 1917; GS Memo no. 27 14 July 1917, 1 Div WD July 1917; GS Memo no. 29, 1 Div WD August 1917.
62 Stevenson, *To Win the Battle*, 95; Letters Headquarters no. 1 (A) Group AIF to GOC 1st Australian Division 17 July 1917, 2 August 1917, 10/17, and 10 November 1917, AWM: AWM27 303/1.
63 *Melbourne Herald*, 19 June 1918, 19.
64 Telegram, Fifth Army to I ANZAC, 9 April 1917, in Letters from Birdwood to Munro Ferguson 1917, AWM: AWM3DRL 3376 6/4.
65 Viney, 'Sir H.B. (Hooky) Walker', 3.
66 Letter, Walker to Bean, 13 August 1928.

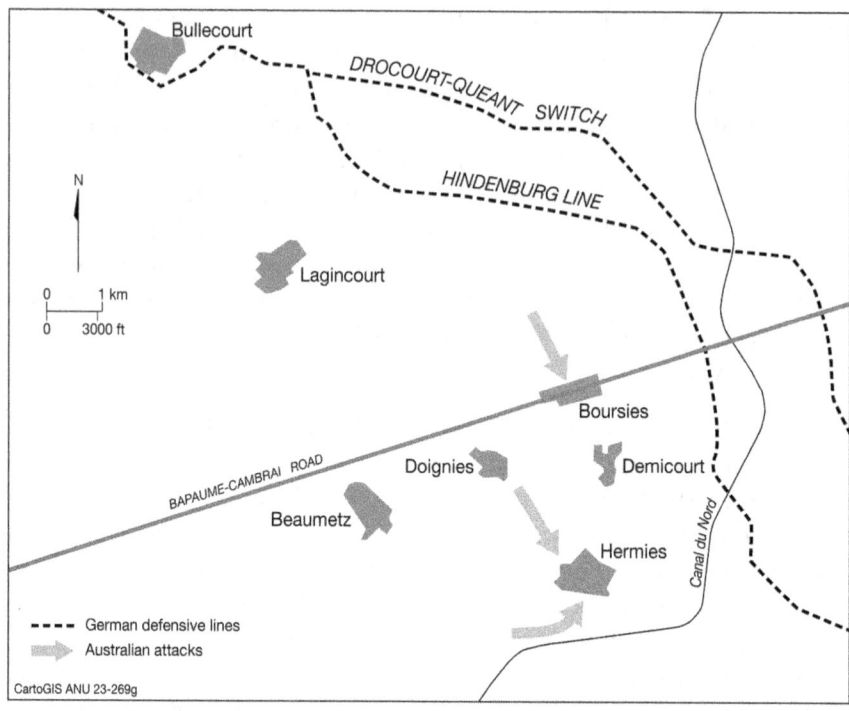

Map 7.5: First Australian Division operations against Boursies, Demicourt and Hermies, 8–9 April 1917

Fortunately, the 1st Division served the rest of Walker's tenure in command in General Sir Herbert Plumer's Second Army, first with I ANZAC during Third Ypres in the second half of 1917, and from April to late July 1918 on the Lys under XV Corps. Throughout this period, he appears not to have contested plans, and to have felt comfortable with the operations the division undertook. This was probably because Plumer was a commander in his own image, careful and competent. Nor had Walker lost any of his moral courage. While commanding the 48th (South Midland) Division in Italy in the latter half of 1918, he refused to participate in an attack ordered by his Italian corps commander. His action, he said, left him sitting 'on a very "slippery seat"', but that 'subsequent events justified my refusal'. The matter was referred to the Earl of Cavan, Commander-in-Chief of British Forces in Italy, who upheld Walker's decision because the proposed attack would have involved 'an entirely unnecessary loss of life'.[67]

---

67 Sir Harold Walker, 'Against Austrians: 48th Division's Campaign, *Reveille* 6, no. 9 (1 May 1933): 11; KW Mitchinson, *The 48th (South Midland) Division 1908–1919* (Solihull: Helion & Company Ltd, 2017), 230.

7. FILLING THE GAP

At Third Ypres, during the battles of the Menin Road and Broodseinde, Walker worked within Second Army's and I ANZAC's plans. These involved the 1st Division advancing on a narrow front between the divisions on either flank. Consequently, his contribution as to how the attacks were carried out was limited. Nonetheless, prior to both of them, Walker closely observed the German barrage lines. Noting where they fell on the ground, he decided to assemble his attacking waves as far forward as possible, as 'numerous casualties could be saved' by 'avoiding the hostile barrage as far as possible'.[68]

Concerning Walker's insistence on reducing casualties, Viney wrote:

> [H]e was probably far more careful regarding his division than many [Australian commanders] ... and he would not commit his troops to an attack (if he could possibly avoid it) unless convinced that the results ... would more than justify any loss which might necessarily be incurred. Even then he was most particular to see that every possible precaution was taken to make the task of the attacking troops as easy as possible and to reduce casualties to a minimum. In this regard he was governed not only by a genuine regard for his troops, but also because he considered them too valuable to be wasted on what he termed "mere eyewash stunts." I remember hearing him say on one occasion that the Australians were far too valuable as assault troops to be wasted on unnecessary attacks undertaken merely to gratify the personal vanity and ambition of their commanders ... I have known him refuse outright to commit his division to what he termed needless slaughter, and even threaten to resign his command and return to the British forces rather than do so.[69]

When the German Operation Georgette broke through the Allied line in French Flanders on 9 April 1918, the 1st Division was rushed north to help stem the offensive. By 11 April, the Germans were eight kilometres from Hazebrouk, a key railway junction that, if lost, would sever the Allied north–south lines of communications. Arriving that day, the division was told it 'was the only formed body of troops between here and the Channel ports'.[70] Faced with a desperate situation, Walker deployed his 1st and 2nd brigades along a perilously thin nine kilometre arc east of Hazebrouk, occupying the high ground where it was available. Sensibly, he asked that the intermingled

---

68 Report on Operations, 17–22 September, 1 Div WD September 1917, AWM: AWM4 1/42/32 Part 2; Report on Operations, 4/5 October 1917, 1 Div WD October 1917, AWM: AWM4 1/42/33 Part 2.
69 Viney, 'Sir H.B. (Hooky) Walker', 13.
70 Peter Pedersen, *The Anzacs: Gallipoli to the Western Front* (Camberwell: Penguin Viking, 2007), 332.

British units desperately fighting to his front be withdrawn to avoid any confusion should they be driven back by the advancing Germans.[71] When the blow fell on the 1st Division, it was repulsed. A second attack met the same fate on 17 April, and the front stabilised. Walker then began a series of minor aggressive operations. In taking fortified villages, he sought to envelop them rather than attacking directly, although an attempt to retake Mèteran by the 3rd Brigade by this means on 23 April failed. Nibbling away at the German line during the remaining tenure of Walker's command, the division gained ground and unchallenged ascendancy over its opponents. When leaving the XV Corps in early August 1918, Lieutenant General Sir Henry De Lisle recorded his appreciation of the division's 'exceptional service rendered during the past four months'.[72]

Conclusion

In *To Win the Battle*, his excellent study of the 1st Australian Division, Robert Stevenson observes that 'it was not born great, it *became* great', and shows that the division began hitting its peak in 1917, becoming one of the finest divisions in the AIF.[73] Plumer certainly held it in high regard, commenting in mid-1918 'there is no division, certainly in my army, perhaps in the whole British Army, which has done more to destroy the morale of the enemy than the 1st Australian Division'.[74] That it became a first-class division was due to several factors, not the least of which was the role Walker played as its commander. As Stevenson records, '[f]or the 1st Division the influence of the commanding general was paramount and all pervasive'.[75]

Walker was undoubtedly the most competent divisional commander at Anzac, and arguably one of the AIF's best on the Western Front. Sound judgement and common sense underpinned his considerable tactical acumen. Nor was his courage wanting. He was a general who regularly visited the front line to see things for himself, sharing in the process the same dangers as his men.

---

71 CEW Bean, *The Australian Imperial Force in France During the German Offensive, 1918*, vol. V of the Official History of Australia in the War of 1914–18, 4th ed. (Sydney: Angus & Robertson, 1938), 463.
72 GOC XV Corps no. 128/28G 4 August 1918 to GOC 1 Div, AWM: AWM27 354/1.
73 Stevenson, *To Win the Battle*, Chapter 7, 211.
74 Eric Wren, *Randwick to Hargicourt. History of the 3rd Battalion AIF* (Sydney: Ronald G Donald, 1935), 298–99; CEW Bean, *The Australian Imperial Force in France During the Allied Offensive, 1918*, vol. VI of The Official History of Australia in the War of 1914–18 (Sydney: Angus & Robertson, 1942), 440.
75 Stevenson, *To Win the Battle*, 216.

Moreover, he cared about them. Nor did Walker lack moral courage, refusing to be bullied into carrying out rushed operations, and regularly arguing against operations that he thought would involve unnecessary casualties or had little chance of success. He supervised training closely and took great pains to ensure that his men were thoroughly familiar with their tasks. For all these reasons, he won the respect, confidence and affection of all those he led. The 1st Australian Division reached and maintained a consistently high level of operational and administrative efficiency under him.

As a leader who took care of his team, Walker was nothing if not a team player. He never acted alone. Not being staff-college trained, he left his staff to get on with the details after giving them his intent, outline plan and the issues he deemed important. He also consulted extensively with his subordinates, including junior officers and non-commissioned officers. For example, choosing to gain ground at Anzac by sapping or mining, rather than assaulting, Walker held a conference to consider the options that included his engineers. It determined that tunnelling was safer than sapping.[76] In France, Major Drake-Brockman remembered being called to see Walker one night: 'He arose from his bed and discussed the problems at the front. His decisions and instructions were lucid and to the point.'[77] After an attack during Third Ypres in October 1917, Walker invited Company Sergeant-Major John Palmer of the 6th Battalion to breakfast to discuss it.[78]

Walker also appreciated the character of his Australians and exhibited a sense of humour. When Private Larry Shean bemoaned he was penniless, his mates bet him he wasn't game to touch the 'Old Man' for a loan. Seeing Walker's staff car approaching, Shean stepped out into the middle of the road, held up his hand and walked to the rear door of the now stationary car. A few hurried words were exchanged, after which a hand was extended through the window, and Shean returned to his mates with a 10-franc note.[79]

Had it not been for the Australian Government's intention to have all AIF commands held by Australians, Walker, rather than Monash, may have replaced Birdwood as commander of the Australian Corps when Birdwood took over the Fifth Army. Besides being highly regarded, Walker

---

76 Casey Diary 7 June 1915; 1 Div Engineers WD August 1915, 6 June 1915, AWM: AWM4 14/7/1 Part 1; Bean, Official History, vol. II, 262.
77 Drake-Brockman, *The Turning Wheel*, 102.
78 Ronald J Austin, *Rough as Bags: The History of the 6th Battalion, 1st AIF, 1914–1919* (McCrea: RJ and SP Austin, 1992), 220.
79 Austin, *Rough as Bags*, 204.

was, after all, the senior and most experienced divisional commander, was competent and was highly regarded by his men. After hearing of Monash's appointment, Chauvel confided to his wife that the Australian infantry 'would infinitely rather be led by W[alker] than M[onash]'.[80] According to the British historian Robert Rhodes James, Australian Prime Minister William Hughes:

> considered for a very long time whether Walker should command the Australian Corps in preference to Monash, and subsequently stated that if the British Government had not accepted Monash, he would have insisted on Walker.[81]

Far from 'filling a gap', Walker made a significant contribution to the AIF. That this is not well known is probably due to the overly nationalistic nature of Australian military history. As a study in command, he is an exemplar. For moulding the 1st Division into one of the finest in the AIF, and for his insistence on reducing casualties wherever possible, Australia owes him a debt. He deserves to be remembered as one of the finest commanders of the AIF.

---

80   AJ Hill, *Chauvel of the Light Horse* (Melbourne: Melbourne University Press, 1978), 157.
81   James, *Gallipoli*, 242.

Image 1: David Horner, aged 17, in his Prince Alfred College uniform, Adelaide, 1965
Note: This was the image that was attached to his application for entry to the Royal Military College, Duntroon.
Source: RMC–Duntroon Museum.

Image 2: Lieutenant David Horner after joining the 3rd Battalion, the Royal Australian Regiment, 1970
Source: David Horner.

Image 3: Lieutenant David Horner with his Platoon Sergeant Brian Payne, Nui Dat, South Vietnam, 1971

Note: Horner enjoyed a good working relationship with Payne: 'He understood things like loyalty.'

Source: David Horner.

Image 4: A very lean Lieutenant David Horner showing the effects of the extensive patrolling that characterised his deployment, South Vietnam, 1971
Note: He is shown with his signaller Private Sony Chater.
Source: David Horner.

Image 5: Lieutenant Colonel David Horner describing the battle for Finschhafen during a Joint Services Staff College (JSSC) tour, Papua New Guinea, 1989
Note: His posting to JSSC was the last of his Australian Regular Army Career.
Source: David Horner.

Image 6: Dr David Horner filming an interview for the documentary *Kokoda: The Bloody Track*, Canberra, 1992

Note: It was one of many to which he contributed, both on and off screen, during his career.

Source: David Horner.

Image 7: Professor David Horner with the Governor-General, Quentin Bryce, after being made a Member of the Order of Australia for 'service to higher education in the area of Australian military history and heritage as a researcher, author and academic', Canberra, 2009
Source: David Horner.

Image 8: Professor David Horner speaking at the launch of Volume I of the Official History of Australian Peacekeeping, Humanitarian and Post–Cold War Operations, Australian War Memorial, Canberra, 2013

Note: He was the sole author of this volume and would contribute to another three in the six-volume series.

Source: David Horner.

Part IV: Coalition warfare

8

The four pillars of human interoperability for multinational military integration: the Australian experience

Steven Paget

David Horner's publications have predominated in the fields of Australian military history and strategic studies, but his reputation as a research scholar has meant that his contribution to the development of generations of students is not as prominent as it deserves to be. I was fortunate enough to be David's final PhD student and, even though those days now seem a long time ago, the legacy of his supervision has endured. This volume is a testament to the vast catalogue of publications that David has produced, but it is also a reflection of his influence on the scholars that have followed him. David's guidance and support was invaluable to me, as it has been for many others. The scholarly standards that he has reached over more than four decades of research have set a benchmark for others to aspire to.

Michael McKernan described David Horner in 2004 as 'undoubtedly the stand-out Australian military historian of his generation'.¹ While Horner's mastery of Australian military history is well-established, his contribution to our understanding of multinational operations is not as widely appreciated.² Titles such as *High Command: Australia's Struggle for an Independent War Strategy 1939–1945* and *Strategy and Command: Issues in Australia's Twentieth-Century Wars*, alongside a volume of the Australian Centenary History of Defence, histories of the RAR, the Royal Australian Artillery and the Australian Special Air Service, may imply an Australia-centric approach, but the dynamics of coalition warfare and multinational operations are, in fact, carefully interwoven into Horner's work.³

In his 2021 review of the nation's involvement in the Second World War, Horner surmised: 'The experience of coalition warfare … became the most important influence in shaping Australian defence and foreign policy and Australian military concepts for the next seventy years.'⁴ Cooperation between Australia's armed forces and their international counterparts, both before and after the Second World War, has been central to Horner's publications. In overseeing the Official History of Australian Peacekeeping, Humanitarian and Post-Cold War Operations series, for example, Horner was conscious that 'all the Australian deployments had been part of a multinational force' and that it was necessary to address the 'the problems of operating as part of a coalition'.⁵

---

1   Michael McKernan, Review: 'The Australian Army, and: The Royal Australian Air Force, and: The Royal Australian Navy, and: Making the Australian Defence Force, and: The Department of Defence, and: Australian Defence: Sources and Statistics, and: An Atlas of Australia's Wars', *The Journal of Military History* 68, no. 1 (2004): 315, doi.org/10.1353/jmh.2003.0396.
2   Rather than being merely an Australian or multinational military historian, Horner has spanned the defence and security fields in his work. For example, see David Horner, *The Spy Catchers: The Official History of ASIO 1949–1963*, vol. I of The Official History of ASIO (Sydney: Allen & Unwin, 2014).
3   David Horner, *Strategy and Command: Issues in Australia's Twentieth-Century Wars* (Cambridge: Cambridge University Press, 2021), doi.org/10.1017/9781009067041; David Horner, *High Command: Australia's Struggle for an Independent War Strategy, 1939–1945* (Abingdon: Routledge, 2021), doi.org/10.4324/9781003120193; David Horner, *Making the Australian Defence Force*, vol. 4 of The Australian Centenary History of Defence (Melbourne: Oxford University Press, 2001); David Horner, *The Gunners: A History of Australian Artillery* (Sydney: Allen & Unwin, 1995); David Horner and Jean Bou, *Duty First: A History of the Royal Australian Regiment* (Sydney: Allen & Unwin, 2008); David Horner, *SAS: Phantoms of War: A History of the Australian Special Air Service* (Sydney: Allen & Unwin, 2002).
4   Horner, *Strategy and Command*, 143.
5   David Horner, 'The Evolution of Australian Official War Histories', in *War, Strategy and History*, edited by Daniel Marston and Tamara Leahy (Canberra: ANU Press, 2016), 85–86, doi.org/10.22459/wsh.05.2016.

Horner's analysis of Australia's integration with international military partners is significant given the nation's longstanding and enduring contributions to multinational endeavours as part of a 'largely alliance-based strategic culture' and a resultant 'way of war that is fundamentally coalition focused'.[6] Australia has not only been a willing and regular multinational contributor but has also proven to be a deeply respected one, with a reputation for high-quality personnel and a readiness to deploy them overseas to operate alongside allies.[7] Australia's enduring commitment to multinational endeavours is significant not only as part of the nation's military history but also as an exemplar of coalition integration.

This chapter addresses Australia's approach to enhancing procedural and human interoperability with multinational armed forces. The development of interoperability with the UK and the US, which have long been positioned as the nation's 'great and powerful friends' and have also most frequently led coalitions, will be explored, alongside Australia's wider defence relationships. A detailed review of the history of Australia's strategic and defence policies is beyond the scope of the chapter and, while it is recognised that alignment with both the UK and the US has prompted debates about whether particular decisions and actions were in the national interest, this work focuses on the efficacy of measures enacted to achieve interoperability, particularly as the nation's alliance-based strategy and expeditionary way of war have driven the requirement for interoperability, not vice versa.

The chapter will focus on four key pillars in the development of multinational interoperability: experience, education, exchanges and exercises. Australia's extensive involvement in multinational operations and the resultant benefits of experience in the achievement of interoperability will be explored. While the value of experience cannot be overstated, pre-emptive measures to enhance interoperability provide a foundation that can be built upon during operations. Notably, Australia has demonstrated a long-term commitment to defence cooperation and engagement.[8] Defence engagement includes conferences, seminars, staff talks and high-level military visits, while defence cooperation

---

6   Peter J Dean, 'The Alliance, Australia's Strategic Culture and Ways of War', in *Australia's American Alliance: Towards a New Era?*, edited by Peter J Dean, Stephan Frühling and Brendan Taylor (Melbourne: MUP Academic Digital, 2016), 193–94.
7   Jeffrey Grey, *A Military History of Australia* (Cambridge: Cambridge University Press, 2008), 3.
8   There are subtle differences in the meaning of terminology, although other scholars have preferred the term 'defence diplomacy' to encapsulate similar activities. See: Daniel Baldino and Andrew Carr, 'Defence Diplomacy and the Australian Defence Force: Smokescreen or Strategy?', *Australian Journal of International Affairs* 70, no. 2 (2016): 140, doi.org/10.1080/10357718.2015.1113229; Michael L'Estrange, 'International Defence Engagement: Potential and Limitations', *Security Challenges* 9, no. 2 (2013): 27.

incorporates capacity building, international education and training, and multinational exercises.[9] Defence engagement and cooperation have various aims, including enhancing interoperability with likely multinational partners.[10] James Goldrick assessed in 2016 that 'perhaps the most important contribution' that Australia can make to the enhancement of interoperability 'will be to create and sustain the personal links that have proved so important in operations'.[11] This chapter will examine how those vital connections have been generated through international education and training opportunities, personnel exchanges, and multinational military exercises.

Multinational operations and interoperability

Coalitions are as old as documented warfare and have been formed on every continent except Antarctica.[12] Notwithstanding their longevity, there was a surge in scholarly interest in multinational operations following operations in Iraq and Afghanistan, with their prevalence leading to them being recognised as 'the dominant form of Western democracies' involvement in military conflict'.[13] Yet, despite this frequency, the successful integration of forces from different nations has proven challenging for a multitude of reasons, including technological incompatibilities, variations in the application of doctrine and operating procedures, differing rules of

---

9   Jennifer DP Moroney, Celeste Ward Gventer, Stephanie Pezard and Laurence Smallman, *Lessons from U.S. Allies in Security Cooperation with Third Countries: The Cases of Australia, France, and the United Kingdom* (Santa Monica: RAND Corporation, 2011), 9.
10 Daniel Baldino, 'An Exercise in Management: Defence Engagement in the Indo-Pacific', *Security Challenges* 12, no. 1 (2016): 153.
11 James Goldrick, 'Interoperability', in *Australia's American Alliance: Towards a New Era?*, edited by Peter J Dean, Brendan Taylor and Stephan Frühling, (Melbourne: MUP Academic Digital, 2016).
12 Stéfanie von Hlatky and Thomas Juneau, 'When the Coalition Determines the Mission: NATO's Detour in Libya', *Journal of Strategic Studies* 45, no. 2 (2022): 259, doi.org/10.1080/01402390.2021.2011234; Rosella Cappella Zielinski and Ryan Grauer, 'A Century of Coalitions in Battle: Incidence, Composition, and Performance, 1900–2003', *Journal of Strategic Studies* 45, no. 2 (2022): 186, doi.org/10.1080/01402390.2021.2011233.
13 Patrick A Mello, 'National Restrictions in Multinational Military Operations: A Conceptual Framework', *Contemporary Security Policy* 40, no. 1 (2019): 50. For example, see Marina E Henke, *Constructing Allied Cooperation: Diplomacy, Payments, and Power in Multilateral Military Coalitions* (Ithaca: Cornell University Press, 2019), doi.org/10.7591/cornell/9781501739699.001.0001; Patricia Weitsman, *Waging War: Alliances, Coalitions, and Institutions of Interstate Violence* (Stanford: Stanford University Press, 2013), doi.org/10.1515/9780804788946; Olivier Schmitt, *Allies That Count: Junior Partners in Coalition Warfare*, (Washington, DC: Georgetown University Press, 2018); Scott Wolford, *The Politics of Military Coalitions* (New York: Cambridge University Press, 2015), doi.org/10.1017/CBO9781316179154; Sarah E Kreps, *Coalitions of Convenience: United States Military Interventions after the Cold War* (New York: Oxford University Press), 2011.

engagement and cultural friction.[14] Interoperability is, consequently, an essential consideration for military planners in the formation and operation of multinational forces.

Multinational interoperability, at its broadest level, relates to the capacity of the armed forces of different nations to operate together efficiently and effectively.[15] Interoperability is a broad term and has been sub-classified in various ways. NATO has separated interoperability into three categories: human, procedural and technical.[16] The human element includes key issues such as language and culture, and relates to the ability of military personnel to form cohesive working relationships and cooperate effectively. Procedural interoperability encompasses doctrine and tactics, techniques, and procedures, while the technical element covers the compatibility of equipment and communication systems.[17] There is also a vertical element to interoperability across the tactical, operational and strategic levels. Strategic-level interoperability has been defined as the 'integration of world outlook, values and interests', whereas, at the operational level, it represents the ability of different nations to 'operate side by side and/or as different parts of a command echelon or hierarchy'.[18] Tactical-level interoperability encapsulates the 'fungibility' of military forces, particularly in the areas of tactics, techniques and procedures.[19] Importantly, the levels are interconnected, with interoperability at the tactical and operational levels generating benefits at the strategic level.[20]

---

14   Eric Min, 'Speaking with One Voice: Coalitions and Wartime Diplomacy', *Journal of Strategic Studies* 45, no. 2 (2022): 323, doi.org/10.1080/01402390.2021.2011232; Patricia A Weitsman, 'Wartime Alliances Versus Coalition Warfare: How Institutional Structure Matters in the Multilateral Prosecution of Wars', *Strategic Studies Quarterly* 4, no. 2 (2010): 114.
15   Anna Danielsson, 'Producing the Military Urban(s): Interoperability, Space-making, and Epistemic Distinctions between Military Services in Urban Operations', *Political Geography* 97 (2022): 3, doi.org/10.1016/j.polgeo.2022.102649; John R Deni, 'Maintaining Transatlantic Strategic, Operational and Tactical Interoperability in an Era of Austerity', *International Affairs* 90, no. 3 (2014): 586, doi.org/10.1111/1468-2346.12128.
16   Joakim Erma Møller, 'Trilateral Defence Cooperation in the North: An Assessment of Interoperability Between Norway, Sweden and Finland', *Defence Studies* 19, no. 3 (2019): 240, doi.org/10.1080/14702436.2019.1634473.
17   Major General Duane A Gamble and Colonel Michelle MT Letcher, 'The Three Dimensions of Interoperability for Multinational Training at the JMRC', *Army Sustainment*, September–October (2016): 17–18.
18   Deni, 'Maintaining Transatlantic Interoperability', 585.
19   Myron Hura et al., *Interoperability: A Continuing Challenge in Coalition Air Operations* (Santa Monica: RAND Corporation, 2000), 12, doi.org/10.7249/mr1235.
20   Derrick V Frazier and J Wesley Hutto, 'The Socialization of Military Power: Security Cooperation and Doctrine Development Through Multinational Military Exercises', *Defence Studies* 17, no. 4 (2017): 387, doi.org/10.1080/14702436.2017.1377050; Alastair Finlan, Anna Danielsson and Stefan Lundqvist, 'Critically Engaging the Concept of Joint Operations: Origins, Reflexivity and the Case of Sweden', *Defence Studies* 21, no. 3 (2021): 368, doi.org/10.1080/14702436.2021.1932476.

Interoperability must be understood as 'more a journey than a goal', given the complexity and interconnectedness of its different elements.[21] It presents an inherent challenge: while potential friction points need to be anticipated and addressed in advance of operations, the baseline of interoperability is constantly fluctuating due to various factors, including shifts in the strategic environment, emerging technologies and changes in doctrine.[22] Interoperability is also an expensive endeavour, particularly when the acquisition of common platforms is pursued, as demonstrated by the Australian purchase of the F-35 aircraft.[23]

Moreover, the identity, culture and outlook of national armed forces are inevitably shaped by their environment and history, and they will not always share obvious similarities with multinational counterparts. Despite close associations with the UK and, later, the US, as well as the imperial influence on the foundation of the nation's armed forces, Australia is often considered to have a distinctive 'military identity', forged at Gallipoli and shaped over the course of more than a century. Interoperability represents a careful balancing act between preserving national military identity and culture, and cooperating effectively with other national armed forces.[24] Therefore, procedural interoperability needs to be reviewed constantly and refreshed, while human and organisational relationships have to be cultivated and continually strengthened. The achievement of human interoperability, including intersecting cultural elements, is complex but worthwhile, as it has been identified as the component that binds multilateral forces together.[25]

It should be noted that interoperability has proven to be a contentious issue in Australia's military history, particularly during the First World War, interwar years and early stages of the Second World War, as it was underpinned by, and intersected with, imperialism. While interoperability was central to cooperation between armed forces across the British Empire, it is necessary to draw a distinction between the ability to interoperate and the limitations on sovereignty imposed by imperialism. Indeed, the

---

21 Goldrick, 'Interoperability'.
22 Michelle L Pryor, Thomas Labouche, Mario Wilke and Charles C Pattillo, Jr, 'The Multinational Interoperability Council Enhancing Coalition Operations', *JFQ* 82, 3rd Quarter (2016): 112.
23 See Adam Lockyer, 'The Logic of Interoperability: Australia's Acquisition of the F-35 Joint Strike Fighter', *International Journal: Canada's Journal of Global Policy Analysis* 68, no. 1 (2013): 71–91.
24 Thomas Moore, 'An Australian Approach to Ethical Warfare? Australia and the "War on Terror"', in *War, Ethics and Justice: New Perspectives on a Post–9/11 World*, edited by Annika Bergman-Rosamond and Mark Phythian (Abingdon: Routledge, 2011), 42, doi.org/10.4324/9780203868522-8.
25 Thomas Crowson, 'Breaking it Down Barney Style: A Framework for Cultural Interoperability', *Canadian Foreign Policy Journal* 22, no. 2 (2016), 109, doi.org/10.1080/11926422.2016.1186704.

principles of interoperability have endured throughout Australia's military history. For example, while it was later determined efficacious for Australia to have its own staff college, rather than send officers to Britain or India, international exchanges continued, owing to the benefits accrued from them. In short, multinational operations require an ability to interoperate rather than replicate. Therefore, Australia's earliest experiences of achieving interoperability are relevant, as they demonstrate the validity of the principles, which have endured into the contemporary era through measures that more appropriately preserve sovereignty and national interests.

'Great and powerful friends'

Australia's ability to operate alongside multinational partners, particularly lead nations in coalitions, has been shaped by its historic strategic alignment with so-called 'great and powerful friends': first, the UK and, in turn, the US.[26] Extensive efforts to cultivate interoperability with those keystone partners have been accompanied by frequent participation in multinational operations, leading to Australia developing a reputation as 'the "first follower" of its great power ally'.[27] Multinational cooperation has not been without its challenges. As Horner reminds us:

> Australia's strategy has often been part of a wider allied strategy, either because of Australia's place in the British Empire, or more recently as part of the United States Alliance or Western Alliance. This raises questions as to how much influence Australia can have over allied strategy.[28]

While the onset of the Second South African War (1899–1902) predated Federation on 1 January 1901, the deployment of troops from all Australian colonies, for the first time in history, represented an imperial

---

26 Laura Seddelmeyer, '"Great and Powerful Friends of Yesteryear": Australia's Dilemma with "East of Suez"', 1967–71', *Australian Journal of Politics and History* 67, no. 1 (2021): 18, doi.org/10.1111/ajph.12764; Joan Beaumont, 'The State of Australian History of War', *Australian Historical Studies* 34, no. 121 (2003): 166, doi.org/10.1080/10314610308596243; Jeffrey Grey, 'In Every War but One? Myth, History and Vietnam', in *Zombie Myths of Australian Military History*, edited by Craig Stockings (Sydney: NewSouth, 2010), 194.
27 Maryanne Kelton and Aaron P Jackson, 'Australia: Terrorism, Regional Security, and the US Alliance', in *Coalition Challenges in Afghanistan: The Politics of Alliance*, edited by Gale A Mattox and Stephen M Grenier (Stanford: Stanford University Press, 2015), 238, doi.org/10.1515/9780804796293-018.
28 Horner, *Strategy and Command*, 1–2.

initiative and commenced a trend of participation in coalition warfare.[29] Australia's subsequent experiences during the First World War must be contextualised within the wider British imperial defence strategy.[30] The agreement made by Prime Minister Edmund Barton at the 1902 Imperial Conference to standardise the equipment and organisation of the Australian Army with its British counterpart laid the foundations for integration and interchangeability.[31] Compatibility of the armed forces of the 'imperial family' was considered essential.[32] Rhys Crawley has emphasised: 'Reflecting the ideal of "Greater Britain", the AIF and the RAN were both Australian and British, and knew that the strength of the imperial war effort was its combined weight, controlled and underpinned by Britain.'[33]

Although the Australian military emerged from the First World War far more experienced, the interconnectedness of the British Empire's armed forces remained central to its development. Tellingly, Prime Minister Stanley Bruce declared at the 1926 Imperial Conference:

> The guiding principle on which all our defence preparations are based … is uniformity in every respect—organisation, methods of training, equipment—with the fighting services of Great Britain, in order that in time of emergency we may dovetail into any formation with which our forces may be needed to co-operate.[34]

Manifesting the legacy of an interwar imperial defence policy, Australian forces were deployed overseas at the onset of the Second World War to operate under British commanders-in-chief.[35] The first years of the conflict nevertheless exposed fractures in the relationship with Britain, as evidenced by the campaign in Greece, and led to the strengthening of Australia–US

---

29 Effie Karageorgos, '"Jingo Dingo Insanity" and Mafeking Day: Articulating Madness in Federation-era Australia', *History Australia* 19, no. 1 (2022): 74, doi.org/10.1080/14490854.2022.2028553.
30 David Horner, 'The AIF's Commanders: Learning on the Job', in *The AIF in Battle: How the Australian Imperial Force Fought, 1914–1918*, edited by Jean Bou (Melbourne: MUP Academic Digital, 2016), 62.
31 Horner, *Strategy and Command*, 35.
32 Gary Sheffield, 'Manpower, Training, and the Battlefield Leadership of British Army Officers in the Era of the Two World Wars', in *Manpower and the Armies of the British Empire in the Two World Wars*, edited by Douglas E Delaney, Mark Frost and Andrew L Brown (Ithaca: Cornell University Press, 2021), 82, doi.org/10.7591/cornell/9781501755835.003.0008.
33 Rhys Crawley, 'Marching to the Beat of an Imperial Drum: Contextualising Australia's Military Effort During the First World War', *Australian Historical Studies* 46, no. 1 (2015): 80, doi.org/10.1080/1031461x.2014.994540.
34 Quoted in Horner, *High Command*, 5.
35 David Horner, 'Advancing National Interests: Deciding Australia's War Strategy, 1944–45', in *Australia 1944–45: Victory in the Pacific*, edited by Peter Dean (Cambridge: Cambridge University Press, 2016), 10, doi.org/10.1017/cbo9781316015445.004.

defence ties, with the arrival of American General Douglas MacArthur in 1942 being deemed 'a pivotal event in Australia's military alliance relationships'.[36] Although the relationship with the UK, and the legacy of its influence on the Australian military, would endure beyond the Second World War, there was an increasing emphasis on defence cooperation with the US.[37]

Throughout the 1950s and 1960s, a variety of initiatives strengthened ties and improved interoperability between the armed forces of Australia and the US, including the ANZUS Treaty (Australia, New Zealand and United States Security Treaty, 1951), the Radford-Collins Agreement (1951), the Southeast Asia Treaty Organization (SEATO) (1955) and the Military Standardization Agreement (1960).[38] The very fact that Percy Spender, Australian Ambassador to the US (1951–58), reportedly informed President Harry Truman that he wished to form 'substantially the same relationship as exists with the British Commonwealth' with the US was testament to the shift in Australian strategic alignment.[39] Notably, Sir Philip McBride, Minister for Defence, proclaimed at a meeting at the Pentagon on 6 June 1956 that the Australians had decided 'our forces should be equipped with modern equipment, standard or compatible with that of the U.S. forces'.[40] Consequently, Australian forces, particularly the RAAF and RAN, embarked upon a significant shift in platform acquisitions that saw a transition away from British equipment to that of the US.[41] This realignment was solidified through Australia's participation in the Vietnam War in support of the US.[42]

---

36 David Horner, 'Australia in 1942: A Pivotal Year', in *Australia 1942: In the Shadow of War*, edited by Peter Dean (Cambridge: Cambridge University Press, 2012), 25, doi.org/10.1017/cbo9781139540681.004.
37 John Blaxland, *The Australian Army from Whitlam to Howard* (Port Melbourne: Cambridge University Press, 2013), 11, doi.org/10.1017/cbo9781107445246.
38 Steven Paget, 'Loaning Ships and Leveraging Influence? American and British Responses to the HMAS *Voyager* Tragedy', *The International History Review* 43, no. 4 (2021): 539, doi.org/10.1080/07075332.2020.1846587.
39 David Lowe, *Australian Between Empires: The Life of Percy Spender* (Abingdon: Routledge, 2016), 143, doi.org/10.4324/9781315656199.
40 'Minutes of Australian Mission Meeting, 6th June 1957', 20 June 1957, Bureau of Far Eastern Affairs, Office of the Country Director for Australia and New Zealand, Box 2, Record Group 59, National Archives at College Park, MD (NARA).
41 Ian McNeill, 'The Australian Army and the Vietnam War', in *Australia's Vietnam War*, edited by Jeff Doyle, Jeffrey Grey and Peter Pierce (College Station: Texas A&M University Press, 2002), 49.
42 For more on the significance of Australian–US interoperability in the lead-up to and during the Vietnam War, see Steven Paget, 'On a New Bearing: The Re-organised Royal Australian Navy at War in Vietnam', *The Mariner's Mirror* 101, no. 3 (2015): 283–303, doi.org/10.1080/00253359.2015.1054686; Steven Paget, 'Magpies and Eagles: Number 2 Squadron, Royal Australian Air Force, and the Experience of Coalition Warfare in Vietnam', in *Allies in Air Power: A History of Multinational Air Operations*, edited by Steven Paget (Lexington: The University Press of Kentucky, 2021), 142–67, doi.org/10.2307/j.ctv190k9zf.

The relationship with the US evolved over the succeeding decades to encompass 'deep ... defence cooperation' and, ultimately, occupy a position of 'centrality'.[43] The trend of purchasing US-designed high-end technology has been accompanied by contributions to US-led coalitions to maintain and enhance Australia's alliance 'credentials',[44] resulting in a reputation as 'the United States' most reliable partner'.[45]

Despite the increased focus on cooperation with the US, it is important not to overlook Australia's continuing relationship with the UK. Australia's involvement in operations with only one of the UK or the US, such as the Malayan Emergency and the Vietnam War respectively, were the exception rather than the rule. Operations in Afghanistan and Iraq, for example, have been viewed as emphasising the 'trilateral "special relationship"' between Australia, the UK and the US.[46] Recent operations involving the three nations have built on a longstanding relationship that stretches back to the First World War but was solidified during the Second World War.[47] Following the Second World War, initiatives such as the America Britain Canada Australia (ABCA) Armies Standardisation Program, and its air force and naval equivalents, effectively created a 'cousinhood of like-minded nations', reinforced by the 'Five Eyes' intelligence sharing arrangements.[48] Moreover, Australia's adoption of NATO standardisation agreements strengthened interoperability with the 'greater Western defence community'.[49] Australia's participation in multinational endeavours has been far broader, however, than cooperation with the UK and the US, particularly in the case of peacekeeping operations.[50]

---

43   Joanne Wallis and Anna Powles, 'Burden-sharing: The US, Australia and New Zealand Alliances in the Pacific Islands', *International Affairs* 97, no. 4 (2021): 1049, doi.org/10.1093/ia/iiab081; Dougal Robinson, 'A Sustained Tantrum: How the Joint Chiefs of Staff Shaped the ANZUS Treaty', *Australian Journal of International Affairs* 74, no. 5 (2020): 495, doi.org/10.1080/10357718.2020.1721430.
44   Iain D Henry, 'Adapt or Atrophy? The Australia-U.S. Alliance in an Age of Power Transition', *Contemporary Politics* 26, no. 4 (2020): 402, doi.org/10.1080/13569775.2020.1777043.
45   Stéfanie von Hlatky, *American Allies in Times of War: The Great Asymmetry* (New York: Oxford University Press, 2013), 115–16, doi.org/10.1017/s1537592714002060.
46   Gabriele Abbondanza, 'Australia the "Good International Citizen"? The Limits of a Traditional Middle Power', *Australian Journal of International Affairs* 75, no. 2 (2021): 184, doi.org/10.1080/10357718.2020.1831436.
47   Horner, *Strategy and Command*, 143.
48   Blaxland, *The Australian Army*, 12.
49   Stephan Frühling, '"Key to the Defense of the Free World": The Past, Present and Future Relevance of NATO for US Allies in the Asia–Pacific', *Journal of Transatlantic Studies* 17 (2019): 249, doi.org/10.1057/s42738-019-00014-0.
50   David Horner, 'Chronicling the Peacekeepers: Problems of Writing the Official History of Australian Peacekeeping, Humanitarian and Post–Cold War Operations', *History Australia* 5, no. 1 (2008): 10.7, doi.org/10.2104/ha080010.

An experienced multinational contributor

In observing that almost all Australian deaths recorded on the Australian War Memorial's Roll of Honour have resulted from 'conflicts in other countries, often as a function of alliance diplomacy', Joan Beaumont has noted that the nation has 'a remarkable record of projecting military force overseas'.[51]

While not their primary purpose, multinational operations provide significant learning opportunities and the potential to solidify and enhance interoperability.[52] Unsurprisingly, given the length and magnitude of the conflicts, Australia's armed forces 'learned several lessons' during both world wars.[53] Through a process of 'learning on the job' from the British and other dominions during the First World War, Australia generated a 'reservoir of expertise' that was further enhanced through the experience of operating alongside Commonwealth forces and, later, the US military during the Second World War.[54]

Cold War operations provided further experience and strengthened relationships between individuals and armed forces. Australia's commitments to the Malayan Emergency (1950–60), the Korean War (1950–53), the Indonesian Confrontation (1963–66) and the Vietnam War (1962–73) provided extensive experience of multinational operations.[55] The career of Lieutenant General Sir John Wilton, Chief of the General Staff (CGS) from 1963 to 1966, provides a noteworthy example of the snowball effect of multinational experience. Wilton served in the British Army prior to the Second World War and the Australian Army during that conflict, in which

---

51 Joan Beaumont, 'Australia's Memorial Building on the Western Front, 1916–2015', in *War Memories: Commemoration, Recollections, and Writings on War*, edited by AH Blanger and Rene Dickason (Montréal: McGill-Queen's University Press, 2017), 55, doi.org/10.1515/9780773548510-006; Joan Beaumont, 'Australia's Global Memory Footprint: Memorial Building on the Western Front, 1916–2015', *Australian Historical Studies* 46, no. 1 (2015): 45, doi.org/10.1080/1031461x.2014.998246.
52 Jon Rahbek-Clemmensen, 'The Strategic Purpose of Individual Augmentee Officers for Junior Partners in Multinational Military Operations', *Defense & Security Analysis* 35, no. 4 (2019): 348, doi.org/10.1080/14751798.2019.1675937; Sara Bjerg Moller, 'Learning from Losing: How Defeat Shapes Coalition Dynamics in Wartime', *Journal of Strategic Studies* 45, no. 2 (2022): 282, doi.org/10.1080/01402390.2022.2030716.
53 David Horner, 'Australian Higher Command in the Korean War: The Experience of Brigadier John Wilton', in *In from the Cold: Reflections on Australia's Korean War*, edited by John Blaxland, Michael Kelly and Liam Brewin Higgins (Canberra: ANU Press, 2020), 167, doi.org/10.22459/iftc.2019.08.
54 Horner, 'The AIF's Commanders', 62.
55 The dates for Australia's involvement in these conflicts are taken from the Australian War Memorial. See www.awm.gov.au/articles/encyclopedia.

he operated alongside both British and American forces, before being posted to the Australian Military Mission in Washington, DC.[56] Wilton later visited Malaya during the Emergency to report on the British Commonwealth operations and commanded the 28th British Commonwealth Brigade during the Korean War. That command built on, and was informed by, his earlier experience of operating alongside the British and Americans, but it also introduced him to a range of personnel from both countries that he later encountered through either SEATO or service in Malaysia and Vietnam.[57]

By the end of the Cold War, and following the 1991 Gulf War, Australia was accustomed to the role of 'junior coalition partner' as a result of long-term experience.[58] The ADF faced the opposite problem in 1999 when it was thrust into the role of significant coalition leader with the formation of the International Force East Timor (INTERFET).[59] Although changes were required to adjust to that role, the ADF could call on experience gained from regularly participating in coalition operations and subsequently learned a number of lessons about leading them.[60] Notably, White Papers and Defence Updates in the decade after INTERFET stated a requirement for the ADF to be able to 'lead' coalition operations in the South-West Pacific.[61]

Although the ADF needed to prepare to lead multinational operations, it once again found itself operating as a junior partner in coalitions during the two decades following INTERFET. The value of enduring commitments was evidenced during the RAN's involvement in the 2003 Iraq War, which built upon Australian ships serving in the Persian Gulf or the Red Sea almost continuously following Iraq's invasion of Kuwait in 1990. That experience contributed to the 'high level of interoperability' within the naval coalition.[62]

---

56 David Horner, 'Why was 5 RAR Stationed at Nui Dat?', in *Vietnam Vanguard: The 5th Battalion's Approach to Counter-Insurgency, 1966*, edited by Ron Boxall and Robert O'Neill (Canberra: ANU Press, 2020), 22, doi.org/10.22459/vv.2019.02.
57 Horner, 'Australian Higher Command in the Korean War', 180–81.
58 Kelton and Jackson, 'Australia', 236.
59 Chris Barrie, 'A Chief of Defence Force's Perspective', in *Niche Wars: Australia in Afghanistan and Iraq, 2001–2014*, edited by John Blaxland, Marcus Fielding and Thea Gellerfy (Canberra: ANU Press, 2020), 47, doi.org/10.22459/nw.2020.
60 Sir Peter Cosgrove, 'Commanding INTERFET', in *East Timor Intervention: A Retrospective on INTERFET*, edited by John Blaxland (Melbourne: MUP Academic Digital, 2015), 53.
61 Stephan Frühling, 'Australian Defence Policy and the Concept of Self-reliance', *Australian Journal of International Affairs* 68, no. 5 (2014): 536, doi.org/10.1080/10357718.2014.899310.
62 Peter Jones, 'Maritime Operations', in *Niche Wars: Australia in Afghanistan and Iraq, 2001–2014*, edited by John Blaxland, Marcus Fielding and Thea Gellerfy, (Canberra: ANU Press, 2020), 146, doi.org/10.22459/nw.2020.

Ultimately, the experience of international force projection alongside multinational partners over more than a century not only drove the need for Australian forces to be interoperable, but it also afforded extensive learning opportunities, thereby providing a platform for improved interoperability.

Multinational exchanges

Personnel exchanges have been considered an essential vehicle to 'better align bilateral and multilateral approaches to improving capability, capacity, and interoperability'.[63] The network of loans and exchanges established by the War Office in Britain played a pivotal role in the dominion armies' development and in promoting standardisation with the British Army prior to the First World War.[64] While Australia had only two imperial loan officers in 1907, the number had risen to 20 by 1914, with those personnel occupying most of the military instructor positions at the RMC – Duntroon. That the dominion armies were more capable and better able to cooperate with the British Army by the outbreak of the First World War was due, in part, to the work done by imperial loan officers.[65] Tellingly, 16 of the 20 imperial officers on loan with the Australian Military Forces (AMF) in August 1914 were still with the AIF in 1916.[66] Colonel (later Major General) Ewen Sinclair-MacLagan, an instructor at Duntroon prior to the outbreak of the First World War, was given command of the 3rd Infantry Brigade and served with the AIF throughout the duration of the conflict, taking command of the 4th Division in mid-1917.[67] It was perhaps telling that Sinclair-MacLagan was considered an 'honorary Australian' when command of all five AIF divisions was Australianised in 1918.[68] The relevance of interoperability beyond the British Empire was emphasised by Sinclair-MacLagan's appointment to lead an Australian mission of 217 men to advise the Americans on operational planning on the Western Front,

---

63 David Gayvert, 'Building Joint Personnel Recovery Through Multinational Collaboration', *Joint Force Quarterly* 91, 4th Quarter (2018): 109.
64 Douglas E Delaney, 'Army Apostles: Imperial Officers on Loan and the Standardization of the Canadian, Australian and New Zealand Armies, 1904–1914', *War in History* 23, no. 2 (2016): 176, doi.org/10.1177/0968344514552436.
65 Delaney, 'Army Apostles', 176, 189.
66 Douglas Delaney, *The Imperial Army Project: Britain and the Land Forces of the Dominions and India, 1902–1945* (Oxford: Oxford University Press, 2018), 131.
67 Aimée Fox, *Learning to Fight: Military Innovation and Change in the British Army, 1914–1918* (Cambridge: Cambridge University Press, 2018), 209; Horner, *Strategy and Command*, 47.
68 Joan Beaumont, '"Unitedly We Have Fought": Imperial Loyalty and the Australian War Effort', *International Affairs* 90, no. 2 (2014): 406, doi.org/10.1111/1468-2346.12116.

thereby demonstrating the integral role of imperial loan officers, with Monash noting that despite not being 'Australian-born', he was 'wholeheartedly Australian'.[69]

Attachments did not work only one way. Permanent Military Forces officers served on exchange with the British and Indian armies, affording them opportunities to obtain regimental experience in view of the limited chances to undertake unit or sub-unit command in Australia, but also to facilitate standardisation among the dominion forces.[70] Royal Australian Naval College graduates also spent approximately half of their service during the interwar years with the Royal Navy (RN).[71] Those exchanges effectively represented an 'on-the-job training scheme', but they were also critical in promoting standardisation and developing professional networks that would underpin multinational cooperation.[72]

The experience of Field Marshal Thomas Blamey, who undertook several attachments, was testament to the significance of international exchanges. Attendance at the staff college in Quetta facilitated attachments with the Indian Army, including the 13th Lancers, 14th Sikhs and the 76th Battery, Royal Field Artillery, between 1912 and 1913. In December 1913, Blamey took part in battalion, brigade and inter-brigade exercises as part of his attachment to 4th Battalion King's Royal Rifles in Rawalpindi, and he later spent two months with the staff of the Kohat Brigade in the North-West Frontier Province during February and March 1914. He completed his attachments with the General Staff at Army Headquarters in Simla, which provided exposure to the work being undertaken to train and organise for war. Blamey's experiences in India were soon followed by attachments in Britain with the 4th Dragoon Guards beginning on 1 July 1914 and, from 22 July, with the staff of the Wessex (Territorial) Division.[73] Having arrived at Quetta as the only staff officer without regimental experience and been considered 'uneducated (in the military sense)', Blamey's experiences in India and Britain served him well for the extensive staff work requirements

---

69   See Mitchell A Yockelson, *Borrowed Soldiers: Americans Under British Command, 1918* (Norman: University of Oklahoma Press, 2008); John Monash, *The Australian Victories in France in 1918* (Collingwood: Black Inc., 2015), 238–39.
70   Garth Pratten, *Australian Battalion Commanders in the Second World War* (Port Melbourne: Cambridge University Press, 2009), 38, doi.org/10.1017/cbo9781139194686; John C Mitcham, *Race and Imperial Defence in the British World* (Cambridge: Cambridge University Press, 2016), 198.
71   Horner, *High Command*, 5.
72   Delaney, 'Army Apostles', 176.
73   David Horner, *Blamey: The Commander-In-Chief* (Sydney: Allen & Unwin, 1998), 20–24.

of the First World War.[74] Indeed, during the period when Blamey served as Major General Harold Walker's COS on the Western Front, the 1st Australian Division 'earned a reputation for solid staff work in a rapidly expanded army where competent staff work was in woefully short supply'.[75]

Blamey's openness to learning from international counterparts continued into and beyond the First World War.[76] Blamey served as a member of the directing staff at a significant War Office exercise in April 1923, which was especially useful as participation in British manoeuvres provided access to 'the type of professional experience that was not available to officers in Australia'.[77] Blamey learned much about operating alongside his British counterparts and forged enduring professional relationships during his periods on exchange.[78] Tellingly, when Blamey was appointed as the Commander of the 2nd AIF in the early stages of the Second World War, Sir Henry Gullett, External Affairs Minister, recognised the need for him to 'take his place with our Allied commanders', commenting: 'His military record and experience are good. He knows the English, and he is most intelligent.'[79]

Blamey's experiences not only stood him in good stead to cooperate with the British, but also to take a firm line when he considered plans or decisions not to be in Australian interests. Although he demonstrated a willingness to cooperate with the British while serving as Commander of the 2nd AIF in the Middle East, Brigadier Sydney Rowell, his COS, recorded that Blamey 'never ceased to make it clear that he owed his duty to his Government. He made it clear that the British could not simply order Australian units about as they liked'.[80] Following extensive service alongside the British, Blamey was 'sympathetic' to the position and requirements of General Sir Archibald Wavell, British Commander-in-Chief in the Middle East, but

---

74 Horner, *Blamey*, 21.
75 Robert C Stevenson, *To Win the Battle: The 1st Australian Division in the Great War 1914–1918* (Port Melbourne: Cambridge University Press, 2012), 5, doi.org/10.1017/CBO9781139524322.
76 For example, Blamey discussed the challenges presented by an assault at Pozières with the British 7 and 19 Divisions, who had previously conducted operations there prior to the attack by the 1st Australian Division. Robin Prior and Trevor Wilson, *The Somme* (New Haven: Yale University Press, 2005), 176.
77 Horner, *Blamey*, 69–70; Peter Dean, *The Architect of Victory: The Military Career of Lieutenant General Sir Frank Horton Berryman* (Cambridge: Cambridge University Press, 2011), 59, doi.org/10.1017/cbo9780511974991.
78 Horner, *Blamey*, 74.
79 Horner, *Blamey*, 129.
80 David Horner, 'Field Marshal Sir Thomas Blamey: Commander-in-Chief, Australian Military Forces', in *The Commanders: Australian Military Leadership in the Twentieth Century*, edited by David Horner (Sydney: George Allen & Unwin, 1984), 205, doi.org/10.4324/9781003119708-13.

that did not preclude fervent objections when it was deemed necessary to protect the integrity of Australian forces.[81] Blamey's subsequent dispute with Wavell's replacement, General Sir Claude Auchinleck, over the relief of Tobruk typified the tenacity with which Blamey defended Australian interests.[82] Although Blamey's educational and exchange experiences enhanced his ability to interoperate with the British, he retained a distinctive Australian outlook.

During the Vietnam War, personnel exchanges proved to be important in providing Australian and American forces with insight into their counterpart's culture and tactics, techniques, and procedures. The Radford-Collins Agreement created a platform for the exchange of staff officers in peacetime, but the RAN and the United States Navy (USN) still found it judicious to swap personnel for limited periods to promote mutual understanding during the conflict.[83] HMAS *Perth*, for example, exchanged personnel with USS *New Jersey* in October 1967 and USS *Newport News* in January 1968.[84] Similarly, 2 Squadron RAAF personnel and US forward air controllers (FACs) were exchanged for brief periods to generate an understanding of how each other operated and provide American personnel with experience of the Australian Canberra aircraft.[85]

The value of personnel exchanges was underscored by RAN operations in the Persian Gulf before and during the Iraq War, with several Australian officers benefiting from significant multinational experience. Commander Mark McIntosh, an RAN liaison officer with the USN, recorded: 'During my brief periods ashore in Bahrain and among my peers at sea, I was mixing with many RN officers, many of whom I had come across when serving in Flag Officer Sea Training Group in the UK several years earlier.'[86] A number of RAN officers had established professional relationships with their international counterparts, particularly from the RN, during reciprocal exchanges.[87] The then Captain Peter Jones, who served as the Maritime

---

81 Iain E Johnstone-White, *The British Commonwealth and Victory in the Second World War* (London: Palgrave Macmillan, 2016), 239.
82 Horner, 'Field Marshal Sir Thomas Blamey', 205.
83 Ian Pfennigwerth, *Tiger Territory: The Untold Story of the Royal Australian Navy from 1948 to 1971* (Sydney: Rosenberg, 2008), 25.
84 Steven Paget, *The Dynamics of Coalition Naval Warfare: The Special Relationship at Sea* (Abingdon: Routledge, 2017), 133, doi.org/10.4324/9781315552545.
85 Paget, 'Magpies and Eagles', 152.
86 Mark McIntosh, 'Reflections on Persian Gulf Naval Operations', *Australian Defence Force Journal* 184 (2011): 70.
87 Paget, *The Dynamics of Coalition Naval Warfare*, 222.

Interception Operations Screen Commander, worked closely with Rear Admiral David Snelson, Commander, UK Maritime Force and de facto maritime coalition deputy commander. Jones was familiar with the RN through completion of principal warfare officer training in Britain, while Snelson had a good understanding of the RAN as well as being acquainted with Australian personnel following a period on exchange with HMAS *Derwent* that began in 1980. The high level of interoperability between the RAN and RN was exemplified by the interchangeability of personnel and their ability to represent both Australian and British perspectives during planning meetings if officers were required to attend to national commitments.[88]

The opportunity to learn from the experience of other nations has also shaped force-restructuring decisions in Australia. One junior officer commented on the experiences of the Australian Army in 1980s: 'Exchange personnel were key. We had combat-experienced Americans and Brits here and we had Australians scooping up information and experience there. This was a matter of survival in our eyes as we were asking force structure questions.'[89] The subsequent employment of exchange officers as instructors on their return to Australia created a snowball effect that facilitated the dissemination of information to a wider audience, thereby enabling the Australian Army to keep 'abreast of tactical, technical and procedural developments in fellow ABCA [America Britain Canada Australia] partner armies'.[90]

The development of Australia's amphibious capability, centred on the two Canberra-class amphibious assault ships, HMA Ships *Adelaide* and *Canberra*, demonstrated the ongoing utility of exchange officers.[91] Cultural change to adapt to a maritime strategy was deemed an essential consideration in the development of amphibious capability, and while a thorough understanding of its 'historical roots' was advocated, the absence of institutional memory ensured that engagement with multinational counterparts, particularly from the UK and the US was also essential.[92] The ADF benefited from the input of an experienced US Marine Corps

---

88   Steven Paget, 'Mind over Matter? Multinational Naval Interoperability During Operation Iraqi Freedom', *Defense & Security Analysis* 36, no. 1 (2020): 78–79, doi.org/10.1080/14751798.2020.1712 025.
89   Blaxland, *The Australian Army*, 61.
90   Blaxland, *The Australian Army*, 61.
91   For more on Australia's amphibious capability and the potential to operate with the US, see Maren Leed, JD McCreary, George Flynn, Alvaro Genie, Jaimie Hoskins and Andrew Metrick, *Advancing U.S.-Australian Combined Amphibious Capabilities* (Lanham: Rowman & Littlefield, 2015).
92   Dean, 'Amphibious Warfare', 58, 73.

officer serving as 'Colonel, Amphibious'—the Deployable Joint Force Headquarters' amphibious capability development lead—and a Royal Marines colonel.[93] The exchange officers, in addition to lateral transfers from the RN and Royal Marines, aided the generation of an amphibious culture and promoted interoperability with both the UK and the US. Ultimately, Australia's experience has substantiated the conclusion of a RAND study on coalition operations: 'Training exchange tours and those involving personnel serving in organizations other than their own further serve as valuable preparation for later interorganization service.'[94]

Internationalised education

Attendance at overseas military educational establishments, and the involvement of international instructors in Australia, have been a vital subset of personnel exchanges in the formulation of multinational interoperability. Although originally born out of necessity, support for international learning opportunities has continued and been enhanced through the involvement of overseas personnel in Australian Professional Military Education (PME) institutions. The internationalisation of PME has helped to 'develop understanding and trust and offer a window into the culture and practices' of international armed forces.[95] As well as cultivating a multinational mindset, international educational exchanges also offer a means to develop both personal and professional networks that can be maintained both throughout and beyond military careers, which is particularly significant given that personnel selected to attend prestigious overseas PME institutions often progress to senior military and, sometimes, political roles.[96] Carol Atkinson determined, following an extensive study of educational exchanges, that 'professional military networks increase interoperability in times of war'.[97] The Australian experience, over more than a century, has validated that conclusion.

---

93   Steven Paget, 'Coming Full Circle: The Renaissance of Anzac Amphibiosity', *Naval War College Review* 70, no. 2 (2017): 117–18.
94   Russell W Glenn, *Band of Brothers or Dysfunctional Family? A Military Perspective on Coalition Challenges During Stability Operations* (Santa Monica: RAND Corporation, 2011), 102.
95   Paget, 'Mind over Matter?', 79.
96   Steven Paget, '"Interoperability of the Mind": Professional Military Education and the Development of Interoperability', *The RUSI Journal* 161, no. 4 (2016): 45, 47, doi.org/10.1080/03071847.2016.1224496.
97   Carol Atkinson, *Military Soft Power: Public Diplomacy Through Educational Exchanges* (Lanham: Rowman & Littlefield, 2014), 58.

8. THE FOUR PILLARS OF HUMAN INTEROPERABILITY

Following Barton's commitment to standardisation with the British Army in 1902, attendance at overseas staff colleges and training establishments was organised for Australian personnel.[98] A December 1908 War Office Memorandum explicitly instructed: '[E]ach self-governing dominion should arrange as soon as possible to prepare and send a suitable number of officers to undergo a Staff College Course at Camberley or Quetta.'[99] The posting of imperial officers to those staff colleges, in the UK and India (later Pakistan) respectively, was vital for the continuation and enhancement of standardisation across 'the Anglophone security network'.[100] The need for standardisation was shared by both the RN and, later, the Royal Air Force (RAF). When the Commonwealth Naval Forces became the RAN in July 1911, an agreement was reached that led to Australian sailors being trained by the RN.[101] A new scheme to enable the dominions to select personnel for training at RAF College Cranwell, and a subsequent four-year stint serving in the RAF, with the intention of enabling cooperation among the various air services was publicised at the 1923 Imperial Conference.[102]

The importance of standardisation efforts directed through educational exchanges was emphasised by the AIF command structure at the outset of the First World War. Although Major General William Bridges, the General Officer Commanding the AIF, has faced criticism for a predominantly imperial outlook that overshadowed Australian national interests, his British origins and Canadian military education may have been fundamental to his selection for the prestigious position.[103] Chris Coulthard-Clark went as far as to suggest that despite his tendency to place imperial interests above Australian national interests, Bridges 'contributed more to the achievement of a national identity for the AIF than is realised' as it is 'probable' that 'only because the first commander of the AIF bore a striking similarity to any other British general did the Australian division have a local officer at its

---

98 Horner, *Strategy and Command*, 35.
99 Horner, *Blamey*, 15.
100 Vipul Dutta, 'The "Indian" Staff College: Politics and Practices of Military Institution-Building in Twentieth Century India', *Journal of Strategic Studies* 42, no. 5 (2019): 612, doi.org/10.1080/01402390.2019.1570148.
101 Horner, *Strategy and Command*, 42.
102 Alex M Spencer, *British Imperial Air Power: The Royal Air Forces and the Defense of Australia and New Zealand Between the World Wars* (West Lafayette: Purdue University Press, 2020), 68–69.
103 Although Bridges did not graduate from the Canadian military academy in Kingston due to his relocation to Australia, he did leave with a Certificate of Military Qualifications. Chris Clark, 'Duntroon to the Dardanelles: Major-General Sir William Bridges', in *The Shadow Men: The Leaders Who Shaped the Australian Army from the Veldt to Vietnam*, edited by Craig Stockings and John Connor (Sydney: NewSouth, 2017), 41.

head when the troops went ashore at Gallipoli to give birth to the "Digger" tradition'.[104] Following the selection of Bridges to command the AIF and the 1st Infantry Division in 1914, he appointed Lieutenant Colonel Cyril Brudenell White, a Camberley graduate, as his COS, and formed his divisional staff around the limited number of staff college graduates.[105] That decision was significant, as graduates of those institutions 'formed the spine' of the British Expeditionary Force during the First World War.[106] Aimée Fox-Godden has noted the importance of 'connectedness', resulting from shared education and training as '[k]nowledge does not simply result from processes or activities; it comes from people and communities of people'.[107] Peter Stanley stated that White's attendance at the British Army Staff College at Camberley in 1906 provided him with 'entrée to a circle of rising and influential British officers, many of whom rose to senior commands in the Great War'.[108]

Education and training in the UK remained significant in the interwar period. Lieutenant General Sir Frank Horton Berryman explained of his time at Camberley:

> At the Staff College we were trained in a common school of thought. The advantage of this was that in war we had the same doctrine of tactics and administration, which was essential if we were to work together. More than that, the officers who had to carry out their duties in co-operation formations knew each other personally.[109]

As well as facilitating a collective mindset, multinational education was also invaluable from a networking perspective. Sir Sydney Rowell, who later served as both CGS and Chairman of the Chiefs of Staff Committee, wrote of his time at Camberley between 1925 and 1926: 'I lived and worked with many of the British and Indian officers with whom I was to deal with in two later tours of duty in the UK and Middle East during the

---

104 Chris Coulthard-Clark, 'Major-General Sir William Bridges: Australia's First Field Commander', in *The Commanders: Australian Military Leadership in the Twentieth Century*, edited by David Horner (Sydney: George Allen & Unwin, 1984), 21, doi.org/10.4324/9781003119708-3.
105 Horner, 'The AIF's Commanders', 62; Stevenson, *To Win the Battle*, 99.
106 Simon Robbins, *British Generalship on the Western Front 1914–1918: Defeat into Victory* (Abingdon: Routledge, 2005), 41.
107 Aimée Fox-Godden, 'Beyond the Western Front: The Practice of Inter-Theatre Learning in the British Army During the First World War', *War in History* 23, no. 2 (2016): 206, doi.org/10.1177/0968344514559873.
108 Peter Stanley, 'The Enigma: General Sir Cyril Brudenell Bingham White', in *The Shadow Men: The Leaders Who Shaped the Australian Army from the Veldt to Vietnam*, edited by Craig Stockings and John Connor (Sydney: NewSouth, 2017), 62.
109 Dean, *The Architect of Victory*, 57.

Second World War. Better to know one's associates in advance than learn their good and not so good points from bitter experience.'[110] The potential for international education to provide opportunities for interaction with future senior military leaders was demonstrated by the Australian officers that were sent overseas. The number of permanent officers sent for staff training increased from six prior to the First World War to 61 during the interwar years, with almost all participants returning to 'key command and staff appointments'.[111] The creation of the Imperial Defence College (IDC) in 1927, which provided education in a range of subjects to personnel from the British armed services and Civil Service, as well as a more limited number of dominion officers, exemplified the potential to interact with 'future leaders'.[112] Attendance at IDC was considered evidence that an Australian officer was being considered for senior rank in the future and fostered productive professional relationships that transcended national boundaries, which could be called upon to aid cohesion during the course of multinational operations.[113]

Douglas Delaney has contended that standardised education for imperial officers at the staff colleges was 'the investment that had the highest payoff, by far' in maintaining interoperability during the interwar years because it 'imparted a common language that allowed them to work together in war'.[114] Similarly, Horner pertinently observed that there was 'little wonder that during the Second World War Australian units were absorbed so smoothly into British formations'.[115] Conversely, the absence of shared experience with the Americans at military schools in the interwar years, and the use of different doctrine, meant that Australian military forces did not cooperate as easily on the battlefield with them as they did with the British.[116]

---

110 Horner, *High Command*, 5.
111 Douglas E Delaney, 'The Eighth Army at the Gothic Line, August–September 1944: A Study in Staff Compatibility and Coalition Command', *War in History* 27, no. 2 (2020): 300, doi.org/10.1177/0968344518776494.
112 Horner, *High Command*, 6.
113 Robert Stevenson, 'The Quiet Achiever: Lieutenant General Sir John Northcott', in *The Shadow Men: The Leaders Who Shaped the Australian Army from the Veldt to Vietnam*, edited by Craig Stockings and John Connor (Sydney: NewSouth, 2017), 123; Jeffrey Grey, *A Soldier's Soldier: A Biography of Lieutenant-General Sir Thomas Daly* (Port Melbourne: Cambridge University Press, 2012), 86, doi.org/10.1017/cbo9781107294240; Tristan Moss, 'Post-war Planner: Lieutenant General Sir Mervyn Brogan', in *The Shadow Men: The Leaders Who Shaped the Australian Army from the Veldt to Vietnam*, edited by Craig Stockings and John Connor (Sydney: NewSouth, 2017), 216.
114 Delaney, 'The Eighth Army at the Gothic Line', 300–01.
115 Horner, *High Command*, 6, 8.
116 Horner, *Strategy and Command*, 229.

As well as sending personnel overseas, interoperability with British and dominion personnel was enhanced through the hosting of international instructional staff in Australia. In addition to the imperial loan officer instructors at Duntroon prior to the First World War, a request was also made to the War Office to support the establishment of the Department of Military Studies at the University of Sydney by dispatching an officer to serve as the Director of Military Studies. Notably, the military courses delivered at the University of Sydney had received support from George Kirkpatrick during an earlier visit to Australia, prior to him serving as Inspector General of the AMF between 1910 and 1914 as an imperial loan officer.[117] British influence and leadership over the department helped to promote interoperability during the First World War by inculcating Australian officers in British doctrine, mindset and procedures.[118] General Sir John Monash, who attended two courses at the Department of Military Studies in 1909 and 1911, praised the crucial preparation that they afforded for operations and staff work in the First World War.[119]

The foundations for cooperation created by internationalised education did not mean that Australian commanders acceded to their British counterparts when they felt the situation warranted opposition, as Blamey demonstrated in the Middle East. While First World War commanders such Henry Chauvel have been criticised for being too accommodating of the British, it could be considered that his actions were a reflection of an Army that had not yet 'come of age'.[120] International exchanges and involvement in overseas education enhanced the potential to cooperate with multinational counterparts, but they did not necessarily lead to an assimilation of perspective. For example, as a result of knowledge of the strategic and political situation garnered through two years attached to the British Army in the First World War and a collective three years at both Staff College at Camberley, and, later, the IDC, John Lavarack felt compelled to forthrightly

---

117 John Connor, 'Australian Military Education, 1901–18', in *Military Education and the British Empire, 1815–1949,* edited by Douglas E Delaney, Robert C Engen and Meghan Fitzpatrick (Vancouver: UBC Press, 2018), 72.
118 William Westerman, 'More than a Mere Footnote: The Department of Military Studies, University of Sydney, 1907–1915', *History of Education* 49, no. 1 (2020): 63, 75, doi.org/10.1080/0046760x.2019.1657507.
119 Peter Pedersen, *Monash as Military Commander* (Newport: Big Sky Publishing, 2018), 50–52.
120 AJ Hill, 'General Sir Harry Chauvel: Australia's First Corps Commander', in *The Commanders: Australian Military Leadership in the Twentieth Century,* edited by David Horner (Sydney: George Allen & Unwin, 1984), 84, doi.org/10.4324/9781003119708-6.

oppose the Singapore Strategy.[121] Lavarack's position demonstrated that while international education can facilitate interoperability, it does not compromise independence of thought and the maintenance of outlooks grounded in national interest.

While there was a clear emphasis on sending Australian personnel overseas in the decades after Federation, Australia also hosted international personnel for education and training, a trend that has increased over time. New Zealand, for example, dispatched candidates to Duntroon for officer training from the time of its establishment and, after 1932, sent naval ratings for training at RAN facilities.[122] Those measures, while limited in nature, helped to provide a platform for later military cooperation between the two nations.

More recent and contemporary operations have also highlighted the benefits of working relationships developed through cross-cultural engagement during educational exchanges. Commodore Don Chalmers' command of Task Group 627.4, which conducted maritime interception operations in the Gulf of Oman between 3 September and 3 December 1990, was aided by his previous experience of international engagement. Chalmers had not only worked alongside Rear Admiral Jerry Unruh, commander of the *Independence* battlegroup and coordinator of sanction operations in the northern Arabian Sea and Gulf of Oman, during the Rim of the Pacific Exercise (RIMPAC), he also benefited from existing relationships with a variety of international personnel through his time at both the Royal College of Defence Studies (RCDS) in the UK and the USNWC.[123] Chalmers was acquainted with various USN staff officers and knew the chief of the Royal Omani Navy from his time at RCDS, which paid dividends when he was able to achieve a relaxation of the restriction on contacts being pursued in Omani territorial waters.[124]

---

121 AB Lodge, 'Lieutenant-General Sir John Lavarack: From Chief of the General Staff to Corps Commander', in *The Commanders: Australian Military Leadership in the Twentieth Century*, edited by David Horner (Sydney: George Allen & Unwin, 1984), 133–34, doi.org/10.4324/9781003119708-9.
122 It is worth mentioning that 10 out of the first 41 cadets at Duntroon were New Zealanders. Daniel Leach, 'Trans-Tasman Liaison: Australasian Defence Coordination and the New Zealand Military Liaison Offices in Australia, 1932–48', *The Journal of Imperial and Commonwealth History* 50, no. 2 (2022): 388, doi.org/10.1080/03086534.2021.2020408.
123 RCDS is a successor to IDC.
124 David Horner, *Australia and the New World Order: From Peacekeeping to Peace Enforcement: 1988–1991*, vol. II of The Official History of Australian Peacekeeping, Humanitarian and Post–Cold War Operations (Port Melbourne: Cambridge University Press, 2011), 367.

The extensive and diverse international experience generated through international PME has both imbued Australian personnel with different perspectives on operations and formed the bedrock of effective working relationships. John Blaxland has assessed that 'the cross-pollination of American and British experiences and approaches, facilitated by Australian officers being trained in US and UK military schools and sent on exchange postings, helped create a remarkably professional Army, despite the comparatively limited funding expended on the Army in Australia'.[125]

The role of international PME in enhancing interoperability is just as relevant for coalition leaders as junior partners, as participants can obtain an 'indication of the viewpoints, skills and limitations' of potential coalition participants.[126] The then Major General Peter Cosgrove's command of INTERFET from September 1999 until February 2000 was facilitated, in part, through his experiences as a student at the Indian National Defence College and the US Marine Command and Staff College, as well as an instructor at both the Australian Joint Services Staff College (JSSC) and the British Army Staff College, which provided him with a detailed understanding of the current 'operational thinking' in those countries.[127] Ash Power, who served as Colonel Operations INTERFET, found it valuable that six of the staff in the headquarters of Major General Songkitti Jaggabatara, deputy INTERFET commander, had been his classmates at the Royal Thai Army Staff College.[128] Although educational exchanges have sometimes been viewed solely through the lens of defence diplomacy, the potential to enhance procedural and especially human interoperability have been demonstrated repeatedly.

While pre-emptive measures were vital in promoting interoperability, it has also been forged through Australia's participation in wartime educational and training exigencies. The establishment of the Joint Overseas Operational Training School (JOOTS), a combined Australian–US initiative to develop multinational amphibious capability during the Second World War, highlighted the need for cooperative education and training.[129] Equally, although very much a US Air Force (USAF) initiative, briefings given to

---

125 Blaxland, *The Australian Army*, 12.
126 Steven Paget, '"A Truly Global Approach": Opportunities for Increased Internationalisation in Professional Military Education', *Canadian Military Journal* 20, no. 1 (2019): 27.
127 JR Ballard, 'Mastering Coalition Command in Modern Peace Operations: Operations "Stabilise" in East Timor', *Small Wars and Insurgencies* 13, no. 1 (2002): 88, doi.org/10.1080/714005413.
128 Power, 'Managing INTERFET and Regional Multinational Coalitions', 105.
129 For more on JOOTS, see Peter J Dean, 'Amphibious Warfare: Lessons from the Past for the ADF's Future', *Security Challenges* 8, no. 1 (2012): 57–76.

FACs by 2 Squadron, RAAF, personnel at the 504th Theater Indoctrination School—better known as FAC University—in Phan Rang during the Vietnam War addressed an urgent operational need by ensuring that an understanding of the capabilities of the Canberra aircraft and Australian tactics, techniques and procedures was maintained by American personnel as they rotated in and out of theatre.[130]

Multinational exercises

Military exercises have long been recognised as an opportunity to develop and enhance interoperability between multinational forces.[131] Indeed, Michael Smith deemed that collective training is 'the "centre of gravity" for successful coalition operations'.[132] Multinational military exercises enhance procedural interoperability by 'exchanging shared techniques, ideas, and practices in simulated operations' and in helping to 'identify gaps' that can be rectified through amendments to doctrine and tactics, techniques and procedures.[133] Where incompatibilities remain, they can at least be factored into planning and mitigated to the greatest extent possible. Human interoperability can also be enhanced as exercises 'help to break down barriers and build bridges' and provide participants with an opportunity to obtain 'a better understanding of the attitude, culture, and values' of their international colleagues.[134] Such exercises also offer a platform for networking and the formulation of professional associations, which can 'provide means for overcoming obstacles otherwise likely to hinder operational effectiveness'.[135]

The value of multinational exercises in enhancing procedural interoperability was illustrated during the Iraq War. The RAAF's successful integration with both the USAF and the RAF was a reflection of the experience accumulated

---

130 Paget, 'Magpies and Eagles', 152.
131 Frega Wenas Inkiriwang, 'Multilateral Naval Exercise Komodo: Enhancing Indonesia's Multilateral Defence Diplomacy?', *Journal of Current Southeast Asian Affairs* 40, no. 3 (2021), 420, doi.org/10.1177/ 18681034211008905; Danylo Kubai, 'Military Exercises as a Part of NATO Deterrence Strategy', *Comparative Strategy* 41, no. 2 (2022): 155, doi.org/10.1080/01495933.2022.2039009.
132 Michael Smith, 'Doctrine and Training: The Foundation of Effective Coalition Operations', in *Problems and Solutions in Future Coalition Operations*, edited by Thomas Marshall, Philip Kaiser and Jon Kessimer (Carlisle: Strategic Studies Institute, 1997), 69.
133 Frazier and Hutto, 'The Socialization of Military Power', 387.
134 Steven Paget, 'Multinational Air Power: The Outlook', in *Allies in Air Power: A History of Multinational Air Operations*, edited by Steven Paget (Lexington: The University Press of Kentucky, 2021), 284, doi.org/10.2307/j.ctv190k9zf.15.
135 Glenn, *Band of Brothers or Dysfunctional Family?*, 33.

during multinational exercises and operations.[136] The RAAF had engaged in a range of multinational exercises over the proceeding decades, but the USAF's Red Flag exercises were especially useful in enabling integration by generating greater mutual understanding of tactics, techniques and procedures, as well as facilitating international working relationships.[137] The exercises provided long-term engagement with the USAF in realistic scenarios, as well as a range of international air forces, including the RAF.[138] The inauguration of the Coalition Flag Exercise, consisting of Australian, UK and US air forces, at Nellis Air Force Base in January 2006 was both a testament to the value of multinational exercises and a recognition of the importance of sustaining interoperability between likely coalition partners.[139]

As well as extensive experience accumulated through sustained involvement in the Red Sea and Persian Gulf, interoperability between the RAN, the RN and the USN, was underpinned by a track record of participating in multinational exercises.[140] Involvement in RIMPAC exercises has provided the RAN with regular interaction with both the USN and (since 1986) the RN and was considered necessary to enable integration into a multinational task force in the event of operations.[141] Although RIMPAC is often regarded as the foremost maritime exercise, Australia's participation in an extensive series of bilateral and multilateral activities, including Five Power Defence Arrangements initiatives and Talisman Sabre, has enabled the honing of procedural interoperability.[142] In the case of naval gunfire support, for example, RAN participation in the NATO Joint Warrior exercise off Cape Wrath in Scotland afforded an opportunity for Australian ships to work with spotters from other countries, thereby refining the use of standardised procedures and enabling interaction with likely coalition partners.[143] The Commander, Task Force 55, then Rear Admiral Barry Costello (USN),

---

136 Benjamin Lambeth, 'Operation Iraqi Freedom: The Allied Contribution', in *Allies in Air Power: A History of Multinational Air Operations*, edited by Steven Paget (Lexington: The University Press of Kentucky, 2021), 245, doi.org/10.2307/j.ctv190k9zf.13.
137 Benjamin Lambeth, *The Unseen War: Allied Air Power and the Takedown of Saddam Hussein* (Annapolis: Naval Institute Press, 2013), 149.
138 For more on the Red Flag exercises, see Brian D Laslie, *The Air Force Way of War: U.S. Tactics and Training after Vietnam* (Lexington: The University Press of Kentucky, 2015), doi.org/10.5810/kentucky/9780813160597.001.0001.
139 Lambeth, *The Unseen War*, 177.
140 Geoffrey Till, 'Trafalgar and the Decisive Naval Battles of the 21st Century', *Cambridge Review of International Affairs* 18, no. 3 (2005): 466, doi.org/10.1080/09557570500238100.
141 Horner, *Australia and the New World Order*, 33.
142 Paget, 'Mind over Matter?', 75–76.
143 Paget, *The Dynamics of Coalition Naval Warfare*, 221.

concluded that participation by key coalition participants in multinational exercises and training reaped 'significant dividends' during the conduct of operations due to the familiarity that existed among the navies.[144]

The capacity for procedural and human interoperability to be strengthened during exercises was further exhibited by the multinational participants in INTERFET. Cosgrove and his staff benefited from participating in Exercise Rainbow Serpent, a command post exercise in November 1998, which afforded access to staff officers from Canada, New Zealand, the UK and the US. Significantly, the exercise rehearsed the deployment of a multinational force for peace enforcement operations in a fictional country.[145] The exercise 'helped to ensure that techniques and procedures were well understood and practised in advance'.[146] Furthermore, John Blaxland, the principal intelligence staff officer in Headquarters 3rd Brigade, had participated in a command post exercise at the Royal Thai Army Command and Staff College in 1997, which involved a combined Association of Southeast Asian Nations and allied forces conducting a fictional coalition military operation. When INTERFET was formed, most participants from that exercise were involved, including officers from Japan, Malaysia, the Philippines, the Republic of Korea, Singapore and the US. Blaxland, furthermore, interacted with a number of his Thai classmates who were serving with INTERFET in Dili.[147] Equally, the infantry battalion from the Royal Thai Army that participated in INTERFET was the same one that exercised with a 2 RAR company during Exercise Chapel Gold in July 1999.[148] The New Zealand Army regiment deployed for INTERFET also profited from having exercised with Australia's 3rd Brigade in northern Australia two years before the operation.[149] In reflecting on INTERFET, Power concluded that it is 'important' for likely multinational partners to 'train and exercise together, and establish personal links'.[150]

---

144 Barry Costello, *Fortune Favors Boldness: The Story of Naval Valor During Operation Iraqi Freedom* (Jacksonville: Fortis, 2019), 91.
145 Horner, *Strategy and Command*, 252.
146 John C Blaxland, *Strategic Cousins: Australian and Canadian Expeditionary Forces and the British and American Empires* (Montréal: McGill-Queen's University Press, 2006), 189, doi.org/10.1515/9780773576940.
147 John Blaxland, 'Introduction: Marking Fifteen Years on for INTERFET', in *East Timor Intervention: A Retrospective on INTERFET*, edited by John Blaxland (Melbourne: MUP Academic Digital, 2015), 13.
148 Blaxland, *The Australian Army*, 135.
149 Blaxland, *The Australian Army*, 157.
150 Power, 'Managing INTERFET and Regional Multinational Coalitions', 106.

Conclusion

While Charles Bean has often been lauded for his focus on 'the wartime achievements of the Australian infantry soldier' in the Official Histories of the First World War, scholars have increasingly emphasised that Australia's military experience must be considered within a multinational environment.[151] Despite being best known as an Australian military historian, Horner has expertly interlaced the national experience, from Federation to the contemporary period, into its multilateral context. Given recent calls for scholars and practitioners to obtain a 'better understanding' of 'the practicalities of military integration', the Australian experience is particularly pertinent.[152] Indeed, Australia's expeditionary way of war has ensured that effective integration with multinational partners has been of paramount importance. Interoperability is perishable and can diminish over time, but Australia's extensive history of multinational operations, punctuated by defence engagement in peacetime, has underpinned the ability of the nation's armed forces to integrate with international counterparts.

There can be no doubting the significance of equipment interoperability and standardised doctrine and procedures in enabling Australia's relatively smooth integration in multinational military formations. Human interoperability, however, has been the glue that has held together the relationship between Australia's armed forces and their closest multinational partners. Among other factors, the four 'Es'—experience, education, exchanges and exercises—have been pivotal in fostering multinational integration. The ADF (and its antecedents) is a seasoned contributor to multinational military operations alongside the UK and the US. Cumulative experience, built over more than a century of multinational operations, has enabled lessons to be learned that have eased integration and mitigated friction. Enduring relationships of both a personal and an institutional nature have been forged, solidified and recalled during operations. Regular involvement in multinational operations has not only eased Australia's assimilation as a junior partner but has also provided the foundation for a coalition leadership role in the case of INTERFET.

---

151 John Connor, 'The Empire's War Recalled: Recent Writing on the Western Front Experience of Britain, Ireland, Australia, Canada, India, New Zealand, South Africa and the West Indies', *History Compass* 7, no. 4 (2009): 1125, doi.org/10.1111/j.1478-0542.2009.00616.x.
152 Olivier Schmitt, 'More Allies, Weaker Missions? How Junior Partners Contribute to Multinational Military Operations', *Contemporary Security Policy* 40, no. 1 (2019): 81, doi.org/10.1080/13523260.2018.1501999.

While that experience has been fundamental to the high level of interoperability achieved with key coalition partners such as the UK and the US, it has been enhanced, as well as sustained in times of peace, through extensive defence cooperation and engagement activities. Internationalised education, from attempts to standardise the dominion armies through shared education and training at Camberley or Quetta staff colleges to modern reciprocal educational exchanges, as well as broader personnel exchanges, have not only helped to promote procedural interoperability but have also cultivated shared understanding and respect across national boundaries and forged strong professional working relationships that have underpinned human interoperability during subsequent operations.[153] Similarly, exercises have provided an opportunity for multinational forces to 'gain further understanding of each other's values, experiences and practices'.[154] Australian forces have been able to enhance procedural interoperability by rehearsing realistic scenarios with likely multinational partners and form close and productive working relationships with their international counterparts.

Given the qualitative nature of human interoperability, it has been considered virtually impossible to quantify precisely the benefits that accrue from participation in multinational activities, but the 'genuine utility of face-to-face interaction and the establishment of personal bonds of friendship and trust' has been evidenced by the Australian experience.[155] The potential for internationalised PME, personnel exchanges and multinational exercises to enhance interoperability has proven to be timeless and to transcend service boundaries. Indeed, the foundation for interoperability during multinational operations has been laid by extensive pre-emptive engagement. Whether through defence cooperation and engagement or being deployed on multinational operations, Australia has garnered a reputation for 'trustworthy mateship and reliable partnership' through an enduring commitment to international military cooperation.[156]

---

153 Steven Paget, 'Harvesting the Rewards of Multinational Cooperation: The Royal Air Force's Project Seedcorn', *Air & Space Power Journal* 35, no. 2 (2021): 92.
154 Maria E Burczynska, 'Multinational Cooperation: Building Capabilities in Small Air Forces', *European Security* 28, no. 1 (2019): 99, doi.org/10.1080/09662839.2019.1584102.
155 Blaxland, *The Australian Army*, 305.
156 Christopher Hubbard, *Australian and US Military Cooperation: Fighting Common Enemies* (Aldershot: Ashgate, 2005), 134.

—

9

'Everybody doing their thing': coalition warfare in southern Afghanistan, 2006–10

Rhys Crawley and Garth Pratten

When American General Stanley McChrystal assumed command of NATO's International Security Assistance Force in 2009, each of his five subordinate regional commands across Afghanistan was 'fighting completely different wars'.[1] This was especially the case in the largest, Regional Command South (RC South), where command rotated between the UK, Canada and the Netherlands, and where provincial efforts—in Helmand, Kandahar, Uruzgan and Zabul—were often conducted without cooperation or cohesion and along national lines.[2] There 'wasn't a unified effort in the south', said one of the International Security Assistance Force's earlier commanders, American General Dan McNeill, who characterised the situation as 'everybody doing their thing'.[3] Different nations had different priorities, approaches, constraints and appetites for casualties. Missions varied, as did the resources allocated to prosecute them. Inconsistent operational tour durations and carefully crafted caveats made the task of exercising command and control even more challenging.

---

1 Stanley McChrystal, interview with Rhys Crawley, 2018.
2 While Daykundi and Nimroz Provinces were formally part of RC South, there were no coalition forces in either province.
3 Daniel McNeill, interview as part of the Combat Studies Institute Oral History Program, 2009.

Unlike the vast majority of David Horner's work, this chapter is not an Australian-centred story. Australia was just one among many nations contributing troops to RC South. Although, as this chapter will show, its role was considered important by its allies, Australia's contribution was not the largest and its voice not the most influential. The chapter adopts a multinational view, which is still rare in much of the literature about the war in Afghanistan. An examination of RC South between mid-2006, when the International Security Assistance Force (ISAF) assumed responsibility for southern Afghanistan, and mid-2010, when its provinces were split to form two separate commands, constitutes a case study in the complexities of coalition warfare.

The approach of this chapter, however, is still very much in harmony with the themes and approach of Horner's work, despite its lack of an Australian focus. A holistic examination of the assembly, functioning and effectiveness of RC South provides the international context to Australia's involvement, an aspect of Horner's work that dates back to *High Command* and which he continued in titles such as his biography of General John Wilton, *Strategic Command*.[4] Furthermore, many of the issues that Horner highlighted about Australia's place as a smaller nation operating in a coalition feature in the analysis that follows, including: balancing national policy aims—among them, domestic visibility—with coalition objectives; maintaining credibility and influence with a smaller force; and the role of the United States (US) as a unifying influence and provider of critical enablers.

Based on interviews, correspondence and a growing body of literature on national experiences of the war in Afghanistan, this chapter is heavily influenced by David Horner's approach—as is to be expected from two authors gratefully mentored by him. Rhys Crawley, to whom Horner gave his first full-time job, has recalled how Horner patiently explained everything from split infinitives and organising archival documents in lever arch files to interview techniques and the particular requirements of writing Official Histories. As Horner explained to Rhys, the role of the historian is to bring order to chaos and make the complex seem simple, advice particularly applicable to the mishmash of national approaches, caveats and capabilities that determined the effectiveness of RC South for much of the first three years of its existence. Our argument is that the experience of

---

4   David M Horner, *High Command: Australia's Struggle for an Independent War Strategy, 1939–1945* (Sydney: Allen & Unwin, 1992), doi.org/10.4324/9781003120193; *Strategic Command: General Sir John Wilton and Australia's Asian Wars* (Melbourne: Oxford University Press, 2005).

war in southern Afghanistan presents a case study of how not to prosecute coalition operations, and that it took the development of a campaign mindset in 2009–10, as well as the resources and leadership of the US, to create order from RC South's chaos.

Forming RC South

ISAF was a product of the Bonn Agreement signed on 5 December 2001 to guide the rebuilding of the Afghan state following the toppling of the Taliban government by the US-led Operation Enduring Freedom (OEF). While the agreement recognised that 'the responsibility for providing security and law and order' resided 'with the Afghans themselves', it called upon the international community to assist with creating new indigenous security forces and for a United Nations–mandated force to be established to maintain security in Kabul and its surrounds in the interim. It was envisaged that 'such a force could, as appropriate, be progressively expanded to other urban centres and other areas'.[5]

ISAF was on the ground in Kabul by the end of December 2001, restricted by its UN Security Council mandate to Kabul and operating under separate command to OEF; British efforts to have ISAF placed under the command of the US's Central Command had been blocked by other contributors.[6] There was initially little international appetite for ISAF to expand to the rest of the country, although it was supported by many Afghans.[7] By 2003, however, accelerating aid to Afghanistan beyond Kabul was seen as a way of extending governance and bringing stability. Furthermore, the US had assembled another coalition to invade Iraq, which not only placed another heavy demand on its armed forces but caused a rift with several allies inside NATO, such as France and Germany. NATO's assumption of command of ISAF in April 2003, and its subsequent decision to expand beyond Kabul (Map 9.1), has thus been described both as it seeking to remain relevant and mending relationships within the alliance by sharing the burden in Afghanistan.[8]

---

5 'Agreement on Provisional Arrangements in Afghanistan Pending the Re-Establishment of Permanent Government Institutions', Annex 1, United Nations, S/2001/1154 (5 December 2001).
6 UN Security Council, Resolution 1386, S/RES/1386 (20 December 2001); Theo Farrell, *Unwinnable: Britain's War in Afghanistan 2001–2014* (London: The Bodley Head, 2017), 96.
7 Farrell, *Unwinnable*, 99–100, 136.
8 Farrell, *Unwinnable*, 137–39; Michael Clarke, 'The Helmand Decision', in *The Afghan Papers: Committing Britain to War in Helmand, 2005–06*, edited by Michael Clarke (Abingdon: Routledge, 2011), 11, doi.org/10.4324/9780203096284; Sten Rynning, *NATO in Afghanistan: The Liberal Disconnect* (Stanford: Stanford University Press, 2012), 46, doi.org/10.1515/9780804784948.

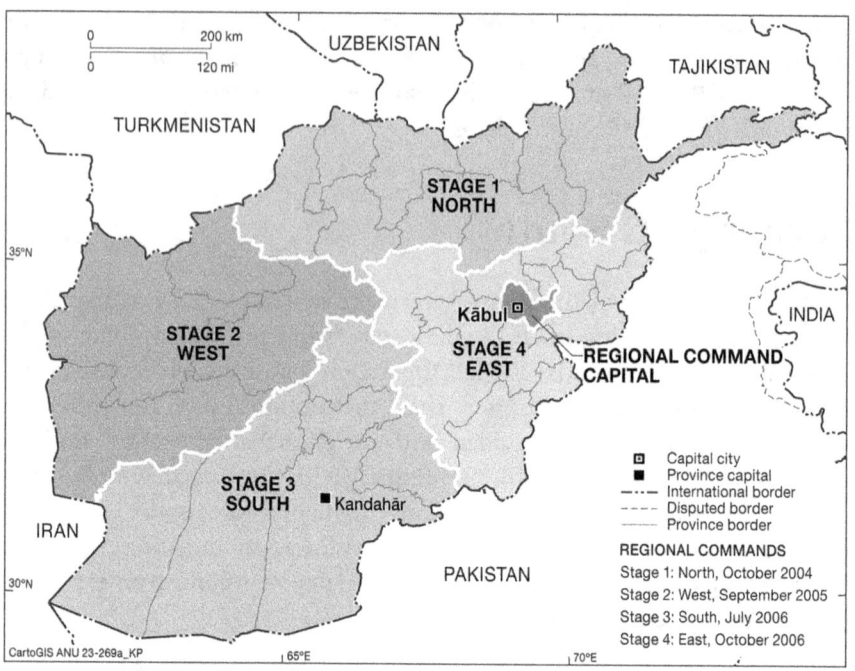

Map 9.1: ISAF expansion, 2003–06

NATO's plans, endorsed by a new UN Security Council mandate, involved the progressive expansion of ISAF between 2004 and 2006 into five regional commands, moving counterclockwise around the country from north to east.⁹ The principal means of aid delivery and assisting the reestablishment of governance were to be civil–military Provincial Reconstruction Teams (PRTs) supported by security forces.¹⁰ While the immediate concern for NATO was to elicit national contributions and allocate areas of responsibility, the move was underpinned by two interrelated imperatives: the first to demonstrate NATO's credibility as a functional military alliance and global actor, and the second to keep the US engaged despite its travails in Iraq. Stabilising the whole of Afghanistan would require US troops, but to trigger an increased deployment, its NATO allies would need to make significant commitments of their own.

---

9   UN Security Council, Resolution 1510, The Situation in Afghanistan, S/RES/1510 (13 October 2003); Steve Bowman and Catherine Dale, *War in Afghanistan: Strategy, Military Operations, and Issues for Congress*, CRS Report for Congress R40156, at 13–14 (3 December 2009).
10 Rynning, *NATO in Afghanistan*, 49. For the background to the PRT concept see Farrell, *Unwinnable*, 132–36.

The process involved much diplomatic horsetrading and highlighted a divide among NATO nations that would continue to blight relationships within the coalition. The further plans moved around the clock face, the fewer volunteers came forward. In particular, many NATO stalwarts refused to consider deployment in southern Afghanistan, where American forces still operated as part of OEF, and where regular combat was guaranteed, as the OEF combat mission was regarded as incompatible with ISAF's reconstruction agenda. Ironically, some NATO members were also concerned that a quick expansion into the south would result in a rapid US withdrawal, thereby depriving ISAF of key enablers such as fixed and rotary wing aircraft, along with intelligence, surveillance and reconnaissance (ISR) platforms.[11]

The south and, in particular, the province of Kandahar, however, could not be avoided. Kandahar, and Kandahar City within it, was, and remains, the key to southern Afghanistan. Kandahar is the heartland of the Pashtun people, who have dominated Afghan politics for hundreds of years, and was the birthplace of the Taliban. Kandahar City, which was the Taliban capital until its flight in the face of coalition offensive operations in December 2001, is the second-largest city in Afghanistan. In 2009 it was estimated to have a population of close to 1 million due to displacement of people from the surrounding insurgency-wracked districts.[12]

Kandahar City stands at the western end of the historical trade route to Quetta in Pakistan, where, in 2003, the surviving members of the Taliban government established a council of leaders—known as the Quetta Shura—that directed the infiltration of fighters back into Afghanistan. Their mission was to reassert Taliban influence by exploiting intertribal rivalry, popular discontent with the predatory rule of local warlords-cum-government officials, and perceived excesses of coalition troops.[13] From Kandahar City, by road, it is just 238 kilometres to Quetta; Kabul is 496 kilometres away. For a multinational effort committed to bringing about a stable, unified Afghanistan ruled from

---

11   Janet Gross Stein and Eugene Lang, *The Unexpected War: Canada in Kandahar* (Toronto: Penguin Canada, 2007), 202–03; Clarke, 'The Helmand Decision', 11–12, 13; Matthew Willis, 'Canada in Regional Command South: Alliance Dynamics and National Imperatives', in *The Afghan Papers: Committing Britain to War in Helmand, 2005–06*, edited by Michael Clarke (Abingdon: Routledge, 2011), 53.
12   Carl Forsberg, *Afghanistan Report 3: The Taliban's Campaign for Kandahar* (Washington, DC: Institute for the Study of War, December 2009), 12, www.understandingwar.org/report/talibans-campaign-kandahar.
13   Theo Farrell and Antonio Giustozzi, 'The Taliban at War: Inside the Helmand Insurgency, 2004–2012', *International Affairs* 89, no. 4 (July 2013): 845–71, doi.org/10.1111/1468-2346.12048; Farrell, *Unwinnable*, 164. A more fulsome discussion of Taliban strategy can be found in Antonio Giustozzi, *Koran, Kalashnikov and Laptop: The Neo-Taliban Insurgency in Afghanistan* (London: Hurst and Company, 2007), 97–139.

Kabul, Kandahar was vital ground. Furthermore, with a large coalition base already established at Kandahar International Airport (Kandahar Airfield), the province provided a secure point of entry and logistics hub.

Aware of both the south's significance and their allies' reluctance to go there, key proponents of ISAF's expansion such as the UK and Canada realised that they would need to lead the way. The laydown of what became known as RC South (Map 9.2) was determined in bi-, tri- and eventually multilateral discussions through 2004 and 2005, and was shaped by interlocking political and military imperatives. The UK, which had long sought more extensive Canadian involvement in NATO, first engaged Canada in early 2004. It initially envisaged Kandahar as the destination for its troops but rapidly conceded the province when it became apparent that the Canadians also favoured a deployment there. The UK instead sidestepped west to Helmand.[14] The key feature of Helmand is the river of the same name, which irrigates a green zone once described as a potential breadbasket for Afghanistan.[15] In 2005, its main crop, however, was opium poppy, which accounted for 25 per cent of nationwide production. At the 2001 Bonn Conference, convened by the UN to manage Afghanistan's transition to a post-Taliban government, the UK had been appointed as the counter-narcotics lead, and it has been suggested that this played a role in the UK's decision to focus its efforts on Helmand.[16]

Canada, seeking to keep faith with the US after declining to participate in its proposed ballistic missile defence program, was seeking a prominent continuing role in Afghanistan.[17] It offered NATO a PRT in late 2003 but subsequently passed up two opportunities to deploy the PRT as part of Stage II of ISAF's expansion into western Afghanistan. In the first instance, Canada was suspicious of a proposed partnership with the Italians in Herat, and, in the second, dissatisfied with the likely obscurity of a base in the central Afghanistan town of Chaghcharan. Furthermore, Canada's army already knew Kandahar, having operated in the province in 2002 as part of OEF, and elements of its leadership favoured a robust role in order to reorient from a peacekeeping-centric outlook.[18]

---

14 Matthew Willis, 'An Unexpected War, a Not-Unexpected Mission: The Origins of Kandahar 2005', *International Journal: Canada's Journal of Global Policy Analysis* 67, no. 4 (Autumn 2012): 994, doi.org/10.1177/002070201206700408; Michael Clarke, 'The Helmand Decision', 15–16.
15 Institute for the Study of War, 'Regional Command South', www.understandingwar.org/region/regional-command-south-0.
16 Willis, 'An Unexpected War', 994.
17 Gross Stein and Lang, *The Unexpected War,* 181–84.
18 Willis, 'An Unexpected War', 988, 992, 997; Willis, 'Canada in Regional Command South', 54–55.

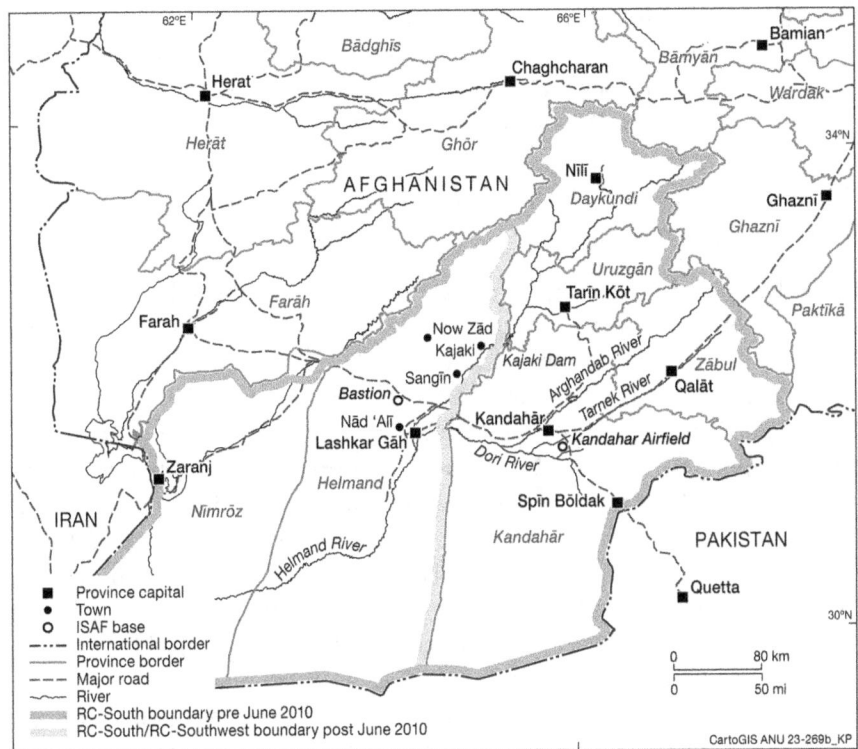

Map 9.2: Regional Command South, 2006–10

The Netherlands, also already engaged in Afghanistan, had been eyeing a move into the southern provinces for some time, for reasons similar to those of Canada. Like Canada, the Dutch military preferred Kandahar because of its base, airfield and their own familiarity with the province.[19] By the time it engaged in conversations with the UK, however, a deal had already been stitched up with Canada for Kandahar; Uruzgan, in which a like-minded partner was considered essential due to the access the province provided to its southern neighbours, was offered in its stead.[20] Nervous about routes into Uruzgan from the east, the Dutch campaigned unsuccessfully for a strong US presence in Zabul, which would eventually see the deployment

---

19 Lenny Hazelbag, 'Political Decision Making of the Mission in Uruzgan, a Reconstruction', in *Netherlands Annual Review of Military Studies, 2009: Complex Operations: Studies on Lebanon (2006) and Afghanistan (2006–present)*, edited by Michiel De Weger, Frans Osingan and Harry Kirkels (Breda: Netherlands Defense Academy, 2009), 251–76.

20 The Dutch also considered the southern provinces of Daykundi and Nimruz but ultimately settled on Uruzgan. See Mirjam Grandia, 'Deadly Embrace: The Decision Paths to Uruzgan and Helmand' (PhD thesis, Leiden University, 2015), 116–25; Clarke, 'The Helmand Decision', 15.

of a Romanian battlegroup and a continuation of the American PRT in Qalat.[21] Meeting independently of NATO, the UK, Canada and the Netherlands hammered out the force laydown of RC South before ISAF's Phase II expansion—RC West—was complete. Command would rotate between the three nations, with Canada taking the first turn, replicating their shared command of Multi-National Division (South-West) in Bosnia between 2000 and 2002.[22]

Each of these nations, along with NATO's Dutch Secretary-General, Jaap de Hoop Scheffer, lobbied vigorously for Australian involvement in southern Afghanistan. The Dutch wanted and needed the Australians. The UK's original hope was for an Australian contribution to Helmand, and the Canadians were happy to have the Australians in Kandahar, but once it became apparent that the Netherlands' contribution would not happen without a credible partner in Uruzgan, Australia was willingly manoeuvred into filling this role.[23] In August 2005, Australia deployed a special forces task group to Uruzgan for 12 months as part of OEF. When announcing this commitment, the Australian Government acknowledged that it was also looking at the possibility of contributing to an ISAF-led PRT. This duly occurred in August 2006, when an engineer-heavy reconstruction task force deployed as part of the Dutch-led Task Force Uruzgan. Evolving through multiple reconstruction, mentoring, advisory and combat roles, Australia remained in Uruzgan until December 2013.[24]

---

21   Grandia, 'Deadly Embrace', 131–32; Gross Stein and Lang, *The Unexpected War*, 206–07.
22   Willis, 'An Unexpected War', 993; Martijn van der Vorm, 'The Crucible of War: Dutch and British Military Learning Processes in and Beyond Southern Afghanistan' (PhD thesis, Leiden University, 2023), 142; Willis, 'Canada in Regional Command South', 55, 60–61.
23   Karen Middleton, *An Unwinnable War: Australia in Afghanistan* (Melbourne: Melbourne University Press, 2011): 172–78; Vince Williams, interview with Garth Pratten, 2017; HQ Task Force Kandahar staff, interviews with Garth Pratten, 2008; Ross Peake, 'Howard: No plan to withdraw Aust soldiers in Iraq', *The Age*, 12 September 2007. Australia did ultimately provide a small contribution to the UK effort in Helmand. Exchange personnel were permitted to remain with their host units if they deployed, and a troop of Australian gunners was attached to Royal Artillery regiments between 2008 and 2011.
24   Rhys Crawley, 'Australia's Lessons', *Parameters* 49, no. 4 (Winter 2019): 53–57, doi.org/10.55540/0031-1723.3119.

9. 'EVERYBODY DOING THEIR THING'

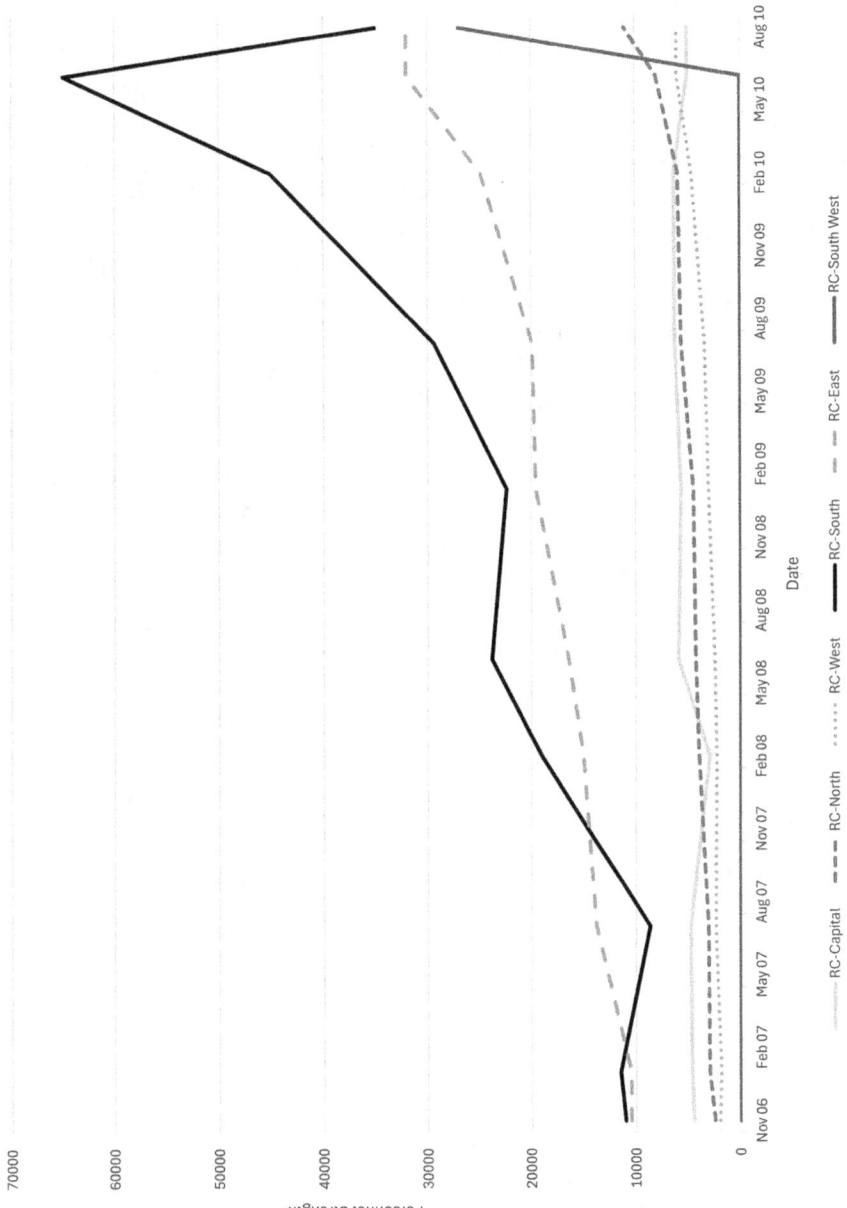

Figure 9.1: ISAF Regional Command strengths, 2006–10[25]

---

25   ISAF Placemats, 2006–10, www.nato.int/cps/en/natolive/107995.htm. Released periodically by NATO, the ISAF placemats provided a summary of organisational details, force laydown and troop numbers for ISAF and, from March 2009, the Afghan National Army.

ISAF's Stage III transfer of authority of RC South from US to NATO command occurred on 31 July 2006. In an instant, the southern provinces became ISAF's 'tactical main effort'.[26] Kandahar was the top priority, then Helmand, Zabul and Uruzgan.[27] ISAF's British commander, Lieutenant General David Richards, told his force the south's security situation 'is a greater challenge than the other Regions'.[28] Responsibility for delivering ISAF's security–reconstruction–development trifecta fell to RC South's first commander, Canada's Brigadier General David Fraser. Though staffed predominantly by Canadians, Fraser's multinational brigade headquarters in Kandahar comprised personnel from each of RC South's contributing nations: he had a British COS, Dutch and American deputies, and an Australian Chief of Operations and Plans.[29] Reporting to this headquarters were four provincial task forces: Canada led and manned Task Force Kandahar's PRT and battlegroup; the UK, supported by Danish and Estonian troops, did the same for Task Force Helmand, the headquarters of which was in Lashkar-Gah; Romanians and Americans formed Task Force Zabul in Qalat. Dutch and Australian elements made up the Tarin Kot–based Task Force Uruzgan.[30] In time, the UK provided an additional battlegroup, based at Kandahar Airfield, as the regional commander's airmobile reserve, to be sent wherever required across the southern provinces—a critical capability when most of the national task forces were tied to holding ground.[31] With an initial target strength of 8,000, RC South progressively increased in size over time (Figure 9.1) and, reflecting this, after Fraser its commander was elevated in rank to Major General. Its basic structure, however, remained relatively unaltered until 2009.

---

26 David Richards, 'Commander's Foreword', *ISAF Mirror* 30 (July 2006): 4.
27 David Fraser, interview with Rhys Crawley, 2018.
28 David Richards, 'Commander's Foreword', *ISAF Mirror* 31 (August 2006): 3.
29 David Fraser and Brian Hanington, *Operation Medusa: The Furious Battle that Saved Afghanistan from the Taliban* (Toronto: McClelland and Stewart, 2018), xiii, 31; Fraser, interview.
30 North Atlantic Treaty Organisation, 'International Security Assistance Force' [hereafter ISAF Placemat], 10 November 2006, www.europarl.europa.eu/meetdocs/2004_2009/documents/dv/placemat_is/placemat_isaf.pdf.
31 House of Commons Defence Committee, 'Thirteenth Report', Session 2006–07, para 79; 3rd Battalion, The Royal Regiment of Scotland, *Aviation Assault Battle Group: The 2009 Afghanistan Tour of The Black Watch 3rd Battalion: The Royal Regiment of Scotland* (Barnsley: Pen and Sword Military, 2011), 12–13.

9. 'EVERYBODY DOING THEIR THING'

Serving together, serving apart

'When NATO took over responsibility for the south of Afghanistan', said Fraser, 'most Afghans and Americans in military-diplomatic circles were hugely sceptical that NATO was even remotely ready for the challenge.'[32] Fraser's headquarters arrived at Kandahar in February 2006 and operated as part of OEF until 31 July. The commander of the US 10th Mountain Division (which ISAF replaced in RC South), Major General Benjamin Freakley, did not think Fraser's force was ready: it, like NATO more generally, seemed to have a peacekeeping mindset. Freakley left Fraser in no doubt that 'he was coming to Afghanistan in a combat operation'.[33] Aside from adopting an offensive mindset, the Canadians had to relearn 'how to conduct brigade operations in combat'.[34] In an honest appraisal of their shortcomings, Fraser admitted that his headquarters had 'a hell of a time figuring out how to manage multiple battalions, international partners, aviation, matériel, medical care, reporting up multiple chains of command, and the gnarly politics of a coalition operating in an area of one million square kilometres'.[35] The challenges, however, were not wholly—indeed, not even mostly—born of inexperience. Instead, they go to some of the inherent structural inadequacies of the ISAF coalition.

Given the emphasis on finding like-minded partners to deploy into RC South, the initial intent seems to have been to provide the basis for coordinated action across the southern provinces. However, a combination of national agendas and caveats, poor command and control infrastructure, shortages of personnel and equipment, and the husbanding thereof, and corrosive misunderstanding and distrust undermined this goal. Fault lines appeared early. The operational tempo of the first couple of engagements after 31 July overwhelmed ISAF. In the Afghan spring and summer of 2006, coalition forces were hard-pressed by an aggressive Taliban. More forces deployed into areas where they knew the Taliban to be, and, unsurprisingly, the Taliban responded.[36] British forces, for instance, were strung out and pinned down among a series of isolated outposts in the northern Helmand Valley; and in the Kandahar districts of Zari and Panjwai, the Canadians fought a succession of bruising encounters with a dug-in enemy prepared to stand and fight.

---

32 Fraser and Hanington, *Operation Medusa*, 63.
33 Fraser and Hanington, *Operation Medusa*, 25–32.
34 Fraser and Hanington, *Operation Medusa*, 27.
35 Fraser and Hanington, *Operation Medusa*, 76.
36 Fraser, interview.

Troops were shuttled about, stretching RC South even thinner, and recriminations flowed thick and fast, usually without much basis. The Canadians accused the British of being reluctant to fight, and US officers claimed the Canadians lacked aggression.[37] The same mud was flung at the Dutch who, along with the Australians, were still finding their feet in Uruzgan. Political interference from The Hague, and Canberra's operational constraints, stymied what others thought they ought to be accomplishing.[38] Criticism did not always follow national lines. Richards, the British Commander of ISAF, noted with frustration in his diary that the UK 'had to be brought kicking and screaming to the party' as ISAF sought to muster forces to respond to over 1,000 Taliban fighters who had assembled in Panjwai district.[39]

For Fraser, transferring RC South from OEF to ISAF made things harder, not easier; the coalition force was worse, not better. Moreover, command and control arrangements were the most 'complicated' and 'horrendous' that he had seen.[40] Theoretically, ISAF's military chain of command ran from NATO's Supreme Allied Commander Europe in Mons, Belgium, to Joint Forces Command (JFC) Brunssum in the Netherlands, to the Commander ISAF (COMISAF) in Kabul, and thence to the regional commanders.[41] Practically, though, it was never this neat. Until Afghanistan, JFC Brunssum had only ever experienced operational command on exercises.[42] When it came to the real thing, it was exposed as being 'ill-equipped' and 'too far removed from the realities of Afghanistan to provide the necessary planning or operational guidance'.[43] For his part, Richards found JFC Brunssum's operationally inexperienced and undermanned staff to be 'distinctly second or third eleven' and confused about its role. They were more of a hindrance than a help.[44]

---

37 David Richards, *Taking Command* (London: Headline, 2014), 237–38.
38 Fraser, interview; Rhys Crawley, 'Mobilising for War: Case Studies from the ADF's Afghanistan Commitments', 2005–06' (paper presented at Chief of Army History Conference, held virtually, 10 November 2021), www.youtube.com/watch?v=H2QMCXUGk24; 'Australian Troops Labelled "Lighthouses"', *9 News*, 29 May 2008, www.9news.com.au/national/australian-troops-labelled-lighthouses/5fb25d2b-3574-4a36-ad4e-b21f4f653120; Middleton, *An Unwinnable War*, 185. Far from criticising the Dutch, Richards thought they performed 'brilliantly'. Quoted in House of Commons Defence Committee, 'Thirteenth Report', Session 2006–07, para 82.
39 Richards, *Taking Command*, 235.
40 Fraser, interview.
41 J5PLANS/7340-093/05–106409, SACEUR OPLAN 10302 (Revise 1) (Unclassified), December 2005.
42 Steve Beckman, 'From Assumption to Expansion: Planning and Executing NATO's First Year in Afghanistan at the Strategic Level' (Master of Strategic Studies thesis, US Army War College, 2005), 6.
43 Ian Hope, *Unity of Command in Afghanistan: A Forsaken Principle of War* (Carlisle: Strategic Studies Institute, US Army War College, 2008), 10, apps.dtic.mil/sti/citations/ADA482251.
44 Richards, *Taking Command*, 224.

None of this was aided by the fact that there were two quite different, and often competing, missions in Afghanistan: ISAF's was stabilisation-focused and OEF's counterterrorism-focused. In a command sense, neither JFC Brunssum nor ISAF had authority over what OEF forces did, nor where they did it. The continuing activities of US special operations forces as part of OEF posed an almost universal frustration among conventional force elements in all of RC South's provincial task forces. RC South did not have sole control of its battlespace, and OEF forces routinely conducted independent operations in the same provinces. Canadian Colonel Ian Hope, who commanded 1st Battalion Princess Patricia's Canadian Light Infantry Battle Group (Task Force Orion) in Kandahar from January to August 2006, saw this firsthand and concluded that unity of command was desperately needed.[45] The implications of command and mission disunity featured in a US Army history: 'Without clarifying guidance from Washington or Brussels, the commanders in Afghanistan had to make do with an informal command structure.'[46] Richards' successor, General Dan McNeill, raised the prospect of dual-hatting the COMISAF (who, after Richards, was always an American), making him Commander US Forces Afghanistan and, thus, also the commander of OEF. This eventually occurred under his successor, General David McKiernan.[47]

Over 2006–08, the various RC South task forces developed into what have been described as a series of fiefdoms waging 'four provincially-based national campaigns'.[48] This state of affairs was epitomised by the nicknames given to each of the provinces: Helmandshire, Canadahar and Uruzdam.[49] From the start, RC South's three lines of operation (governance, defence and security, and development) broke down along national lines.[50] As one US Army official history noted:

> The disjoined nature of NATO's command structure meant that each national battle group arrived with its own perception of their respective missions and vastly different capabilities. Some were prohibited by their respective governments from engaging in combat

---

45 Hope, *Unity of Command in Afghanistan*, 12.
46 Brian F Neumann and Colin J Williams, *The United States Army in Afghanistan: Operation Enduring Freedom, May 2005–January 2009* (Washington DC: Center of Military History, 2020), 31.
47 McNeill, interview; Heather Hrychuk, 'Decision Making at the Theatre Strategic Level: ISAF HQ', *Journal of Military and Strategic Studies* 14, no. 3 & 4 (February 2012): 6.
48 Bowman and Dale, *War in Afghanistan*, 18.
49 Observations by Garth Pratten during visits to Afghanistan 2008–2010; Rajiv Chandrasekaran, 'Troops Face New Tests in Afghanistan', *Washington Post*, online edition, 15 March 2009.
50 Fraser, interview.

operations. Others had more operational flexibility, but did not have the personnel or combat support elements to conduct offensive operations. Finally, none were on a unified rotation schedule. In effect, each national contingent engaged in its own mission within the boundaries of its province, without coordinating with neighbouring NATO forces.'[51]

This remained a major problem for the duration of General McNeill's COMISAF tenure. Unlike the other ISAF regional commands, where one nation had ongoing command responsibility, the rotating command arrangements in RC South between the Canadians, Dutch and British was another brake on achieving unity of effort and unity of command. As much as he was positive about his subordinates' efforts, McNeill had three RC South commanders from three countries in the space of 16 months—Major Generals Ton van Loon (Netherlands), 'Jacko' Page (UK) and Marc Lessard (Canada)—and each naturally arrived with his own national nuances and notions of how the war should be fought (Figure 9.2).[52] Lieutenant General Douglas Lute, who reported on the campaign as a member of President Bush's National Security Council in 2008, similarly observed that the headquarters were not incompetent, but that the 'design flaw' of the command structure facilitated neither continuity of command nor campaign coherence.[53]

During Major General Page's time, RC South operations tended to be split into first and second echelon: the former were those clear–hold–build missions conducted daily by provincial task forces. Although RC South was kept abreast of such efforts, these operations did not require extensive coordination with other elements; thus, task forces took the lead. The trouble with this, as we have seen, was that the national objectives of each task force differed; therefore, the types of first-echelon operations were different in each province. RC South was more involved in controlling second-echelon operations, which generally aimed to disrupt, interdict and defeat the enemy across provinces, thus requiring assets such as the reserve battlegroup.[54]

---

51 Neumann and Williams, *The US Army in Afghanistan*, 32.
52 McNeill, interview; McChrystal, interview.
53 Douglas Lute, interview with Garth Pratten, 7 November 2023.
54 Hainse, interview, 2017.

9. 'EVERYBODY DOING THEIR THING'

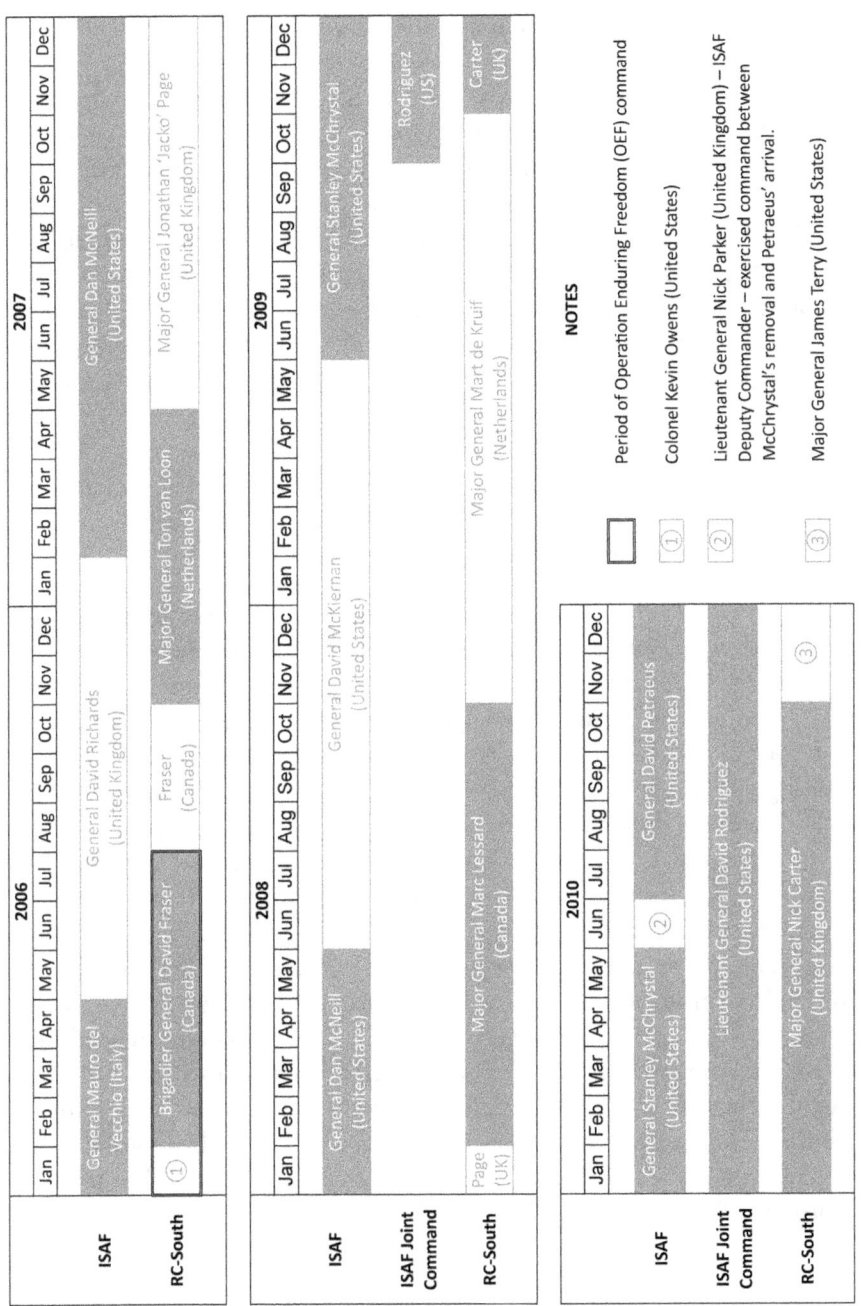

Figure 9.2: ISAF and RC South commanders, 2006–10

With the exception of the Dutch, who gave their military and civilian commanders equal authority, there were still no coordinated 'whole-of-government' national approaches. Within each province there were differences in the approaches, procedures and cultures, as well as the civilian–military–non-government organisation (NGO) relationships of each nation. Some countries saw the problem of Afghanistan as one of a failed or failing state and, therefore, prioritised state-building; others saw the problem in terms of terrorism, meaning that combating terrorism was the priority. Everyone had different ideas of what was meant by the concepts of counterinsurgency—indeed, many refused to use the term until 2009—or comprehensive approach: some thought it was to improve governance, others that it was improving physical infrastructure. Lessard has recalled that he had to understand those differences and try to implement his direction from COMISAF in line with the concomitant views and their associated caveats. It did not take him long to realise the challenge of achieving unity of purpose in such circumstances.[55]

Not only did this prevent the task forces working in unison on region-wide projects that transcended provincial borders, it also angered Afghans, who compared what each province received (from the lead nation) and knew that things were not equal. Nor were the national task forces equal: neither in outlook, nor in emphasis, resources or experience. Though formally running operations in Zabul, for example, the Romanians had no capacity to lead because they had no logistics, medical elements, communications or intelligence. Instead, the US provided the resources.[56] There was no single coalition commander in Zabul in 2007, but there were three lieutenant colonels: a Romanian battlegroup commander, an American responsible for training the Afghan National Army (ANA) and another American commanding the US PRT. Aiming to bring some coherence to the province's leadership, RC South's deputy commander stepped in as de facto commander and visited every week for two to three days to assist. The leaders were capable but needed someone to coordinate their efforts.[57] Similar ad hoc arrangements were still in place in 2008, when Headquarters RC South despatched a colonel and some staff officers to Zabul to try to coordinate Romanian and American efforts.[58]

---

55 Marc Lessard, interview with Rhys Crawley, 2018.
56 Fraser, interview.
57 Hainse, interview.
58 Lessard, interview.

Beyond combat, each PRT responded principally to direction from its respective national capital, and in-country officials lobbied the relevant Afghan ministers in Kabul for assistance to 'their' province, including the allocation of newly created *kandaks* (infantry battalions) to bolster Afghan National Security Forces (ANSF) numbers.[59] In his memoir, *Dust of Uruzgan*, Australian diplomat Fred Smith recounts the reaction of an Afghan official to a visit by Australian representatives: 'On their arrival the local bureaucrat had sighed and said: "You are Australian? You must be here to talk about Uruzgan."'[60]

As a shared province, Uruzgan—like Zabul—lacked the unity of effort brought to Helmand and Kandahar by single national commands. The Deputy Commander—Operations at RC South subsequently observed: 'The Australians saw themselves as an independent actor and did what they thought was right. They weren't much interested in regional plans and were good at finding a fight.'[61] When it came down to exerting influence, however, RC South dealt directly with task force commanders (that is, the Dutch), not their subordinate units (as Australia was).[62] Unfortunately for both, some—including Fraser—questioned whether the Netherlands was suited to running a province.[63] Fellow Canadian, Marquis Hainse, RC South deputy commander in 2007, was more sympathetic and believed the Dutch deserved more credit than they received, a view shared by some of his successors.[64] The reality, as Hainse saw it, was that the Dutch military downplayed what they were doing in Uruzgan for political reasons: they never admitted that they were in combat because of the way that would play out in the Netherlands.[65]

Initially, the commander of RC South was not empowered to give comprehensive guidance to national contingents within the command.[66] 'An alarming spectrum of national caveats', both declared and undeclared, limited what contingents could be asked to do and where they could do it, restricting RC South's actions.[67] Even more frustrating than these caveats were those nations that prioritised their national plans over the regional mission.

---

59 Dale and Bowman, *War in Afghanistan*, 17.
60 Fred Smith, *The Dust of Uruzgan* (Sydney: Allen & Unwin, 2016), 256.
61 David Hook, interview with Garth Pratten, 2017.
62 Hainse, interview.
63 Fraser, interview.
64 Hainse, interview; Hook, interview, 2017; Nick Carter, interview with Garth Pratten, 2017.
65 Hainse, interview.
66 Bowman and Dale, *War in Afghanistan*, 17.
67 Fraser and Hanington, *Operation Medusa*, 27.

'Caveats for me were not a big issue. It was having nations understand that sometimes, when I give direction, it might be a little different to their national plan,' said Major General Lessard. The problem was not that the national plans existed per se, but that they were so proscriptive. With little wriggle room to impress his own will upon each nation's predetermined plan, Lessard questioned his own ability to command effectively. Where he could not command, he tried to influence. Ultimately, task force plans were not entirely misaligned, but RC South had to try to ensure they were as closely aligned as possible—with each other and with ISAF's mission.[68]

The Dutch were perhaps the most constrained, with the political environment in the Netherlands meaning that Task Force Uruzgan was subject to intense political scrutiny. All operations with the possibility of contact with enemy, or probability of a confrontation, had to be approved in The Hague. Dutch officers thus had to be able to 'tell a good story' to gain approval and acted pre-emptively by declining ISAF missions they did not think would be approved, thereby contributing to views held by others in the force, including many Australians, that they were unduly timid or passive.[69] Australia's caveats on deployment outside of Uruzgan, which applied at various times both to Australian conventional and special forces, frustrated some in RC South. In an interview in 2009, Brigadier David Hook, the Deputy Commander—Operations expressed his disbelief that a request for Australian engineers to repair bridges outside of Uruzgan had to go all the way to the prime minister.[70]

Quite apart from all these constraints on commanding coalition operations, Headquarters RC South was, in fact, not resourced to exert much control over them. It had few organic enablers and functioned essentially as a clearing house for support from ISAF assets, principally those of the US. At no point did Major General Lessard feel he had nearly enough resources to meet all his requirements. Staff numbers were a problem, too. Of the roughly 300 personnel in Lessard's headquarters, for example, 120 were from the signals squadron. Most cells had enough staff to function effectively, but Lessard felt deficient in the intelligence and planning cells. More planners were required just to 'answer the mail' from ISAF headquarters. Given the dispersion of RC South's forces, and the threat from improvised

---

68 Lessard, interview.
69 David P Auerswald and Stephen M Saideman, *NATO in Afghanistan: Fighting Together, Fighting Alone* (Princeton: Princeton University Press, 2014), 159.
70 David Hook, interview with Garth Pratten, 2009.

explosive devices, air support was critical. Lessard had a small but effective cell responsible for calculating the residual capacity of Dutch, British and American aircraft, as the command had none of its own. These would then be allocated according to the priorities at the time. Without divisional-level resources, however, the task forces had to make do with whatever assets they had available within their provinces, or what they were temporarily allocated from ISAF. For Lessard, this went directly to his (and Canada's) credibility: he, as a Canadian divisional commander, was not able to bring any assets with him, be it a reserve battle group, a signals intelligence element or a special counter–improvised explosive devices (counter-IEDs) force.[71]

Going 'where the population was': prioritising a regional approach

The year 2009 was a watershed in the history of ISAF's operations in Afghanistan. Multiple reviews concluded that the campaign was under-resourced, poorly coordinated and going nowhere fast.[72] Successive ISAF commanders General David McKeirnan (June 2008 – May 2009) and General Stanley McCrystal (June 2009 – May 2010) worked to reinforce the ISAF effort and unify its direction, and the major beneficiary was RC South. This said, 2009 also marked the beginning of what could be described as an Americanisation of the war in the south as the influx of US reinforcements overwhelmed the contributions of RC South's founding partners.

Appointed as both Commander of the International Security Assistance Force in Afghanistan (COMIASF) and Commander US Forces Afghanistan (USFOR-A), McKeirnan was the first officer to unify the NATO and United States (OEF) command structures.[73] Like his predecessors, however, he inherited a mission without an integrated civil–military campaign plan. As he later observed: '[T]he regional campaigns were all operating to different drumbeats, and a lot of those dictated by the drum being played back in national capitals.' The south, where he assessed that 'there were

---

71 Lessard, interview.
72 Jack Fairweather, *The Good War: Why We Couldn't Win the War or the Peace in Afghanistan* (London: Vintage, 2015), 290–91, 301–02, 304; Lute, interview.
73 Auerswald and Saideman, *NATO in Afghanistan*, 69; Rynning, *NATO in Afghanistan*, 164–65.

really four different campaigns going on', was particularly troubling.[74] While McKeirnan's initial instincts were to reinforce hard-pressed American forces in RC East, he eventually decided the focus of his command would be RC South, but he sought to bring unity of effort through the development of a counterinsurgency campaign plan.[75] Accompanying requests for more troops resulted in the first significant US reinforcements since the invasion of Iraq, with 3,500 approved in the last months of the Bush administration and another 21,000 in the first months of Barak Obama's presidency.[76]

Despite these efforts, McKeirnan lost the confidence of the Obama administration and was 'abruptly replaced' in June 2009 by General Stanley McCrystal.[77] McCrystal is widely portrayed as changing ISAF's conduct of the war, although his tenure predominantly represented evolution rather than drastic change, with the exception of his efforts to reduce civilian casualties. He promulgated a revised 'population-centric' counterinsurgency campaign plan that emphasised 'protecting the Afghan people', facilitating Afghan governance and partnering with the ANSF at every level.[78] Emphasising the need for the campaign to be 'properly resourced', he requested another 40,000 reinforcements, of which 30,000 were approved by Obama.[79] Recognising the need for ISAF to regain the initiative in 'seriously threatened' areas and 'focus its full range of civilian and military resources where they [would] have the greatest effect on the people', McChrystal retained McKeirnan's emphasis on the south.[80]

Reiterating that 'ISAF's subordinate headquarters must stop fighting separate campaigns', McChrystal further reformed ISAF command arrangements, including the creation of ISAF Joint Command (IJC), an operational-level headquarters under a US lieutenant general. IJC was to coordinate

---

74 Daniel McKeirnan, cited in Edmund J Degen and Mark J Reardon, *Modern War in an Ancient Land: The United States Army in Afghanistan, 2001–2014*, vol. II, *Global War on Terrorism* series (Washington, DC: Center of Military History, 2021), 176.
75 Degen and Reardon, *Modern War in an Ancient Land*, vol. II, 205–07, 209–11, 219–20; Fairweather, *The Good War*, 289–90.
76 Bowman and Dale, *War in Afghanistan*, 7 (9 March 2011).
77 Degen and Reardon, *Modern War in an Ancient Land*, vol. II, 203. For an analysis of McKeirnan's demise, see Rynning, *NATO in Afghanistan*, 160–66.
78 Stanley McChrystal, 'Commander's Initial Assessment', 30 August 2009, 2-1, 2-12, 2-15–2-17, 2-19–2-20.
79 McChrystal, 'Commander's Initial Assessment', 2, 20–21. For discussion on the decision-making surrounding the second tranche of the Obama surge, see: Carter Malkasian, *The American War in Afghanistan: A History* (Oxford: Oxford University Press, 2021), 234–37, doi.org/10.1093/oso/9780197550779.001.0001.
80 McChrystal, 'Commander's Initial Assessment': 2-18–2-19; Malkasian, *The American War in Afghanistan*, 231.

and support the operations of the regional commands while McChrystal and ISAF headquarters (HQ) focused on strategy and political engagement with the government of Afghanistan, NATO and troop-contributing nations, including the US.[81] He also enforced the concept of the battlespace commander, which meant that no OEF military operations would be planned or executed in the regional commands without the consent of their commander.[82]

Spanning 2008–09 and the commands of McKiernan and McChrystal, Major General Mart de Kruif's command of RC South was one of contrasting halves, reflecting the decisions made in Kabul and Washington. In the first six months, RC South lacked the capabilities and soldiers to have any 'permanent and lasting effect'.[83] When de Kruif assumed command in 2008, RC South was starting to plan and implement some actions with regional effect, such as the upgrade of the Kajaki Dam hydro-electric power plant with the installation of a third turbine. This operation serves to highlight both the potential for combined effort and the challenges to achieving it in southern Afghanistan. The dam refurbishment project was led by USAID and projected to raise generating capacity from 3 to 150 watts, providing power for 1.7 million homes. Due to the dam's location in northern Helmand, the UK task force mounted the operation to move the turbine on the last stage of its journey. British civilian officials, however, dismissed the worth of the operation because the main beneficiaries would be the citizens of Kandahar City; there 'was no discernible benefit to Helmand', and the operations would distract from the implementation of the British-conceived Helmand Road Map.[84] As this example demonstrates, RC South's task forces were mostly still primarily, or completely, focused on what was happening in their province. The Romanians remained short of assets, and Dutch caveats reduced their effectiveness.[85] RC South lacked region-wide governance, reconstruction and development programs.

---

81 Department of Defense, *Report on Progress Towards Security and Stability in Afghanistan* (Washington, DC: Department of Defense, 2010), 13–14.
82 Mart de Kruif, correspondence with Rhys Crawley; McChrystal, 'Commander's Initial Assessment', 2–14.
83 de Kruif, correspondence.
84 Although the operation to move the turbine was tactically successful, it proved to be a strategic failure. See: Farrell, *Unwinnable*, 239–43; Mike Martin, *An Intimate War: An Oral History of the Helmand Conflict* (London: Hurst and Company, 2014), 211–12.
85 de Kruif, correspondence.

De Kruif assessed RC South was losing and was struggling to regain the initiative from the Taliban and other insurgents. He needed more military forces to turn this around. Obama's surge provided just that, giving RC South 'the mobility, manpower and dominance to regain the initiative and significantly limit the freedom of action of the insurgents'.[86] Designation as the ISAF main effort brought with it the majority of the US reinforcements—which saw the strength of the command grow from 17,900 in November 2008, to 34,855 in October 2009—and priority access to additional ISAF assets, including air support, ISR and elements of Task Force Paladin, the counter-IED task force.[87] Most notable was the arrival of a US combat aviation brigade, which brought with it 140 helicopters. The significance of this deployment can be gauged by the fact that it trebled the number of helicopters in Afghanistan. Such an increase in enablers increased RC South's capacity to support task force operations, thereby increasing its significance to them.[88]

The surge also changed RC South headquarters, which was expanded and saw its planning processes and battle rhythm revised. A Combined Joint Operations Centre was constructed to better monitor and support operations across the command. In particular, a synchronisation process provided the foundations for the coordination of task force operations to achieve a combined effect. To give practical effect to the concept of battlespace ownership, a liaison cell was established within the headquarters to effect better coordination of special operations inside RC South, including their approval by the commander or his representative.[89] As Hook later observed, RC South was transformed from a regional support headquarters to one that had the capacity to command the region.[90]

A civil–military planning cell had also been formed in November 2008 to produce a 'comprehensive, long range regional strategy'. It commenced work early in the new year on a 24-month campaign plan. The cell was focused on fostering economic development, a key component of which was securing the two major settled areas in the southern provinces, Kandahar City and its environs, and central Helmand, which represented 80 per cent of the population. Concerned that the British were most in need of

---

86   de Kruif, correspondence.
87   ISAF Placemats, 25 November 2008, 1 October 2009; Hook, interview, 2017.
88   Hook, interview, 2017.
89   Hook, interview, 2017. See also Anthony King, *Command: The Twenty-First-Century General* (Cambridge: Cambridge University Press, 2019), 239.
90   Hook, interview, 2017.

9. 'EVERYBODY DOING THEIR THING'

support, de Kruif prioritised Helmand.[91] Two major operations followed in mid-2009: *Panchai Palang* (Panther's Claw), conducted by Task Force Helmand to clear the Babaji area[92] north-west of the provincial capital of Lashkar Gar; and *Khanjar* (Strike of the Sword), conducted by the recently arrived 2nd Marine Expeditionary Brigade to secure several towns in southern Helmand. Along with integrating new US forces and regaining the initiative, the other major focus during de Kruif's command was expanding projects from provincial to regional level. To that end, provincial governors and Kabul's leaders were brought together for regional conferences led by the UN Assistance Mission to Afghanistan to discuss regional plans for agriculture, energy, infrastructure and banking systems.

The command of de Kruif's successor, British Major General Nick Carter, has received more scholarly attention than that of the officers who preceded him. The crux of those studies is that, by dint of timing, resources, intellect and personality, Carter was able to bring RC South's task forces together as a formation in a way that had not previously been seen.[93] As this chapter has demonstrated, Carter's command followed a long period of trial, error and reform in ISAF's war in Afghanistan. By the time he assumed command in November 2009, the first tranche of Obama reinforcements were on the ground, and the second was about to be announced. With a headquarters of 800 personnel, Carter had both the capacity and authority to command the region. Brigadier General Jon Vance, who commanded Task Force Kandahar for two separate periods under de Kruif and Carter,[94] noted that Headquarters RC South 'became more directive as McChrystal's efforts to regionalise the mission took hold'.[95]

Carter's period of command was the most intensive period of activity of the campaign in the south. His operational design represented an evolution of the efforts made in both ISAF and RC South headquarters since 2008

---

91 Fairweather, *The Good War*, 295.
92 Farrell has pointed out that the use of 'Babaji' as shorthand for the *Panchai Palang* operational area is a misnomer, as the operation also embraced the adjacent areas of Malgir and Spin Masjid: Farrell, *Unwinnable*, 255.
93 See King, *Command*, 214–48; Anthony King, 'Operation Moshtarak: Counter-insurgency Command in Kandahar 2009–10', *Journal of Strategic Studies* 44, no. 1 (2021): 36–62, doi.org/10.1080/01402390. 2019.1672160; Malkasian, *The American War in Afghanistan*, 274.
94 Vance commanded TFK during de Kruif's tenure from February to November 2009. He was brought back to Afghanistan in June 2010 when his successor, Brigadier General Daniel Menard, was sacked for an inappropriate relationship with a female subordinate. See Sonia Verma, 'General Who Crafted Afghan Strategy Returns to Put it in Practice', *The Globe and Mail*, online edition, 30 May 2010; Ingrid Peritz, 'Former Canadian General Fined, Demoted for Affair', *The Globe and Mail*, online edition, 21 July 2011.
95 Auerswald and Saideman, *NATO in Afghanistan*, 130.

to provide a coherent, unified campaign plan with appropriate priorities, sequencing and resources. As one of his principal staff officers noted, Carter was 'determined to conduct a division fight'.[96] It is not correct, however, as suggested by one source, that 'there was, in short, no plan when Carter took over'.[97] Although Carter conceived of his mission differently to his predecessor—namely, as winning support for the government of Afghanistan by connecting the people with governance—its essential requirement was the same: to 'go where the population was'.[98] Carter, like McChrystal, saw Kandahar City as the priority for all the reasons described earlier in this chapter, but both were pushed towards further action in central Helmand first due to a number of factors: the decisions of their predecessors, the timeline for the arrival of reinforcements, the conditions attached to the deployment of some of those reinforcements and the need for McChrystal to demonstrate progress in Washington.[99]

The scale and scope of the operations conducted during 2010 reflect the growth in both size and capability of RC South and its ability to achieve both unity of command and effort. Operation *Moshtarak* (Dari for 'together') in February 2010 included one of the largest air assaults since the Vietnam War. Over 100 helicopters from four nations landed or supported United States Marine Corps (USMC) and UK forces and their Afghan partners to capture Marjah and Nad e Ali west of Lashkar Gar in Central Helmand. Additional troops were involved in ground-based components of the operation, contributing to an overall force of 1,200 from Task Force Helmand (UK, Denmark and Estonia), 3,000 from the USMC and 4,400 from the ANSF.[100]

Largely dependent on forces from the second tranche of the Obama surge, RC South's focus switched to Kandahar in June. In keeping with Kandahar City's densely packed civilian population and its economic importance, the

---

96   Benjamin Hodges, interview with Garth Pratten, 20 December 2023.
97   King, *Command*, 228. Brigadier General (later Lieutenant General) Ben Hodges, who served in both de Kruif's and Carter's headquarters, has observed it is unfair to the former to suggest he and his team 'just trudged along' (Hodges, interview). David Hook has likewise observed that de Kruif was the 'unsung hero of campaign transition' in southern Afghanistan (Hook, interview, 2017).
98   Carter, interview.
99   Malkasian, *The American War in Afghanistan*, 241.
100 Farrell, *Unwinnable*, 310; Malkasian, *The American War in Afghanistan*, 250; The Associated Press, 'Coalition attacks Taliban stronghold', *CBC News* online, 12 February 2010. The Moshtarak helicopter force comprised airframes from the US (Army and USMC), the UK and Canada. It is difficult to precisely establish the number of helicopters involved. Sixty transport airframes carried the USMC force and three waves of 36 the UK force. The total number of attack and utility helicopters carrying out escort and overwatch missions is not detailed in available open sources.

9. 'EVERYBODY DOING THEIR THING'

concept of *Hamkari* (Dari and Pashto for 'cooperation') meant limiting civilian casualties and the destruction of property by surrounding the city with successive layers of security. Afghan National Police, mentored by US military police, would secure the city itself, ANA units would guard the outskirts of the city, and further ANA elements, alongside US and Canadian combat troops, would clear the settled areas along the Arghandab River. All told, eight coalition and nine ANSF manoeuvre battalions, as well as a US battlefield surveillance brigade, were involved. This represented an unprecedented massing of combat power in the province, which, as the US Army's official historians observed, 'for the first time devoted enough forces to clear and hold Kandahar City's outlying districts while simultaneously interdicting infiltration routes from Pakistan'.[101]

Despite the priority placed on the major population centres in the emphasis on a regional approach, national political imperatives continued to complicate command in RC South. In line with his emphasis on Kandahar, and to make operational space for the growing USMC contingent in Helmand, early in his command Carter sought the redeployment of the UK contingent from Helmand. As Theo Farrell has noted, it was politically a 'forlorn hope' and financially unacceptable to the UK, given the prolonged investment of the lives of its soldiers and the contents of its treasury in Helmand.[102] As forces were concentrated in Helmand and Kandahar, Uruzgan became an economy-of-force effort. Australian commanders and officials ostensibly accepted the necessity of such prioritisation, but tension remained between coalition and national imperatives. There is a sense of the tail trying to wag the dog in the reflections of Major General John Cantwell, the commander of Australian forces in the Middle East Area of Operations:

> The most important is my encounter with the British two-star general in command of the whole southern region of Afghanistan, Major General Nick Carter. Uruzgan province falls within his command and I must establish a good working relationship with him, to ensure that we get the right level of support and *that our mission is properly understood* [my emphasis] and aligned with the troubled south of the country … We get off to a good start, although I sense we will not be friends. His attention is firmly—and understandably—on

---

101 Malkasian, *The American War in Afghanistan*, 283, 292–93; Degen and Reardon, *Modern War in an Ancient Land*, vol. II, 296.
102 Farrell, *Unwinnable*, 301; Rynning, *NATO in Afghanistan*, 191.

> combat operations in Helmand province, to the west of Kandahar ... In the months ahead I will be a frequent visitor to Carter's office in a bid to ensure vital resources are not bled away from our own area of responsibility.[103]

National 'red cards' were still played, such as when Brigadier General Vance withheld Canadian troops until ISR support he considered necessary was provided.[104]

McChrystal's emphasis on Afghan ownership of the campaign helped Carter to corral the resources necessary to implement his plans. When ANA *kandaks* needed to be redeployed from Uruzgan to reinforce Operation *Moshtarak*, Dutch and Australian officials protested, as both saw the development of capable Afghan security forces in the province as fundamental to their exit strategy. Plans for *Moshtarak* had been developed in concert with the commander of 205 Corps of the ANA, which allowed Carter to respond: 'I'm not ordering it, the Afghans are.'[105] Although Carter was enabled like no previous RC South commander, to realise his intent he still relied heavily on the exercise of influence rather than command. Technically, he had no control over the PRTs, which remained national relief efforts, and a number of civilian agencies also operated within and across his boundaries.[106] As Anthony King, who periodically visited Carter's headquarters, has observed: he 'had to manipulate, negotiate and enjoin. He had [to] act as a diplomat and an ambassador, asking for support, rather than simply commanding in a traditional military fashion'.[107] Carter saw the cornerstone of command in this coalition environment as building confidence: demonstrating to both subordinates and national capitals that there was a sensible plan, sufficiently resourced, that managed risks and took account of national objectives.[108]

---

103 John Cantwell, *Exit Wounds: One Man's War on Terror* (Melbourne: Melbourne University Press, 2012), 255–56.
104 Auerswald and Saideman, *NATO in Afghanistan*, 130.
105 Carter, interview; King, *Command*, 233–34.
106 Carter, interview.
107 King, *Command*, 234.
108 Carter, interview.

'The Americans are coming!'

The American reinforcements transformed the war in the south. They provided the means to carry out the RC South campaign plan but also overwhelmed the contributions of the command's founding nations. Less than 3,000 Canadian soldiers had been responsible for the 50,000 square kilometres of Kandahar province prior to 2009; by the middle of 2010, 20,000 US troops were also there.[109] In Helmand, 9,000 UK troops were initially joined by 10,700 US Marines, and by the time the build-up of 1 Marine Expeditionary Force was complete, they would be outnumbered two to one.[110]

Enabling as it was, the increased American presence brought its own complications. It was a significant policy decision to place 30,000 US troops under the command of a British general and a UK-led coalition HQ.[111] US brigadier generals, John 'Mick' Nicholson and Benjamin 'Ben' Hodges, successively occupied senior positions within de Kruif's and Carter's headquarters.[112] They had a role within the US non-operational national command chain, the ear of senior Americans in Kabul, and proved key intermediaries.[113] Hodges, who served as Carter's Deputy Chief of Staff—Operations, has been described as a US 'control measure', but he has described his role in different terms.[114] His responsibility was to ensure the provision of US support to Carter; his role was not to protect America's interests, but rather ensure its contribution was fully, and effectively, utilised.[115] One of Hodges's British peers observed his value was twofold: he understood what Carter wanted and could 'talk in American'; he was the '[US] national support bloke'.[116] At times Hodges, who wore an RC South shoulder patch rather than a US one, sometimes felt embarrassed by

---

109 Caroline Leprince, 'The Canadian-led Kandahar Provincial Reconstruction Team: A Success Story?', *International Journal* 68, no. 2 (June 2013): 374.
110 Malkasian, *The American War in Afghanistan*, 242, 249; Degen and Reardon, *Modern War in an Ancient Land*, vol. II, 283–84.
111 Benjamin Hodges, 'Command at the Two Star Level—Kandahar' (panel presentation at Command in the 21st Century conference, University of Warwick, UK, 5 September 2017).
112 Brigadier General Nicholson served periods as both Deputy Commander–Stabilisation and Deputy Commander–Operations in HQ RC South 2008–09. He was replaced by Brigadier General Hodges in September 2009.
113 Fairweather, *The Good War*, 294–95; Hook, interview 2017; Hodges, interview.
114 Unnamed HQ RC South staff member cited in King, *Command*, 240.
115 Hodges, interview.
116 Hodges, panel presentation at Command in the 21st Century conference 2017; Dickie Davis, cited in King, *Command*, 240.

the arrogant 'we're in charge' attitude of some of his countrymen and on at least one occasion had to 'raise … hell' to insure Carter had access to key intelligence.[117] There were some issues, however, that were beyond the wit of even the most senior officers to solve: for example, it took three months for Carter to be equipped with his own terminal to access the US secret network.[118]

Issues of national prestige and influence weighed on the minds of British and Canadian politicians, officials and commanders. Still smarting from accusations that the British Army had 'cut and run' in Iraq, some British senior officers feared being marginalised in Helmand.[119] Ahead of the arrival of the first tranche of USMC reinforcements, the commander of Task Force Helmand told one of his battalions: 'Gentlemen … the Americans are coming! We risk being put in a corner, sidelined and forgotten. The Americans think we're wet and present only problems.'[120] The Canadians were initially loathe to accept USMC reinforcements in Kandahar due to a similar fear of being overshadowed.[121] Although US Army units were eventually received with a sense of relief, the Canadians remained hesitant to give up control.[122] The reduction of the Canadian footprint was most strongly opposed by civilian officials in Ottawa, rather than their commander in the field; they clung to 'maps, plans and benchmarks in parts of the province for which Canadian forces no longer had responsibility'.[123] The commander of Task Force Helmand faced similar difficulties when the UK Prime Minister, Gordon Brown, blocked moves to hand over the notorious northern Helmand outpost of Sangin to the USMC to achieve a greater concentration of forces in the centre of the province.[124]

The USMC had its own agendas in Afghanistan. In Washington, the USMC's Commandant had negotiated the conditions of the Corps' large-scale return to Afghanistan. The marines would deploy in their own distinct and united area of operations to enable them to operate, in accordance with their doctrine, as an integrated air-ground task force. Operational control

---

117 Hodges, interview.
118 Hodges, panel presentation at Command in the 21st Century conference 2017.
119 Farrell, *Unwinnable*, 263. See also Toby Harnden, *Dead Men Risen: The Welsh Guards and the Defining Story of Britain's War in Afghanistan* (London: Quercus, 2011), 108–09.
120 Mark Carleton-Smith, cited in Farrell, *Unwinnable*, 239.
121 Malkasian, *The American War in Afghanistan*, 241.
122 Carter, interview.
123 Auerswald and Saideman, *NATO in Afghanistan*, 131.
124 Fairweather, *The Good War*, 367–69. Close to third of all fatal casualties of the UK in Afghanistan were sustained in Sangin: Farrell, *Unwinnable*, 356.

of the USMC forces would be retained by the Commander USMC Forces at US Central Command in Florida. While the ISAF chain of command could direct tactical tasks and impose local control measures on the marines, they could be neither reorganised nor divided.[125] The US Ambassador to Afghanistan joked that the USMC should be considered a separate nation within the ISAF coalition because it acted so independently of the other US forces.[126] The marines' conditions essentially dictated their deployment to Helmand—'the least crowded part of the theatre, where they could run their own show'—and were a significant factor determining the plans of McKeirnan and McChrystal, and de Kruif and Carter, discussed earlier.[127]

Once the marines reached divisional strength, a new regional command—Regional Command Southwest (RCSW), comprising Helmand and Nimruz provinces—was created under the command of Major General Richard Mills. Although in part prompted by US inter-service politics, the move was justified on the grounds of reducing RC South's span of command. At its high point in June 2010, RC South controlled 65,000 coalition troops and operated in partnership with various components of the ANSF, comprising another 30,000 personnel. The split enabled Carter and his headquarters to focus on *Hamkari* without the distraction of Helmand and halved the number of troops under command.[128] In an echo of recent history, RC Southwest was quickly nicknamed 'Marineistan'.[129]

The arrival of the marines and the advent of RC Southwest resulted in a curious set of circumstances, highlighted by the US Army's official history. In a campaign strategy that emphasised the protection of the population, the marines, comprising 20 per cent of the US force, were now deployed in an area containing 5 per cent of the population. A USMC-led headquarters was commanding the UK task force it was initially called upon to reinforce, and a UK-led headquarters was commanding what was now an essentially US Army division with limited allied supplementation.[130] This situation,

---

125 Degen and Reardon, *Modern War in an Ancient Land*, vol. II, 220.
126 Fairweather, *The Good War*, 313.
127 Douglas Lute, 'Integrating a Military and Peace Strategy for Afghanistan: Making Ends, Ways and Means Meet', *Accord* 27 (June 2018): 70–71; Farrell, *Unwinnable*, 277; Degen and Reardon, *Modern War in an Ancient Land*, vol. II, 222–23. Carter sought, unsuccessfully, to have some USMC elements diverted to Kandahar: Farrell, *Unwinnable*, 300–01.
128 Carter, interview.
129 *U.S. Marines in Afghanistan, 2010-2014: Anthology and Annotated Bibliography*, edited by Paul Westermeyer and Christopher N Blaker (Quantico: History Division United States Marine Corps, 2017), 3.
130 Degen and Reardon, *Modern War in an Ancient Land*, vol. II, 285.

however, would not last beyond the end of 2010; plans to end RC South's rotating command and replace Carter, at the end of his tenure, with an American general were already well advanced.

In his 2008 review of the Afghanistan campaign, Lieutenant General Lute had reported that 'nobody was running the show and there was no common purpose'. Among his recommendations were the dispatch of American troops to southern Afghanistan, a focus on Kandahar, and the replacement of the rotating NATO headquarters with an American one.[131] While Lute doubts there was a direct chain of action between his non-executive report and the transfer of authority from Carter to Major General James L Terry of the US 10th Mountain Division on 2 November 2010, these recommendations had essentially come to pass.[132] The Netherlands Government had decided to leave Afghanistan, and the bulk of its forces had departed in August 2010. With the Australians declining leadership in Uruzgan, sufficient US forces had been scraped together to partner with them and form Combined Team Uruzgan. The Canadians had also confirmed their intent to depart in 2011. Their battlegroup was operating in an area just a fraction of the size of its original area of responsibility, and two US Army brigades were continuing the clearance of Taliban heartland in the rural districts of Kandahar. The three most active regional commands—South, Southwest and East—were headed by Americans, with 106,000 US troops split almost equally between them. In Kabul, both operational coordination and strategic direction were the responsibility of US generals. As Sten Rynning observed in his examination of NATO in Afghanistan, the war was now 'squarely in American hands'.[133]

Conclusion

The RC South that Carter inherited from de Kruif in late 2009, then built upon through 2010, looked nothing like that which had existed in the period 2006–08. What came before could best be characterised as an inefficient coordinating headquarters, unable to bring cohesion to the disparate efforts of individual provincial task forces. Successive commanders—Fraser, Van Loon, Page and Lessard—tried, with little luck and much frustration, but

---

131 Fairweather, *The Good War*, 291.
132 Lute, interview.
133 Degen and Reardon, *Modern War in an Ancient Land*, vol. II, 205; Rynning, *NATO in Afghanistan*, 191.

none was ever in a position to impose his will on a coalition force that was only nominally under his command. Individual nations, resourced and constrained differently, and balancing their own political objectives and coalition goals, adopted approaches they thought most appropriate for the problem confronting them. Where some saw security issues, others saw development challenges. There was little consistent attempt to link efforts or approaches across provincial boundaries. As a result, there was neither unity of command nor unity of effort. As the authors of the US Army's official history have observed, there was no wider 'coalition consensus on what the problem in Afghanistan was and how best to solve it', resulting in a dearth of leadership from ISAF headquarters in Kabul.[134] Watching on, Afghans—whether aligned with the government, the insurgency, or neither—could not have helped but see the imbalance.

The troubling assessments of 2008, however, brought renewed US attention to Afghanistan, resulting in reforms in the command structure, the imposition of a counterinsurgency-based strategy, reinforcements and geographic prioritisation. These new circumstances provided first de Kruif, and then Carter, with the capabilities, authority and resources to command RC South as a region, instil a campaign mindset across its constituent parts, and prioritise effort in accordance with the ISAF campaign plan. The fact that US leadership was required to unite ISAF, and RC South, however, raises a fundamental question whether coalitions can operate effectively without a dominant lead nation to impose campaign coherence and reinforce the varied will and limited means of other partners.

---

134 Degen and Reardon, *Modern War in an Ancient Land*, vol. II, 183.

Part V: Intelligence

10

Codebreaking in the Asia-Pacific War: struggle and triumph, May 1942 to December 1944

Richard Frank

The foundation of my relationship with David Horner arose from common service as platoon leaders in the Republic of Vietnam. Even before I met him, I recognised not only the superb quality of his work as a historian, but also certain subtle ways of looking at events that someone with combat experience would radiate. Of these perspectives, I would particularly stress four. First, a deeply ingrained sense of war's complexity, driving deep research to gather a full picture of events. Second, a balancing regard for the 'fog of war'. A historian will know more about the situation than a leader does at the time. Before entering any damning judgement about decisions, one instinctively distinguishes sharply between what one knows now compared to what one knew as a leader then. Third, humility, derived from the memory of the role of chance in events small or great. Finally, a habitual respect for all combatants. To the degree the following reflects these principles, they shine a light on this topic and on David. Finally, we share a particular interest in radio intelligence. When I was asked to participate in this worthy endeavour, I had just found some important and new archival documents adding an important part to that story.

The release of archival holdings on Allied radio intelligence work against Imperial Japan since the 1970s disclosed a complex story. Following failure to unmask Japanese plans from December 1941 to February 1942, progressive breakthroughs from March to May 1942 set up the celebrated engagement at Coral Sea and the stunning victory at Midway in June. Another great triumph against Japan unrolled through 1945 as Japanese naval, military and diplomatic traffic surrendered their contents wholesale. But from May 1942 to December 1944, Japanese communications security measures duelled often effectively against Allied radio intelligence organisations. Each side scored successes and failures in a roller coaster pattern. Then, in December 1944, a Japanese initiative to improve both security and ease of communications spectacularly backfired, setting the stage for massive Allied reading of Japanese Navy traffic in 1945.[1]

This paper addresses the far less covered, though still important, interval between May 1942 and December 1944. Overall, security measures of Japanese communications, particularly those of the Imperial Navy, drive the story. From a September 1940 breakthrough onwards, the main Japanese diplomatic cipher machine, dubbed 'Purple' by the US, was read consistently. Over 1942 to early 1943, compromises of the codes and ciphers of the Imperial Navy, and then the Imperial Army, concerning movements of merchant vessels proved important in the destruction of Japanese shipping. Prior to early 1944, however, the Imperial Army systems resisted large-scale, timely compromises. Penetration of Imperial Navy systems proved uneven.

Because the fighting on sea and in the air between the US and Japan dominated, Imperial Navy communications form the key story. Further, although the attack on Japanese radio communications involved the Americans, the British and the Australians, the sources used here are primarily American. This choice was dictated by the fact that very extensive American records, now declassified, tell the comprehensive wartime story, albeit without full acknowledgement of Allied contributions, or, for that matter, of US centres in Hawaii and Australia. Nothing in the following should be understood as a singularly American (or solely Washington) success or failure.[2]

---

1   For a measure of the massive penetration of Japanese diplomatic, military and naval communications coded in 1945, see Richard B Frank, *Downfall: The End of the Imperial Japanese Empire* (New York: Random House, 1990) xvii, 80, Chapters 7 and 13–15.
2   Regarding the break of the 'Purple' diplomatic cipher machine, the break into code and ciphers for merchant ship movement, and the breakthrough on Imperial Army coded communications, see Richard B Frank, *Tower of Skulls: A History of the Asia Pacific War July 1937–May 1942* (New York: WW Norton & Company, 2020), 148–52; Edward J Drea, *MacArthur's ULTRA: Codebreaking and the War Against Japan, 1942–1945* (Lawrence: University Press of Kansas, 1992), 74–75, 92–93.

By way of context, between Pearl Harbor and the August 1945 surrender, the Imperial Navy created 184 coded communications systems that employed some 1,007 ciphers. From an intelligence perspective, a handful of major systems towered in importance, and those are the focus here.[3]

The Battle of Midway

Communications intelligence, and especially Lieutenant Commander Joseph Rochefort's brilliant interpretation of the fragments of evidence at the Fleet Radio Unit at Pearl Harbor, enabled the Pacific Fleet Commander, Admiral Chester W Nimitz, to orchestrate a victorious strategic ambush of the Japanese carrier striking force at the Battle of Midway, 3–7 June 1942.[4] That triumph owed much to the fact that the unexpectedly rapid extent of Japan's opening offensives prevented the planned early replacement of the main fleet code. The American communications organisations designed this system as JN-25B8. This nomenclature stood for Japan (JN), one basic 5-digit coded and enciphered communications system (25), code books identified in sequence by letters in alphabetical order (B), and all ciphers identified in sequential numerical order (8). On 28 May (Japan time), the Imperial Navy shifted the general-purpose fleet code under American nomenclature from JN-25B8 to JN-25C9. This represented a different code book (C) and cipher (9). While codebreaking proved invaluable in setting up the Midway battle, it played no vital role in the actual engagement.[5]

---

3   For the overall number of Imperial Navy code and ciphers system, see 5750/119 CNSG-OP-20GY-P History for World War II Era (Part 2 of 3) Chapter 3, page 2 [in this document the pagination changes in mid-file from linear to a new order based on its original label as 'Chapter 3', which starts again at page 1], Box 116, CNSG Library, Record Group [hereafter RG] 38, National Archives and Records Center [hereafter NARA], College Park, MD [hereafter File 5750/119 CNSG-OP-20GY-P, History for World War II Era (2 of 3)].
4   Elliot Carlson, *Joe Rochefort's War: The Odyssey of the Codebreaker Who Outwitted Yamamoto at Midway* (Annapolis: Naval Institute Press, 2011) provides the best overall account on radio intelligence for the Battle of Midway, particularly in Chapters 19 to 27. See Jon Parshall and Andrew Tully, *Shattered Sword: The Untold Story of the Battle of Midway* (Dulles: Potomac Books, 2005) for a comprehensive overview of the battle; see also John B Lundstrom, *The First Team: Pacific Naval Air Combat from Pearl Harbor to Midway* (Annapolis: Naval Institute Press, 1984), Part III. Lundstrom was groundbreaking on radio intelligence and is still the gold standard on US naval aviators at Midway.
5   For the basic JN-25 system, see File 5750/119 CNSG-OP-20GY-P, History for World War II Era (1 of 3), 6–7, BOX 115 CNSG Library, RG 38, NARA [hereafter File 5750/119 CNSG-OP-20GY-P, History for World War II Era (1 of 3)].

Technically, JN-25A and B and subsequent systems were enciphered codes. Code operators took the original plain-text message and converted it into coded text first. For that purpose, the code book (at this point JN-25B) contained some 50,000 possible five-digit code groups representing a word, a phrase, a term, a ship, a location, etc. For frequently used text, there could be multiple code groups. After creating the coded text, the code operator then went to an additive book. This consisted of hundreds of pages laid out in a grid of lines and columns, originally 10 by 10. In each box in the grid there was a random five-digit number. The code operator created the text that was radioed, adding to the code group the random five-digit number in the additive book using "false" or modulo arithmetic (no carrying or borrowing, thus "9" plus "4" gave "3"). For example:

Plain text: aircraft carrier
Original code group: 91113
Additive random number: –52139
Final message text: 43242

The code operator receiving the message reversed this process.[6]

Maintaining secrecy about radio intelligence

A discussion about communications intelligence in the Asia-Pacific theatre in the Second World War requires acknowledgement of the most noteworthy threats to the secret program between 1942 and 1944. Shortly after the Battle of Midway, a severe jolt hit all the Allied communications intelligence organisations. A *Chicago Tribune* newspaper correspondent, Stanley Johnston, sailed with the carrier USS *Lexington* through the Battle of the Coral Sea. Swayed by Johnston's admirable performance as a shipmate when *Lexington* was sunk, the carrier's executive officer, Commander Morton Seligman, disastrously misplaced trust in the journalist. Violating stringent restrictions on the dissemination of radio intelligence information, Seligman exhibited to Johnston a key message detailing the Imperial Navy forces earmarked

---

6   For the JN-25 encipher code, see, from the following documents all in RG 38, CNSG Library, NARA: Box 115, File 5750/197, History of GYP-1, pages 1–4, 7–9, 12–13; Box 115, File 5750/198 Op-20 GY [Monthly Reports] February 1940 to January 1942, especially March 1940, January to March and August to December 1941, and January 1942; Box 116, File 5750/199 (2 of 3), Op-20-GYP History World War II, pages 1–4, 7, 12–13; Box 116, File 5750/202 CNSG-History of OP-20-GYP-1 WWII (1 of 2), pages1–52, especially pages 1–7, 11–14, 17–22, 25–26, 29.

10. CODEBREAKING IN THE ASIA-PACIFIC WAR

for the Midway operation. Johnston wrote an article incorporating this detailed order of battle information including ship identifications by name. Likewise displaying a gross lack of sensitivity to manifestly secret information, Johnston's editors printed this article on 7 June.

Then the premier military affairs analyst for the leading American newspaper, the *New York Times*, Hanson Baldwin, removed any ambiguity about Allied penetration of Japanese codes. In an article on 8 June, Baldwin wrote that Japanese based their plans on surprise, but they failed, one cause being 'radio intelligence, which played so large a role in the Battle of Jutland'. The roster of specific ships deployed for Midway eliminated all plausible sources except espionage and 'radio intelligence', and Baldwin told the Japanese it was not espionage.

Navy furore about the breach led to the US Justice Department convening a grand jury that potentially could have indicted various journalists. Federal authorities, however, only targeted the *Chicago Tribune*, a rabid opponent of the Roosevelt Administration, exempting the *New York Times*, normally a solid supporter of the administration. Ultimately, the administration terminated the legal proceedings based on the judgement that a public trial (there could be no other in the US at that time) would threaten to further damage secrecy.[7]

Evidence appeared still later that the secret was widely known at Pearl Harbor. Historian John Lundstrom discovered a June 1942 diary entry by a newly arrived Navy fighter pilot, Ensign JP Altemus, assigned to USS *Enterprise* (CV-6), that word was out about the pending Japanese attack on Midway and the breaking of Japanese codes. In a postwar memoir, *Crossing the Line*, Alvin Kernan, an enlisted ordnance man in Torpedo Squadron 6 on the *Enterprise*, likewise affirmed the story was all over the ship.[8]

The 1943 episode then involved Major General Alexander Patch, who turned in a respectable performance as the US Army XIV Corps commander in the final months of the Guadalcanal campaign. In May 1943, Patch

---

7   On security violations by the *Chicago Tribune* and *New York Times* post–Battle of Midway, see Elliot Carlson, *Stanley Johnston's Blunder: The Reporter Who Spilled the Secret Behind the U.S. Navy's Victory at Midway* (Annapolis: Naval Institute Press, 2017); Hansen W. Baldwin, 'Midway Surprise Failed', *New York Times*, 9 June 1942, 8.
8   The personal log of Lt(jg) JP Altemus AV(N) USNR, 1 June 1942, kindly provided by John Lundstrom via email 10 March 2022, contains widespread knowledge of codebreaking success; see also Alvin Kernan, *Crossing the Line: A Bluejackets Odyssey in World War II*, Yale Library of Military History series (New Haven and London: Yale University Press, 2007), 52–53, 56.

was dining with a small party when the conversation turned to the recent Japanese public announcement that Fleet Admiral Isoroku Yamamoto, the architect of the Pearl Harbor attack, had been killed in an air engagement in the South Pacific. Patch attributed the success to codebreaking before a group of civilian diners. One participant reported Patch's comments, which reached US Army COS General George C Marshall.

When Marshall demanded an explanation, Patch did not deny his codebreaking disclosure, but he added the disturbing comment that 'little or no secrecy' existed in the South Pacific about the availability and use of codebreaking information. Marshall stopped the process at a severe dressing down of Patch, again for fear that further action might increase the likely secrecy breach rather than lessen it. Thanks to Marshall's mercy, Patch would go on to effectively command the US Seventh Army in the European theatre in 1944–45.[9]

The 1944 episode reached the highest stakes. Evidence suggested that the Republican 1944 presidential nominee, Governor Thomas E Dewey, might foreground allegations the administration had advanced knowledge from codebreaking of the Pearl Harbor attack. This galvanised Marshall to take extraordinary action. He took it upon himself to write a letter to Dewey. Marshall maintained he was acting on his own initiative without prompting from any administration official, and that his purpose was to explain that public disclosure of American codebreaking success might have dire consequences in alerting the Axis to this invaluable source of intelligence against Japan as well as Germany.

Colonel Carter Clarke, a key figure in the US program, dressed in civilian clothes, carried the letter by hand to Dewey and delivered it in secret. Dewey expressed deep scepticism that President Franklin D Roosevelt was not behind Marshall's initiative and that the true purpose of the letter was to block public exposure of a shocking administration failure. Based on Clarke's report, Marshall drafted a second, much more discursive letter. Marshall itemised the triumphs of codebreaking both against Germany and Japan, and their supreme value to the Allied cause. Dewey remained sceptical that

---

9   On the Alexander Patch security breach, see *The Papers of George Catlett Marshall*, edited by Larry I. Bland and Sharon Ritenour Stevens, vol. 4 (Lexington: The George C Marshall Foundation, 1981). For an electronic version based on *The Papers of George Catlett Marshall*, vol. 4, see *'Aggressive and Determined Leadership,' June 1, 1943–December 31, 1944* (Baltimore and London: The Johns Hopkins University Press, 1996), 39–40.

Roosevelt had not initiated the effort. Alarmingly, Dewey insisted that 'there was little in this letter that I did not already know'. In the end, however, Dewey did not pursue the matter during the election campaign.[10]

It is vital to understand that these disclosures carried not only implications for the security of Japanese codes and ciphers, but also indications that the codes and ciphers of other Axis powers were under attack and might be compromised.

Guadalcanal code book recoveries

The capture of the Guadalcanal airfield on 8 August 1942 yielded a treasure. Although the Japanese garrison partially destroyed their cryptographic holdings with acid, the Marines recovered a mass of code materials, including JN-25C9. When the Japanese changed the main general-purpose fleet code and cipher to JN-25D10 on 15 August, American intelligence organisations feared the public disclosure of the codebreaking success behind the Battle of Midway might have triggered this change. However, a later decrypted JN-25C9 message sent prior to the Guadalcanal landing noted a scheduled change to JN-25D on 15 August.

JN-25D10 presented the most daunting of cryptographic challenges: a 'triple lock' of simultaneous change of code, cipher and rules of usage. Rules of usage explained how cipher operators would identify the system in which the message was written, indicators or 'keys' identifying where to begin ciphering or deciphering messages in additive books, and other information. Although the first small breaks occurred in October, the calendar showed November 1942 before Allied codebreakers fully solved the system and began to derive significant current intelligence from JN-25D10. Meanwhile, with the important exception of traffic analysis by volume and some direction finding, this sweeping JN-25 revision produced an almost total blackout of up-to-date, high-value tactical and operational intelligence from August until October/November.

---

10 For Marshall's communications with Thomas Dewey, see 'Statement for the Record of Participation of Brig. Gen. Carter W. Clarke, GSC in the Transmittal of Letters from Gen. George C. Marshall to Gov. Thomas E. Dewey the Later Part of September 1944', NARA, RG 457, Studies on Cryptology, SRH-043; The Papers of George Catlett Marshall, vol. 4, 39–40, 293–94, 607–11.

The shift on 15 August to JN-25D10 marked the end of one system employing a single code and cipher. Instead, JN-25D introduced, in US terminology, four (by Japanese count: five) separate 'channels', each to carry its own different brand of traffic, each with its own code and cipher combination, and each identified by a separate system indicator so that addressees of messages would know what code and cipher combination to apply. Moreover, the system incorporated one dominant 'major' channel (JN-25D10) and a second 'minor' channel (JN-25E11) that differed in terms of volume and importance. One 'channel' contained high command messages (two, and later more, separate 'channels' by Japanese count), but 'microscopic' volume rendered them impervious to codebreaking throughout the war. This is a very important distinction. As at Midway, the critical penetrations of coded communications were not in the highest command traffic but at lesser levels, where, normally, the penetrations only cumulatively disclosed partial intentions and plans. These pieces then had to be assembled into a full or partial picture. A final separate channel was used by minor vessels.[11]

Initial breaks into JN-25D

JN-25D baffled Allied codebreakers for months. They only passed the basic research stage in the last 10 days of September. In early October, it finally dawned on the codebreakers that some messages did not break out in JN-25D10. This established that JN-25 was no longer a single channel but multiple channels. More investigation determined that one newly discovered 'channel' used a different code and cipher; it was classed as JN-25E11. It would be roughly mid-October before useful intelligence began to seep out from literally thousands of messages, most of which yielded only trivial content. Even those of great significance contained blanks formed by unknown code groups or garbles. Most of this process was not fully recorded.[12]

Codebreaking finally produced golden intelligence on 7 and 8 November. On the former date, a message disclosed a major operation was set for Z-Day, soon deduced to be 13 November. The operation would employ a 'large

---

11   On the introduction of JN-25D and its dramatic effects, see File 5750/119 CNSG-OP-20GY-P, History for World War II Era (1 of 3), 7–9, 20–21; File 5750/202 History of OP-20-GYP-1 World War II (1 of 2) 63–65, 72, 77–80, 95, Box 116, CNSG Library, RG 38, NARA [hereafter File 5750/202 History of OP-20-GYP-1 World War II (1 of 2)].
12   On early struggles with JN-25D and 'triple lock', see File 5750/202 History of OP-20-GYP-1 World War II (1 of 2), 71–72.

number' of troop transports that would reach Guadalcanal at 2200 on 13 November. A detachment of *Kongo*-class fast battleships would pummel Guadalcanal with a 'vigorous bombardment' the night before Z-Day. The Japanese obviously intended to replicate the devastating bombardment by the same types of battleships on 13 October that had impaired American airpower on Guadalcanal. The main fleet component, styled the Advanced Force, would remain north of Guadalcanal from Z-Day minus 1 in support of the operation.

A second message of 8 November from Admiral Yamamoto confirmed a huge troop convoy as the main object of the operation. (The record here is not explicit, but in view of repeated assertions in the historical accounts that high command channels remained secure, it is far more likely this was not Yamamoto's original message but a retransmission in a lesser system.) A massive Japanese aerial assault on Guadalcanal airfields would commence Z-Day minus 3 (10 November). There was also reference to a Striking Force (standard Japanese title for aircraft carrier unit), but the composition and exact mission of this element remained unclear. This intelligence proved vital for victory in the Naval Battle of Guadalcanal, 12–15 November, that ultimately decided the campaign.[13]

On 17 November 1942, Nimitz signalled:

> Once again Radio Intelligence has enabled the fighting forces of the Pacific and Southwest Pacific to know where and when to hit the enemy. My only regret is that our appreciation, which is unlimited, can only be extended to those who read this system.

King added the very high accolade of 'Well done'—his third such message in three weeks.[14]

Codebreaking success from November 1942 to December 1944, however, proved far more intermittent than continuous. The first conspicuous example of this occurred between December 1942 and February 1943. After five months of desperate struggle, Japanese leaders determined to mount yet another, even larger-scale offensive to take Guadalcanal. Eventually, logistical calculations, particularly about shipping, demonstrated that this

---

13 On the decryption of 7 and 8 November messages, see File 5750/202 CNSG Library RG 38 History of OP-20-GYP-1 World War II (1 of 2), 75–77; Richard B Frank, *Guadalcanal: The Definitive Account of the Landmark Battle* (New York: Random House, 1990), Chapters 17–18, 534–39.
14 Nimitz and King congratulate radio intelligence organisations—see File 5750/202 CNSG Library RG 38 History of OP-20-GYP-1 World War II (1 of 2), 76.

scale of offensive would come at the cost of completely unacceptable effects on Japan's entire war economy. Accordingly, late in December the emperor sanctioned an order to withdraw surviving forces from Guadalcanal. American intelligence failed to detect this intention until literally the very last few days. Manifestly, this demonstrated the codebreaking was not betraying top-level Japanese plans. Other forms of radio intelligence, particularly traffic analysis, continued to provide valuable insights. But traffic analysis only involved the external characteristics of Japanese communications, not the content of encoded and encrypted messages.[15]

Chance and the Yamamoto mission

The now familiar story that codebreaking intelligence led to the fatal rendezvous of US Army Air Force P-38s based on Guadalcanal with the plane bearing Fleet Admiral Isoroku Yamamoto just off the coast of Bougainville on 18 April 1943 failed to divulge the complicated story of the state of Allied command of Japanese naval communications in 1943. On 14 April, a message first from Admiral Yamamoto disclosed his personal intention (his name was spelled in the message) to fly down from Rabaul on 18 April to visit Buin at the southern end of Bougainville and Ballale in the Shortland Islands, off Bougainville's southern point. This message was broken by both Pearl Harbor and Washington. The message disclosed the composition of his flight as two G4M (Allied codename 'Betty') bombers with a six-fighter escort and an itinerary down to the minute for his arrival at Ballale Island (now Ballalae) in the Shortland Islands at 1000 local time. A second decrypted message from the Commander-in-Chief, Southwest Area Fleet, confirmed the composition of the flight and the itinerary down to the minute of arrival at Ballale.

This information permitted the planning of the interception. This proved an extremely challenging feat that required a complex, low-level flight path to avoid detection of the interception force. Exceptional dead-reckoning navigation was brilliantly executed by the flight leader, Major John Mitchell. The flight arrived on time and shot down the two Betty bombers, killing Yamamoto and many members of his staff. One P-38 was lost.[16]

---

15   On the failure to detect the Japanese plan to withdraw from Guadalcanal, see Frank, *Guadalcanal*, 534–39, 597.
16   On critical decryptions of messages on Yamamoto's flight, 18 April 1943, see File 5750/324 (4 of 4), 'The Death of Admiral Yamamoto, May 27, 1943', CNSG Library, Box 138, RG 38, NARA. For a detailed account of the mission, see Dick Lehr, *Dead Reckoning* (New York: Harper, 2020).

Decades later, the release of more information about radio intelligence revealed a remarkable twist of fortune. The system usage rules 'radically changed' for the two critical messages on 15 April. This created a huge obstacle in locating the key indicator, the starting point for all attempts at decryption. This change shut down decryption of current intelligence from those sources from that point for 38 days. Thus, had Yamamoto's trip been between two and 36 days later, with a parallel delay in the messages providing his itinerary, no attempt to intercept his flight would have been feasible.[17]

Key documents captured in the Gilberts and Marshalls

By later 1943, the latest J Code version of JN-25 had been recovered cryptanalytically. However, the new ciphers J36 and J38 proved tougher to master because the 'indicator groups', which revealed the page, line and column to begin encryption and decryption, resisted identification. At Tarawa, during the Gilbert Islands operation in November 1943, captured additive sheets divulged the critical information that the sheets were no longer 10 (columns) by 10 (lines) but now 12 by 15. Further, the sheets revealed that single indicator groups no longer marked the starting point for encryption. Instead, the new system used 'ordinates' of two- or three-digit numbers to mark the line, column and page of the starting point in the additive groups. These numbers were cleverly hidden in a mixed random sequence.[18]

Fear arose that the Japanese suspected a compromise with the loss of the Gilberts when they initiated an emergency usage, but they continued the J36 and J38 additive books until 9 January 1944. A change came the next day, and anxiety surged that the Japanese had changed the code, cipher and usage rules, threatening another drastic setback in codebreaking, as had occurred in the 'triple lock' of August 1942.[19]

---

17 On the codebreaking blackout and Yamamoto's flight, see File 5750/119, History of Op-20-GP (part 2 of 3) Chapter 3, 10–12; File 5750/202, History of OP-20-GYP-1 World War II (1 of 2), 117; File 5750/324 (4 of 4), 'The Death of Admiral Yamamoto, May 27, 1943', Box 116, CNSG Library, Box 138, RG 38, NARA.
18 On the Tarawa recoveries, see File 5750/119 CNSG-OP-20GY-P, History for World War II Era (1 of 3), 10–12.
19 On the change of additive books, 10 January 1943, see File 5750/119 CNSG-OP-20GY-P, History for World War II Era (1 of 3), 11–12.

A secret history noted that the capture of Kwajalein in the Marshall Islands in February 1944 produced 'one of the richest hauls of enemy documents captured during the war' and, specifically, 'the most valuable capture of the war insofar [sic] as JN 25 [was] concerned'. The cryptanalytic attack on the new system introduced on 10 January, JN-25G, with new code and cipher (G42), was 'slowly advance[ing]' when the electric news came from cryptanalytic detachment in Honolulu on 7 February that the complete cipher G42 had been recovered. This information was photocopied and given to a messenger for expedited delivery to Washington. He encountered repeated flight delays because he could not divulge the import of the contents of his baggage. He was fortuitously denied a seat on one plane. Accordingly, he and the photocopy survived when that plane crashed into the Mississippi River.

The recoveries included not only cipher G42, but additive tables J36 and J38, from 12 January 1943 to 1 October 1944. Other recoveries include the complete JN-25J code book (now little used). Additional key captures were the 'MU KOO2' and 'MU HEI 2' discriminates. The discriminates provided the means for code clerks to indicate to recipients the 'channel' of each JN-25 message. Even though these two discriminant systems were outdated, they provided valuable insight into the practice. With the Marshall Islands haul, the G code group values rapidly fell. Altogether, these captures permitted current decryption, possibly for three months, to 7 June.[20] This corresponded to the first large-scale, timely break-ins of Imperial Army codes, thanks to the Australian discovery of the Imperial Army's 20th Division's crypto library at Sio, New Guinea. During this interval, General Douglas MacArthur was able to 'see the board' of Japanese dispositions on New Guinea and brilliantly advance by passing major Japanese concentrations. At the same time, codebreaking against Japanese shipping messages permitted even higher overall levels of sinking, as well as the specific targeting of reinforcements intended for western New Guinea.[21]

Mike code

The Japanese suspected that the US had captured a G code book, and ciphers G58 and G59, on Biak in June 1944. In fact, just the code book was captured. But the feared compromise prompted the Japanese to switch to the new Mike

---

20 On the Marshall Island recoveries, see File 5750/119 CNSG-OP-20GY-P, History for World War II Era (1 of 3), 10–14.
21 On the breakthrough on Imperial Army codes and increased submarine successes, see Edward J. Drea, *MacArthur's ULTRA: Codebreaking,* 62, 89–93, 129–31, 142–43.

code (JN-25M) and ciphers M60 and M61 on 7 June. In a further emergency measure, they also redirected traffic in the two then active JN-25 channels, diverting it into the RU channel, which used the K code (more on this below). This markedly reduced traffic in JN-25. Captures permitted some reading of the K Code, but a combination of limited traffic, a 1,000-page additive book and the use of as many keys as additives (50,100) made the K Code difficult to read, even with parts of the code book.[22]

In a major change, the Japanese introduced grilles with the Mike code and ciphers M60 and M61 (they also were retroactively adapted for the G ciphers). ('Grille' meant a screen, not a cooking device.) The grilles comprised six different celluloid sheets, identical in size to additive book pages. Each sheet was either pierced or blacked out in a different pattern so certain cells on each page of the additive sheets remained visible and others masked. The grilles changed daily. Not only that, but each day the Japanese also changed the line order. Instead of progressing from top to bottom (line 1 to line 15) of the grille sheet, the daily line order might be 7-2-11 and so on.

Cipher operators no longer could choose a starting point and then proceed in simple sequence in the additive book. Instead, to cipher a message they identified a starting page and then laid the day's grille over that and each successive page of the additive book. They then applied the daily line order, so the sequence of additives became irregular—a much greater challenge for recovery. In the first month of Mike code and ciphers M60 and M61, little progress was made on keys, additives and code groups, though primarily due to lack of traffic. This blackout explains the absence of any important radio intelligence (apart from some confusing direction-finding fixes) during the major fleet action known as the Battle of the Philippine Sea. Some message sheets captured on Saipan reached Washington on 17 July. Few messages in Mike had been read when the Nan code (JN-25N) was introduced on 25 July.[23]

---

22 On the fear of a Biak compromise of the code and ciphers, and the switch to Mike Code, see 5750/119 CNSG-OP-20GY-P, History for World War II Era (2 of 3) Chapter 3, 14–15; File 5750/202 History of OP-20-GYP-1 World War II (1 of 2), 110.
23 On the Mike Code, ciphers M60 and M61 and grilles, see File 5750/119 CNSG-OP-20GY-P, History for World War II Era (1 of 3), 18–19; 5750/119 CNSG-OP-20GY-P, History for World War II Era (2 of 3) Chapter 3, 15–17; File 5750/202 CNSG-OP-20GY-P History of OP-20-GYP-1 World War II (1 of 2), 110–12. By comparison, recovery of JN-25D-10 required 1,000 pages of keys, 50,100 text additives, and the underlying code of 50,000 values. JN-24M-60/61 required recovery of 1,000 page keys, 1,000 line keys, 1,000 column keys, 6 basic grilles, the daily grille line order for each day's cipher in effect, 13,527 coordinates as placed on 501 pages, 90,180 text additives and the underlying code.

Codebreakers gleaned their first actual hint of the employment of grilles on 15 June, when a message in JN-25G refused to read beyond the first group, although keys, placement and additives were indisputably correct. This shifted attention to a previously read message that spoke of celluloid grilles. It became evident that the message was grilled (the G and M ciphers employed the same grilles, but the specific grille and line order changed). This meant that GYP-1 (the key codebreaking office in Washington focused on the main fleet codes of the Japanese Navy) faced the same problem as that of the Mike code: namely, of recovering grilles as well as keys, ordinates, additives and code.

The relatively short use of M60 and M61 meant their importance for current intelligence remained 'relatively small'. Nevertheless, coping with them had major cryptographic benefits in revealing the grille and sophisticated understanding of 'dummy' messages. (Dummy traffic was a security measure designed to frustrate codebreaking with nonsense messages that would generate doubt about code and additive values and usage rules.)

Another facet of the situation was that many Japanese units were now cut off, making it impossible to provide them the most updated cryptographic systems. Hence, 'holdover' use of Mike (and earlier systems) continued and proved valuable in compromising later systems. Then, on 21 September 1944, the grilles were dropped and traffic continued to be sent with only the complications inherent in the new cipher.[24]

Nan code

For a long time, American codebreakers apprehensively anticipated that at some point 'the Japanese by accident or design would achieve the right combination of novelty and elaboration to cause GYP-1 serious difficulty. This combination, long anticipated, finally arrived on 25 July 1944, in the form of Nan-62. This was 'the finest JN-25 cipher. It introduced simultaneously a new cipher, a new code and a new usage and there were no major compromises'. Current decryption halted for almost four months.

---

24   For the 'Holdover' systems, see File 5750/202 CNSG-OP-20GY-P History of OP-20-GYP-1 World War II (1 of 2), 116.

The most significant upshot of this blackout was the concealment of useful codebreaking clues on specific Japanese plans for the Battle of Leyte Gulf, 23–25 October.[25]

From 12 October and after, traffic showed messages with 160 to 180 groups staying on a page, 'unmistakable evidence that the grilled usage had been lifted'. GYP-1 was about to shift emphasis to N66 when, on 15 October, N66 was replaced by N-70. Within another two weeks, examination confirmed that the additive book pages had slightly increased to a 10-column, 20-line format with 200 additives per page. The 20 lines were grouped in pairs. Messages sent at odd hours used the first half of the doubled line, and messages at even hours the second.[26]

The now incredibly convoluted additive concealment measures made Japanese communications secure but sparked confusion and ultimately a passive revolt of the code operators. The use of grilles and half lines confused the operators, so they started messages in the wrong half line, enciphering the wrong columns, using the wrong grille, or getting half of the wrong line order—'in short making every possible error'. The system became so mind-bogglingly cumbersome and a such snare for errors that originators of messages fled from JN-25 (traffic fell by 50 per cent) to other systems, principally to one called RU in American terminology.[27]

The RU ciphers

The story of the RU ciphers commenced in the fall of 1942, when JN-25 subdivided into four channels. Until the summer of 1944, two of these, the so-called 'Major' and 'Minor' channels, accounted for all but a fraction of the five-digit traffic; thus, they became the focus of the codebreaking story. The third or 'High Command' channel (unworkable due to lack of traffic) itself divided into two or more sub-channels.

---

25 On the lack of important code breaking success during the Battle of Leyte Gulf, see John Prados, *Combined Fleet Decoded: The Secret History of American Intelligence and the Japanese Navy in World War II* (New York: Random House, 1995), 617–87. This detailed account covers all available forms of intelligence but itemises code-breaking contribution in just four pages. None of these provided more than a generic warning of a pending Japanese operation without anything like a detailed breakdown.
26 Nan Code; N62 to 70: File 5750/202 CNSG Library History of OP-20-GYP-1 World War II (1 of 2), 117–18, 125–26; 5750/119 CNSG-OP-20GY-P History for World War II Era (2 of 3), Chapter 3, 18.
27 Revolt of the code clerks: 5750/119 CNSG-OP-20GY-P History for World War II Era (2 of 3), Chapter 3, 18; File 5750/202 CNSG Library RG 38 History of OP-20-GYP-1 World War II (1 of 2), 126–28.

RU first appeared on 1 November 1942. The system remained of low priority because it transmitted personnel and material information rated 'confidential' rather than 'secret'. American analysts dismissed it on the basis that the Japanese themselves 'had no high opinion of the RU channel'. The system 'died' on 20 December 1943. Then, unexpectedly, the channel rose from the 'dead' on 1 February 1944. It used the same King code (JN-25K), but with a new, 1,000-page additive book that gave even more security. Even though the complete King code book was captured in February in the Marshalls, and 16 pages of additives in March, the volume was still too low to permit effective attack.

Meanwhile, on 8 June, the Imperial Navy imposed code and cipher changes on the other JN-25 channels. When the central cryptographic authorities found it impossible to suppress use of the G58 and G59 ciphers altogether in these waves of changes, they retroactively applied the grilles to G58 and G59, backdating a feature deployed first on M60 and M61. 'The result of all these sudden changes was to so upset the established routine of JN-25 that it was never to be the same again.'

The evidence of the passive revolt by disgruntled cipher operators manifested in the abruptly soaring use of the grille-less RU cipher traffic, raising it far above its intended station to make it a major channel. This did not bring joy to Allied hearts, for it looked like the codebreakers now had on their hands 'two large systems [JN-25M and the RU channel] neither of which had been broken'. Worse, prospects for a break looked dismal.[28]

Ransuuban and the 'Christmas present'

Resources of the Washington-based cryptographic offices were 'severely taxed in August and September 1944', as the first two Nan ciphers defied solution. The codebreakers greeted with relief the third Nan cipher, N70, introduced on 15 October, because the Japanese had at last abandoned grilles. But no immediate intelligence could be drawn until N70 was solved. That period of blackout would include the vast Battle of Leyte Gulf, when the Imperial Navy suffered massive losses that reduced it to near impotence against the might of the US Navy.

---

28   On the RU Ciphers, see File 5750/119 CNSG-OP-20GY-P History for World War II Era (1 of 2), 117–18; File 5750/202, History of OP-20-GYP-1 World War II (1 of 2), 132–36.

10. CODEBREAKING IN THE ASIA-PACIFIC WAR

Codebreakers read a 27 September Tokyo message in M60 that outlined cryptographic changes for November, including the use of Ransuuban. This was the first indication of a new JN-25 system. Predictions on the new system hinged on the meaning of Ransuuban. Literally, it meant 'jumbled numbers board'. October intercepts about Ransuuban failed to mention any underlying code. As the later historical summary observed, the codebreaking horizon looked so glum in November 1944 that no one 'would have believed that the greatest period of cipher recovery in JN-25 was about to begin'.[29]

By 3 December, Washington notified the field that the Ransuuban was an additive system. Still, a black cloud of pessimism over breaking Ransuuban lingered at the end of December. Then one Japanese code clerk sent what became celebrated as the 'Christmas present'. On 31 December, two messages that had been sent just two minutes apart on 25 December came to light, originating from Ominato, a naval base on Honshu. In the processing of the messages, a lucky break turned up from the heading (Honden Giden) indicating probable dummy traffic. At first, originators of dummy traffic created a jumble of code groups, but over time some, like the Ominato operator, became lazy or complacent and composed messages with entire sequential blocks of code groups divulging entire pages of the code book. Other characteristics of dummy messages facilitated additive recovery. Out popped Nan as the underlying code. On 31 December, Washington triumphantly outlined the Ransuuban system. It was a strip cipher, using 100 additive strips, each 20 digits long (a total of 2,000 digits), that changed each day, and with certain other technical features. By 2 January, decryption of the Ransuuban system began.

Ransuuban's fatal weakness was that all the traffic of a given cipher was enciphered by a scrambling of 2,000 digits by strips of 20. Once all the digits were recovered, one had only to determine which 40 strips were used on a given day, and once the strip key was recovered, all the day's traffic was immediately decryptable. This was incomparably easier than solving one Nan book cipher running concurrently that would have required recovery of 100,200 unique text additives, an utter impossibility in terms of traffic volume alone. Even so, there could be gaps in a Nan book cipher due to incomplete recovery. In the strip ciphers, there were no gaps. With each day's strips identified, the day's traffic would be read in its entirety.

---

29   Ransuuban appears: File 5750/119 CNSG-OP-20GY-P History for World War II Era (1 of 2), 117–18; File 5750/202 CNSG Library RG 38 History of OP-20-GYP-1 World War II (1 of 2), 158–60.

A further weakness in the system made recovery of the daily key susceptible to use of IBM punch cards to process current message cards with master cards for the underlying keys. By the end of January, the daily break was accomplished by 0500, Washington time. Thereafter, all incoming traffic could be sent immediately to the decryption line. When the system reached peak efficiency, each day started with a race to see which station could break the day's traffic first. For the period from 1 January 1945 to the end of the war, more than 75 per cent of the strip cipher traffic was decrypted currently. This was an unprecedented rate of success for the whole war.[30]

Conclusion

In American eyes, three basic reasons largely explained the success against Imperial Navy communications systems. First, because the Japanese reposed such confidence in their systems, they never suspected that such a basic mistake as using an old cipher with a new code could result in compromises. This accounted for a good deal of GYP-1 success. Second, not only was the American effort massively staffed, but also the powerful aid of IBM equipment enormously multiplied its effectiveness. These machines produced success in problems like the RU channel ciphers that would have overwhelmed a small staff with only hand methods. Third, the Americans worked and solved nearly all systems that offered sufficient volume. This wide spectrum of effort proved invaluable: when one intelligence channel was temporarily stymied, another could often take its place. Further, the many systems the Japanese used compromised each other.[31]

Nevertheless, the overall story of Allied codebreaking from May 1942 to December 1944 is a complex mix of failure and success.

---

30   'Christmas present': File 5750/202 CNSG Library RG 38 History of OP-20-GYP-1 World War II (1 of 2), 160–73, 180–81.
31   Three reasons for success against Imperial Navy communications systems: File 5750 CNSG-OP-20GY-P History for World War II Era (3 of 3), Chapters 4 and 10.

11

David Horner, intelligence history and Venona

John Blaxland

David Horner is a soldier–scholar who, for most of his career, has focused on authoritative, research-based Australian military history. In addition, he has made a mark as a historian of intelligence, helping us to understand the early days of the Cold War, the formation of the ASIO and the decrypts of Soviet diplomatic cables, codenamed Venona, as they affected Australia. Together with his ANU colleague Desmond (Des) Ball AO, Horner has also significantly expanded our understanding of the 'Five Eyes' partnership of Anglosphere countries: the US, the UK, Canada, New Zealand and Australia. This chapter revisits Horner's scholarship, considering the long-lasting legacies of the Venona decrypts for Australia's national intelligence arrangements and international security networks.

Over time, the term 'Five Eyes' would come to refer to the trusted bonds between the above five countries. Signals intelligence (Sigint) reports would increasingly be written for release to officials from the five countries, but for their eyes only and not for further distribution outside the trusted circle. Nowhere would this trusted collaboration manifest itself in a more significant and enduring way than in the Sigint domain, in which the Venona decrypts would continue to cast a long shadow.

In the mid-1980s, I was a cadet at the RMC – Duntroon, studying in the history honours program of the University of New South Wales' Faculty of Military Studies. The then Lieutenant Colonel Horner had recently completed his doctoral thesis, published in 1982 as *High Command: Australia and Allied Strategy, 1939–1945*, and had been posted by the Army to Duntroon (and, later, to the ADFA, Canberra) as a Visiting Military Fellow.[1] In his tutorial group, we examined the pitfalls of Australia's command and control arrangements during the Second World War. Horner's *High Command* served as an eye-opening, warts-and-all study of how Australia managed—or, at times, did not manage—the higher levels of command and control of Australia's military forces when the nation faced an existential crisis in 1941–42. He elevated the focus of scholarship from the tactical level that had dominated much of the work of CEW Bean on the First World War and the Official Histories of the Second World War.

Horner's work also included a helpful diagram explaining the complicated intelligence control arrangements at the height of the Pacific War (Figure 11.1). Many of the elements of this diagram went on to be reflected in the postwar intelligence arrangements that emerged from 1947 onwards and about which Horner would write later.

The discussion on higher command arrangements, even if dating from the Second World War, was particularly significant in the early to mid-1980s. At this time, the Australian Government was reorienting its defence policy away from Forward Defence: that is, the policy pursued from the 1950s through to the early 1970s that focused on deploying defence forces alongside British and US elements to bolster security and stability in South-East Asia and beyond. Instead, the focus from the mid-1970s, which accelerated in the mid-1980s, was on the defence of the continent itself, with Australia ostensibly taking principal carriage for its own territorial defence. This redirection of effort helped fuel a fresh interest in how Australia would exercise command and control over its armed forces in what were deemed to be credible contingencies, where self-reliance became critically important. It also helped to generate a greater focus on Australia's national security arrangements, particularly its intelligence agencies. Horner's work was both timely and useful for those of us interested in exploring such issues.

---

1   DM Horner, *High Command: Australia and Allied Strategy, 1939–1945* (Sydney: George Allen & Unwin, 1982).

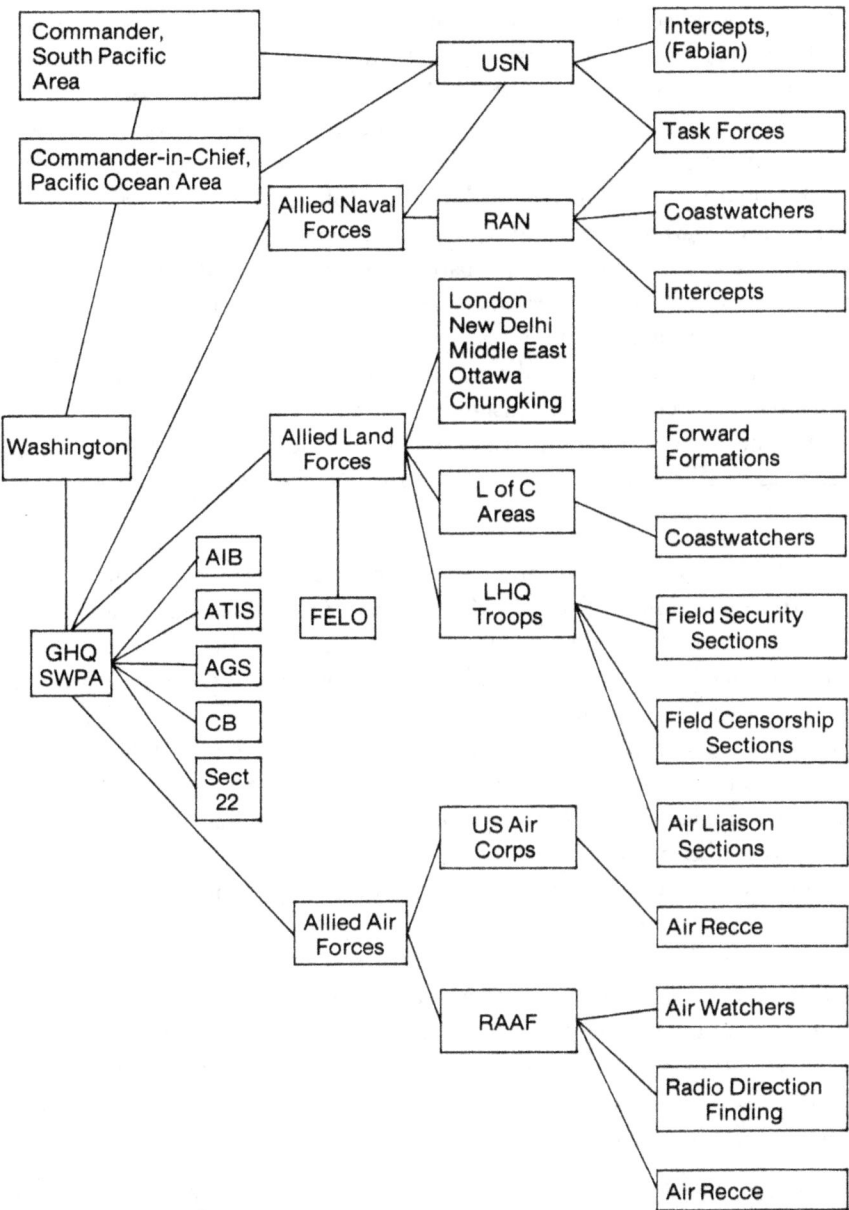

Figure 11.1: Allied intelligence organisation in the South-West Pacific Area, May 1943[2]

---

2   Horner, *High Command*, 241.

Horner's approach to the writing of intelligence history bears the same hallmarks as his military history work. It involves measured judgements drawn from deep empirical research, including from among various archival records in Australia and abroad, supplemented by interviews, a review of other contemporaneous records, such as newspaper articles, and reference to secondary sources, in that order. His approach eschews theorising but emphasises narrative and measured judgements substantiated by clear evidence trails. To some, he is frustratingly even-handed, too reluctant to engage in controversy. Nevertheless, Horner's methods are perhaps the most appropriate to navigate the murky world of intelligence organisations and avoid the popular sensationalism and conspiracy theories the subject often attracts. These tendencies are just one of the challenges intelligence historians face. The necessary compartmentalisation and secrecy of intelligence agencies conflicts with the desire of historians for fearless exposure of the archival record.

It is in the organisational antecedents in intelligence collection, analysis and dissemination of Second World War information that much of the groundwork was laid for the modern intelligence architecture of today—an issue that Horner appreciated well and was writing on before others recognised its significance. It was partly on the basis of these credentials—Horner was also the Official Historian of Peacekeeping, post–Cold War and Humanitarian Operations—that he was hired by ASIO to lead a team to write its Official History. Horner's commitment to accuracy and integrity led to occasional confrontations with ASIO's mid-level management, who were involved in reviewing drafts of the Official History manuscripts. In the face of pressure to remove awkward and embarrassing narratives, Horner stuck to his principles. In the end, successive directors general of ASIO, David Irvine and Duncan Lewis, recognised that Horner's approach would, in the end, be a more creditable one to take. Better to follow Horner's principled approach, they recognised, than to take a more minimalist path focused more on reputation management and secrecy than providing a fulsome and authoritative account.

Integral to the story of this human intelligence–focused organisation, ASIO, was a series of developments that came to light through another medium of intelligence collection known as signals intelligence, or Sigint. This involved collection of often encrypted messages generated with the use of electricity and transmitted (via wireless radio or over a line) by another party that were then intercepted for exploitation by parties other than the intended recipient. In the latter years of the Second World War, Sigint derived from decrypted Japanese messages indicated there were people passing classified information to the Russians in Canberra, who were then transmitting this information to be shared with Japanese authorities. This bizarre development was an apparent attempt to assist Japan to extend the Pacific War for long enough for the Soviet Union to enter the fight after having won against Nazi Germany.[3] Little had I appreciated, before commencing work with Horner on the Official History of ASIO, just how much Sigint was a part of the founding of that organisation: its history was most famously connected with Venona.

The Venona decrypts

A brief explanation of Venona is necessary at this juncture. The official historian of the British General Communications Headquarters (GCHQ), John Ferris, described Venona thus: 'a counterintelligence program of interception aimed at unearthing Soviet spies in Western governments'.[4] 'Venona' was the code word that counterespionage practitioners eventually settled upon to represent a collection of almost 3,000 partly decrypted Soviet secret messages, transmitted between 1941 and 1948, mostly by radio, and intercepted by US and UK radio intercept sites around the world. The recovered records mostly concerned clandestine activities of the Soviet security and military intelligence arms known as the NKVD and the GRU.[5] They revealed widespread Soviet espionage networks in Australia, the UK, Canada and the US.[6]

Venona was initiated during the Second World War by the US Army Signal Intelligence Service, a precursor organisation to the National Security Agency (NSA), but its story began earlier. In 1927, British Prime Minister Stanley Baldwin made a startling revelation in the House of Commons. In a boastful manner, he read out decrypted and translated Soviet messages, failing to realise that, in so doing, he exposed to the Soviets critical vulnerabilities in the security measures they were applying to diplomatic reporting. These relied on machine-generated codes for encryption of Soviet messages, but

---

3 This case is made in Desmond Ball and David Horner, *Breaking the Codes: Australia's KGB Network 1944–1950* (Sydney: Allen & Unwin, 1998); David Horner, *The Spy Catchers: The Official History of ASIO 1949–1963*, vol. I of The Official History of ASIO (Sydney: Allen & Unwin, 2014), 54–56.
4 John Ferris, *Behind the Enigma: The Authorised History of GCHQ Britain's Secret Cyber-Intelligence Agency* (London: Bloomsbury, 2020), 347.
5 Nigel West, *Historical Directions of Signals Intelligence* (Plymouth: Scarecrow Press, 2012), 223–27.
6 Horner, *The Spy Catchers*, 55.

through pattern and frequency analysis, as well as occasional security lapses and some resourceful and clever mathematicians, such codes could be broken. This humiliating exposure taught the Soviet Union to rely thereafter on one-time pads: that is, sets of codes for which there was only one set at each end of a radio circuit and only one occasion (one time) on which the code (in the pad) could be applied to encipher and decipher a message. This system was seen as a fail-safe way of making encrypted messages unbreakable by even the most advanced and experienced cryptographers.

With the German army on the outskirts of Moscow in late 1941, and the Soviets' ability to generate one-time pads disrupted, however, emergency measures were taken. These involved the production of a duplicate batch of one-time pads to cover a critical shortfall in cipher-keying material, and their use continued after the end of the Second World War. This practice provided a window of limited duration to break into the Soviets' secret diplomatic communications. However, when the Soviets realised this critical vulnerability in their system, the portal of insight into Soviet activities, 'left ever so slightly ajar by this fatal slip slammed shut once again'.[7] While Venona material ceased being used operationally by the Soviet Union in 1948, it remained challenging to piece together all elements of the puzzle. Indeed, incremental progress continued to be made on extracting useful information from the Venona decrypts for over 30 years, with the program not winding up until 1980.

The use of the duplicate one-time pads ceased to be employed for live communications in 1948—a development that some attribute to the reporting of evidence of Soviet leaks by members of the ring of Soviet spies inside British intelligence organisations recruited from Cambridge University in the 1930s. Matthew Aid, however, has identified an alternative source: William Weisband, a Russian linguist working at the US Army Security Agency who 'told the KGB everything he knew about the US's Russian codebreaking efforts'. Aid notes that 'for reasons of security', Weisband was not put on trial for espionage and was considered 'the traitor that got away'.[8]

---

7   Stephen Budiansky, *Code Warriors: NSA's Codebreakers and the Secret Intelligence War Against the Soviet Union* (New York: Alfred A. Knopf, 2016), 68.
8   Matthew M Aid, *The Secret Sentry: The Untold History of the National Security Agency* (New York: Bloomsbury Press, 2000), 19.

Considered the 'holy grail' of counterintelligence, Venona decrypts revealed clues as to the identities and activities of thousands of Soviet spies across the globe.[9] It was through Venona, for example, that the US gained proof of Soviet infiltration into the network of scientists working on the Manhattan project that built the atomic bombs used at Hiroshima and Nagasaki. This included one of the most consequential Soviet spies, the German-born theoretical physicist Klaus Fuchs, who passed secrets to the Soviets from 1942 before he was exposed in 1949.[10] The Venona program also provided substantive evidence pointing to the espionage of Alger Hiss and Julius Rosenberg. The British joined the Venona program in 1948, and further exploitation of the high-grade Soviet intelligence and diplomatic service communications continued for decades afterwards.[11]

Venona was so sensitive that the circle of 'indoctrinated' personnel (that is, those briefed on the tightly held 'compartmented' information) was far smaller than was the case with the ultra-top-secret, or 'Ultra', Sigint reporting (involving message interception, transcription, decryption, translation and dissemination) of the Second World War. Ultra remained behind the veil for three decades after the end of the war, receiving widespread publicity from 1974 onwards.[12] The secrecy around Venona, however, outlasted that by nearly two decades.

Venona and the Australian connection

While numerous scholars explored the Venona revelations on espionage in the UK and the US, it was Horner and Ball who first examined its history and significance for Australia, Australian defence and Australian intelligence scholarship. Their truly groundbreaking 1998 work *Breaking the Codes* dug deep to help explain with forensic rigour how the Venona decrypts pointed to a nest of spies in Australia.[13] Ball brought his deep knowledge of Sigint, and Horner his encyclopedic knowledge and understanding of wartime arrangements. Never before had the significance of Sigint to Australia's postwar intelligence arrangements been spelled out so clearly.

---

9   West, *Historical Directions of Signals Intelligence*, 223–27.
10 Anon, 'Klaus Fuchs' at *Security Service MI5*, www.mi5.gov.uk/klaus-fuchs.
11 Robert L. Benson, *The Venona Story* (Fort Meade: Center for Cryptologic History, NSA, 2012), 3–11.
12 See Aid, *The Secret Sentry*, 19; and Benson, *The Venona Story*.
13 Desmond Ball and David Horner, *Breaking the Codes: Australia's KGB Network, 1944–1950* (Sydney: Allen & Unwin, 1998).

Horner's 2014 *The Spy Catchers* (the first volume of the Official History of ASIO) built upon this work, elaborating on the significance of the Venona decrypts for ASIO's foundation in 1949.[14] While *Breaking the Codes* made the direct causal link between Sigint and the creation of ASIO, *The Spy Catchers* explained how this happened with a level of depth and insight that had never before been seen. The obvious difference between the two publications was that Horner had unfettered access to ASIO's unredacted records, which he scoured for relevant material to include.

As I reflect on the significance of these works, a few salient points emerge. Government officials observed that as the Second World War was drawing to a close, there was a need to establish Australia's intelligence organisation on a postwar footing. Australia had learned much from its wartime experience; notably, the need to be forewarned about emerging threats in order to be forearmed. This meant developing intelligence collection and analysis agencies that were responsive to Australian Government priorities and concerns, not just dependent on drip-fed information from London or Washington. In addition, postwar defence planners were concerned with ensuring that the organisation and status of Australia's intelligence bodies had greater equality with its allies. A report of 3 August 1945 reflected the government's decision to establish agencies that were considered to warrant higher-level oversight. That oversight was seen as necessary for coordinating their responsibilities and functions, and for ensuring that their requirements (including funding needs) were adequately represented in government. Initially, these arrangements included an intelligence collection agency and an assessments agency: the Defence Signals Bureau (DSB, the precursor of the modern-day ASD) for Sigint collection and reporting; and, for assessments, the Joint Intelligence Organisation (JIO), covering the functions of the Defence Intelligence Organisation (DIO) and what would later become the Office of Natonal Intelligence (ONI). Both were to be grouped as part of a Joint Intelligence Board that would be headed by a retired Brigadier tasked with providing managerial oversight and representation on higher Defence and security-related committees. Furthermore, 'in view of the need to combine military and political intelligence', it was agreed that the Board 'should include a member of the Department of External Affairs'.[15] That meant that the intelligence function was no longer be the exclusive purview of the Defence bureaucracy.

---

14 Horner, *The Spy Catchers*.
15 Report by Joint Planning Committee, 'Higher Defence Organisation–Joint Intelligence Committee-Proposed Terms of Reference', CG Oldham, Secretary Joint Planning Committee, NAA: Box 2363, File 1, 3.

Finding the right balance between a more independent, national set of intelligence arrangements and the continuing need for collaboration with the US and UK remained a challenge. This was exacerbated by emerging concerns immediately after the Second World War about Australia's reliability as a trusted partner in handling the most sensitive of intelligence secrets shared by the US and UK.

Indeed, as Horner explains in *High Command*, the Americans had not signed any alliance arrangements with Australia and had been distancing themselves from their Australian partners incrementally as the war moved north. This was evidenced particularly when General MacArthur excluded Australian land combat forces from involvement in the Philippines campaign and tightly restricted potential Australian land-force engagement in the plans for seizing Japan.

Both US and British agencies had evidence of Soviet espionage in Australia that went back to late 1943. US Sigint decrypts from 1943 to 1948 included over 200 messages to and from the KGB residency operating from inside the Russian Embassy in Canberra.[16] Much of this Sigint material was intercepted and decrypted in near-real time, but, eager to protect its sensitive and valuable source, investigators sought corroborating evidence before any further action arising from the revelations was taken.[17] In 1947, the British, likewise, decrypted some KGB messages sent from the Soviet Embassy in Canberra that contained classified British military estimates. It appeared that an Australian was passing information to the embassy. Indeed, the Soviet Embassy had several friends in Australia. Between the German invasion of Russia and the end of the war, the Soviet Union had been an ally. And several prominent Australians remained inclined to continue to view it sympathetically, even when it was clear that it was becoming a threat with the emerging Cold War. Throughout this period, the Soviet Union maintained an active espionage program targeting its wartime allies. Many messages were passed between agents and their handlers, and between Soviet diplomatic missions and their headquarters back in Moscow.[18]

---

16   Horner, *The Spy Catchers*, 55.
17   See, for instance, 'Reissue: Biographical Details relating to Francisca Burny Alias "Sister"', 25 April 1945, Ref. No: S/NBF/T11 of 21 January 1955, in archive.org/details/1945_25apr_francisca_burny. See also 'Reissue: "Klod" to Recommend Sources From Progressive Parties For Study of Internal Australian Affairs (1945)', 1 July 1945, Ref No. 3/NBF/T320, issued 15 December 1955, in archive.org/details/1945_1jul_study_internal_australian_affairs; and Benson, *The Venona Story*, 53.
18   Horner, *The Spy Catchers*, 54.

As evidence from Venona decrypts mounted, concern grew in the US and the UK about the seemingly lax security measures in place concerning Australian officials with access to highly classified documents. Through clever and persistent detective work, many of the cover names in the decrypts were correlated with individuals involved in passing classified and sensitive information to the Soviet Embassy in Canberra.[19] In March 1948, Sir Percy Sillitoe, Director General of Britain's MI5, was despatched, along with the head of MI5's protective security division, Roger Hollis (later head of MI5 from 1956 to 1965), to discuss the matter with Australia's Prime Minister, Ben Chifley. However, when presenting the case to Chifley and government officials, including Brigadier Frederick Chilton (appointed from among the cohort of demobilising senior military officers to become the first postwar Defence Department Chief of Joint Intelligence in 1946), and Defence Secretary Sir Frederick Shedden, Sillitoe was constrained by the fact that he was under instructions not to reveal the source of his information. When Chifley asked for proof, Sillitoe could offer only an unconvincing cover story about a possible mole.[20] The Australian Government rejected the accusations, and no suspect was arrested.

Meanwhile, the Pentagon banned all classified information, including Sigint and other classified and operationally sensitive reports, flowing to Australia. The Americans regarded the Chifley Labor government as too friendly by far towards the Soviet Union. They suspected, particularly, the Minister for External Affairs, Dr Herbert Vere Evatt, and the Secretary of the Department of External Affairs, John Burton.[21] In *Breaking the Codes*, Horner and Ball, too, remained deeply sceptical of Burton, accusing him of being a Soviet spy.[22] In *The Spy Catchers*, however, Horner is less categorical in his assessment about how compelling the evidence was of Burton being an active Soviet operative. In essence, Horner notes, the circumstantial evidence is strong but probably inconclusive, and not something that would be taken in court as proving the case beyond reasonable doubt. As in other cases of espionage, security and intelligence agencies are deeply reluctant to expose their intelligence evidence to cross-examination in a court of law. This reticence springs in part from the sense that, in the espionage business, the

---

19 Horner, *The Spy Catchers*, 55–56.
20 See Horner, *The Spy Catchers*, 56–59.
21 See Rob Foot, 'The Curious Case of Dr John Burton', *Quadrant*, 1 October 2013, www.quadrant. org.au/magazine/2013/11/curious-case-dr-john-burton/.
22 Desmond Ball, 'The Moles at the Very Heart of Government', in *The Weekend Australian*, 16 April 2011, www.theaustralian.com.au/nation/politics/the-moles-at-the-very-heart-of-government/news-story/cdfaf618ed39b562057f9df7a20433e4.

secret of success is in keeping one's successes secret lest one's adversary learns of them and adjusts practices to prevent any further eavesdropping. This phenomenon of restricted access, and the difficulty of accurately reaching a judgement on incomplete information, have long plagued intelligence historians, Horner being one example. Such scholars are eager to be as accurate and truthful as possible but find themselves constrained by delayed release of sensitive documents, redactions obscuring important details or, in the case of official historians with access to unredacted documents, agency insistence on protecting sensitive information from being published because an adversary may find it advantageous.

While the British took security extremely seriously, their attitude to Australia's lapse was more forgiving than that of the Americans. They were motivated to have Australia remain an intelligence partner because, for the UK's postwar plans, Australia mattered as an imperial partner in the 'Far East' (Australia's near north). As Clare Birgin and I explain in *Revealing Secrets: An Unofficial History of Australian Signals Intelligence & the Advent of Cyber*, the UK would come to rely on Australia carrying a substantial part of the load, assisting with intelligence and security tasks related to British holdings in Hong Kong and South-East Asia.[23] This manifested itself with Navy, Army and RAAF deployments as part of the British Commonwealth Far Eastern Strategic Reserve. What was less well known, but arguably more significant in London, was the intelligence collection and reporting contribution from Australians working in Melbourne, as well as those alongside British colleagues in Hong Kong and Singapore. Sillitoe and Hollis convinced Australian officials and politicians that Australia could solve its security problem by creating a local version of MI5, which became ASIO. Then British authorities launched a diplomatic campaign, aimed at convincing their American counterparts to accept the proposed solution.[24] Britain's Prime Minister, Clement Attlee, interceded with the Americans on Australia's behalf.[25] His appeal was not enough to sway President Harry Truman, but Shedden was sent to Washington to plead Australia's case. Horner, of course, wrote *Defence Supremo*, the definitive Shedden

---

23   Clare Birgin and John Blaxland, *Revealing Secrets: An Unofficial History of Australian Signals Intelligence and the Advent of Cyber* (Sydney: UNSW Press, 2023).

24   This is the subject of Horner, *The Spy Catchers*, Chapters 3 and 4, and is also covered in Ferris, *Behind the Enigma* (see page 374).

25   Letter from copies of papers from the Harry S Truman Presidential Library in Independence, Missouri, in CCH Series XVI, cited in Thomas R Johnson, *American Cryptology During the Cold War, 1945–1989* (Washington, DC: National Security Agency, 1995), 19.

biography.²⁶ Shedden, for his part, failed to win over the Americans.²⁷ This awkward circumstance persisted through 1948 and well into the following year, when Chifley eventually established ASIO.

Continuing American concerns about Australia's security, and their reluctance to turn on the flow of sensitive intelligence, generated teething problems with the new Australian Sigint agency. This body was initially known to insiders as the Melbourne Signals Intelligence Centre and, to the uninitiated, as the Defence Signals Branch, or DSB. Its establishment predated the formation of ASIO by more than two years, DSB having been established on 1 April 1947. While DSB could collect intercepted messages from its eavesdropping stations across the country, there was little by way of reciprocal sharing of Sigint. The American, and in turn British, unwillingness to share Sigint continued until the election defeat of the Chifley government in 1949, which brought about a sea change in international Sigint information exchange.²⁸ The victorious Liberal government, under Robert Menzies, was able to distance itself sufficiently in the eyes of the Americans from perceived leftists in the Labor government. This was critical because, through the Venona program, the source of the leaks was known to be two Soviet sympathisers in Australia's Department of External Affairs associated with 'Doc' Evatt, now Labor leader. With Menzies in power and those associates removed from positions of influence, the US allowed a limited resumption of cryptological exchange with Australia early in 1950.²⁹

The Petrov defection and Venona

The defection in April 1954 of Vladimir Petrov, Third Secretary of the Soviet Embassy in Canberra and a KGB Colonel, along with his wife Evdokia, a Soviet cipher operator and senior to Petrov in KGB rank, more than justified Australia's reinstatement. The most significant Soviet defection to the West at the time, it was a timely intelligence victory for Australia. Petrov provided documents to ASIO confirming what Venona had already revealed: a Soviet spy network had been operating in Australia. The establishment of ASIO was premised on countering espionage—hence the title of Horner's

---

26   See David Horner, *Defence Supremo: Sir Frederick Shedden and the Making of Australian Defence Policy* (Sydney: Allen & Unwin, 2000).
27   See David Horner, *Defence Supremo*; and Johnson, *American Cryptology*, 19.
28   See Horner, *The Spy Catchers*, 120.
29   Horner, *The Spy Catchers,* 134–38.

first volume of the ASIO Official History, *The Spy Catchers*. ASIO was explicitly set up with a mission to address that Soviet spy network. The Petrov papers also suggested that members of the Australian Labor Party had passed information to the Soviet Union. Menzies announced a royal commission on espionage on parliament's last sitting day before the 1954 general election. The establishment of a royal commission made sense, but its timing suggested a political stunt to bolster Menzies' re-election prospects. The lack of any convictions arising from the royal commission also led some to see it as a witch-hunt. While critical to validating many of the judgements exercised by the government, the Venona decrypts were not allowed to be exposed to the public or used as evidence in the commission. In reality, insiders relied on details supplied by the Petrovs, and other circumstantial evidence, to make their case. In intelligence operations, it seems, the truth is guarded by a bodyguard of alibis. The challenge of not being lost in the wilderness of mirrors is a real one for intelligence historians struggling to write accurately while constrained by redacted, delayed release, and sometimes misleading, documents and reports.

The value to Western intelligence of the Petrovs' defection went beyond the information supplied to the royal commission. On the basis of their interrogations, ASIO prepared detailed reports on aspects of Soviet intelligence that were shared with allied agencies. Furthermore, both Petrovs provided very useful information on Soviet codes and ciphers. Above all, the corroborating information they supplied during their interviews by ASIO and others contributed to the further breaking-into and more comprehensive interpretation of some of the encrypted KGB cables that had been uncovered under the Venona program.[30] The Petrov defection thus provided reassurance that Venona-sourced reports were reliable, and that the counterespionage efforts had been relatively successful to that point in winding back Soviet penetration of the Australian Government bureaucracy.[31]

Despite its self-evident importance, the code word 'Venona' for decades remained little known or understood outside a small circle of interested history buffs. Until the 1990s, when the Cold War had ended, and the evident utility of maintaining secrecy over the Venona material had lapsed, historical works on intelligence in the Second World War and Cold War

---

30   Horner, *The Spy Catchers*, 378.
31   Christopher Andrew and Oleg Gordievsky, *KGB: The Inside Story of Its Foreign Operations from Lenin to Gorbachev* (London: Hodder & Stoughton, 1990), 375.

years were not able to observe the significance of Venona. The work of Ball and Horner was revisionist in the sense that, with access to previously undisclosed primary-source archival material, they were able to recast an important set of chapters in Australia's military and intelligence history. Notably, the American reserve towards Australia that was manifest in the later stages of the Second World War, and the degree of mistrust of Australia over its lax approach to security, came into sharp focus in their work.

The legacy of Venona

For intelligence historians, Venona illustrates the challenge of writing about a secretive domain in which important information is retained in closed repositories until the operational utility and sensitivity wanes. Once the Venona program closed in 1980, there was a 15-year lag before the public release of archival records in 1995, but once they were released they led to significant revision, with numerous publications that emerged in the late 1990s factoring Venona into their narratives.[32] Horner, with Ball, led the way when it came to exploring the extensive implications arising for military, security and intelligence historians from the Australian angle on Venona. What their work has shown is that the legacy of Venona in the history of Australian intelligence was lasting and multifaceted. First, Venona demonstrated the efficacy of having national Sigint agencies in the principal capitals of Washington DC and London, and encouraged the expansion of the Sigint arrangements of the Second World War to include Australia, Canada and New Zealand. This investment stood in marked contrast to the period after the First World War, when British and American Sigint functions were largely starved of resources and atrophied for much of the interwar period. The Venona decrypts made clear that, while the Second World War was over, the emerging Cold War would demand unprecedented peacetime attention by the defence and national security arms of government. In Australia's case, the British returned after the war and worked closely with their Australian counterparts to fill the gap left by the departing Americans, who from 1942 to 1945 had filled critical appointments in the two Australia-based allied Sigint organisations: the Central Bureau (General MacArthur's combined wartime US–Australian Sigint agency) and the Fleet Radio Unit (also known as FRUMEL), a US–Australian–UK signals intelligence unit founded in Melbourne. Those Australians who avoided being demobilised,

---

32 See Aid, *The Secret Sentry*.

and who were retained for their core knowledge and skills, remained on the government payroll and would go on to form DSB. These people tended to be expert at traffic analysis, translation and reporting, but they were not so strong in some of the higher-order cryptographic skills required for decryption. They also lacked some of the cryptographic and computational expertise of their American counterparts (as well as their IBM computers). These gaps were filled by the arrival in Melbourne of a cohort of skilled British Siginters, ably led by a wartime Sigint expert, Commander 'Teddy' Poulden, who would become the first Director of DSB in 1947. After a few years, Poulden would be replaced as Director DSB by an Australian, Ralph Thompson. In essence, Australia in 1947 could not have done it without British assistance. That support would continue for the next decade while Australia's own capabilities matured, but this direct British support with UK staff on secondment to Australia tapered off, particularly after the Suez Crisis of 1956.[33]

In reflecting on how this came to be, it is worth remembering that Venona material helped crystalise the scale of the Soviet challenge and, in turn, pointed to the need to retain trusted partners and allies. Thus, Venona effectively contributed to the strengthening of American resolve to sustain its wartime connections with the UK as the Cold War emerged. The isolationist retreat from international leadership after 1919 was not to be repeated after 1945. With Australia emerging from under British wings over time, the United States' more internationalist approach would apply to what would become known as the 'Five Eyes'. Australia, Canada and New Zealand had been trusted members of the Allied wartime arrangements, and as they increasingly asserted their sovereign rights and responsibilities after the war, the US came to appreciate their utility, not just as British adjuncts but as contributing entities in their own right. At the same time, while the UK's political and economic influence was waning globally, its connections with Australia and the other partners in the Five Eyes indirectly helped extend the longevity and efficacy of British power and influence, not just in its remaining colonial possessions (notably in the Far East), but its influence in Washington. While Australian Sigint activity in Australia, Hong Kong, Singapore and elsewhere helped its governments to understand challenging security dynamics in the region, it also directly assisted the British, with scarce resources and a light regional footprint, to manage their slow retreat from empire in the Far East.

33 See Blaxland and Birgin, *Revealing Secrets*, 228.

Beyond this, Venona cast a long shadow over the architecture of the Australian intelligence organisations in the post-1945 period. First, the legacy of 'compartmented' secrecy would endure as a signature of work in the intelligence community. Venona had always been managed as a closely held (that is, compartmented) secret about which only a small circle of insiders were briefed. Security clearances date back to the early, and fairly rudimentary, arrangements for handling Sigint in the Second World War, which evolved and matured over time. Today, they are a pre-requisite for employment as an insider in the intelligence agencies. Contemporary government security clearance processes, notably, the negative and positive vetting practices with their extensive and rigorous historical checks, can trace their antecedents to the revelations of trusted senior insiders passing information to those who were not authorised to view the material. Over time, they have been refined further to reduce the prospects of those who betrayed their own for a variety of motives summarised in the acronym MICE: money, ideology, coercion and ego. The list of candidates includes the likes of the Cambridge Five from the UK, others like Robert Hanssen and Aldrich Ames in the US, as well as people like Jean-Philippe Wispelaere in Australia.[34]

Beyond this, the connections with Anglosphere partners, and the trusted collaborative and distributed nature of intelligence collection and reporting, can also be directly and causally linked to the Venona decrypts. ASIO, as we have noted, emerged from the Venona revelations. Although suspicions arising from Venona lasted for several years, ASIO's establishment in 1949 went a long way towards re-establishing confidence and trust. The creation of an external human intelligence agency, the Australian Security Intelligence Service (ASIS), in 1952 further demonstrated to Australia's international intelligence partners that it treated intelligence and security as of fundamental importance to statecraft. Indirectly, at least (few were included or 'briefed in' on its existence), Venona would serve also to remind practitioners for the duration of the Cold War of the nature of the espionage challenge presented by the Soviet Union. Responding to this within Australia was a responsibility that fell principally to ASIO, but other agencies were also acutely aware of the expansive approach to intelligence collection taken by the Soviet Union, and of the challenging nature of the task in collecting intelligence on Soviet targets.

---

34   See Nino Bucci and Michael Inman, 'Wispelaere: The Spy Who Stayed Out in the Cold', *The Age*, 10 July 2012, www.theage.com.au/national/victoria/wispelaere-the-spy-who-stayed-out-in-the-cold-20120709-21rui.html.

DSB, meanwhile, built on the technical prowess of Australian Sigint teams that were seen as playing a constructive role in bolstering and supplementing the resources of, successively, the British and the Americans. Much of the manner in which DSB emerged, the technology it was assigned to use, and the networked and trusted sharing of information can be traced to the way the Australian Government chose to respond to the challenge that Venona represented. Once appraised of the gravity of the leaks pointed out by Venona, the Chifley government moved resolutely to sideline the Commonwealth Investigation Service and establish ASIO as the principal national security intelligence organisation. It did so in a way that largely mirrored the functions and capabilities of the UK's MI5. Once the superstructure for stronger security and robust counterintelligence initiatives had been built, confidence could be restored in sharing Sigint and other sensitive intelligence material, capabilities, procedures and technologies.

In 1953, a tripartite conference with the US and the UK in Melbourne examined the procedural and technical mechanisms for intelligence sharing, the distribution of responsibilities and the arrangements for routine and enduring liaison. This conference firmly set DSB, the antecedent of today's ASD, on a firm footing as a trusted and equal, albeit significantly smaller, partner in an international intelligence enterprise. The conference saw DSB recognised with its own Australian director, working and responsive to Australian Government direction, but informed and aided by seconded British personnel and increasingly assisted by access to American cryptological and computing power.

In later decades, after the establishment of DSB and the JIO in 1947, and ASIO in 1949, Australia's national intelligence community would be buffeted by reviews and royal commissions. The royal commission inspired by the Petrov defection was followed by royal commissions in the 1970s and 1980s, undertaken at the behest of prime ministers Gough Whitlam and Bob Hawke, and led by Justice Robert Marsden Hope. These reviews examined controversies that had emerged around the way business was conducted by the intelligence agencies. ASIO came out with the harshest criticism; ASIS and JIO less so, while the Defence Signals Directorate (formerly DSB) emerged with the greatest praise from Hope. Behind Hope's praise was a recognition of the professional and collaborative approach to Sigint collection and reporting, which drew on shared techniques and technologies that UK and US authorities entrusted in the Defence Signals Directorate (DSD). Much of this was due to the confidence they evinced that the troubles exposed by Venona had been addressed.

In addition, much of this buffeting can be traced to the transformation of the intelligence community, over a number of years, from one based on prime ministerial executive directives to ones based on explicit provisions set out in legislation and open to public scrutiny. Similar transformations occurred in other countries in the trusted intelligence circle abbreviated as the 'Five Eyes'.

Australia's intelligence community also expanded in 2018 to cover 10 agencies that between them were responsible for intelligence assessment (DIO and ONA), foreign human intelligence collection (ASIS), Sigint (ASD), geospatial intelligence (AGO), domestic security intelligence (ASIO), police intelligence (Australia Federal Police), financial intelligence (AUSTRAC), transnational organised crime (ACIC) and border and immigration security matters (Home Affairs). The expansion of the intelligence community reflects a more technological, connected, web-enabled, web-dependent and web-vulnerable world that has emerged since the proliferation of computers and the onset of the digital revolution, or what is sometimes described as the fourth industrial revolution.

Oversight mechanisms and legislative provisions have established guardrails and limits of authority for these numerous agencies as well. It is not often recognised, however, that many of these agencies are linked via highly classified ICT networks with counterparts across the globe, often accessing Sigint that is shared routinely. Those arrangements rest on the foundations made possible by the extraordinary revelations associated with the Venona decrypts. They rest on the intelligence architecture developed in the early postwar years that built on those foundations.

Australia in the 2020s has a robust national intelligence community that, after decades of operations, along with a number of reviews and reforms, has emerged as a set of instrumentalities that successive governments have valued and supported, while also seeking to ensure they are properly supervised and held to account. ASIO came under legislation with the *ASIO Act* in 1956. The other principal intelligence agencies would come under legislation incrementally, commencing with the *Office of National Assessments Act* in 1977 and, later, additional legislation such as the *Intelligence Services Act* of 2001. Related legislation affecting other intelligence instrumentalities within the Defence, Home Affairs and Attorney-General portfolios would follow.

While secrecy has been a hallmark of the nation's intelligence bodies, one thing is clear. The legacy of Venona is profound and enduring. In helping us understand that, and how it contributed to the emergence of ASIO, ASD, ONA and other intelligence bodies, we are indebted to Horner and Ball. Their intellectual influence continued in the structure and content of *Revealing Secrets*. This work consciously builds on the authoritative and informative foundations that Horner and Ball laid. The book explores the antecedents of Australia's modern-day Sigint and cyber capabilities. It reaches back to ancient cryptology as the conceptual foundation of modern Sigint, before tracing the tentative steps early in the twentieth century, followed by the dramatic expansion of Sigint and electro-mechanical computers in the Second World War. It also examines the postwar arrangements, the experience on military operations in Korea, Borneo, Vietnam, Timor and Afghanistan, followed by the emergence of legal oversight arrangements after a succession of royal commissions. The book ends considering the transformation of a secretive, attention-shy Cold War directorate into a more publicly engaged cybersecurity agency with a shopfront in capital cities, following its coming out as the nation's go-to cyber-assistance authority after the onset of the digital revolution. This work leans heavily on the foundations of Ball and Horner. In opening up the field of Australian intelligence history, Horner has been a pathfinder, not just for myself, but also for scholars who will find many more opportunities for research and writing in this field into the future.

Part VI: Changing environments

12

The history of the Australian Defence Force and space

Tristan Moss

Space has been used in the service of Australia's defence since the 1950s. As with Australia's civil space efforts, the manner in which the defence departments, the ADF and other agencies have used space and seen space in national security terms has been shaped by the country's geography and its historical ties to the US, and, to a lesser extent, the UK. These factors saw Australia acting as an important node in US space capabilities from the late 1950s and an Australian Defence department, the Department of Supply, managing the world's largest rocket range alongside British partners. However, Australia's defence space activities have also been influenced by the significant barriers to accessing space, most notably, the cost. As a result, much of the country's past use of space has been characterised by the perception of the domain in terms of discrete capabilities, such as satellites or imagery, rather than as a domain in which Australia could operate in the service of its security. Indeed, there was, until 2022, no single structure to oversee the ADF's approach to space.

In its simplest form, 'space' refers to the physical region beyond the earth's atmosphere, defined by the ADF as beyond 100 kilometres above sea level. Yet the word 'space' is often used as a shorthand for human activities beyond earth's atmosphere, which include a multitude of overlapping areas: research, human travel, navigation, sensing and communications, and ground-based infrastructure that includes launch facilities, tracking, command and control. It is through these activities that countries become space actors: they need not have their own nationals or objects in space to be counted as such, despite a public focus on astronauts and spacecraft. The use of space in service of national security is, at its core, a joint concern, with the capabilities that derive from space affecting each armed service and other elements of the defence organisation. The nature of space, with high financial and technical barriers to entry, reliance on complex technology and the difficulty of operating in the medium, has presented challenges for militaries around the world. Importantly, these challenges are not merely technical, but are also structural and doctrinal, and few countries operate alone in meeting them.

While space is often considered 'new', epitomising progress and the future, the way nations perceive and use space for national ends reflects their history, values and institutional structures. It is therefore fitting that this chapter appears in a collection of works reflecting on the scholarship of David Horner, whose work illuminates these vital themes in the study of the Australian military. During my PhD studies at the Strategic and Defence Studies Centre (SDSC) at The Australian National Univeristy (ANU), his work was a starting point for my own study of the military during the Cold War, while as a senior academic he was always generous with his time. No military historian better exemplifies the importance of rigorous research in laying the foundation for analysis, and no history of any aspect of Australia's defence from the Second World War to today can examine its subject without reference to Horner's work. The structure, activities and experiences of the ADF and the organisations that support it are not a product of single decisions by military leaders, but rather are shaped by myriad factors, from geography, strategic circumstances, budgets and technology to international relationships and institutional structures. Horner, who has written on every conflict and deployment in which Australia participated over the last 70 years, demonstrates this more than any other military historian. His work thus lays the foundation for a discussion of how the ADF has grappled with space, its first new domain since the creation of the Australian Flying Corps during the First World War.

Two broad themes stand out in analysing the ADF and space. The first is alliance relationships and their pervasive effect on the whole defence organisation. Horner's second book, *High Command: Australia's Struggle for an Independent War Strategy, 1939–1945*, speaks to the enduring theme within Australia's military past of reconciling Australia's own interests with the benefits and challenges of working with allies.[1] Horner's later work, on

---

1 David Horner, *High Command: Australia's Struggle for an Independent War Strategy, 1939–1945* (Canberra: Australian War Memorial and Sydney: George Allen & Unwin, 1982), doi.org/10.4324/9781003120193.

Vietnam, peacekeeping and post–Cold War operations, and on the creation of the ADF, all examine the influence played by the need to work with allies. In the Second World War, as today, Australia's geography, economic size and identity as a Western democracy have all shaped the way the country has entered into these relationships. Australian military space activities, ironically, do not occur in a vacuum; they are profoundly shaped by the global geopolitical context and the concerns of its friends, the nation's reliance on others and what it offers its allies in return.

The second theme is the importance of institutional structures in how the ADF is led, conducts operations and prepares for future conflict. Horner argues that command is not simply a matter of leadership but also a function of effective structures. While the act of leadership is well studied in Australian military history, particularly in the two world wars, Horner's work offers an avenue to understand not just how individuals shaped Australia's military past, but also how the institution of the ADF, as an instrument of the Australian state, shaped the trajectory of Australia's military experience.[2] Horner's body of work shows that developing effective structures to carry out government direction is as central to the ADF's business as leadership from individual officers, and that the creation of such structures is an essential part of the military's ability to come to terms with the shifting political, strategic and technical world around it.[3]

Space in Australian defence history

There have been three periods of Australia's engagement with space and defence. The first saw Australia involved in space activities initiated by other countries, which made it a small but important participant that was largely reactive to others' plans. This period, between the start of the space age in the late 1950s and the early 1970s, saw Australia involved in rocket testing at the Woomera testing range and hosting American defence facilities related to space, such as Pine Gap and Nurrungar. These mirrored Australia's participation in American civilian space endeavours, most notably, support for human spaceflight efforts through the establishment

---

2   See, in particular, David Horner, *Strategic Command: General Sir John Wilton and Australia's Asian Wars* (Melbourne: Oxford University Press, 2005); David Horner, *Making the Australian Defence Force* (South Melbourne: Oxford University Press, 2001).
3   David Horner, *Strategy and Command: Issues in Australia's Twentieth-Century Wars*, Australian Army History Series (Cambridge: Cambridge University Press, 2021), 264.

of spaceflight tracking stations around the country. Here, too, space was seen as a medium through which to achieve other national security ends, namely, alliance management. The second period, from the 1970s to the early 2000s, saw Australia gradually investigate its own defence needs in space, adding specific capabilities to meet particular needs, ever mindful of costs. This period was markedly less spectacular but laid the foundations for Australia's own space requirements to be met in the longer term. Finally, the third period, from the 2010s, saw Australia begin to see space as a warfighting domain, and one in which Australia might realistically seek to ensure its own sovereign needs beyond cooperation with allies.

The scholarly discussion of Australia's defence space history, like its space history more broadly, is patchy and reflects the fragmented nature of the country's space efforts in which there were few large projects to catch the eye of the public (or scholars) and no coherent national strategy.[4] Because much of Australia's interaction with the space domain has stemmed from the intelligence relationship, the highly classified and politically sensitive nature of these capabilities dominated conceptions of space in defence thinking in Australia and stifled public discussion. Moreover, as British space power theorist Bleddyn Bowen argues, academic discussions of space and national security tend to be dictated by the policy foci of the day and are invariably American-centric.[5] Thus, the US dominated Australia's space history, both military and civilian.[6] The relationship with the US continues to be one of the central pillars of Australia's current space efforts.[7] Until the 1970s, Australia was also closely involved in British and European space activities

---

[4] For a discussion of Australia's civilian space history literature, see Tristan Moss, '"There Are Many Other Things More Important to Us Than Space Research": The Australian Government and the Dawn of the Space Age, 1956–62', *Australian Historical Studies* 51, no. 4 (November 2020): 442–58, doi.org/10.1080/1031461X.2020.1766522.

[5] Bleddyn Bowen, *War in Space: Strategy, Spacepower, Geopolitics* (Edinburgh: Edinburgh University Press, 2020), 3.

[6] See particularly the work by Desmond Ball. Desmond Ball, *A Suitable Piece of Real Estate: American Installations in Australia* (Sydney: Hale & Iremonger, 1980), trove.nla.gov.au/work/10099484/version/45430140%20295453069; Desmond Ball, *Defence Aspects of Australia's Space Activities* (Canberra: Strategic and Defence Studies Centre, Research School of Pacific Studies, The Australian National University, 1992), openresearch-repository.anu.edu.au/handle/1885/216542; Desmond Ball, Bill Robinson, and Richard Tanter, 'Australia's Participation in the Pine Gap Enterprise', NAPSNet Special Reports, (June 08, 2016), nautilus.org/napsnet/napsnet-special-reports/australias-participation-in-the-pine-gap-enterprise/.

[7] For an analysis of this relationship, see Tristan Moss, 'The space between alliance and self-reliance: The evolution of the Australia-US defence space relationship', United States Studies Centre at the University of Sydney, August 2023.

at Woomera, the scale of which is detailed in Peter Morton's *Fire Across the Desert: Woomera and the Anglo-Australian Joint Project*, which serves as the most rigorous and comprehensive history of Australia's space activities.[8]

For smaller countries outside the archetype presented by the larger space actors—of significant space expenditure focused on human spaceflight, satellites and rockets, facing different strategic contexts—there are even fewer scholarly appreciations of how space might be used.[9] Australian thinking on the national security uses of space has, until recently, largely originated from within the military, often among those who have studied in the US.[10] While the relative importance of space to Australian defence planning increased over the decades, a number of themes thread their way through Australian thinking on space and its use in service of the country's defence. The lack of a government space policy, military or civilian, the absence of space structures and coordination with the defence organisation, and the poor management of space knowledge and the defence space workforce are constants in writing about national security space from the

---

8   Peter Morton, *Fire Across the Desert: Woomera and the Anglo-Australian Joint Project, 1946–1980* (Canberra: AGPS Press, 1989). There are a range of other studies of Woomera, ranging in detail. Kerrie Dougherty has written a number of short pieces on different aspects of Woomera. See, for instance, Kerrie Dougherty, 'The Weapons Research Establishment: An Administrative History', International Astronautical Congress proceedings, IAC-16-E4.2.6 (2006). Michael Wohltmann's more recent history of Woomera is detailed in its description, if polemical. See Michael Wohltmann, *Looking Back to See the Future: A Revisionist History of Woomera 1947–1980* (Adelaide: Digital Print, 2022). Geoffrey Gray has written about Indigenous experiences on the range, in Geoffrey Gray, 'Aborigines, Elkin and the Guided Projectiles Project', *Aboriginal History* 15, no. 1/2 (1991): 153–162. Alice Gorman similarly centres Indigenous experiences in her work. See, for instance, Alice Gorman, 'The archaeology of space exploration', *The Sociological Review* 57, no. 1 (2009): 132–145.
9   John J Klein, *Understanding Space Strategy: The Art of War in Space* (Abingdon: Routledge, 2019), 151, doi.org/10.4324/9780429424724; Wade Huntley, 'The Mice that Soar: Smaller States' Perspectives on Space Weaponisation', in *Securing Outer Space: International Relations Theory and the Politics of Space*, edited by Natalie Bormann and Michael Sheehan (London: Taylor & Francis Group, 2009), 147–67, doi.org/10.4324/9780203882023.
10   AM Forestier, *Into the Fourth Dimension: An ADF Guide to Space* (Canberra: Air Power Studies Centre, Royal Australian Air Force, 1992); Wayne Gale, *The Potential of Satellites for Wide Area Surveillance of Australia* (Canberra: Air Power Studies Centre, Royal Australian Air Force, 1992); Scott Wallis, DAB Fogg and RAAF Aerospace Centre, *Space Operations: An Australian Perspective* (Canberra: Aerospace Centre, 2001); Dominic Sims, 'Initiating a Coherent Approach to the Development of RAAF Space Doctrine', Air Power Development Centre Working Paper 09 (2008), airpower.airforce.gov.au/sites/default/files/2021-03/WP09-Initiating-a-Coherent-Approach-to-the-Development-of-RAAF-Space-Doctrine.pdf; Stephen B Cook, *A Potential Policy for Australian Military Space* (Canberra: Air Power Development Centre, Royal Australian Air Force, 2014); Darin J Lovett, *Space Power for Australia's Security: Grand Strategy or Strategy of Grandeur* (Canberra: Air Power Development Centre, Royal Australian Air Force, 2015); Chris Westwood, 'Securing Space: Australia's Urgent Security Policy Challenge for the 21st Century', *Australian Defence Force Journal* 201 (2017): 35–45.

1980s to the 2020s.[11] A common argument is the need for a more robust discussion of Australia's approach to space, and one that sees space not just as a collection of capabilities, but as a coherent policy area.[12]

'There, bare and fair': 1950s and 1960s

Australia's membership of the British Commonwealth and, later, its close relationship with the US, as formalised in the 1951 ANZUS Treaty, have shaped choices of who it has cooperated with in defence and space. Australia is useful to other nations for a variety of reasons: as one former NASA representative in Australia has put it, Australia is 'there, bare and fair', referring to its location in the southern hemisphere, its sparsely populated centre, away from sources of electromagnetic interference, and its stable democracy aligned to the West.[13] Throughout the Cold War, the Australian Government was conscious that it could trade its geography for access to American security and technology and, in this way, Australia was sometimes more interested in space for what it could do for its relationship with the US and others than it was in space per se.

The testing facilities at Woomera rocket range were at the heart of Australian space policy, acting as a centre of gravity that led to and shaped not only Australia's defence interest in space, but all its space efforts. The range, often simply referred to as 'Woomera', was established in 1947 as a joint project with the UK, the result of a need to develop missiles and other technology in the wake of the Second World War. The range itself encompassed an arc from Woomera to Talgarno on the Western Australian coast, through which rockets were tested, although the bulk of the facilities were housed around Woomera, a town about 450 km north of Adelaide whose population grew to over 6,000 people. The range was supplemented by research laboratories at Salisbury, close to Adelaide. In 1955, the two facilities became known as the Weapons Research Establishment (WRE), which was overseen by

---

11 For an overview of space during this period, see Brett Biddington, 'Space Security in the 21st Century' (PhD diss., University of New South Wales, 2019).
12 See, for instance, Tristan Moss, ed., *The Foundations of Australian Space Policy*, Regional Commentary, (Brisbane: Griffith Asia Institute, Griffith University, 2023); Tristan Moss, 'Unifying Space: Australia Needs a Whole of Government Space Policy', Black Swan Strategy Paper, (Perth: UWA Defence and Security Institute, 2021); Cassandra Steer, 'Australia as a Space Power: Combining Civil, Defence and Diplomatic Efforts', Policy Options Paper, National Security College, The Australian National University, 2021, 4.
13 Biddington, 'Space Security in the 21st Century', 97.

the Department of Supply, one of a number of defence-related government departments.[14] Being defence-related, activities at Woomera by extension involved the three armed services.

Woomera's long history saw it host a variety of military tests. These included V2 rockets taken from Germany after the Second World War, the Australian-designed Ikara anti-submarine missile, the Jindavik target drone and a variety of British-designed missiles. Woomera's involvement with space began with the British program of intercontinental ballistic missile (ICBM) tests from the 1950s.[15] As part of the design process, the joint project used the Black Knight rocket to test re-entry phenomena and tracking, a vital but not yet fully understood aspect of a missile's flight profile with the aim of both improving a missile's ability to hit its target without interception and at the same time to facilitate better tracking of enemy missiles. During the late 1950s, the Woomera range was also configured for tests of the British-designed Blue Streak ICBM. However, this project was cancelled in the face of British concerns about the vulnerability and cost of a land-based missile system. In an effort to save some of the sunk costs, Blue Streak became the first stage of a cooperative launcher designed by a consortium of European nations, under the banner of the European Launch Development Organisation. The resulting Europa rocket was tested at Woomera in the late 1960s and early 1970s, but when launches were moved to French Guiana, Australia declined further involvement in European space efforts because investing in a rocket and satellites designed primarily to service European needs did not suit its interests.[16]

The presence of a substantial range and modern instrumentation also made Woomera attractive to the US as a location for a spacecraft tracking station, and from 1957 the range hosted the Minitrack system. This was the first of a series of civilian stations based around Australia, which are best known for supporting the American moon landings, such as the Honeysuckle Creek, Orroral Valley and Tidbinbilla stations outside Canberra. Australia has hosted more American civilian and military tracking stations than any other country apart from the US itself. The government's reasons for agreeing to these facilities and other cooperative projects were intimately

---

14   For a detailed overview of the Woomera range, see Morton, *Fire Across the Desert*.
15   While the British tested both ICBMs and the nuclear weapons in Australia, and the Maralinga testing area was adjacent to the Woomera range, these two programs were administratively separate.
16   For a discussion of the Australian Government's policy on ELDO, see Moss, '"There Are Many Other Things More Important to Us Than Space Research"'.

tied to national security. Allen Fairhall, Minister for Supply in the Menzies government during the early 1960s, and therefore responsible for Woomera, clearly laid out Australia's interests in a 1964 submission to Cabinet:

> Our considerable dependence on the United States in Defence places some emphasis on the development of our existing friendly relations with the United States, and this can be advanced by encouraging US activities in Australia on reasonable terms. In addition, the projects involved are of great significance to the western world and offer important advantages to Australia, economically and scientifically.'[17]

While the government acknowledged that there were some economic and scientific benefits to the arrangements, later internal government correspondence contained the admission that in many cases, growth within Australia's own technological knowledge through cooperation with the US during the 1960s, such as in the case of tracking stations, was sometimes overstated.[18] Instead, it was the benefit to the alliance that hosting tracking stations accrued that mattered.

Military communications satellites were the first space-based capabilities Australia seriously investigated procuring for its own needs. As such, they reflect some of Defence's early thinking on space capabilities as desirable but not yet worth significant expenditure, given access was available more quickly and at less cost through the US. The advantages of communications satellites were obvious: not only is Australia a large, sparsely populated continent, but the ADF had commitments throughout the Asia-Pacific region. Defence planners were aware of US efforts to create a network of communications satellites, and Australia had been approached by the US to host tracking and data relay stations for their first program, named Advent. In 1964, the Chiefs of Staff Committee considered the satellite communications question, finding that 'it was in Australia's interests' to participate in cooperative defence satellite communications programs with the US and the UK, in addition to its cooperation in the civilian Intelsat communications system. However, it did not act on this finding immediately.[19]

---

17   Allen Fairhall, Cabinet Submission No. 562, 'Approval and Provision of site for tracking station for United States Project Apollo', November 1964, NAA, A5619, C754.
18   See White to Casey, nd, and Casey to White, 10 September 1963, NAA, M1148, USA – GENERAL.
19   Joint Communications-Electronics Committee Report 11/66, 'Australian Participation in the United States Defence Satellite Communications System', 6 July 1966, NAA, A1838, 694/7/48.

12. THE HISTORY OF THE AUSTRALIAN DEFENCE FORCE AND SPACE

While recognising the capability was appropriate for Australia's needs, Defence took its time deciding on satellite communications. In 1966, the Joint Planning Committee examined the question, identifying a strategic requirement for access to satellites. There was no telling where Australian forces might be deployed, and given that it was constructed around small, mobile forces that might be spread across a large geographic area, there was a need for 'flexible, reliable and continuous long-distance military communications'. Satellites were one option for meeting this need.[20] Demonstrating that the concerns about sovereign control of space assets are not new, some officials were worried about the possibility of foreign control of communications if Australia did not own the satellites it used.[21] However, the committee tasked with examining Australia's long-range defence communications found that the country's needs were already met through 1966 agreements with the US and the UK for terrestrial links.[22]

In addition to tracking stations, Australia participated in a range of US and British military space projects from the 1960s. These were broadly focused on missile technology, nuclear test detection, communications, mapping and intelligence gathering. Some saw Australian involvement in the test of hardware, such as the sequential Projects Gaslight, Dazzle and Sparta, which measured aspects of ballistic missile re-entry and were important in the early development of antiballistic missile systems. Similarly, Project Falstaff explored hypersonics.[23] Other projects, such as Project Quarterstaff, sought to map Australia's region from space. Project Sparta (Special Antimissile Research Tests, Australia) saw nine US-built Redstone rockets launched from Woomera in a joint project between Australia, the UK and the US. The success of the project resulted in one rocket being left unused; this was subsequently donated to Australia, allowing Australia's only domestically built and launched satellite, WRESAT, to enter orbit in 1967. The development of a satellite from scratch in just 11 months was a significant achievement for the WRE, but while it conducted civilian research in space, the program was firmly rooted in military space efforts. The rocket range, tracking equipment and many of the parts came from military tests at Woomera. The single-minded focus on this goal over other

---

20   Joint Communications-Electronics Committee Report 11/66, 'Australian Participation in the United States Defence Satellite Communications System', 6 July 1966, NAA, A1838, 694/7/48.
21   Cable, Washington to Canberra, 4 August 1966, NAA, A1838, 694/7/48.
22   Joint Communications-Electronics Committee Report 11/66, 'Australian Participation in the United States Defence Satellite Communications System', 6 July 1966, NAA, A1838, 694/7/48.
23   For a description of Falstaff, see Wohltmann, *Looking Back to See the Future*.

projects was in part justified as a test of the organisation's ability to launch a military satellite in a time of crisis. In addition, the launch of WRESAT is best seen as an example of the importance of foreign funds and equipment to Australia's early space history.[24]

Space and intelligence gathering from the 1970s

The second period of Australia's defence space history was marked by the increasing ADF utilisation of certain space capabilities, where before the military had only been a participant in others' projects. While those projects that capitalised on Australia's favourable geography continued, the ADF, created in 1976, sought access to communications, intelligence and navigation space capabilities. It did so in a range of ways, from commercial leases and allied partnerships to, in a few cases, its own sovereign control. In some cases, planners and commentators recognised the utility of space but understood that other options were cheaper. As barriers to access came down, most notably costs, Australia signed up. However, this was a gradual process. One article in the *Australian Defence Force Journal* in 1978, for instance, suggested that Australia buy time on a US surveillance satellite (noting that the idea was 'Fanciful? Perhaps, but it would be a damned good system!'), without suggesting there was any pressure to do so, while in 1983 another author demonstrated that space was still desirable but not yet vital, asking: 'Should Australia use satellites to support maritime operations?'[25]

The best-known intersection between Australia's defence and space experience has been its hosting of US defence facilities at Pine Gap and Nurrungar. Negotiated in 1966 and opened four years later, the Joint Defence Facility Pine Gap was established to support a joint Central Intelligence Agency and National Reconnaissance Office satellite program that intercepted telemetry from Soviet and Chinese missile tests and VHF and UHF communications. Nurrungar opened in 1969 and served the USAF Defence Support Program, which tracked Soviet missile launches through a series of geosynchronous

---

24 For a detailed analysis of the WRESAT project, see Morton, *Fire Across the Desert*, Chapter 24.
25 COG Williams, 'Spy in the Sky', *Australian Defence Force Journal* 9, March–April (1978): 52 and GA Spence, 'The Effect of Satellites on Australian Maritime Strategy During the 1980s', *Australian Defence Force Journal* 39, March–April (1983): 41–47.

satellites.[26] Situated deep within the Australian landmass, the position of these stations made them largely immune to seaborne jamming, compared with other sites in the Pacific.[27] Australians were always present, working alongside Americans in these facilities, although controversially it took time for them to gain access to the highest and most classified areas.[28]

Australia has also built its own space intelligence-gathering facilities. In 1979, Australia also embarked on a sovereign satellite intelligence-collecting capability with the creation of the Shoal Bay Receiving Station, a signals intelligence facility outside Darwin. One of Shoal Bay's primary functions was the interception of Indonesian satellite communications. In 1993, the then-DSD opened the Australian Defence Satellite Communications Station (ADSCS) at Korajena, outside Geraldton, Western Australia. Like Shoal Bay, Korajena collects signals intelligence from satellites, with a focus on the Indo-Pacific region. When opened, it lay under the orbits of a number of Soviet, regional and commercial communications satellites; the number of satellites it can observe has increased exponentially since.[29] ADSCS and Shoal Bay are entirely Australian managed, albeit it with some US and British staff in several key positions. From its inception, ADSCS formed part of the wider Five Eyes intelligence sharing network, made up of the US, the UK, Canada, Australia and New Zealand, and raw data was sent directly to partners. However, the same has not occurred with information collected at Shoal Bay. In 2000, shortly after the Five Eyes relationship was publicly revealed, Australia was not sharing raw intelligence data from Shoal Bay with partners.[30] That Australia held information relating to Indonesia more closely than other data reflected the tensions with that country in the late 1990s and early 2000s and suggests that Australia was willing to pay for its own, sovereign facilities in support of those national security priorities it deemed most vital.

---

26 Jeffrey T Richelson, *America's Space Sentinels: The History of the DSP and SBIRS Satellite Systems*, 2nd ed. (Lawrence: University Press of Kansas, 2012), 51.
27 Richelson, *America's Space Sentinels*, 54.
28 Ball, Robinson and Tanter, 'Australia's Participation in the Pine Gap Enterprise', 19; Andrew O'Neil, 'Australia and the "Five Eyes" Intelligence Network: The Perils of an Asymmetric Alliance', *Australian Journal of International Affairs* 71, no. 5 (3 September 2017): 539, doi.org/10.1080/10357718.2017.1342763; Richelson, *America's Space Sentinels*, 55, 147.
29 Ball, *Defence Aspects*, 31–33. See also Australian Defence Satellite Communications Station, Kojarena, *Nautilus Institute*, nautilus.org/publications/books/australian-forces-abroad/defence-facilities/australian-defence-satellite-communications-station-kojarena/; and Gary Adshead, 'Spy Base in Our Backyard', *The West Australian*, 14 October 2013.
30 Jeffrey Richelson, 'Desperately Seeking Signals', *Bulletin of the Atomic Scientists* 56, no. 2 (March 1, 2000): 49, doi.org/10.2968/056002013.

Communications and space services

During this second period of Australian military space, satellite communications grew from merely desirable to important. By 1970, Australia's communication requirements had risen substantially, with Army signals traffic alone growing by 450 per cent in just five years.[31] Both the UK and the US were developing satellite communications, and the Defence Committee considered partnering with both.[32] The findings of the Defence Committee's 1971 examination of the issue were prescient in their understanding of the balance that Australia needed to strike between having its own capability and leveraging international partners. The committee recognised that relying on international partners came with risks and argued that 'wherever practicable Australia should have command and control and should not rely on another country for defence communications not backed up by nationally owned and operated systems'. The issue here was 'not so much the possibility of sudden denial' but the likelihood of being relegated to second-tier status when the system was stretched. At the same time, the committee recognised that because of cost, Australia's relatively small requirements for communications satellites and its inability to produce or launch them, some sort of cooperation was to be accepted.[33] Nonetheless, despite supporting satellite communications for their survivability, bandwidth and coverage, Defence again delayed the decision, and by 1980, Defence's communications needs were still being met by military and commercial radio links.[34]

Australia's first defence satellite communications connection came from linking into US systems. In 1981, a ground terminal for the US Defence Satellite Communications System (DSCS) was opened at Watsonia Barracks, Victoria. While there were other DSCS terminals at US installations around the country, Watsonia provided a link through which information between Australian sources and the US could be transferred. This included links from DSD to the NSA in the US, and joint DSD/

---

31 John Blaxland, *Signals Swift and Sure: A History of the Royal Australian Corps of Signals, 1947 to 1972* (Watsonia: Royal Australian Corps of Signals Corps Committee, 1998), 133.
32 Joint Communications-Electronics Committee Report 3/67, 'Defence Communications Satellite Systems', 20 February 1967, NAA, A1838, 694/7/48.
33 Joint Staff Directive, 'A Study of Satellite Systems for Australian Military Communications Purposes', 31 March 1971, NAA, A1838, 694/7/48 PART 2.
34 Cabinet Decision No. 12359, Memorandum No. 907, 'Defence and Security Implications of the Proposed National Satellite Communications System', 2 July 1980, NAA, A12930, 907.

GCHQ installations then in Hong Kong.[35] Also beginning in 1981 was the first satellite communications provided to the RAN through the US Navy's Western Pacific Fleet Satellite Communications satellites. Using UHF links, this provided limited data transmission to some RAN units, although even a decade later, the capacity was limited to 'receive' only in many ships, with just three frigates, two guided missile destroyers and two auxiliaries able to transmit via satellite as well as receive. By the early 1990s, the ADF also used INMARSAT and Telecom Australia for satellite communications, but these only offered insecure transmissions, and the Army had just eight terminals to support overseas operations.[36] Ultimately, it took the launch of Australia's first civilian communications satellite, AUSSAT, for Defence to gain access to Australian-controlled space-based communications. Utilising the capacity on AUSSAT, launched by NASA's space shuttle *Discovery* in 1985, Defence maintained its own earth stations to access the civilian system.[37] However, Defence lost interest in following up on AUSSAT because of cost and concerns about the security of a civilian system, using a mixture of commercial and US satellites instead.[38]

By the 1990s, the ADF was regularly using space capabilities in a variety of different fields. Weather data was provided through the Bureau of Meteorology, which had access to weather data from commercial sources. The ADF was also able to access the same weather data network for the use of the services' own meteorological units.[39] From the mid-1990s, the ADF also used the global positioning system (GPS) for navigation, replacing the earlier US Transit system used by the RAN, which had been only suitable for slow-moving vehicles, operated in only two dimensions and had a 200 metre circle of error.[40] First approved for trial in 1988, GPS was initially rolled out for high-priority RAN and RAAF users, survey and hydrography, and submarines. The final phases, which saw small GPS receivers given to the Australian Army, occurred during the mid-1990s, with the planned rollout completed around the end of the decade.[41]

---

35 Desmond Ball, *Code 777: Australia and the US Defense Satellite Communications System (DSCS)* (Canberra: Strategic and Defence Studies Centre, Research School of Pacific Studies, The Australian National University, 1989), 167, 170.
36 Forestier, *Into the Fourth Dimension*, 7–12.
37 Ball, *Defence Aspects*, 57.
38 SR Partridge, 'Aussat: The Social Shaping of a Satellite System' (PhD diss., University of Wollongong, 1989), 336.
39 Forestier, *Into the Fourth Dimension*, 6–9.
40 Forestier, *Into the Fourth Dimension*, 8–19.
41 Forestier, *Into the Fourth Dimension*, 8–17.

The Australian shift to continental defence after the Vietnam War (the so-called 'Defence of Australia' period) saw a significant rise in the country's surveillance needs as Defence policy focused on defending the air–sea gap to the continent's north. While the utility of Australian–owned or operated remote sensing satellites was studied by the Defence Science and Technology Organisation, mapping and survey was conducted with either allied data, provided through pre-existing networks or bought commercially.[42] Equally, although there was a clear requirement to observe Australia's northern and north-western approaches, Defence settled on the Jindalee Operational Radar Network (JORN) to meet these needs, rather than a space-based capability. This over-the-horizon radar, able to detect ships and aircraft in the Indonesian archipelago and further, offered the Australian Government 'practical broad area capability at an affordable cost', and Cabinet saw JORN as being far more cost-effective than a satellite.[43] It also had the benefit of being Australian–developed and operated, and was seen as likely to be developed and implemented more quickly than a satellite.[44]

Space during the 1990s and 2000s

Space was a minor part of Australia's defence strategy up to and during the 1990s, with the ADF treating space capabilities as addendums to other areas of defence, with a lower priority than other potential acquisitions.[45] While the 1994 Defence White Paper acknowledged the value of space to Australia's national security, there was no single area of Defence tasked with leading Australia's space activities and, as a result, a lack of coordination. With few advocates for space, no career path for space-qualified personnel, particularly at the policy level, and no government commitment to the use of space in support of the ADF, space was 'the missing dimension in Australia's defence policy', according to one officer.[46] The formation of the Defence Space Directorate in 1995 marked a slow shift towards a centralised

---

42 Graham Wren, 'The Role of Space in Australia's Force Development', *Australian Defence Force Journal* 118 (1996): 8.
43 Cabinet Minute No. 14774, Submission No. 7674, 'Jindalee Operational Network (JORN)', 19 December 1990, NAA, A14039, 7674 and Cabinet Minute No. 5422, Submission No. 2150, 'Project Jindalee – Over-the-Horizon Radar, implementation of stage B', 17 May 1978, NAA, A12909, 2150.
44 Gale, *The Potential of Satellites*, section 7, 4.
45 Forestier, *Into the Fourth Dimension*, 1–7.
46 Kenneth Drover, 'Space Power: The Missing Dimension in Australia's Defence Policy', *Australian Defence Force Journal* 93 (March–April 1992), and Kenneth J Drover, 'Space Power: Military Imperatives in Australia's Environment', Air War College Research Report (March 1989): 37.

12. THE HISTORY OF THE AUSTRALIAN DEFENCE FORCE AND SPACE

and joint approach to space, while the creation of the Defence Imagery and Geospatial Organisation in 2000 reflected the expansion of available data from space and the need for greater analysis capacity. However, there was still no single body coordinating policy on space.[47] By 2002, Squadron Leader Dominic Sims wrote that services like the RAAF used space for a range of activities, from communications to weather, but these activities 'represent dependencies the RAAF does not currently fully understand'.[48] Sims pointedly began his examination of RAAF space doctrine with a quote from the service's strategic document, *The Fundamentals of Australian Aerospace Power*: 'Cost currently prohibits the RAAF from exploiting the space environment.'[49]

The fragmented nature of ADF approaches to space reflected the lack of a broader Australian Government policy on space, which was marked by a perception of space in terms of the task a particular capability might undertake, rather than as a single domain. At a national level, space scholar Brett Biddington describes this period as having 'bifurcated narrative between space as a national security priority and as an industry development priority'.[50] Some sub-departmental structures were set up after the first government-commissioned study of Australia's space policy, the 1985 Madigan review, most notably the Australian Space Office. However, these structures were underfunded and short-lived, and national security was explicitly excluded from their remit.

Throughout the 1990s and early 2000s, Australia did not seek to develop space as an area of significant policymaking in Defence or elsewhere. As outlined in a 1992 report on the Australian Space Office, Australia was a customer, not a developer of space.[51] Even as late as 2003, the Howard government's *Space Engagement Statement* saw no need to pursue self-sufficiency in space in the face of adequate cooperative arrangements with other nations and the availability of commercial space capabilities.[52] As a result, Australian engagement with space in Defence and, more broadly, across government was focused on individual capabilities, bought as needed. The space assets

---

47 Wren, 'The Role of Space in Australia's Force Development', 5; Wallis, Fogg and RAAF Aerospace Centre, *Space Operations*, 2.
48 Sims, 'Initiating a Coherent Approach to the Development of RAAF Space Doctrine', 4–5.
49 Sims, 'Initiating a Coherent Approach to the Development of RAAF Space Doctrine', 2.
50 Biddington, 'Space Security in the 21st Century', 139.
51 Biddington, 'Space Security in the 21st Century', 132.
52 Department of Industry, Tourism and Resources, 'Australia's Space Engagement: The Australian Government's Space Related Activities, Policy Framework and Overview', 2003.

procured or accessed by Defence met each perceived need, but the glue linking these capabilities into a coherent area of Defence interest, such as space workforce management and integration of the space domain into strategic thinking, was missing. Equally, it is easy to see these decisions in hindsight and in light of subsequent efforts to create a space command, rather than as the product of fitting a small but growing area of Defence expenditure alongside a myriad of other demands on resources, from frigates to training to tanks.

To Australian Space Command: 2010s and 2020s

During the 2010s, Defence began to better address the issues, identified in previous decades, that had shaped Australia's approach to military space. There was no single catalyst for change, but, rather, a growing realisation within Defence that in the context of a shifting space environment, space was not a domain that could be ignored, and that ideas, institutional structures and procurement must be adapted. This period was defined by the steady falling cost of access to space, and the subsequent expansion of state and other actors using space. Specific threats, such as Chinese and Russian anti-satellite tests, concentrated Western attention, while the US, in particular, sought to develop institutions that were equipped to tackle these growing threats in space. Australian Defence planners were aware of this, but change was gradual, with the construction of a coherent ADF space strategy and the structures to implement it occurring over more than a decade.

More broadly during this period, there was an Australian discussion of its needs in space as a country, albeit with an industry focus rather than a whole-of-government focus, leading to the creation of an Australian Space Agency (ASA) in 2018. While a significant step forward in the place of space in Australia, the new agency was small in size and purview. It was particularly interested in fostering a space industry, and as such was subordinated within the Department of Industry, Science and Resources. As in previous iterations of Australian civilian space structures, national security was absent from the ASA's remit (although liaison was facilitated between it and Defence), and many space functions remain with other departments, such as the Commonwealth Scientific and Industrial Research Organisation (CSIRO). A significant further limitation in the ASA's approach to space was the continuing absence of a whole-of-government space policy, such that the historical fragmentation of Australia's space efforts was not entirely eliminated.[53]

Within Defence, the 2010s saw a marked move towards including space in strategic planning. The 2009 Defence White Paper, the first such analysis for nine years, identified space as an area of importance and interest, placing the concept of 'self-reliance' alongside a recognition of the need to continue to work with allies in the face of the high costs of space.[54] The White Paper also committed to acquiring a 'satellite with remote sensing capability', although this was discussed in terms of ISR, a subsection of 'information superiority', rather than space capability. This framing was consistent throughout the paper, with it highlighting the importance of satellite communications as a vital element of information and communications technology.[55]

Over the next decade, Australia strengthened its language on space, centring the domain in defence thinking in a new way. Space moved into the spotlight within the ANZUS alliance at the joint Australia–United States Ministerial Consultation (AUSMIN) meeting in 2010, with the release of the Space Situational Awareness Partnership Statement of Principles and a joint statement on space security that acknowledged the crucial nature of satellites to defence activities.[56] The 2012 AUSMIN meetings cemented this new centrality of space in Australia's strategic outlook, with Australia committing to a new joint space facility. The 2013 Defence White Paper noted that Australia's security was reliant on 'assured access to space systems', while the 2016 paper identified space as one of six themes that Defence was to pursue.[57] Finally, in laying out Australia's responses to changes since the 2016 White Paper, the 2020 Defence Strategic Update emphasised space as 'critical to ADF warfighting effectiveness, situational awareness and …

---

53 See Cassandra Steer, 'Who is Australia in Space? The Need for a National Space Policy', in *The Foundations of Australia's Space Policy*, edited by Tristan Moss (Griffith Asia Institute Regional Commentary, 2023), 27–42.
54 Department of Defence, *Defending Australia in the Asia Pacific Century: Force 2030* (Canberra: Commonwealth of Australia, 2009), 62.
55 Department of Defence, *Defending Australia in the Asia Pacific Century: Force 2030*, 82, 120.
56 'Australia–United States Ministerial Consultations 2010 Joint Communiqué', 8 November 2010, www.dfat.gov.au/geo/united-states-of-america/ausmin/Pages/ausmin-joint-communique-2010.
57 Department of Defence, '2013 Defence White Paper' (Canberra: Department of Defence, 2013), 24, www.defence.gov.au/about/strategic-planning/defence-white-paper. Department of Defence, '2016 Defence White Paper' (Canberra: Department of Defence, 2016), 10, www.defence.gov.au/whitepaper/docs/2016-Defence-White-Paper.pdf.

communications' and laid a framework for additional space capabilities, much of them Australian-owned or operated, through the 2020 Force Structure Plan.[58]

Matching the new awareness of space was the growth of the institutional structures within the ADF designed to manage space assets and policy. The Defence Space Coordinating Office (DSCO) was established as a joint office within ADF headquarters in September 2006. DSCO's mission was to provide 'Defence-wide coordination, monitoring and consideration' of all things space. Unlike the Space Directorate, DSCO's functions included an input into policy, increasing the space voice and expertise in Defence.[59] In 2012, Defence created the Australian Space Operations Centre (AUSSpOC), located within Joint Operations Command (JOC) to provide command and control of space operations in support of JOC's wider responsibilities.[60] Following the 2014 Defence First Principles Review, the DSCO was moved to report directly to the Vice Chief of Defence Force, reflecting the growing importance of space.

Satellite communications remained one of the ADF's most pressing space needs into the twenty-first century and, by the 2010s, one for which the benefit clearly now outweighed the cost, for the first time since the idea was examined in the 1960s. Defence launched its own payload for the first time in 2003, attached to the Optus C1 satellite. Prior to 2007, the ADF had still largely used civilian-provided satellite communications for links to its deployed forces in the Middle East.[61] To meet its military communications needs, the Australian Government signed an agreement with the US to participate in the Wideband Global SATCOM (WGS) system in 2007, seeing buying into an established system as cost-effective and quicker than a unique build. Australia contributed funds equivalent to the cost of one of the 10 satellites, although it did not own any specific satellite. Instead, it gained access to a set amount of bandwidth, overwhelmingly in the Australian region but also, when needed, globally.

---

58 Department of Defence, *2020 Defence Strategic Update*, 2020, www.defence.gov.au/about/strategic-planning/2020-defence-strategic-update.
59 Cook, *A Potential Policy for Australian Military Space*, 15.
60 Max Blenkin, 'Polar Orbit', *Australian Defence Business Review* 16 (October 2021); and Royal Australian Air Force, 'Air-Space Integration', Doctrine Note Series ADFN 1–19, (Canberra 2019): 56.
61 Australian National Audit Office, '2009–10 Major Projects Report', 2010, 286.

While Australia was allocated a larger share of the WGS system than all non-US partners combined, Australia's part in the program reflects the balance between military need and sovereign capability that was first identified in the 1970s. The WGS program had a unique procurement regime, in which Australia had no direct relationship with the builder, Boeing, instead dealing with the US Government, which was constrained by the International Traffic in Arms Regulations regime.[62] The agreement with the US sees WGS resources managed by US installations in Hawaii. At least 24 hours' notice is required for requests.[63] The process has been smooth and is sometimes expedited, as during the 2020 bushfires, but is ultimately under the control of the US.[64] Australia also uses a defence payload on the Intelsat 22 satellite over the Indian Ocean, launched in 2012, and contracts with commercial providers.[65] The reliance on both US-controlled WGS and commercial contracts represent potential risks for the ADF in times of crisis, when their priorities might not align with those of partners.[66]

In early 2022, Defence created Defence Space Command, addressing the issues that had shaped the organisation's approach to space by creating what was intended to be a single, high-level and integrated headquarters. Space Command initially reported directly to the Chief of Air Force, as the RAAF had responsibility for space. In 2023, Space Command moved to the Joint Capability Group, reflecting a more 'joint' approach to space.[67] The Command's priorities were to develop strategic planning for space, to aid in the procurement and management of space capabilities, to build a space workforce within the ADF and to advocate for space issues within the organisation.[68] The creation of Space Command was intended to be a first point of call for space within the ADF as well as, importantly, with US space commands and the newly created US Space Force. In turn, this has been facilitated by an increased interest from the US to work with allies in space, marking a break from the tightly held world of military space that

---

62   Australian National Audit Office, '2009–10 Major Projects Report', 286.
63   Memorandum of understanding between the Department of Defence of the United States of America and the Department of Defence of Australia concerning the Production, Operations and Support of Wideband Global Satellite Communications, 14 November 2007, 40–42.
64   Max Blenkin, 'Sovereign SATCOM: the urgent quest for sovereign SATCOM capability', *Australian Defence Business Review*, 23 February 2021.
65   'Govt to buy full Intelsat IS-22 UHF payload', *Australian Defence Magazine* (5 May 2010), www.australiandefence.com.au/news/govt-to-buy-full-intelsat-is-22-uhf-payload.
66   Moss, 'The Space Between Alliance and Self-Reliance', 39.
67   Moss, 'The Space Between Alliance and Self-Reliance', 21.
68   'Defence Space Command', Royal Australian Air Force, www.airforce.gov.au/our-mission/defence-space-command.

the US had maintained during the Cold War. As is the case with the ASA, however, many space functions remain outside the remit of Defence Space Command.

Concurrent with the launch of Defence Space Command, Defence released its Space Strategy and Space Power Manual to guide its approach to the domain. These represented the first step in a publicly articulated approach to space but are perhaps best read as a reflection of the various drivers and themes of Australian space thinking rather than the final word on the country's use of space for national security ends. While the Space Power Manual was perhaps brief in its approach to space power, the Strategy went some way to laying a roadmap for building the ADF's approach to space as an institution. Its five lines of effort continued the concerns of the previous 60 years and attempted to address some of the longstanding weaknesses in approaches to Defence space: ensuring Australian access to space, working with other space actors in Australia and internationally, encouraging the growth of the understanding of space issues, progressing Australian sovereign capability, and the development of Defence's space structures and personnel. The delicate balance between sovereign capability and the need to work with partners also threads throughout the document. The Strategy marked a break from the ADF's past approach in its clear direction in developing the institutional structures, conceptual approaches, relationships and capabilities. For instance, its commitment to strengthening the ADF's doctrinal understating of space power, developing interdepartmental governance around space, and establishing industry priorities might, if undertaken successfully, build a stronger foundation for the use of space.[69]

The institutional and conceptual changes of the 2010s were matched by the development of space capabilities available to Australia. At the time of writing, the ADF is exploring capabilities more within its own control rather than through partnerships. In 2023, having gained experience with the WGS, Defence awarded a contract to Lockheed Martin for an Australian-managed military communications satellite under Joint Project 9102, marking the largest space acquisition project in Australia's history. Yet, this project was cancelled the following year, a victim of the myriad pressures on the Defence budget and space's still-secondary position in Australia's defence. The 2010s also saw an expansion of space domain awareness (SDA) capabilities, with Australia constructing three ground stations integrated into a broader US

---

69   Royal Australian Air Force, *Defence Space Strategy* (2022) and Royal Australian Air Force, *Defence Space Power eManual* (2022).

system to identify and track space objects such as satellites, missiles and debris. These are managed by the RAAF's 1 Remote Sensing Unit, which also manages JORN. Taking advantage once again of Australia's geographic position, these SDA installations offer a means by which Australia provides a capability of value to the US. Equally, the ability to develop a picture of the space environment is a vital foundation for any Australian sovereign defence activity in space.[70] Defence has also openly discussed more independent and offensive capabilities, including a remote sensing satellite similar those run by the National Reconnaissance Office (NRO) in the US and electronic or laser-based anti-satellite infrastructure.[71]

An Australian-run space surveillance capability and the 2022 collaboration between Defence and the NRO in two intelligence satellite launches mark a shift in Australia's conception of the cost of space relative to the need, albeit an incomplete one, as demonstrated by the cancellation of the Australian-owned defence communication satellite.[72]

Conclusion

It should be no surprise that the capabilities that Australia had begun to procure and use by the 2020s were first mooted at least a decade before, and in the case of communications satellites, during the 1960s. Australia has long been involved in space but approached it with reference to its needs and means. Australia's historic experience in defence space was the product of an interplay between its strategic circumstances, the availability of technology, its cost and the country's alliances. In this way, Australia's first, and longest, engagement in space came as a result of the relationships with the UK and the US during the 1960s and saw Australia largely reacting to its allies' needs, willing to trade geography for strategic gain. The ready access to US space capabilities also shaped the way in which Australia approached space. Australia met its space needs through access to foreign systems, gaining

---

70   Joint Standing Committee on Foreign Affairs, Defence and Trade, Inquiry into the Department of Defence Annual Report 2019–20, November 2021, www.aph.gov.au/Parliamentary_Business/Committees/Joint/Foreign_Affairs_Defence_and_Trade/DefenceAReport19-20/Report.
71   Australia's path to a surveillance satellite has two phases: first, working with commercial partners for access to data; and second, developing Australia's own satellite. Joint Standing Committee on Foreign Affairs, Defence and Trade, Inquiry and Jack Norton, 'Russia and China give Australia's space commander the need for speed', *ASPI Strategist*, 23 March 2022, www.aspistrategist.org.au/russia-and-china-give-australias-space-commander-the-need-for-speed/.
72   Moss, 'The Space Between Alliance and Self-Reliance', 37, 41.

intelligence from the broader US intelligence network, navigating with the use of US satellites and communicating using US national or commercial satellites. In turn, this shaped the ADF's approach to space. The creation of effective institutional structures is vital to Defence's ability to meet national need, as Horner points out. However, the particular nature of much of Australia's military space history, shaped by geography and alliances, saw space accessed in an ad hoc fashion, with each service or area of Defence procuring a capability to fit a need, rather than approaching space as a single area of interest.

Only with the lowering of the cost of space, and the increasing integration of space within a wide variety of military functions, from navigation to communication, has the ADF sought to deepen its engagement with space. The shift in approach only occurred in earnest from the 2010s and has yet to be fully realised in the acquisition of capabilities. While it owns or manages ground-based stations, in the early 2020s the ADF did not yet own significant space assets. The road to Australian satellites in orbit is a long and expensive one.[73] Australia's space future will reflect the balance that the country has always tried to strike between cost and need, albeit in changed strategic and technological circumstances. Most likely, Australia will seek to answer its space needs with a spectrum of partnerships, ranging from paying for access to certain systems to cooperative arrangements, to buying its own satellite from US or perhaps local industry.

The history of Australian defence space is, thus, one of gradual growth in acquisitions, structures and thinking, underpinned by geography and alliances. This trajectory is the direct product of the broader context in which the Australian Defence organisation found itself from the 1950s to the 2020s. The ADF's engagement in space has always been a balance between Australia's own needs and what it can reasonably afford. This is no different from other areas of defence; however, the historical use of space to further alliance relationships marks it out from most other capabilities. While there can be a tendency to focus on the concerns of the present in discussions of Australia's military space needs, an understanding of the foundations of the Defence organisation's use of space allows for a nuanced picture of the longstanding issues and the drivers of Australian policy towards space.

---

73   Colin Clark, 'Lockheed Wins Australia's Biggest Ever Space Contract, Worth Estimated $4B AUD', *Breaking Defence*, 3 April 2023, breakingdefense.com/2023/04/lockheed-wins-australias-biggest-ever-space-contract-worth-estimated-4b-aud/.

13

Soldiers as peacekeepers, peacekeepers as soldiers: the Australian experience

Peter Londey

I offer this chapter in gratitude for David Horner's calm and wise leadership of the team that, under his direction as official historian, wrote the six large volumes of the Official History of Australian Peacekeeping, Humanitarian and Post–Cold War Operations, published by Cambridge University Press between 2011 and 2020. The team was, by and large, very harmonious (and a few of us, including David Horner himself, remain drinking friends long after the series was completed).[1]

---

1   I would like to thank Lt Gen John Sanderson for some trenchant and informative comments on an earlier draft of the Cambodia section. I would also like to thank the editors of this volume for their thoughtful comments on an earlier draft, and all the peacekeepers I have been fortunate enough to interview.
Abbreviations:
PKOH = Official History of Australian Peacekeeping, Humanitarian and Post–Cold War Operations
Individual volumes are abbreviated as follows:
PKOH 1 = Peter Londey, Rhys Crawley and David Horner, *The Long Search for Peace: Observer Missions and Beyond, 1947–2006* (Melbourne: Cambridge University Press, 2020)
PKOH 3 = David Horner and John Connor, *The Good International Citizen: Australian Peacekeeping in Asia, Africa and Europe, 1991–1993* (North Melbourne: Cambridge University Press, 2014)
PKOH 4 = Jean Bou et al., *The Limits of Peacekeeping: Australian Missions in Africa and the Americas, 1992–2005* (Melbourne: Cambridge University Press, 2019) [Note: full list of authors is: Jean Bou, Bob Breen, David Horner, Garth Pratten and Miesje de Vogel]
PKOH 5 = Bob Breen, *The Good Neighbour: Australian Peace Support Operations in the Pacific Islands, 1980–2006* (Melbourne: Cambridge University Press, 2016).

Although the team was split between different institutions, in particular the Australian War Memorial (AWM) and The Australian National University (ANU), the project was a very collegiate endeavour. We generally met fortnightly, discussed one or two pre-circulated draft chapters quite frankly, and then retired for drinks to soothe any wounded egos. Thus, almost every chapter of those six volumes passed at a draft stage through a committee of critical peers, including authors of volumes and our exceptionally talented pool of research assistants.

I had an informal title of Deputy General Editor, in recognition of the fact that, more than anybody else on the project, I came to it from a background of writing about peacekeeping. In particular, while working at the AWM in 2004, I had published *Other People's Wars*, the first book-length history of all Australian peacekeeping from 1947 on.[2] David Horner approached the project from a different direction, as one of Australia's most distinguished military historians. Thus, it was not surprising that when David came to comment on my chapters, he sometimes felt that my interest in the multilateral nature of peacekeeping had led me to provide too little institutional history, especially of the Australian Army. And, as my chapters arrived at their final form, he was not averse to inserting into my text short biographical notes detailing the military careers of some of the peacekeepers I was writing about.[3]

David's approach was based on an implicit assumption that, of all aspects of a peacekeeper's past, the military side was the most important, but it would be an enormous research task to test the validity of that assumption. Here, I am more concerned with the degree to which military peacekeepers have, in fact, succeeded in coping with the fuzzy logic of peacekeeping, with all the patience, flexibility, adaptability and improvisation that it necessitates.[4]

---

2   Peter Londey, *Other People's Wars: A History of Australian Peacekeeping* (Sydney: Allen & Unwin, 2004).
3   These were often up to a paragraph, far longer than the brief biographical footnotes that Bean established as a staple of Australian official histories (consider Bean, *The Australian Imperial Force in France 1917* [Sydney: Angus and Robertson, 1933], 25 n. 13, where Blamey's previous career is dealt with in 12 words).
4   I use the words 'military' and 'soldiers' for convenience, partly because most of Australia's peacekeepers have, in fact, come from the Army (and, as peacekeepers, the roles of members of all three services have often been indistinguishable). In the Australian context, I use 'military' to refer to members of the ADF, as against civilian police and other civilians.

The question and terminology

I wish to use the term 'peacekeeping' as a catch-all for a wide range of activities that might be grouped together as 'peace operations'. Not everybody agrees with the use of such a blanket term. Writing on Cambodia, John Sanderson has been at pains to distinguish peacekeeping, the task for which the Military Component of the United Nations Transitional Authority in Cambodia (UNTAC) was authorised and equipped, from 'peace enforcement'.[5] This has developed more recently into the trenchant view that 'peace enforcement is war by another name'.[6] Some have argued that recent UN 'stabilisation operations' in Africa, sometimes working with even more robust 'parallel forces', have moved peacekeeping closer to war fighting,[7] while those fighting wars in Afghanistan and Iraq have tried to present their activities as in some way akin to peacekeeping.

This is not the place to argue the case at length, but I believe the tendency to emphasise the differences between various types of peacekeeping (as broadly defined) and the related tendency to elide the differences between robust peacekeeping and war are both dangerous. Peacekeeping, however robust, has a different moral basis from war fighting, and whether or not the moral basis matters to the military, it matters (in a democratic state) to the public that has authorised the military to operate on its behalf. It would be idle to claim that states never pursue their own interests when contributing peacekeepers (Australia's intervention in Solomon Islands would be an immediate counter-example), but the interests of the local people should overwhelmingly be the criterion by which success is judged. Consequently, engagement with, and support from, the local people are essential elements in any peacekeeping other than the most mechanistic observer mission.[8] In situations where there is an existing, functioning state apparatus, it may still be peacekeeping to support that existing government, as long as the

---

5 On the earlier use of 'peacekeeping'—specifically, to describe what might now be termed 'peace enforcement'—see Londey, PKOH 1, 629.
6 John Sanderson, 'UNTAC: The Military Component View', in *The United Nations Transitional Authority in Cambodia (UNTAC): Debriefing and Lessons*, edited by Nassrine Azimi (London/The Hague/Boston: Kluwer Law International, 1996), 130–33, doi.org/10.1163/9789004633698_025; John Sanderson, 'Assisting Failed States', Lecture to Australian Institute of International Affairs, 29 October 2009, 3 (page number refers to Sanderson's text).
7 Shannon Zimmerman, 'Parallel Lines in the Sand: The Impact of Parallel French Interventions on UN Stabilization Operations in Mali and the Central African Republic', *Global Governance: A Review of Multilateralism and International Organizations* 28 (2022): 60–61, doi.org/10.1163/19426720-02801001.
8 UNMOGIP (UN Military Observer Group India–Pakistan) is a possible example of the latter.

government itself is not a creation of the same powers that are providing the peacekeepers (in which case it is not peacekeeping but a form of colonialism). Force may indeed need to be used, to defend the peacekeepers themselves, to defend the local population, to 'defend the mandate'.[9] In general, however, the use of force under the rules of engagement (ROE) will depend not on the recipient's membership of a particular group but on actual individual behaviour at the time. Peacekeepers may well use drones for reconnaissance and even surveillance, but not, surely, to launch strikes against suspected troublemakers. Above all, peacekeepers should use the minimum level of force consistent with achieving the above objectives. This is where the alleged similarities between the most robust peacekeeping and, say, the war in Afghanistan break down.[10]

Are the military necessary to peacekeeping? As operations have become larger and more complex, the military have, in practice, remained their backbone. It is possible to imagine alternatives. Sandra Whitworth has suggested that:

> wildly impractical but responsible ideas might include contributing not platoons of warriors but contingents of doctors, feminists, linguists, and engineers; regiments of construction workers and carpenters; armies of midwives, cultural critics, anthropologists, and social workers; battalions of artists, musicians, poets, writers, and social critics.[11]

Artists can indeed play a role. In 2011, Australian artist George Gittoes and his partner Hellen Rose founded the Yellow House Jalalabad to foster arts such as painting, performance and film-making, and to give women an artistic voice. Gittoes argues that the Yellow House Jalalabad, which still operates in 2025, has been a more valid and effective a way of fighting for peace and freedom in Afghanistan than the war launched by America and its

---

9   A necessarily woolly term, this would include, for example, the Australians' defence of humanitarian aid convoys and distribution in Somalia.
10 The war crimes alleged against both Australian and British forces in Afghanistan occurred in a context in which the killing of enemy combatants was considered entirely legitimate; compare the Canadian scandal in Somalia (see below). On Australian war crimes, see the 'Brereton report': Inspector General of the Australian Defence Force, *Report of Inquiry … into Questions of Unlawful Conduct Concerning the Special Operations Task Group in Afghanistan* (Canberra: Commonwealth of Australia, 2020). On British allegations, see 'Eighty Afghan civilians may have been summarily killed by SAS, inquiry told', *The Guardian*, 3 July 2023.
11 Sandra Whitworth, *Men, Militarism, and UN Peacekeeping: A Gendered Analysis* (Boulder/London: Lynne Rienner, 2004), 186.

allies.¹² Nevertheless, in what follows, I will argue that, generally, the military do bring crucial skills and capabilities to peacekeeping, although the qualities of individual peacekeepers may, in practice, be equally important.

Antecedents and amnesia

As is often noted, the UN Charter makes no mention of peacekeeping, moving straight from purely diplomatic measures to restore peace in Chapter VI to a full-blown collective security strategy in Chapter VII. The failure of the drafters of the Charter to envisage ways in which the military could be used to restore or protect peace without resorting to fighting is mystifying, because there were plenty of recent antecedents. The League of Nations, the predecessor of the UN, was considered largely discredited by 1945, but the League had, for example, used military observers, and had deployed a number of international forces to protect plebiscites. The largest such force under League auspices was an International Force of 3,300 troops (from Britain, Italy, the Netherlands and Sweden) that supervised and protected the 1935 plebiscite over the future of the Saar territory.¹³ Only five years before the Charter was written, Sarah Wambaugh published an account of the Saar plebiscite, including the role of the International Force.¹⁴ Wambaugh was lavish in her praise for the latter's role, including the way 'the mere moral effect' of its presence had helped to maintain order.¹⁵ A reviewer lamented the book's appearance at a moment 'when Plebiscites have become of purely academic interest to the majority of mankind' and predicted it would be forgotten.¹⁶ And so it was. Just 10 years later, in 1950, when Australian judge and Kashmir mediator, Sir Owen Dixon, was casting around for a method of ensuring a fair plebiscite in the Vale of Kashmir, he was clearly unaware of the precedent of the Saar plebiscite of 1935. Nor did anyone in New York remind him. Rather than a military solution, Dixon proposed a purely civilian UN presence, overseeing the plebiscite itself and the administrative functions of the Vale (which was under Indian

---

12 G. Gittoes, '6/10/22—The New Yellow House', artistprofile.com.au/george-gittoes-the-new-yellow-house/; yellowhousejalalabad.wordpress.com.
13 For a brief summary of peacekeeping under the League, see Londey, PKOH 1, 6–8.
14 Sarah Wambaugh, *The Saar Plebiscite: With a Collection of Official Documents* (Cambridge: Harvard University Press, 1940), doi.org/10.1086/ahr/46.3.649. Wambaugh was something of a League expert on the Saar territory and was closely involved in the plebiscite (vi).
15 Wambaugh, *The Saar Plebiscite*, 317.
16 MS MacDonnell, *International Affairs Review Supplement* 19, no. 2 (1940): 121.

occupation), to reduce pressure on voters.[17] It was left to Australian defence planners, a year later, to follow up a suggestion by Prime Minister Robert Menzies with a proposal for a 30,000-strong joint Commonwealth force, deployed widely across Kashmir and operating under UN 'direction and control', to create conditions for a free plebiscite. Australia's proposed contribution of one battalion and a squadron of ground attack aircraft was too much for Menzies, and the matter was dropped.[18]

Another, even more recent, precedent of wider roles the military could play was the military government of occupied territories towards the end of the Second World War. Occupation of enemy territory is clearly not peacekeeping, but it will often have some similar characteristics, especially in terms of helping and achieving good relations with a civilian population, and in requiring more flexibility than the stereotypical military approach. In 1944, American novelist John Hersey published *A Bell for Adano*, a fictionalised account of the allied occupation of the town of Licata in Sicily, which to some extent addresses these very questions.[19] The hero of Hersey's novel is the American Major Joppolo, the officer of the Allied Military Government of Occupied Territories (AMGOT)[20] placed in charge of the town.[21] At the start of the novel, Joppolo discards the voluminous lists AMGOT has given him of tasks for the first day, passes over his own lengthy notes from AMGOT school lectures, and turns to a single page, 'Notes to Joppolo from Joppolo': 'Don't make yourself cheap. Always be accessible to the public. Don't play favorites. Speak Italian whenever possible. Don't lose your temper. When plans fall down, improvise.'[22]

---

17   UN S/1791, 'Report of Sir Owen Dixon, United Nations Representative for India and Pakistan, to the Security Council', 15 September 1950, 22–25; cf. Londey, PKOH 1, 176–77.
18   Report, 'Proposed British Commonwealth Force for Employment in Kashmir', 6 September 1951; memo, DoD to DEA, 21 September 1951; NAA: A816, 19/313/23. Discussion by Londey, PKOH 1, 182–85. Some of the ideas in fact came from the Department of External Affairs.
19   John Hersey, *A Bell for Adano* (New York: Knopf, 1944). References below are to the 1965 Bantam reprint.
20   On AMGOT, see Thijs W Brocades Zaalberg, *Soldiers and Civil Power: Supporting or Substituting Civil Authorities in Modern Peace Operations* (Amsterdam: Amsterdam University Press, 2006), 25–44, library.oapen.org/handle/20.500.12657/35148.
21   Hersey, *A Bell for Adano*. The novel was a bestseller and won a Pulitzer Prize in 1945. Joppolo is governor of a town called Adano in the novel. Hersey himself was a war correspondent who accompanied the allied invasion of Sicily and spent a few days with Major Frank Toscani, the model for Joppolo. See 'Frank Toscani, 89, inspired novel *A Bell for Adano*', *Chicago Tribune*, 28 January 2001.
22   Hersey, *A Bell for Adano*, 13–14.

Like a peacekeeper implementing a vague or shifting mandate crafted through political compromise far away in New York, Hersey portrays Joppolo as having to make it up as he goes along. In an undated foreword to the novel, Hersey argued that the quality of the individual will be more important than any number of principles and plans:

> Neither the eloquence of Churchill nor the humaneness of Roosevelt, no Charter, no four freedoms or 14 points, no dreamer's diagram so symmetrical and so faultless on paper, no plan, no hope, no treaty—none of these things can guarantee anything. Only men can guarantee, only the behavior of men under pressure, only our Joppolos.[23]

These words could be applied in full to peacekeeping.

The military and UN peacekeeping

This is not the place to rehearse the history of peacekeeping. Rather, I wish to focus on why peacekeeping was invented in 1947, with the military at its core, to fill the gap in the UN Charter, and then discuss a series of peacekeeping operations in the 1990s and early 2000s—in Cambodia, Somalia, Bougainville and Solomon Islands—examining the ways in which military peacekeepers have been challenged by the ambiguities of the peacekeeping environment and have often shown flexibility in dealing with that environment.[24] Since peacekeeping is not foreshadowed in the UN Charter, it had to be invented on the ground, and, ever since, it has demanded initiative, imagination and flexibility of its practitioners. The so-called mandate is rarely, if ever, a clear set of instructions; rather, it is the product of a Byzantine process of conflict and compromise in the Security Council. Where there is a written settlement between the parties that, too, will display the compromises and deliberate vagueness necessary to get a peace agreement over the line. Peacekeepers will always face a complex set of judgements as they set out to protect, restore and rebuild societies wracked by conflict. The question is whether the way soldiers are trained to think will make them less able to adapt to the fluid demands of peacekeeping.

---

23 Hersey, *A Bell for Adano*, 6.
24 Given the nature of this volume, I wish to focus on Australian peacekeeping operations. The age of the case studies reflects the paucity of Australian peacekeeping in the last 20 years.

The first UN peacekeepers, as I have argued at length in the Australian Official History, were the 'military officers' requested by the UN Consular Commission in Indonesia at its very first meeting on 1 September 1947.[25] The context was the ongoing dispute between the Netherlands, colonial masters of Indonesia before the Japanese invasion of 1942, and the Indonesian Republicans, who had declared independence just before the Japanese surrender in 1945. In July 1947, the Dutch launched an invasion of Republican-held territory, leading to a UN-imposed ceasefire.[26] The Security Council asked the consuls in Batavia of the six countries that had career consuls stationed there to organise themselves into a body to report on observance of the UN-imposed ceasefire and on other aspects of the situation.[27] This body was known as the Consular Commission.

The Security Council apparently assumed that the consuls would rely on their diplomatic staff to accomplish the task. However, at their first meeting, the consuls decided not only that they needed more people to help them monitor a particularly messy situation on the ground,[28] but also that the additional personnel should be military officers, to be provided by each of the six countries. This was the key moment when the military entered the world of UN peacekeeping. Why did the consuls make this decision?[29] The key driver was probably the consuls' appreciation of the difficulties of the situation. The American consul-general, Dr Walter A. Foote, reported afterwards that the meeting had decided 'that consular officers alone would be helpless in efforts [to] perform mission effectively'.[30] Hence the need for military officers, who were to be sent to the very scattered locations where the two armies were in contact with each other, to check that all units knew of, and were observing, the ceasefire, and to monitor whether patrolling was consistent with the ceasefire.[31]

---

25 Peter Londey, in Peter Londey, Rhys Crawley and David Horner, PKOH 1, 383–89, doi.org/10.1017/9781108628938. Although I saw it too late to consult it for this chapter, see also Steven Farram, *Indonesia 1947: Australia and the First United Nations Cease-fire Order* (North Melbourne: Australian Scholarly Publishing, 2019), doi.org/10.1017/s0022463423000073.
26 Londey, PKOH 1, 52–6.
27 UN Security Council Resolution 30, 25 August 1947. The six countries were Australia, Belgium, China, France, the United Kingdom and the US.
28 On reasons for the messiness, see Londey, PKOH 1, 64–65.
29 On the personalities involved, see Londey, PKOH 1, 58–63.
30 Cable 344, Batavia (Foote) to Washington, 3 September 1947, FRUS 1947, Far East, vol. 6, doc. 845. The State Department had already foreshadowed the possible provision of military personnel: cable 235, Washington (Acting Secretary of State, Robert A. Lovett) to Batavia (Foote), 27 August 1947, FRUS 1947, Far East, vol. 6, doc. 843.
31 Londey, PKOH 1, 60–61, 64–68.

The observers would need to be self-reliant in the field; to be able to talk as equals to the military on both sides of the conflict; and, above all, to have sufficient understanding of land warfare to understand and assess the behaviour of the two armies. In 1947, the world was awash with both military and civilians with recent military experience, but perhaps the natural default was to use serving officers. Yet, Australia's group of four officers, selected to represent the three services, included a RAN representative, Commander Henry Chesterman (decorated as a liaison officer with the Americans during the war) and Squadron Leader Lou Spence (a fighter pilot). Whether Chesterman and Spence had any insights into whether, for example, aggressive patrolling by either side was within the terms of the (ill-defined) ceasefire, is uncertain.[32] Many civilians with recent service experience could have done the job. However, the Commission may have been more comfortable sending military officers into areas of real potential danger. Only the previous year, three Australian war-crimes investigators from the RAAF and the Army had been ambushed and killed in a Javanese village.[33] Java had been a chaotic enough place before Dutch military action made things even worse.

Regardless of their varied wartime experience, the first four Australian peacekeepers soon found themselves having to make judgements that, while no doubt informed by that experience, also went beyond it. As the first UN peacekeepers to come up against the vagueness of Security Council resolutions, they discussed the various possible meanings to be given to terms such as 'cease fire' and 'cessation of hostilities' (both used but not defined by the Security Council), and devised their own definitions, only to note that since the two parties interpreted these words differently a cessation of hostilities was in fact unachievable. Asked to judge the merits of the Van Mook Line, the Dutch authorities' self-proclaimed front line, they noted that, 'although expedient on administrative grounds, [it] cannot be justified on legal and moral grounds'.[34] The boundaries between the military and the political had already dissolved, and the peacekeepers were drawn into both.

---

32   On the four, see Londey, PKOH 1, 65–66.
33   The case was certainly well known in Australia, because Richard Kirby, soon to be Australia's representative on the UN Committee of Good Offices (UNGOC), had been sent to investigate: Blanche d'Alpuget, *Mediator: A Biography of Sir Richard Kirby* (Melbourne: Melbourne University Press, 1977), 47–68; Londey, PKOH 1, 46–48.
34   Dyke, Chesterman, Campbell and Spence, 'Report of Australian Military Observing Officers to the Consul General for Australia on the Military Situation in Java, August–September 1947', c. 1 October 1947, 2–3, NAA: A4355, 7/1/7/6; Londey, PKOH 1, 68–69.

Cambodia

Over the next 45 years, peacekeeping developed to encompass not only military observers, but also buffer forces, peace enforcement, the use of civilian police, support for elections and much else. With new-found ambition after the end of the Cold War, the UN mounted UNTAC, its largest and most complex mission so far. UNTAC's broad role[35] meant that it faced some of the same conceptual problems raised by military government at the end of the Second World War. UNTAC's civilian and military wings were created as separate entities. The long-time Japanese UN official Yasushi Akashi, who led the mission, did not encourage close coordination even among the six civilian components.[36] As for the military component, commanded by Australian Lieutenant General John Sanderson, the UN's vision was that it would operate almost completely separately from the civilian parts of UNTAC, with little need for coordination between them. In the event, the division of responsibilities proved far more fluid.

The Paris Peace Accords for Cambodia contained the compromises and silences typical of a negotiated settlement. They also contained seeds of disputes that would require an agile refocusing of UNTAC's military tasks in the course of the operation.[37] The military was meant to disarm 70 per cent of the troops of each of the four Cambodian factions, to create an environment within which the civilian components of UNTAC could do their work. Following demobilisation, and well before the elections, six of the force's 12 battalions were to be sent home, leaving internal security in the hands of the police forces of the various factions, supported and monitored by UNTAC's own civilian police component. In fact, the factional civilian police proved either illusory or ill-trained, poorly equipped and politically partisan. Consequently, the Khmer Rouge felt that demobilising 70 per cent of their troops would leave them too vulnerable, and they refused to cooperate. UNTAC's own civilian police component was the largest the UN

---

35 For a summary, see John Connor, in David Horner and John Connor, PKOH 3, 109–10, 139–49, doi.org/10.1017/cbo9781139196437; Brocades Zaalberg, *Soldiers and Civil Power*, 79–102.
36 Connor, PKOH 3, 138–40.
37 The following draws on Sanderson's own account in Sanderson, 'UNTAC: The Military Component View', 127–30, noting, inter alia, that the delay in setting up UNTAC weakened the influence of the moderates in the different factions who had been instrumental in arriving at a negotiated settlement (127). In addition, the Khmer Rouge had called for quadripartite military and police forces, but the Hun Sen government rejected this.

had ever fielded, but it was of variable quality and deployed very slowly.[38] As a result, Sanderson's peacekeeping force remained at full strength for the duration of the mission and provided vital support to the operation in many ways not envisaged by the original planners.[39]

Sanderson himself pushed back against demands that UNTAC adopt a peace enforcement role,[40] for which it had neither the resources nor the political backing. Instead, he argued for the need to forge 'an alliance with the people' in other ways, and he rejected the 'prevailing view' that this was not the business of the military component: 'This misses the point— the military has a much deeper presence, and "hearts and minds" activities always form an essential part of a military component's method of operation in these circumstances.'[41] The general security situation, especially in the provinces, was deteriorating, as demobilised or unpaid soldiers often turned to banditry or extortion; returning refugees included both thieves and their prey.[42] Such law-and-order issues were meant to be solely the preserve of the civilian police,[43] but in practice UNTAC's military also played a role, though this would depend on each battalion's approach.

A battalion of Dutch Royal Marines was stationed in Banteay Meanchey province, around the town of Sisiphon, in the north-west, near the Thai border. Sanderson had a high opinion of the Marines, the closest unit he had to special forces, regarding them as 'thoughtful and strong peacekeepers', and he therefore placed them in this, the most difficult area of the mission, in a region where both the Khmer Rouge and Thai special forces had been active.[44] Given that their primary task of demobilising the factional forces could not be carried out, the Dutch turned pragmatically to supporting security in other ways; the commander of the first rotation, Lieutenant Colonel Herman Dukers, commented: 'If you are unable to execute the

---

38 Brocades Zaalberg, *Soldiers and Civil Power*, 103–05. On problems with the UNTAC civilian police, see KC Roos, 'UNTAC's Civilian Police Operation', in *The United Nations Transitional Authority in Cambodia, Debriefing and Lessons*, edited by Nassrine Azimi (Leiden: Brill/Nijhoff, 1995), 139–45, doi.org/10.1163/9789004633698_026.
39 Connor, PKOH 3, 140–41.
40 By 'peace enforcement', Sanderson meant taking on the Khmer Rouge militarily.
41 Sanderson, 'UNTAC: The Military Component View', 130–34; final quote, 134. On the 'prevailing view', especially the view in New York, see Azimi, *United Nations Transitional Authority in Cambodia*, 10.
42 Brocades Zaalberg, *Soldiers and Civil Power*, 105–06.
43 *Agreement on a Comprehensive Political Settlement of the Cambodia Conflict*, Annex I, Sections B and C (text available at treaties.un.org/doc/Publication/UNTS/Volume%201663/v1663.pdf).
44 Lt Gen John Sanderson, personal communication, 27 June 2023; Brocades Zaalberg, *Soldiers and Civil Power*, 106–24.

mission you have come to perform, you use your common sense.'[45] They did this with Sanderson's full support—early on, he actually went out on night patrol with them—and he tried to use them as an example to the rest of the peacekeeping force.[46] Lacking powers of arrest, the Dutch focused on supporting the local provincial government and police; for example, undertaking joint night patrols with local police. Without the Dutch, the local police did not like to patrol at night and were often attacked by bandits or Khmer Rouge. The Dutch preferred night patrolling, because it was cooler, and their night-vision goggles gave them an edge. In at least one case, the Dutch 'arrested' suspected thieves and handed them over to local authorities.[47] Battalions also engaged directly with the civilian population, providing humanitarian aid (in the Dutch case, mainly medical, educational or construction work). For the Dutch, the virtues of civic action were threefold: they helped win over the Cambodians, improved troop morale and increased support for the deployment at home in the Netherlands.[48]

As the elections approached, the military component took on the vital roles of providing security, organisational support and coordination. In September 1992, with progress in other areas blocked, Sanderson convinced Akashi that they should conduct elections whether or not the Khmer Rouge cooperated. Facilitating and protecting the elections became the military component's chief task, and the deployment of the battalions was adjusted to match the administrative areas of the Civil Administration component.[49] Increasingly, the military took over the planning in addition to the security of the elections, as Sanderson deployed his diplomatic, engineering and organisational skills to good effect.[50] Although there was some resentment at what some have called 'Sanderson's coup',[51] the civilians also saw the value in the technical, logistical and organisational support that the military component could supply.[52] The boundaries between civilian and military tasks had proved porous, aided by Sanderson's own personal qualities not only as a soldier but also as a manager and a diplomat.[53] Soldiers had proved that peacekeeping needed them.

45 Quoted in Brocades Zaalberg, *Soldiers and Civil Power*, 107.
46 Lt Gen John Sanderson, personal communication, 27 June 2023.
47 Brocades Zaalberg, *Soldiers and Civil Power*, 106–16.
48 Brocades Zaalberg, *Soldiers and Civil Power*, 96–102.
49 Connor, PKOH 3, 185–89.
50 For a non-Australian account, see Brocades Zaalberg, *Soldiers and Civil Power*, 125–52.
51 For a graphic description, see Brocades Zaalberg, *Soldiers and Civil Power*, 128–30.
52 See, for example, speech by Civil Administration Component head, Gérard Porcell, January 1993, quoted in Brocades Zaalberg, *Soldiers and Civil Power*, 130.
53 Brocades Zaalberg, *Soldiers and Civil Power*, 130.

13. SOLDIERS AS PEACEKEEPERS, PEACEKEEPERS AS SOLDIERS

Somalia

The year of the elections in Cambodia, 1993, also saw Australia contribute a battalion group, based around the 1st Battalion, Royal Australian Regiment (1 RAR), to the US-led Unified Task Force (UNITAF) in Somalia. Commanded by Lieutenant Colonel David Hurley, for four months from January to May 1993, 1 RAR was responsible for the western Somali town of Baidoa and the surrounding countryside (the Baidoa Humanitarian Relief Sector). The primary task was to provide an environment in which humanitarian aid agencies, non-government organisations (NGOs), could deliver aid, in particular food, to a starving population that was prey to militias, criminals and clan conflict. The battalion was thrust into a policing role for which it was not specifically trained and whose boundaries were a matter of interpretation. Initially, there was no local government with sufficient legitimacy for the Australians to work with them as the Dutch did with the provincial government in Sisiphon. The situation and the task were complex, and there were significant differences of opinion among the Australians as to the appropriate level of aggression to employ, given that the context was peacekeeping (albeit reasonably robust peace enforcement), not war.[54]

From the start, Somali youths would needle and provoke the Australians with aggressive looks, spitting and rock throwing. Many of the soldiers felt they needed to respond to these provocations to avoid losing respect among Somalis and, possibly, coming under fire more often as a consequence. The practice grew up of 'adjusting Somali values', by grabbing the miscreants, roughing them up a little and shouting at them. Hurley, all his company commanders and most of the platoon commanders discouraged this practice.[55] There was also a practical issue that showing a friendly face towards the local population might result in receiving more human intelligence, always the Australians' prime source of situational awareness.[56] Detained Somalis were invariably released,[57] and many of the soldiers found the ROE restrictive. Armed intruders who would have been shot on conventional operations had to be challenged verbally and with warning shots. Only if

---

54 Bob Breen, in Jean Bou et al., PKOH 4, 80–105, doi.org/10.1017/9781316182338; see especially comments at 81.
55 Breen, PKOH 4, 94–6, 105.
56 Breen, PKOH 4, 92.
57 Breen, PKOH 4, 95.

they raised and aimed their weapons could the Australians shoot to kill.[58] Echoing widespread frustration, Lieutenant Andrew Pritchard wrote: 'I sometimes think that it would be easier in some ways if an open war was declared. At least we could feel free to act as an army should rather than as a police force.'[59] Hurley himself felt caught between this desire for action and his own instincts about how a peacekeeping operation should be conducted; he feared that, as a result, he was losing the respect of his soldiers.[60]

The question of how much aggression should be employed was ongoing throughout the mission and remained undecided. When operations moved to the countryside, Hurley was happy to disrupt, and frighten off, bandits and militia. Most of the soldiers and non-commissioned officers (NCOs) disagreed: as Breen puts it, they wanted 'to conduct search and destroy rather than search and clear operations'.[61] There were also differences between the various companies of 1 RAR. For example, Major Anthony 'Ant' Blumer, the commanding officer (CO) of D Company, adopted an aggressive approach to searching for bandits and weapons, not far short of the approach taken by the US Marines who had preceded the Australians in Baidoa; other company commanders, such as A Company's Major Doug Fraser, took a more measured approach.[62] After one nine-day rotation in the town, Fraser commented: 'While [my soldiers] would have liked to have had a fight, in every situation where this could have occurred, they instead disarmed individuals and defused situations, despite incredible peer pressure being placed upon them.'[63] In Baidoa town, Hurley was concerned to maintain sufficient aggression to keep the all-important NGOs onside, without breaching ROE or simply making the situation worse.[64]

Compared with the Official History account, Breen gives a franker account of Australian operations in a recent, popular book, *Chasing Bandits in the Badlands*. On some occasions, Hurley called off ambushes when he learned of them because he believed they contravened the ROE; Breen comments

---

58 Breen, PKOH 4, 84–5.
59 Quoted in B Breen, *Chasing Bandits in the Badlands: Australian Soldiers Adjusting Attitudes in Somalia 1993* (Newport: Big Sky Publishing, 2023), 51.
60 For a telling quotation from Hurley's notes at the time, see Breen, *Chasing Bandits*, 68.
61 Breen, PKOH 4, 115; cf. Breen, *Chasing Bandits*, 164–66.
62 Bob Breen, *A Little Bit of Hope: Australian Force—Somalia* (Sydney: Allen & Unwin, 1998), 102–03, 117–22, 165. Breen seems less inclined to talk about such differences in sub-unit culture in PKOH 4. In Breen, *Chasing Bandits*, 201, Breen declares himself agnostic as to which approach worked better.
63 Maj Doug Fraser, quoted in Breen, *Chasing Bandits*, 120.
64 Breen, PKOH 4, 113.

that some of Hurley's subordinate commanders 'were bordering on being vigilantes'.[65] Breen details incidents such as a corporal returning to the location of a previous firefight to provoke another, culminating in firing a 66-millimetre anti-armour rocket into a building.[66] In an 'untidy' incident, members of Blumer's company attacked an NGO compound they believed was being used as a base for banditry by the Somali guards, killing a half-asleep Somali and throwing grenades into the compound.[67] On another occasion, Australians fixed bayonets to stare down an angry crowd after they had confiscated what they took to be an abandoned shipping container; Hurley ordered the container returned.[68]

In many areas, such as policy on confiscation of weapons, Hurley and his subordinates had to make judgement calls.[69] One such issue was the protection of humanitarian aid convoys into the countryside. It was clear that the soldiers should protect the convoys themselves but, unlike the US Marines before them and the French after them, the Australians took it on themselves to stay and try to ensure an orderly distribution of the aid. This also meant preventing drivers from siphoning off their cut, trying to minimise the amount village elders took to sell on the black market, and trying to stay long enough to allow, for example, women to get home with their share. The Australians did this out of a moral sensibility (shared by commanders and soldiers) that they should support the vulnerable and that simply dropping aid off and driving away did not solve the fundamental problems for much of the population.[70]

Increasingly, Hurley found himself drawn into Baidoa politics, acting in effect as military governor, or perhaps as the 'chief elder' in town. It was an essential role, as the Australians tried to lay the groundwork for new institutions, such as police, judiciary and prisons, but it was also a role for which Hurley felt fundamentally unprepared by his military training.[71] He seems to have risen to the role very effectively, but, clearly, another model is possible, such as that in Solomon Islands where the Regional Assistance Mission to Solomon Islands (RAMSI) was headed by a diplomat, and there

---

65   Breen, *Chasing Bandits*, 175–77.
66   Breen, *Chasing Bandits*, 94–104; a more subdued account at PKOH 4, 110–12.
67   Breen, *Chasing Bandits*, 121–29; brief account at PKOH 4, 133–34.
68   Breen, *Chasing Bandits*, 84–88; brief account, leaving out several key points, at PKOH 4, 109.
69   Breen, PKOH 4, 96–97.
70   Breen, PKOH 4, 103–05, 121, 141.
71   Breen, PKOH 4, 117–23; Hurley's thoughts on lack of training: 120; cf. Brocades Zaalberg, *Soldiers and Civil Power*, 226.

was perhaps a more effective division of labour. Among other things, Hurley felt that the time spent attending meetings took him away from his duties as battalion commander.[72] The Australians' efforts to reform institutions could be seen as not in accord with their primary mission,[73] but the changes made outlasted their presence.[74] A non-Australian commentator, Brocades Zaalberg, suggests that these successes stemmed from the Australian Government's willingness to give the contingent 'substantial latitude to execute their ill-defined mission', together with a commander willing to improvise.[75] As a result, the Australians in Baidoa:

> not only went further than all the other contingents in assuming governmental responsibilities in Somalia, their institution building efforts would remain unrivalled by any military contingent during peace operations in the remainder of the 1990s.[76]

In summary, although there were times when the aggression shown by some Australians in Baidoa risked being counterproductive, overall Baidoa remains one of the best demonstrations of the capacity of soldiers to undertake constructive peacekeeping in a hostile environment.

Bougainville

I shall now deal much more briefly with two missions where there was a balance between civilian and military participation. In Somalia, the military were more or less left to do it on their own. In Cambodia, there was a large set of civilian components in UNTAC, but they were of variable quality and, in the end, it fell to the military component to take over many of their roles. In Bougainville, the New Zealand–led Truce Monitoring Group (TMG) and the Australian-led Peace Monitoring Group (PMG) entered the scene at a point at which peace agreements had been reached,[77] and the security situation was relatively benign. The TMG and the PMG were both

---

72   Breen, PKOH 4, 120. Brocades Zaalberg, *Soldiers and Civil Power*, 214, suggests that the degree of difference between the different companies (discussed above) arose partly because Hurley, increasingly consumed by political duties, had less chance to impose uniformity of approach.

73   Breen at PKOH 4, 125; cf. Brocades Zaalberg, *Soldiers and Civil Power*, 238. Breen is referring especially to Major Mike Kelly's intervention to have notorious bandit Hussein Gutaale arrested, tried and executed.

74   See Brocades Zaalberg, *Soldiers and Civil Power*, 238–40 for examples.

75   Brocades Zaalberg, *Soldiers and Civil Power*, 238–39.

76   Brocades Zaalberg, *Soldiers and Civil Power*, 240.

77   Respectively, the Burnham Truce of 1997 and the Lincoln Agreement of 1998; texts in *Without a Gun: Australians' Experiences Monitoring Peace in Bougainville, 1997–2001*, edited by Monica Wehner and Donald Denoon (Canberra: Pandanus Books, 2001), 160–61, 185–89.

unarmed.[78] Four countries contributed—Australia, New Zealand, Fiji and Vanuatu—but Australia alone provided civilian monitors, drawn from a variety of government departments (in particular Foreign Affairs and Trade (DFAT) and Australian Agency for International Development (AusAID), together with civilian police from the Australian Federal Police (AFP)). Although there were a considerable number of military in both missions, their chief role was less security than logistic support. The operations often acted as a taxi service to facilitate meetings by representatives of the parties, but their core business was travelling to villages and conducting meetings to inform people of, and give them confidence in, the peace process. The civilians, although a small minority among the monitors,[79] did most (or at least a lot) of the talking in the village meetings, while also gathering information about the public mood. Female Australian civilians and military ni-Vanuatu and Fijians (who were culturally close to the Bougainvilleans) played particularly important roles in engaging with the local people.[80]

Inevitably, there are different views as to how this mix of military and civilians worked in practice. One Australian civilian who did three tours was DFAT officer turned folk singer, Fred Smith. Smith's impression was that at least some of the military monitors were uncomfortable with the slow and intangible progress of the village meetings. He felt the military were task-driven in a way not entirely compatible with the slow and deliberative nature of Melanesian culture. On the other hand, when Smith began playing his songs in the meetings—music was a very important part of Bougainville culture—he found the soldiers quite supportive. Smith became something of a celebrity on Bougainville, recording songs with his own band and with other Bougainvilleans—one of Sandra Whitworth's 'battalions of artists, musicians, poets'. In a mission where encouraging hearts and minds to embrace the peace process was the overwhelming priority, civilians could clearly play an important role. Smith's impression was that the soldiers could be unhappy with the lack of specific goals, of a defined end-state:

---

[78] On the situation in general, see Anthony Regan at Wehner and Denoon, *Without a Gun*, 1–41; Bob Breen, PKOH 5, 87–160. On being unarmed, a military operations officer in the PMG, Luke Foster, has commented, 'Relying on the people for the safety of peace monitors reinforces the point that peace is the people's responsibility'. In Luke Foster Wehner and Denoon, *Without a Gun*, 120.
[79] In early 2000, there were just 18 Australian civilians in the 312-strong PMG: Wehner and Denoon, *Without a Gun*, 190.
[80] Breen, PKOH 5, 220; Luke Foster at Wehner and Denoon, *Without a Gun*, 120.

but really we were there to be there; it was not so much what we achieved ... but what sort of signals we sent out about the situation, about who we were ... It was critical that we be seen and that we be trusted.[81]

On the other hand, Breen, in the Official History, suggests that the civilians, who had thought they would take the lead politically, were somewhat taken aback to find that the military officers who commanded monitoring teams or worked at the team sites were also keen to engage politically with Bougainville society.[82] Luke Foster, an operations officer with the PMG, specifically rejected the perception that the military were in Bougainville only in support roles: '[E]veryone in Bougainville is a peace monitor. Their actions, expressions, words and deeds are all examined and evaluated by Bougainvilleans.'[83] In other words, being military or not being military was less important than how each group conducted themselves. Moreover, despite some initial frictions, over time both groups came to respect each other's contributions.[84]

Solomon Islands

Like the TMG and PMG in Bougainville, the RAMSI was a non-UN mission composed of states of the Pacific (Australia, Fiji, New Zealand, Papua New Guinea and Tonga). Furthermore, like the Bougainville missions, RAMSI was innovative in its structure. Although for the initial period, the overwhelming majority of the force was military—1,922 personnel, out of a total force of about 2,225[85]—it was explicitly understood that the lead agency was the civilian Participating Police Force (generally referred to as 'RAMSI police'), mainly consisting of members of the AFP and the Australian Protective service, although all five nations provided some police. The head of mission, the Special Coordinator, was an experienced Australian diplomat, Nick Warner, who as a diplomat had experience working close to

---

81 Iain 'Fred' Smith, interviewed by Peter Londey, 30 March 2005; long quotation at 1:00. Yet, in the same interview, Smith comments that in an earlier mission in Solomon Islands he found military personnel friendlier and more willing to engage with the local people than members of the Australian Federal Police (1:04–05).
82 Breen, PKOH 5, 219–20.
83 Foster in Wehner and Denoon, *Without a Gun*, 121.
84 Breen in Wehner and Denoon, *Without a Gun*, 45–8; Foster in Wehner and Denoon, *Without a Gun*, 121.
85 Numbers: Breen, PKOH 5, 380 n. 2.

13. SOLDIERS AS PEACEKEEPERS, PEACEKEEPERS AS SOLDIERS

Australian peacekeepers in Rhodesia, Namibia and Cambodia.[86] Having a civilian as head of mission was common enough in the UN, but for Australia it possibly represented a new direction.[87]

The situation in Solomon Islands was one of civic disorder and ethnic conflict, especially between the people of the two main islands, Guadalcanal and Malaita. At the same time, and partly as a result of the conflict, the economy was in disarray. In 2000, one of the militant forces, the Malaita Eagle Force, had taken over the capital and forced the government to resign. With an endemic culture of corruption and weakening institutions of government, Australian politicians and members of think tanks began talking about Solomon Islands as a 'failed state'.[88] Nevertheless, the security situation was not as bad as that in Baidoa in 1993, where bandits, criminals and clan leaders had created a place where only well-armed and well-trained infantry could patrol with any degree of safety. In Solomon Islands, a carefully graduated use of force was appropriate. Unarmed RAMSI and Solomon Islands police went out on patrol, but with armed police in the background ready to intervene if necessary.[89] If the situation became very serious, troops could be rapidly deployed. Whereas in Baidoa, the Australians deliberately cultivated a show of force in order to dominate the town, RAMSI carefully cultivated a peaceable, non-threatening image.

At the same time, the visible threat of force, with armed soldiers, ships, aircraft and helicopters, also played a role in RAMSI's ability to make rapid improvements in the security situation. Only three weeks into the mission, one of the most notorious warlords, Howard Keke, head of the Guadalcanal Liberation Front, agreed to surrender. Keke encouraged his followers to disarm and encouraged other Guadalcanal Liberation Front leaders to do likewise. At least some of the opposing Malaita Eagle Force followed this example and handed in their weapons. No doubt war weariness was among the causes, along with Keke's belief that under RAMSI's protection he would at least get a fair trial (he was still sentenced to life in prison for murder). But the other factor was, no doubt, his fear of RAMSI's military strength. Breen comments that Keke's willingness to surrender out of fear

---

86   Breen, PKOH 5, 375, 383–4. The reference at PKOH 5, 384, to the Commonwealth Monitoring Force in Rhodesia as 'a Commonwealth group that had supervised disarmament of militant groups in Rhodesia' is highly misleading: see Londey at PKOH 1, 605–89; and Londey, *Other People's Wars*, 126–32 for accounts of the CMF.
87   See Breen's comments, PKOH 5, 375.
88   Breen, PKOH 5, 364–68.
89   Breen, PKOH 5, 385.

of military action against him 'alone vindicated the deployment of a large military force to Solomon Islands. Thus, so-called soft and hard power combined effectively'.[90]

As a gun amnesty finished and RAMSI needed to arrest those who still held illegal weapons, Warner still favoured 'careful, patient and nuanced action', not aimed at intimidating the population but, rather, relying on the population to report the presence of armed men.[91] The security situation had improved so much that, by the end of October 2003, the military contribution started being greatly reduced, and RAMSI increasingly centred on civilians (mainly Australian) attempting to make changes in the operation of Solomon Islands public administration, and the rebuilding of the Solomon Islands police.[92] In April 2006, however, riots in the wake of a disputed election result overwhelmed the RAMSI and Solomon Islands police. Eye-witness accounts suggested that the situation may have been aggravated by heavy-handed action by members of the AFP.[93] Australian troops were sent back in to restore order, supported by snipers in helicopters. Once again, the military were needed.[94] In the long run, the initial popularity RAMSI had gained by bringing law and order to Solomon Islands wore off, as many Solomon Islanders became increasingly resentful at Australian attempts to bring change to the social norms of Solomon Islands politics.[95]

Military culture, training and peacekeeping

Canada long saw itself as the 'peacekeeping nation' *par excellence*. Apart from Indonesia in the 1940s, Canada contributed to every UN peacekeeping mission during the Cold War.[96] It was, therefore, a great shock to Canadians when they discovered that in March 1993 Canadian soldiers in Somalia

---

90   Breen, PKOH 5, 387–89; quotation at 389.
91   Breen PKOH 5, 389–91. The quotation is from a cable sent by Warner to Canberra.
92   Breen, PKOH 5, 391–93.
93   See the report from aid worker Luke Johnston, quoted by Breen, PKOH 5, 414: police aggressiveness, physical manhandling of people and use of tear gas turned 'a little crowd that was peaceful ... into this raging mob'.
94   Breen, PKOH 5, 418–21.
95   These problems arose very early in the mission: Breen, PKOH 5, 405–06. Breen's comment (405) that 'some Solomon Islanders became indifferent to reform and institution building' reflects the neocolonialist mindset with which Australia approached RAMSI. Conflict between pro- and anti-RAMSI groups underlay the riots in 2006—see Breen, PKOH 5, 412–13.
96   Walter A Dorn, 'Maple Leaf and Blue Beret: The Rise, Fall, and Promise of Canadian Peacekeeping', in *Peacekeeping: Perspectives Old and New*, edited by Howard G Coombs et al. (Kingston, Ontario: Centre for International and Defence Policy, Queen's University, 2023), 58.

13. SOLDIERS AS PEACEKEEPERS, PEACEKEEPERS AS SOLDIERS

had tortured and killed a 16-year-old Somali boy, Shidane Arone, who was suspected of thieving. Once walls of silence were broken down, it was discovered that this event was part of a pattern of maltreatment of Somalis that, going unpunished, gave the perpetrators of this crime the sense that such activities were sanctioned. The entire Airborne regiment, to which the perpetrators belonged, was disbanded.[97] Anthropologist Donna Winslow wrote a study of the causes of these events for the resulting Commission of Inquiry, emphasising that the Canadian Airborne saw themselves as an elite combat force, whose members valued 'sub-unit solidarity at the expense of regimental and army cohesion'.[98] The Airborne felt underprepared for the frustrations of a mission in which the enemy was not clearly identifiable. They confronted a Somali society equally disdainful of outsiders and referred to Somalis dehumanisingly as 'smufty', 'nig nog' and so on. Winslow avoids the conclusion that combat soldiers cannot make good peacekeepers but does reject the notion that the crimes were simply the work of 'a few bad apples'. Rather, she concludes, 'the roots of the death of Shidane Arone go deep into the past of the Airborne Regiment and into the heart of Airborne regimental culture'.[99]

No such scandals have emerged (to my knowledge) regarding Australian peacekeepers, though there is certainly evidence of soldiers who may have fantasised such actions.[100] Nevertheless, in Somalia, as discussed above, Australian soldiers with 1 RAR were in the habit of roughing up Somalis in the process they termed 'adjusting Somali values'. The practice was never condoned at a command level, yet it reveals some of the same frustrations with Somali society that were felt by the Canadian Airborne. In addition (as noted above), some of the Australians deliberately provoked contact in which Somalis were very likely to die. This is a far cry from torturing and killing a prisoner, but it reflects the fact that soldiers in peacekeeping may not always choose the course that leads to the least amount of violence. Soldiers' attitudes are critical here. Many soldiers believed that 'adjusting Somali values' was necessary to ensure Somali respect for the peacekeepers.[101]

---

97 Dorn, 'Maple Leaf and Blue Beret', 47.
98 Donna Winslow, *The Canadian Airborne Regiment in Somalia: A Socio-cultural Inquiry* (Ottawa: Minister of Public Works and Government Services Canada, 1997); quotation, 264. The specific sub-unit involved 'was hyperinvested in an aggressive rebel identity with strong antipathy for out-groups' (265).
99 Winslow, *Canadian Airborne Regiment in Somali*, 261–70; final quotation at 270.
100 I will not cite references because I do not want to identify individuals. It should also be noted that these were soldiers operating in highly stressful situations, and their thoughts at the time may well not have reflected their usual views of the world.
101 Breen, PKOH 4, 94–96; Breen, *Chasing Bandits*, 62–67.

It was, in effect, one warrior culture staring down another. Soldiers may self-identify as 'warriors', 'peacekeepers' or other categories;[102] more important, perhaps, is the degree to which modern military training is expressly designed to strip away aspects of individuality and inhibition that will get in the way of a soldier doing what is deemed necessary, including, if required, killing. It seems plausible that their training, group cohesion and attitudes to outsiders may well make special forces less effective as peacekeepers than regular combat troops.[103]

Yet, at times, outsiders reflect stereotyped views of the military that are not borne out by the evidence.[104] Breen quotes a member of the AFP in Solomon Islands as characterising differences thus:

> [W]hen a soldier is told to jump—they jump. Within the police environment, a police officer will say 'why?' Police are trained to question—soldiers are trained to obey orders.[105]

That is unfair. It is easy to find Australian military of all ranks making their own judgements, and sometimes deliberately going against the judgements of superior officers. 'Adjusting Somali attitudes' would be one example, where soldiers were choosing *not* to obey orders. In Cambodia, Sanderson has praised the initiative shown by Australian signallers, often working in isolated locations with small teams of other nationalities. In Rhodesia in 1980, in the heat of the moment, Lieutenant Jim Truscott resisted those encouraging him to kill a Patriotic Front soldier who was threatening the group with an AK-47. By resisting the soldier's instinct to defend himself, Truscott may have saved the mission politically.[106] From the first four Australians in Indonesia, when they were working out for themselves how to interpret the questions put to them by the Security Council, countless Australian peacekeepers have done more than simply obey orders.

---

102 See, for example, Wendy A Broesder et al., 'Can Soldiers Combine Swords and Ploughshares? The Construction of the Warrior–Peacekeeper Role Identity Survey (WPRIS)', *Armed Forces & Society* 41, no. 3 (2015): 519–40, doi.org/10.1177/0095327x14539326; Iselin Silja Kaspersen, 'New Societies, New Soldiers? A Soldier Typology', *Small Wars and Insurgencies* 32, no. 1 (2021): 1–25, doi.org/10.1080/09592318.2020.1785990.
103 Cf. recent revelations about the Australian and British SAS in Afghanistan (see n. 10): Dorn, 'Maple Leaf and Blue Beret', 47, on the Canadian Airborne. On the other hand, see Sanderson's comments on the Dutch Royal Marines, quoted above.
104 See, for example, comments by Fred Smith, quoted above.
105 Superintendent Rod Walker, quoted by Breen, PKOH 5, 393.
106 See Londey, PKOH 1, 648–49.

13. SOLDIERS AS PEACEKEEPERS, PEACEKEEPERS AS SOLDIERS

Soldiers are not slaves of their training and indoctrination, which will, in any case, differ between countries, between branches of the military and between time periods. In practice, not all of their previous civilian self is stripped away. Lieutenant General Robert Nimmo was a successful commander of the United Nations Military Observer Group in India and Pakistan (UNMOGIP) in Kashmir from 1950 to 1966 because, as a general officer, he had the respect of the Indian and Pakistani senior commanders, and also because of his personal qualities as a diplomat.[107] When Australian Major Roy Skinner confronted Israeli Defence Minister General Moshe Dayan in 1967 over the siting of UN observation posts along the Suez Canal, he himself had never been to war, but nevertheless he impressed Dayan with his spartan living conditions and, no doubt, with his calm, direct, firm manner.[108] These were personal qualities, not intrinsic to being a soldier, and after his service as an observer with the UN Truce Supervision Organization, Skinner had a long civilian career with UN Relief and Works Agency, working with Palestinian refugees, as well as working for UNICEF and the UN Department of Humanitarian Affairs in Iraq.[109] In Rhodesia, Australians assigned to Assembly Places (APs) where Patriotic Force soldiers were cantoned generally performed extremely well in a difficult and dangerous situation. One of the most successful AP commanders was Captain Kevin Byrne, who had lived in Papua New Guinea at the time it gained independence in 1975; drawing on that experience, he emphasised joint Rhodesian/Patriotic Front activities (including patrols around the AP) to prepare for a future after the peacekeepers had gone.[110] Individuals—their experience and character—can be important.

Units also differ from one another. I have discussed above the differences between companies in Somalia. In East Timor there were even greater differences between 5/7 RAR, commanded by Lieutenant Colonel Simon Gould, and 2 RAR, which it replaced on the western border in January 2000. 2 RAR, described as a 'tough scrub battalion' by Bob Breen,[111] had treated operations on the border as a counterinsurgency operation, protecting bases with barbed wire and machine-gun pits, and patrolling aggressively to find and destroy militia. While acknowledging the importance of security, Gould insisted on a lighter touch, with the emphasis on nation-building and

---

107 Londey, PKOH 1, 186–87.
108 Londey, PKOH 1, 270–71; photo of the meeting at B6.
109 I base this assessment partly on having known Skinner well in his later years.
110 Londey, PKOH 1, 675, 688.
111 Bob Breen, *Mission Accomplished East Timor: The Australian Defence Force Participation in the International Forces East Timor (INTERFET)* (Sydney: Allen & Unwin, 2001), 63.

helping the locals. In a discussion of whether it was justified to return fire across the international border against an unseen enemy, Gould argued it was not, stating—in the face of opposition from his superior officer, Brigadier Mark Evans—that 'the Battalion view is that deadly force should be an absolute last resort'. At one incident in February 2000 at a border reunion, Indonesian soldiers fired over the heads of the crowd after East Timorese youths began throwing rocks at the soldiers. Gould remonstrated verbally with the Indonesians; his men did not threaten to use their weapons, but rather rugby-tackled the stone-throwing youths.[112] 2 RAR had, of course, entered the theatre when the security situation was much tenser, but they had not particularly changed their modus operandi. The difference between them and 5/7 RAR is indicative of the wide differences in philosophy that are possible even between combat battalions in the same army.

Conclusion

What qualities do peacekeepers need? That is the subject for a book, but the following might be a brief list (in addition, of course, to the core military skills in which soldiers, sailors and air people are trained). First would be the ability to feel empathy, or at least sympathy, with people of radically different cultures. Peacekeepers must be on the side of the civilian population and try to understand the local culture on its own terms. Peacekeepers need to have internalised the virtue of employing the minimum level of violence consistent with achieving their mission. Peacekeepers need to be adaptable and flexible. As was seen above in the cases of Cambodia and Somalia, the mission envisaged in the planning stage may change radically or may have to be interpreted liberally in accordance with what is possible. Judgements must be made on the ground as to what is needed and what is feasible. The need to make decisions on the ground, and sometimes in the course of an action, means that peacekeepers need to come from a defence force that gives latitude to junior officers and NCOs, and, indeed, that expects private soldiers and their equivalent to make sound judgements in the heat of action. Finally, because peacekeeping is different from war, in its moral basis if nothing else, experience in previous peacekeeping operations must always be an advantage.

---

112 Craig Stockings, *Born of Fire and Ash: Australian Operations in Response to the East Timor Crisis, 1999–2000* (Sydney: UNSW Press, 2022), 788–94. The note about rugby tackling is from interviews I conducted as 5/7 RAR departed (see list in Stockings, *Born of Fire and Ash*, 887–88).

Australian peacekeeping at the end of the 1990s, including, of course, East Timor, benefited greatly from the number of personnel who had been peacekeepers before, in the Middle East, Namibia, Western Sahara, Cambodia, Somalia, Rwanda and elsewhere. Sadly, with Australian peacekeeping at a low ebb for most of the last 20 years, that level of experience can no longer be found in the ADF. Nor does the recent Defence Strategic Review (released on 24 April 2023) offer much hope for the future, with its determined emphasis on war fighting in our own region.[113] Things may change.

Historically, the ADF has been extremely reluctant to train personnel specifically for peacekeeping, but perhaps there is the need to try to inculcate the qualities listed above. No two peacekeeping operations will be the same, but wargaming (peacegaming?) scenarios such as those faced by Sanderson in Cambodia or Hurley in Baidoa would mean that future peacekeeping contingents would arrive with a better idea of the possible adaptations they may have to make, and the sorts of difficult decisions they may face. At the very least, tactics for dealing with spitting, rock-throwing youths could be discussed before deployment, instead of being subject to a rather unstructured debate on the ground in theatre. There is now a wealth of historical material about Australian peacekeeping, which can be mined to find many scenarios worth discussing or gaming. Whether such training would make soldiers worse as soldiers is problematic. Peacekeeping training should produce a more nuanced, thoughtful way of dealing with a dangerous environment and with the civilians who are caught up in it. Whether that is viewed as a help or a hindrance in conflict probably depends on one's views on the likely nature of future war.

To conclude, I am not sure that I would agree with David Horner about the importance of a soldier's previous military career as preparation for his or her role as a peacekeeper (although, clearly, previous peacekeeping experience is important). Individual personality and worldview strike me as equally important or perhaps more so. That said, there is, clearly, nothing about being a member of the ADF that precludes one from being a good peacekeeper. Given that the environment of peacekeeping will often require the ability to operate in a dangerous environment and to use force—if necessary, deadly force—to protect oneself and others, it is fortunate that members of the military can indeed make good peacekeepers.

---

113 Department of Defence, *National Defence: Defence Strategic Review* (Canberra: Commonwealth of Australia, 2023).

14

Disappointing the dragon: an Australian strategy and a fourth armed service for the grey zone

Bob Breen

My education at Duntroon and knowledge of several graduates who became scholars, such as Robert O'Neill, David Horner and John Coates, inspired me to write about Australian military history. I became a journeyman among gifted masters. David Horner influenced me the most by introducing me to my first publisher, John Iremonger, of Allen & Unwin, in the late 1980s, lifting my standards of research and written expression, and supervising my PhD candidature with Paul Dibb and another soldier–scholar, Alan Dupont, in the early 2000s. He then employed me as the author for Volume V and a contributing author for Volume IV of the Official History of Australian Peacekeeping, Humanitarian and Post–Cold War Operations series in the mid-2000s and early 2010s. David Horner has been my academic mentor and inspiration for over 30 years. He and I also share a deep interest in the fortunes of the Sydney Swans Football Club.

This chapter draws on revelations from David Horner's histories of Australian strategy and higher command before and during the Pacific War 1942–45, as well as the development of Australian intelligence services and the Special

Air Service Regiment (SASR).[1] The chapter uses these revelations to suggest that some elements of Australia's history should not be repeated. Horner's strategic histories reveal that in the 1930s, Australia relied on British alliance promises, underinvested in conventional military power, lacked strategic imagination and failed to develop sovereign strategies and capabilities to counter an emerging Asian adversary.

Horner's higher command histories, including the Blamey and Shedden biographies,[2] reveal subordination to American strategy for prosecuting the Pacific War. His histories of the Australian intelligence services reveal the emulation of British models and a struggle to specify civilian and military responsibilities. In the case of the SASR, Horner's history exposes the inappropriateness of following British models for Australian circumstances and the necessity for special operations capabilities to be free from conventional military direction.

This chapter joins the contemporary Australian strategic debate, something David Horner has not and does not do. He produces truthful, comprehensively researched history but does not propose the practical application of historical lessons to present or future Australian defence policy. He debates history and defends his interpretations but does not take a position in the current Australian national security debate. However, as other chapters in this volume show, he does intend his findings to be used by others to inform discussion and decision-making about key issues relating to Australian security and strategy.

---

1   David Horner, *Crisis of Command: Australian Generalship and the Japanese Threat, 1941–1943* (Canberra: Australian National Univeristy Press, 1978); *High Command: Australia and Allied Strategy, 1939–1945* (Canberra: Australian War Memorial and Sydney: George Allen & Unwin, 1982, republished as *High Command: Australia's Struggle for an Independent War Strategy, 1939–1945* (Sydney: Allen & Unwin, 1992), doi.org/10.4324/9781003120193; *Inside the War Cabinet: Directing Australia's War Effort, 1939–1945* (Sydney: Allen & Unwin, 1996); 'Australian Army Strategic Planning Between the Wars', in *Serving Vital Interests: Australia's Strategic Planning in Peace and War*, edited by P Dennis and J Grey (Canberra: School of History, Australian Defence Force Academy, 1996); 'Australian and Allied Intelligence in the Pacific in the Second World War', Working Paper No. 28, Strategic and Defence Studies Centre, Canberra, 1980; *The Spy Catchers: The Official History of ASIO 1949–1963*, vol. I of The Official History of ASIO (Sydney: Allen & Unwin, 2006); *SAS: Phantoms of the Jungle, A History of the Australian Special Air Service* (Sydney: George Allen & Unwin, 1989), republished 1991 and 1992, and updated and republished as *SAS: Phantoms of War, A History of the Australian Special Air Service* (Sydney: Allen & Unwin) in 2002.
2   David Horner, *Blamey: The Commander-in-Chief* (Sydney: Allen & Unwin, 1998); *Defence Supremo: Sir Frederick Shedden and the Making of Australian Defence Policy* (Sydney: Allen & Unwin, 2000).

Informed by Horner, this chapter indeed takes a position in the contemporary Australian strategic policy debate. It calls for a strategy for Australia in the 'grey zone'—a term used to describe a range of illegal violent and nonviolent activities perpetrated by one state against another, intended to coerce or even dominate, but calibrated to stay under the threshold of acts of war. While the chapter does not argue against Australia's investment in military hardware such as submarines, surface vessels and missiles, nor question the value of the US alliance, it does recognise the urgent need for an innovative approach to counter grey-zone threats, which have the potential to circumvent the conventional foundations of Australia's defence and undermine its sovereignty.

In advancing this case, the chapter first explains the grey zone and identifies an escalating Communist Party of China (CPC) grey-zone campaign against Australia. It argues that Australia is vulnerable because this campaign ignores Australia's geographic advantages and bypasses the ADF. Furthermore, while consecutive Australian governments have recognised the grey-zone threat, they have failed to systematically address it. Reflexive legislation against espionage, subversion, foreign interference, cyberattacks and new interdepartmental task forces are tactical, not innovative strategic responses to this new threat. Furthermore, Australia is constrained by alliance-dependent strategic thinking that originated during the Pacific War.

The chapter thus proposes a sovereign Australian grey-zone strategy that does not depend on American or British promises, or urgent investments in conventional military power.[3] This strategy embraces ingenuity and favours unique Australian organisations and operational concepts, rather than American or British models, to counter Australia's contemporary grey-zone threat. It is founded on the concept of response power, which has four pillars: detection, informational actions, deterrence and de-escalation. To enable such a strategy, Australia must establish a fourth armed service, the Response Force, with domestic and international arms. The chapter is an overview of my forthcoming book, *Let's Trade, Not Argue: An Australian Strategy to Secure a Respectful Relationship with China*, which builds on an earlier work published in 2022, *Disappointing the Dragon: How Australia Should Stand Up to the Communist Party of China*.[4]

---

3   The definition of a sovereign strategy is one whereby Australia has the ways and means to implement it autonomously and independently in its national interest while complying with alliance obligations and national and international laws.
4   Bob Breen, *Disappointing the Dragon: How Australia Should Stand Up to the Communist Party of China*, (Woodend: Echo Books, 2022).

Australia and the grey zone

The term 'grey zone' echoes Plato's informal perpetual war between the utopian 'white' of peace and the all-too-real 'black' of war.[5] Grey-zone campaigns involve nonviolent and violent actions by nations or subnational groups that are coercive and often harmful while remaining below the threshold of what are usually considered acts of war. Mazarr describes a grey-zone campaign as 'gradualist and coercive in nature, and … unconventional in the tools it employs'.[6] The ways are 'diverse operations to influence, persuade, and coerce nation-states, organisations and individuals to operate in accord with one's strategic interests without employing kinetic force'.[7] The means are espionage, subversion, propaganda, foreign interference and, when escalated to hybrid warfare, violent actions by unmarked military forces, armed spies, mercenaries and provocateurs: grey-zone combatants.[8]

Contemporary grey-zone campaigns integrate political, economic, cyber, electronic and informational actions. Typically, campaigns oscillate through three electronic and subversion escalations, culminating in hybrid warfare if earlier phases have not succeeded.[9] The label 'hybrid' encompasses centuries-old modalities of conventional and unconventional warfare:

> Hybrid war is conducted through non-attributable proxies and methods to destabilise the target state and achieve the aggressor state's strategic objectives short of war … It intends to achieve military and political objectives rapidly and present a *fait accompli* … before a conventional military response can prevent it.[10]

---

5   Plato surmised: 'Every State is, by a law of nature, engaged perpetually in an informal war with every other State', and '"peace" is nothing but a name'. *Plato in Twelve Volumes*, vol. 10 & 11 (Cambridge: Harvard University Press, 1967), translated by RG Bury, www.perseus.tufts.edu/hopper/text?doc=Perseus%3Atext%3A1999.01.0166%3Abook%3D1%3Apage%3D626.
6   Michael Mazarr, *Mastering the Gray Zone: Understanding a Changing Era of Conflict* (Carlisle: US Army War College, 2015), 4.
7   Ross Babbage, *Stealing a March: Chinese Hybrid Warfare in the Indo-Pacific; Issues and Options for Allied Defense Planners*, vols 1 and 2 (Washington, DC: Centre for Strategic and Budgetary Assessments, 2019), 1.
8   Thomas Paterson, 'The "Grey Zone": Political Warfare is Back', *The Interpreter*, 3 September 2019, www.lowyinstitute.org/the-interpreter/grey-zone-political-warfare-back.
9   Phase 1: political subversion and economic pressure; Phase 2: political subversion, economic pressure and cyber/electronic attack; and Phase 3: political subversion, economic pressure, cyber/electronic attack and hybrid war. These phases are based on the Rand Corporation phases as well as the author's assessment from other research. See LJ Morris et al., *Gaining Competitive Advantage in the Gray Zone: Response Options for Coercive Aggression Below the Threshold of Major War* (Santa Monica: Rand Corporation, 2019), www.rand.org/pubs/research_reports/RR2942.html.
10 US Army, *Multi-Domain Battle: Evolution of Combined Arms for the 21st Century 2025–2040* (Fort Eustis: US Army Training and Doctrine Command, 2017), searchworks.stanford.edu/view/13429861.

There is some academic scepticism, but twenty-first-century grey-zone campaigns that have the potential to escalate to hybrid warfare are dangerous, and they are here now.[11]

China and Russia have started a new grey-zone Cold War. David Kilcullen describes this phenomenon in *The Dragons and the Snakes: How the Rest Learned to Fight the West*. He references China's 20-year-old *Unrestricted Warfare* doctrine to illustrate how the CPC prosecutes its campaigns.[12] Clive Hamilton and Mareike Ohlberg describe the CPC's worldwide grey-zone campaign in *Hidden Hand*.[13] Ross Babbage and colleagues sharpen comprehension of China's grey-zone strategy in *Which Way the Dragon?* and other analyses.[14] There is substantial literature on Chinese and Russian political warfare and grey-zone tactics.[15]

The Australian Government and its security chiefs recognise the grey zone. The former Chief of the Defence Force, General Angus Campbell, opened his remarks to a conference on 'War in 2025' thus: 'So let's start … in the grey zone of political warfare … where our worst nightmare will first emerge, where it has already commenced, and where it's all been done before.' The government's 2020 Strategic Update struck a similar note:

---

11 D Stoker and C Whiteside, 'Blurred Lines: Gray-Zone Conflict and Hybrid War—Two Failures of American Strategic Thinking', *Naval War College Review* 73, no. 1 (2020), www.proquest.com/openview/a60ecb52fe7f98765ad0ef5f1d063591/1?pq-origsite=gscholar&cbl=34989.
12 David Kilcullen, *The Dragons and the Snakes: How the Rest Learned to Fight the West* (London: Scribe, 2020), 200–14, 218, 222–24, 244–45, doi.org/10.1093/oso/9780190265687.001.0001.
13 Clive Hamilton and Mareike Ohlberg, *Hidden Hand: Exposing How the Chinese Communist Party is Reshaping the World* (Sydney: Hardie Grant Books, 2020).
14 Ross Babbage, *Which Way the Dragon: Sharpening Allied Perceptions of China's Strategic Trajectory* (Washington, DC: Centre for Strategic and Budgetary Assessments, 2020); *Winning Without Fighting: Chinese and Russian Political Warfare Campaigns and How the West Can Prevail*, vols 1 and 2 (Washington, DC: Centre for Strategic and Budgetary Assessments, 2019) and Ross Babbage, Tom Mahnken and Toshi Yoshihara, *Countering Comprehensive Coercion: Competitive Strategies Against Authoritarian Political Warfare* (Washington, DC: Centre for Strategic and Budgetary Assessments, 2018).
15 Government of the United Kingdom, *Understanding Hybrid Warfare*, Multinational Capability Development Campaign (MCDC) Project, UK Government, London, 2017, assets.publishing.service.gov.uk/media/5a8228a540f0b62305b92caa/dar_mcdc_hybrid_warfare.pdf; Government of the United Kingdom, *Countering Hybrid Warfare*, MCDC Project, UK Government, London, 2019, www.gov.uk/government/publications/countering-hybrid-warfare-project-understanding-hybrid-warfare; J Norberg, F Westerlund and U Franke, 'The Crimea Operation: Implications for Future Russian Military Interventions', in *A Rude Awakening: Ramifications of Russian Aggression Towards Ukraine*, edited by N Granholm, J Malminen and G Persson (Stockholm: Swedish Defence Research Agency FOI, 2014); O Jonsson, *The Russian Understanding of War: Blurring the Lines Between War and Peace* (Washington, DC: Georgetown University Press, 2019); Mazarr, *Mastering the Gray Zone*; Peter Kouretsos, 'A Literature Review' in Annex A: 'Contextualising Chinese Hybrid Warfare' in Ross Babbage, *Stealing a March: Chinese Hybrid Warfare in the Indo-Pacific* (Washington, DC: Centre for Strategic and Budgetary Assessments, 2019); J Hai-Chi Loo, S Shiu-Hing Lo and S Chung-Fun Hung, *China's New United Front Work in Hong Kong: Penetrative Politics and Its Implications* (Singapore: Palgrave MacMillan, 2019), doi.org/10.1007/978-981-13-8483-7.

Grey zone is one of a range of terms used to describe activities designed to coerce countries in ways that seek to avoid military conflict. Examples include using para-military forces, militarisation of disputed features, exploiting influence, interference operations and the coercive use of trade and economic levers. These tactics are not new. But they are now being used in our immediate region against shared interests in security and stability. They are facilitated by technological developments, including cyber warfare.[16]

The ASIO, the Australian Strategic Policy Institute (ASPI) and several writers also confirm that the grey-zone Cold War has come to Australia.[17] In his Annual Threat Assessment of 24 February 2020, the ASIO Director General, Mike Burgess, opined:

The level of threat we face from foreign espionage and interference activities is currently unprecedented. *It is higher now than it was at the height of the Cold War* [author's emphasis].[18]

Further, in the ASIO Annual Report 2020–21, Burgess said: 'I remain concerned about the potential for Australia's adversaries to ... undermine Australia's sovereignty, democratic institutions, economy and national security capabilities.'[19]

While ASIO is not politically free to name China, in 2022, ASPI published an Australian state and territory assessment of CPC grey-zone penetration.[20] There are warnings about the CPC's grey-zone campaign in South-East Asia, New Zealand and the Pacific Islands.[21]

---

16 Department of Defence, *2020 Defence Strategic Update*, (Canberra: Commonwealth of Australia, 2020), 12, www.defence.gov.au/about/strategic-planning/2020-defence-strategic-update.
17 Clive Hamilton, *Silent Invasion: China's Influence in Australia* (Melbourne: Hardie Grant Books, 2018); Peter Hartcher, *Red Zone: China's Challenge and Australia's Future* (Melbourne: Black Inc, 2021); Alex Joske, 'The Party Speaks for You: Foreign Interference and the Chinese Communist Party's United Front System', *Policy Brief*, Report no. 32/2020, 9 June (ASPI, Canberra, 2020), www.aspi.org.au/report/party-speaks-you.
18 M Burgess, 'Director General's Annual Threat Assessment 2020', ASIO, 24 February 2020.
19 Australian Security Intelligence Organisation, *ASIO Annual Report 2020–21*, 5, www.asio.gov.au/sites/default/files/Annual%20Report%202020-21%20WEB.pdf.
20 John Fitzgerald, ed., *Taking the Low Road: China's Influences in Australia's States and Territories* (Canberra: Australian Strategic Policy Institute, 2022).
21 Jim Molan, *Danger on Our Doorstep* (Sydney: HarperCollins Publishers, 2022); Ross Babbage, *Countering Chinese Adventurism in the South China Sea* (Washington, DC: Centre for Strategic and Budgetary Assessments, 2016); Babbage, Mahnken and Yoshihara, *Countering Comprehensive Coercion*; Babbage, *Winning Without Fighting*; Babbage, *Stealing a March*.

The ASIS Director General does not issue annual threat assessments. Still, ASIS is engaged in the grey zone, attempting to detect and disrupt threats to Australia's national interests 'upstream' overseas, while ASIO does so 'downstream' in Australia.[22] Unlike ASIO, which can inform law enforcement agencies to act against law-breaking and special forces to thwart violent terrorist acts, ASIS does not have the authority to employ armed force to counter grey-zone threats to Australia's national interests overseas.[23] The CPC has the escalation initiative there—metaphorically, it can 'punch' with impunity in the grey zone while Australia is left to complain with impunity.

The vulnerability

The 2020s are historically rhyming with the 1930s, when Australia previously faced the possibility of conflict with a major Asian trading partner, Japan. The difference is that, unlike hegemonic China today, Japan in the 1930s did not have a sophisticated grey- zone strategy, or the ways and means to coerce Australian governments politically, informationally, electronically (cyber) and economically in an escalatory manner. Nonetheless, this history provides a call to action. Horner observes that Australian governments did not formulate a sovereign national defence strategy in the 1930s. Australia had not prepared for conflict with the obvious regional enemy with a viable middle power strategy and the right capabilities. A 'Sovereign' strategy is one that Australia has the ways and means to implement autonomously and independently in its national interest while still meeting alliance obligations and complying with national and international law. There is no evidence that 'Australia's politicians and military leaders [before or] during the Second World War used the terms national strategy, military strategy or grand strategy'.[24] 'The likelihood that Japan would attack when British fleets were elsewhere, and that Singapore would be taken by the Japanese from the landward side' was prominent in public discourse but prompted little government action.[25] As Horner masterfully describes, Australia's preference was for the promises of the British Singapore Strategy.[26]

---

22 Australian Government, *Intelligence Services Act 2001*, www.legislation.gov.au/Details/C2022C00153 (site discontinued).
23 Australian Government, *Intelligence Services Act 2001*, Sections 6 and 11.
24 Horner, *High Command: Australia's Struggle*, 2.
25 Gavin Long, *The Final Campaigns, Australia in the War of 1939–1945*, vol. VII, series 1–Army (Canberra: Australian War Memorial, 1963), 585.
26 David Horner, *Strategy and Command: Issues in Australia's Twentieth-Century Wars* (Melbourne: Cambridge University Press, 2022), Chapters 5 and 6.

But what of the 2020s? How might Australia, at best a middle power, deter another Asian trading partner with hegemonic ambitions and a massive navy, army and air force? Should Australia replicate the 1930s and remain dependent on allies for strategic guidance and protection? Is it time for Australia to defend itself against an obvious threat with a sovereign strategy that guides the development and employment of the right capabilities?

Unlike in the 1930s, there is a surfeit of twenty-first strategic guidance. The 2020 Strategic Update and the 2023 Defence Strategic Review (DSR) reflect bipartisan preferences for enhancing conventional military capabilities to meet the challenges of the rise of China.[27] While the 2020 Update mentioned the grey zone, there is no strategy or planning for enhancing Australian grey-zone capabilities. The more recent DSR begins by acknowledging the grey zone indirectly as 'other actions that fall short of kinetic conflict, including economic coercion, are encroaching on the ability of countries to exercise their own agency and decide their own destinies', but then focuses on accelerating the acquisition of nuclear-powered submarines, longer-range missiles and conventional force projection from Australia's northern homeland military bases.[28]

Australia released a new national defence strategy in 2024 to implement the DSR. This strategy confirmed that Australia is following strategic traditions emanating from the Pacific War: reliance on powerful allies and overdue investment in conventional military capabilities.[29] The AUKUS agreement affirms a 'forever partnership' and dependence.[30] In the 2020s and beyond, the Australian Navy and Air Force will not be able to operate

---

27 Department of Defence, *National Defence: Defence Strategic Review 2023* (Canberra: Commonwealth of Australia, 2023) www.defence.gov.au/about/reviews-inquiries/defence-strategic-review.
28 Department of Defence, *Defence Strategic Review 2023* 4, 7, and Executive Summary, 17–21; Anthony Albanese and Richard Marles, 'Release of the Defence Strategic Review', media release (Joint Statement), 24 April 2023, www.minister.defence.gov.au/media-releases/2023-04-24/release-defence-strategic-review.
29 Department of Defence, *2024 National Defence Strategy* (Canberra: Commonwealth of Australia, 2024), 6–8, 38–43, 46.
30 Australian Government, 'Prime Minister of Australia, President of the United States and Prime Minister of the United Kingdom, Joint Leaders Statement on AUKUS', media release, 14 March 2023, www.pm.gov.au/media/joint-leaders-statement-aukus; Andrew Tillett, 'PM Hails New Subs Deal as "Forever Partnership"', *Australian Financial Review*, 16 September 2023, www.afr.com/politics/federal/pm-hails-new-subs-deal-as-forever-partnership-20210916-p58s3t.

optimally without American aircraft, naval vessels, submarines, supply chains, fuel reserves, technical maintenance and upgrades of operating systems.[31]

Some influential alternative voices in the strategic debate also largely ignore the grey zone. In a sustained body of work, Hugh White has consistently argued that China's rise to a military superpower is inexorable and America's decline in the Asia-Pacific region inevitable. Australia should thus not rely solely on the US to defend its national interests in a more contested Asia.[32] He highlights the risks of both entrapment in America's wars, especially with China, and abandonment by America if China threatens Australia. White urges Australia to adopt an independent defence posture but remains focused on conventional capabilities offering a 'defence from invasion' grand strategy through 'sea denial' based on a 32-strong submarine fleet and more strike aircraft, and consigning the Army to homeland defence.[33]

White, however, is silent about responding to political and hybrid warfare in the grey zone, dismissing cyber activities as neither a decisive strategy nor a viable warfare domain because of the mutually assured destructive effects.[34] White rightly questions the utility of Australian conventional land force projection but has not considered unconventional land force projection used to enhance targeting and the precise application of Australian maritime and air power. He is silent on the disruption and mauling of shipping in home ports, and supply lines and communications being cut by the employment of sovereign unconventional warfare capabilities, including cyber. This silence echoes the failure of imagination of Australian civilian and military leaders concerning Japanese shipping in 1942–43 that was molested only briefly in Singapore Harbour. Australian leaders did not develop sovereign capabilities to attack Japanese ships in port and elsewhere, or cut fuel and other supply lines, and destroy Japanese aircraft before they took off from forward airfields.[35]

---

31 Duncan Tchakalian, 'The Future of Air Superiority', Air/space blog (Air and Space Power Centre, Canberra), 9 May 2022, airpower.airforce.gov.au/blog/BP24698623; Secretary of Air Force Public Affairs, 'RAAF, USAF Leaders Sign Joint Vision Statement in Washington', Air Force Public Affairs, 29 September 2022, www.af.mil/News/Article-Display/Article/3174233/raaf-usaf-leaders-sign-joint-vision-statement-in-washington/.
32 Hugh White, *How to Defend Australia*, (Melbourne: Latrobe University Press, 2020), 296.
33 White, *How to Defend Australia*, Chapters 16 and 18.
34 White, *How to Defend Australia*, 27–28.
35 Horner, *High Command; Blamey*.

The obvious question is: 'Does a sovereign Australian grey-zone strategy in the 2020s matter if Australia increases Defence expenditure and remains close to traditional allies?' The difference in the 2020s compared to the 1930s is that, unlike Japanese nationalists, the CPC is coming for Australia in the grey zone first, and that is where Australia should have a strategy. The ADF is not designed to counter a grey-zone campaign that aims to escalate through nonviolent to violent phases to subjugate Australia without war. Australia's geographic advantages and armed forces become less effective when the economy, standard of living, political system and societal cohesion and wellbeing are attacked in the grey zone. Based on precedents in the South China Sea, the Philippines, Vietnam, India and Hong Kong, the CPC campaign will bypass conventional armed forces and geographical battle spaces to infiltrate and coerce rather than invade.[36] Taiwan, possibly China's 'Crimea', may succumb to a grey-zone campaign rather than an invasion.[37] Though a massive strategic surprise attack—an electronic Pearl Harbor— cannot be ruled out, according to Jim Molan in *Danger at Our Doorstep*, the CPC campaign will likely be incremental rather than sudden—covert and challenging to detect.[38] It will oscillate to confuse. There will be periods of political honeymoon and tensions, sometimes characterised as bullying.[39] The CPC will deny its grey-zone actions assiduously while employing political, economic, information and cyber tactics relentlessly. Chinese escalations will be beyond regular diplomatic and economic activities but below the use of violent coercion unless nonviolent escalations fail.[40] Australia needs a lawful response beyond regular diplomatic activity and below the threshold of military action. This response echoes Western intelligence agencies' special operations and covert action responses to Russia and China during the first Cold War. It has de-escalation objectives and is different: technologically enhanced and more sophisticated.[41]

---

36   Bonny Lin et al., *Competition in the Gray Zone: Countering China's Coercion Against U.S. Allies and Partners in the Indo-Pacific* (Santa Monica: Rand Corporation, 2022). www.rand.org/pubs/research_reports/RRA594-1.html#download.
37   The author's reference to Crimea relates to Russia's successful escalatory grey-zone campaign in Crimea in 2014. For Taiwanese grey-zone scenarios see Linda Jakobson, 'Why Should Australia Be Concerned About Rising Tensions in the Taiwan Straits?' *China Matters Explores*, 9 February 2021, chinamatters.org.au/policy-brief/policy-brief-february-2021/; Simone Gao, 'The Chinese Communist Party's Plan A to Take Taiwan', *The Wall Street Journal*, 22 March 2023, www.wsj.com/articles/the-chinese-communist-partys-plan-b-to-take-taiwan-jinping-united-front-influence-invasion-weapons-1653cc84.
38   Molan, *Danger on Our Doorstep*, Prologue, 13–30 and 31.
39   Corey Lee Bell and Elena Collinson, 'Australia-China Relations: The Outlook for 2023', *The Diplomat*, 22 December 2022, thediplomat.com/2022/12/australia-china-relations-the-outlook-for-2023/.
40   Lin et al., *Competition in the Gray Zone*.
41   See Ian Dudgeon, 'Intelligence Support to the Development and Implementation of Foreign Policies and Strategies', *Security Challenges* 2, no. 2, (July 2006), for discussion about enabling ASIS to engage in special operations and covert action.

This chapter does not argue against Australia's traditional strategic posture, except that Australia's sovereign capacity to deter an invasion fleet with submarines is decades away.[42] It argues for a strategy to meet the CPC in the grey zone as soon as possible to thwart escalations designed to coerce a subordinate relationship that subjugates Australia's sovereignty in favour of China's national interests. The proposed strategy focuses on preventative de-escalation to complement Australia's traditional defence posture.

The aim is to remove the CPC's temptations to escalate from 'light grey' political and economic intimidation to darker grey hybrid warfare. While understanding that Australia must communicate carefully with one of its major trading partners, CPC cyber attacks, espionage, political interference, arbitrary economic embargos, and the intimidation of Australian citizens in Australia and overseas warrant more than communicating concerns through diplomacy and declaring progress through meetings.[43]

Meeting the challenge of a second Cold War

How might Australia defend itself in the grey zone during a second Cold War that might, through miscalculation, escalate into another conflict in the Asia-Pacific region? A sovereign grey-zone de-escalation strategy is about proportional and lawful pre-emptive responses to escalating illegal activities. The power to respond when land, maritime and air power do not apply underpins it. A de-escalation strategy paces the shades of grey from nonviolent political, economic and informational pressure to violent, disruptive, destructive coercion. More particularly, response power detects, informs, deters and de-escalates at home and abroad to counter the three phases of grey-zone campaigns. When CPC coercion escalates to destructive

---

42 Parliament of Australia, 'Fact Sheet: Trilateral Australia–UK–US Partnership on Nuclear-Powered Submarines', 13 March 2023, parlinfo.aph.gov.au/parlInfo/search/display/display.w3p;query=Id%3A%22media%2Fpressrel%2F9066413%22.
43 Department of Foreign Affairs and Trade (DFAT), 'Meeting with China's State Councilor and Minister of Foreign Affairs Wang Yi', media release, Canberra, 21 December 2022, www.foreignminister.gov.au/minister/penny-wong/media-release/meeting-chinas-state-councilor-and-minister-foreign-affairs-wang-yi-1; DFAT, 'Step Forward to Resolve Barley Dispute with China', joint media release, Canberra, 11 April 2023, www.foreignminister.gov.au/minister/penny-wong/media-release/step-forward-resolve-barley-dispute-china.

cyber attacks and the deployment of grey-zone combatants with capabilities to disrupt Australia's political system, social cohesion and economy, Australia must have real, ready and lethal countermeasures.

Detection

The first pillar is knowing what is going on. The first Cold War instruments for detection still apply for a second Cold War. According to David Horner, in 1949 the Australian Government founded ASIO, realising that the nation needed 'its own counter-espionage organisation. It also needed to cooperate with and retain the confidence of similar agencies in allied countries'.[44] In 1952, Prime Minister Robert Menzies secretly founded an armed ASIS by charter to collect intelligence overseas and collaborate with allied counterpart organisations.[45] While referring only to ASIO directly because ASIS was still secret, Menzies stated: '[T]he Organisation is the "fourth arm" of Australian defence, after the Navy, Army and Air Force.'[46]

Fortunately, the Global War on Terrorism has consolidated the detection pillar. Australia's intelligence agencies have converged into the National Intelligence Community (NIC), which has increased detection and surveillance—'staring'—capabilities.[47] There is a suite of laws aimed at detecting and punishing foreign espionage, subversion, interference and international investments that are not in Australia's national interests.[48] The NIC meets these threats through strengthened integration across Australia's

---

44 Horner, *The Spy Catchers*, 32.
45 'Protecting Australia since 1952', home page, Australian Secret Intelligence Service (ASIS), last modified 2023, www.asis.gov.au/About-Us/ASIS-Overview/History/.
46 Horner, *The Spy Catchers*, 561.
47 Horner, *The Spy Catchers*, 145–50. The National Intelligence Community (NIC) was officially formed following the Australian Government's adoption of the 2017 Independent Intelligence Review's (IIR) recommendations. See Australian Government, *2017 Independent Intelligence Review*, 2017, www.pmc.gov.au/publications/report-2017-independent-intelligence-review. The NIC is comprised of the Office of National Intelligence (ONI), ASIO, ASIS, Defence Intelligence Organisation (DIO), Australian Geospatial Intelligence Organisation (AGIO), Australian Transactions Reports and Analysis Centre (AUSTRAC), Australian Signals Directorate (ASD), Australian Criminal Intelligence Commission (ACIC), AFP and Department of Home Affairs (Home Affairs); see 'Our Mission', Office of National Intelligence, www.oni.gov.au/national-intelligence-community. The NIC now has over 7,000 employees and an annual budget of over $2 billion. See 'Australian National Security', Australian Government, n.d., www.nationalsecurity.gov.au/.
48 *National Security Legislation Amendment (Espionage and Foreign Interference) Act, Amendment to Criminal Code Act 1995, 2018* (Cth); Foreign Influence Transparency Scheme Amendment Bill 2019 (Cth).

national intelligence enterprise. The current proficiency of these ways and means suggests that the detection pillar of response power is already in place and persistent.

Informational actions

The government can take informational actions once the NIC detects and 'stares' at the CPC campaign. The 'battle of the narratives' is about understanding, shaping, and influencing the decisions of governments and populations' attitudes. A nation that can change international public opinion and perceptions has an enormous advantage. Revelations and information directed at the CPC campaign inflicts hurt by discrediting its narratives. Diplomacy and negotiations that seek rapprochement accompany informational actions. Detection and surveillance do not counter the CPC grey-zone campaign until there is astute media exposure of CPC activities.

Public exposure and discourse about the CPC campaign deliver low-level deterrence. The more significant challenge is to deliver increasing levels of deterrence to meet each escalation. If diplomacy and negotiation fail and CPC grey-zone escalation continues, Australia can only deter and de-escalate if it has armed and potent special operations capabilities. Counterterrorism legislation has given Australian special forces lawful authority to act against violent grey-zone combatants behaving like terrorists. Still, this level of deterrence is ad hoc and not enough. The Australian Government's 2020 Force Structure Update mentions the connection between special forces and countering grey-zone activities in the future.[49] Legislation and institutional machinery to deter escalation well before the need for ADF special forces when things have gone wrong are needed now, not in the future.

Deterrence

During the first Cold War, an eminent American strategic theorist, Thomas Schelling, described deterrence as the 'art of coercion and intimidation'.[50] It involves communicating the power to hurt. It is based on what nations know other nations can do to hurt them. Deterrence is a form of firm

---

49 Australian Government, *2020 Force Structure Plan* (Canberra: Australian Government, 2020), para 7.15, www.defence.gov.au/about/strategic-planning/2020-force-structure-plan#:~:text=The%20 2020%20Force%20Structure%20Plan,the%202020%20Defence%20Strategic%20Update.
50 Thomas Schelling, *Arms and Influence* (New Haven: Yale University Press, 1966, reprinted 1980 and 2008), 10.

communication backed by a credible, forceful capability that can also be a bargaining power that underpins negotiation for reconciliation.[51] Schelling, who wrote in the context of the first Cold War, calls it 'The Diplomacy of Violence', but the preference for this chapter's exposition is deterrent diplomacy.[52]

British–American strategic thinker, Colin Gray, agrees with Schelling and opines that deterrence without the capability to 'hurt' is futile.[53] The prospect of coercive force must be real and credible. Schelling observes: 'We [the Western alliance] have learned that the threat [of coercive force] has to be credible to be efficacious.'[54] For Australia to create sufficient grey-zone deterrence, it has to have a well-communicated capability to hurt with well-calibrated capabilities and informational actions that mitigate the risk of disproportionate retaliation.

Schelling's most important idea in the context of an Australian de-escalation strategy is that most international relations conflict situations are about bargaining.[55] Bargaining to deter escalation in the grey zone with hurtful deterrent capabilities is feasible because the threat of conventional warfare, and undoubtedly nuclear war, is metaphorically 'off the table', even when a significant power like China is bullying a middle power like Australia. The CPC will not contemplate a conventional military or a nuclear response to Australia's calibrating a deterrent grey-zone response capability to persuade the CPC to reconcile rather than continue bullying.

Deterrence must be lawful, proportional and justifiable to the community of nations, and to China's political leadership and people. In short, Australia has to affirm that it wishes to get along with the CPC but can stand up to the CPC firmly and hurtfully if bullied. The challenge is to identify focal points, not only to optimise the timing and nature of hurt but to open up lines of conciliatory communication immediately in a hostile environment if deterrence has failed and a hurtful response has occurred.[56]

---

51 Schelling, *Arms and Influence*, Chapter 1.
52 Schelling, *Arms and Influence*, Chapter 1.
53 Colin Gray, 'Gaining Compliance: The Theory of Deterrence and its Modern Application', *Comparative Strategy* 29, no. 3 (22 July 2010), 278–83, www.tandfonline.com/doi/full/10.1080/01495933.2010.492198?scroll=top&needAccess=true.
54 Thomas Schelling, *The Strategy of Conflict* (New Haven: Yale University Press, 1980), 6.
55 Schelling, *The Strategy of Conflict*, 5.
56 Schelling, *Arms and Influence*, 103.

14. DISAPPOINTING THE DRAGON

One analogy is a bully, unwilling to communicate or negotiate, choosing to ignore a person who has a guard dog on the lead. The bully would most likely pay attention and communicate after the dog has bitten them once. A jab to the nose or a sting to the ear can force a bully to pay attention and communicate. Metaphorical bites, jabs and stings are carefully calibrated responses to bullying. They are hurtful and annoying, but they are insufficient justification for massive lethal retaliation because the reasons for hurtful responses are explained and warned about in the spirit of 'Look at what you have forced me to do. Let's see if we can work things out now'.

Deterrence based on pre-meditated, carefully calibrated 'stings' is about surprise and deception, but stings only occur within deterrent diplomacy after a private warning about uncomfortable consequences for unreasonable behaviour. Initial stings may be the public exposure of a plot, arrest and detention of grey-zone combatants or a raid on a facility accompanied by publicity to optimise the exposure of illegality. A lethal sting is a last resort. It must always come after the CPC is about to take, or has taken, Australian lives and destroyed Australian property. Even in these circumstances, there is a fair warning and an invitation to negotiate unless surprise and safety are paramount.

The success of deterrence depends on the CPC understanding the risks it will take if grey-zone combatants are detected planning for or executing violent acts against Australia's national interests. The CPC must inspect legislation and comprehend the hurtfulness of responses available to the Australian Government. This realisation may prompt another list of grievances, but the Australian Government will have clarified the consequences of escalating illegal activities.[57] Metaphorically, Australia is putting a sign on an entrance gate, 'Beware of the dog' rather than 'Beware of the dog we plan to buy'.

---

57   Of 14 grievances issued in 2020, 11 related to Australian national security, legislative and informational actions that countered the CPC grey-zone campaign: 1. Banning Chinese investment projects. 2. Banning Huawei from the 5G network. 3. Introducing foreign interference legislation. 4. Revoking visas of some Chinese nationals. 5. Criticising China in international fora. 6. Criticising Chinese encroachments in the South China Sea. 7. Funding ASPI, an anti-China think tank. 8. Introducing anti-China foreign investment legislation. 9. AFP/ASIO raids and deportation of Chinese journalists. 10. Accusing China of cyber attacks. 11. Anti-China media reports. Three that are unrelated are: 1. A call for an independent inquiry into origins of the COVID pandemic. 2. Siding with America's anti-China campaign. 3. Racist attacks on the CPC and Chinese people.

De-escalation capabilities

A de-escalation strategy without real and ready capabilities is not viable. Although not unified in common purpose by a strategy, some grey-zone capabilities, such as the NIC, are postured for detection. Collaborative arrangements between Home Affairs, ASIO and the AFP for law enforcement, and between state and territory police forces and ADF special forces for counterterrorism, are firm foundations for deterrence and de-escalation in the Australian homeland. Hierarchical arrangements for federal government departmental communications are foundations for informational actions. Home Affairs has legislation and capabilities for countering cyber attacks. Defence can protect access to the electromagnetic spectrum and deny access to an adversary. The question is whether these national capabilities are sufficiently joined up and hard enough for de-escalation if CPC grey-zone combatants deploy to the Australian homeland to work with locally recruited individuals and groups.

Beyond the homeland, DFAT and ASIS are the foundations for international detection and informational actions. Still, there has been a lack of deterrent sting since ASIS disarmed in 1983, after a training exercise went wrong in Melbourne.[58] The major weakness in international de-escalation is the lack of anywhere, anytime armed response capabilities to underpin deterrent diplomacy. Synergies between armed and unarmed ASIS elements that rehearse regularly for contingencies are better than expedient collaborations between ASIS and special forces overseas. An armed ASIS with sophisticated technological capabilities would restore Robert Menzies' fourth armed service for Cold War duties.

Responsibilities

Internationally, DFAT should be responsible for countering CPC grey-zone escalations in the nonviolent phases because coercive diplomacy, and political, economic and informational actions, constitute the first phase of a grey-zone campaign. Deterrent diplomacy, backed by capabilities vested in an armed ASIS Response Force to 'sting' China anywhere and anytime, should constitute the frontline of Australia's 'upstream' grey-zone deterrence and defence to thwart escalation to violent phases.

---

58   Diny Slamet, Ian Davis, Paul Chadwick, and Andrew Rule, 'From the Archives, 1983: ASIS Botches Training Drill at the Sheraton Hotel', *The Age*, 29 November 2020, www.theage.com.au/national/victoria/from-the-archives-1983-asis-botches-training-drill-at-the-sheraton-hotel-20201127-p56igg.html.

For 'downstream' defence in the homeland, Home Affairs should be the department for countering CPC grey-zone escalations. A partnership between ASIO and the AFP would enable detection and deterrence in the nonviolent phases, and an enhanced armed AFP Response Force would create an initial deterrent instrument if there were an escalation to violent tactics. The ADF and its special forces would become the ultimate response to counter an escalation to hybrid warfare because Australia will encounter Chinese special forces and armed proxies portrayed as Australian patriots seeking to counter American dominance and achieve a better relationship with China.

Response Force: the fourth armed service

The command and control of Australia's grey-zone Response Force—a fourth armed service—must be at the highest level of government. This is a lesson from the establishment of Special Operations Australia in 1942.[59] Defence and the ADF are responsible for implementing Australia's conventional defence strategy, with special forces capabilities to support ADF operations. The Department of Home Affairs is responsible for homeland security. A Chief of National Security reporting to the Prime Minister and located within a Response Force Headquarters in the Department of PM&C should become responsible for Australia's national and international grey-zone defence. The Chief of National Security would join the Chief of the Defence Force as member of the National Security Committee of Cabinet.

The existing ASIO–AFP partnership is the foundation for the national and near-region arm of Response Force.

In 2024, the AFP had a Counter Terrorism and Special Investigations Command, Specialist Protective Command and the Specialist Response Group (SRG).[60] The SRG has unique skills 'to maximise its response to diverse operations by tailoring deployments to meet a range of operational requirements'.[61] The SRG has a full suite of specialist tactical responses to incidents: search and rescue and crisis; hostage and negotiation operations supported by a bomb response team; and a maritime team. These are backed by command, coordination, planning of extended capabilities

---

59   Horner, *The Spy Catchers*, 20.
60   Australian Federal Police, Australian Federal Police Organisation Structure, AFP website, www.afp.gov.au/about-us/our-agency/chart.
61   Australian Federal Police, Australian Federal Police Organisation Structure.

and a communications response; and logistics and tactical intelligence teams.[62] These are the capabilities for operating effectively in the Australian homeland to deter and de-escalate an escalating grey-zone campaign.

Grey-zone legislation would categorise those preparing, planning and perpetrating disruptive and destructive cyber attacks, and those recruiting and controlling others for violent action, as grey-zone combatants. Response Force would detect and detain in the first instance. If deterrence and negotiations for rapprochement with their sponsors fail, Response Force teams would de-escalate them in proportion to their threat to life and property. If there is a likelihood of an escalation to hybrid warfare, the government can call out the ADF's special forces under the provisions of counterterrorism legislation.

The international arm of Response Force can be built on DFAT and ASIS responsibilities to protect Australia's national interests internationally. It is not an instrument for battle. It uses intelligence, diplomacy, informational actions, deterrence and de-escalation to renew and maintain mutually respectful cooperation with China. While it is an armed force, it is for bargaining, not for employment as a destructive instrument per se. Still, Response Force has to be credible and potent to create deterrence. If deterrence fails, its operations calibrate carefully to cause sufficient hurt to persuade the CPC to return to negotiation and bargaining for agreement, but not constitute acts of war—forceful attention-seeking is not retaliation or provocation for war. However, should the CPC attempt to escalate bullying to violence, the Response Force must have forceful de-escalation attributes in various domains.

The ADF's special forces should not build the international arm of Response Force. History should not be repeated. In David Horner's opinion, the government and the Army had little understanding of the strategic role of armed special operations in Australia's defence during the first Cold War. It took until the International Force East Timor (INTERFET) intervention in 1999–2000, and the aftermath of 9/11 in 2001, for the SASR to become a 'force of choice in handling difficult and delicate situations' anywhere and anytime outside the capabilities of the services.[63] SASR and commandos now operate alongside allied counterparts in the Middle East to deliver

---

62   Australian Federal Police, *Annual Report 2021–22*, 2022, www.afp.gov.au/sites/default/files/PDF/Reports/afp-annual-report-2021-2022-1.pdf.
63   Horner, *Phantoms of War*, 308 and 331.

lethal effects as part of the ongoing War against Terror.[64] That is their core business. Australian special forces are not designed to de-escalate in the grey zone and should not build a response force for international operations. They support conventional military operations and collaborate with allied special forces. They will be a last resort for dealing with grey-zone combatants waging a hybrid warfare campaign, but should not be 'on the frontline' for the initial phases of de-escalating a grey-zone campaign.

Response Force would be an armed intelligence service with special operations capabilities to support the Australian Government's efforts to counter grey-zone campaigns 'upstream' overseas. It would be *like* special forces but is not *of* special forces. There would be a need for more super-intelligent 'geeks' and Australians of Chinese heritage than athletic Anglo-Celtic super-soldiers. Response Force members would be specially selected for individual attributes informed by ASIS and IT skill sets, who possess complex problem-solving skills and mentally and physically resilient characters. They would operate as individuals and in small teams, guided by the law and specific ROE and trained to use technologically advanced equipment. Overseas, they would operate covertly and clandestinely, sometimes in hostile or politically sensitive environments, to achieve strategically important detection, deterrence and de-escalation objectives that are sometimes time sensitive and high risk. Response Force would recruit and employ foreign nationals to detect, stare at and support covert and clandestine operations.

Response Force would take direct and indirect approaches to achieve strategic 'stings'. The direct approach focuses on small-unit precision lethality or surgical strike to seize, destroy, capture, exploit, recover or damage designated targets or influence threats. These capabilities establish credible deterrence but do not presume that a kinetic strike is the first and only option. The deterrence begins with operations to detect and monitor existing and emerging threats. The direct approach calls them out publicly to deter the CPC from further plotting. It culminates—as a last resort—in carefully calibrated stings to de-escalate threats. These actions are preventative warning measures to gain attention and avoid conflict. The indirect approach involves individuals and teams with a deep understanding of cultures and foreign languages, including foreign

---

64 See Department of Defence website, 'Operation Augury', www.defence.gov.au/defence-activities/operations/augury.

nationals. These individuals and teams enable third parties, such as foreign nationals and regional security organisations, to deliver stings that achieve surprise, deception and deniability for Australia.

Response Force should have manoeuvre capabilities in all domains: maritime, land (urban and remote), air, cyber and information. It will be able to create effects along a spectrum that begins with informational embarrassment and progresses through public exposure to warning events, then, if warnings are ignored, covert and public stings to prompt resumption of negotiations aimed at rapprochement. It should be maintained at immediate readiness.

In partnership with diplomats and unarmed ASIS intelligence agents, Response Force would provide understanding and insight into emerging regional and international grey-zone threats. It would conduct covert and clandestine surveillance that detects and stares at threats to understand them, and to identify, analyse and rehearse response options. This attribute incorporates cunning and deception, as well as covert and clandestine infiltration. It encompasses collaboration with international proxies and partners to infiltrate and undermine inimical political, religious, military, racist, extremist and criminal groups—political and hybrid warfare tools. It would be capable of sufficient technological intrusion to retain the strategic escalation initiative.

Politics would permeate all aspects of Response Force operations. Operatives would need to have an astute awareness of politics and socio-political, ethnic and cultural influences, such as tribalism, ethnicity, corruption and parallel structures (also known as 'shadow governments'), and organised criminal networks. They would need to improvise, innovate, apply language skills and cultural awareness, and understand local politics. They should also expand, fuse, and decentralise intelligence functions and targeting while developing proficiency in the assertive use of influence, information and public affairs. Response Force would necessarily be the force of choice for partnering with nations' security forces in Australia's near region to protect their nationhood from an escalating CPC grey-zone campaign.

Response Force would have three functions characterised by the monikers Ghosts, Enablers and Goblins.

Ghosts — covert and clandestine operations

Attempting to counter grey-zone campaigns without lawful, graduated and potent covet and clandestine operations (CCOs) options is fruitless. CCOs are capabilities for defending in the grey zone when no war is declared but hybrid warfare is in the offing. The focus is on secret forms of small-group penetration anywhere worldwide for as long as required for intelligence collection, building situational awareness and targeting.

CCOs can occur both in the physical sphere and through cyber and space vectors. They are about deterrent statecraft across a spectrum, including competing for influence at one end and applying lethal force for strategic effect at the other. They need to be undetectable; response teams need to move in and out of areas without notice: they need to be *ghosts*—never truly discoverable, always a mystery and creators of fear.

Enablers — Neighbourhood Watch

The CPC grey-zone campaign is targeting Australia's neighbours. Enabling operations would involve collaborating with our neighbours and aggregating their contributions into a regional de-escalation strategy. This approach depends on a long-term plan to shape, understand and influence Australia's near region or other priority areas of strategic interest.

Enabling operations involve clandestine Response Force personnel operating in areas of strategic influence. It is a long-term engagement campaign to identify and invest in people and infrastructure to shape and influence political elites, civilian agencies, regional military forces and law enforcement agencies. An enabling 'trade-craft' includes mentoring, training assistance, enablement with niche technologies, targeted diplomatic influence and capacity building through specialised aid.

Goblins — electromagnetic spectrum operations

'Ghosts' and 'Enablers' are not enough. For Australia to have a full spectrum of response capabilities, Response Force must conduct offensive and defensive electromagnetic strike operations (EMSO) anywhere and at any time worldwide. EMSO would strengthen Australia's resilience to CPC 'information confrontation capabilities' by mapping cyberspace to conduct deniable cyber-offensive operations when and where necessary. Cyber stings and electromagnetic storms would feature. EMSO would add a dimension to Australia's independent reconnaissance-sting capabilities, creating Australian-generated 'information confrontation capabilities' that would enable deepfake propaganda and intrusions into IT systems. Narratives would influence CPC grey-zone sponsors' and combatants' will, emotions, behaviour, psychology and morale. Cyber stings would demonstrate the capacity to interrupt supply chains, financial systems and essential services, in emulation of CPC capabilities.

CCOs and enabling operations, incorporating EMSO, facilitate the projection of Australian persuasive influence, initially for warning purposes. If EMSO and CCO warnings were ignored and illegal activities escalated, EMSO would intrude into IT systems and create more disruption. If disruption were not enough and illegal activities became violent, EMSO would accompany high-value time-sensitive CCO. Response Force CCO, EMSO and enabling operations would come with political and physical risks. These risks would increase with the enablement of international partners, foreign nationals and proxy forces. Still, Australia's Response Force could be a risk mitigator because it does not seek or invite a military contest. It aims to slow bullying momentum. At worst, there would be political embarrassment if covert and clandestine activities were compromised. But that would be mitigated because all actions would be designed to ease tensions and de-escalate. There would be no bellicose motives to discover. The narrative would be that the CPC was forcing a response to bullying, but Australia was constantly seeking rapprochement.

Ghosts, Goblins and Enablers are the ways and means of an Australian strategic end-to-end system. CCO, supported by EMSO and enabling operations, would constitute the essence of Australia's international response power projection. They would complement the ways and means of diplomatic, informational, military and economic power. This approach accords with Shemella's prescriptions that integrate diplomatic, informational, military, economic, financial, intelligence and legal efforts to shift the focus from responding to future grey-zone attacks to anticipating and preventing them.[65]

In sum, a domestic and international Response Force would give Australia a fourth armed service capable of detecting threats and generating sufficient well-calibrated warnings and persuasive stings to achieve deterrence

---

65 P Shemella, *Fighting Back: What Governments Can Do About Terrorism* (Redwood City: Stanford University Press, 2011), 135, doi.org/10.1515/9780804778220.

and strategic effects anywhere and anytime. It would offer Australian governments options other than conventional forces to protect threatened sovereignty and national interests. Response Force would detect, warn and push against coercion while diplomats and Australia's political leaders invited discussion and negotiations to achieve rapprochement.

Conclusion

David Horner's strategic and higher-command histories of the Pacific War reveal that Australia relied on allies and was unprepared for conflict in its near region with an Asian power. In the 2020s, reliance on allies is understandable, and increased investment in conventional military deterrence, together with deepening alliance relationships, is wise. To be underprepared in the grey zone is unwise and echoes the lack of Australian strategic imagination and threat perception in the 1930s that Horner's histories reveal.

This chapter identifies a CPC grey-zone threat, anticipates its trajectory and argues that Australia must have a strategy and a fourth armed service designed to detect, deter and de-escalate the threat. The initial aim, which can stop there, is to prompt second thoughts in the CPC about escalating its grey-zone campaign and prompt a return to more respectful relations, evident when Xi Jinping and his wife visited Australia and he addressed the assembled houses of parliament in 2014.

Subsequent events suggest Xi was exploring closer relations with Australia and the Pacific Islands in 2014, but only on his terms. Relations soured when Australia continued to affirm its commitment to the US alliance and reminded China of its human rights obligations. By 2016, the CPC grey-zone campaign was apparent, and the Turnbull and Morrison governments responded reflexively but without a strategy. In 2022–24, the campaign paused to ascertain if the Albanese government might be more amenable to making concessions. The 2023 AUKUS agreement may prompt the resumption of the CPC grey-zone campaign, probably after testing President Donald Trump's resolve in 2025. Australia still lacks a counter grey-zone strategy and the instruments to implement it.

This chapter proposes a fourth armed service called a Response Force to optimise its deterrent effect to back up hardened Australian diplomacy. Deterrent diplomacy is only viable if Response Force possesses real and ready capabilities to hurt the CPC informationally and then to sting if diplomacy and negotiations fail to de-escalate. If deterrence fails, it can sting anywhere and anytime with strategic effect and optimised informational impact but consistently below the threshold of acts of war. If war becomes inevitable, a supplemented and enhanced Response Force becomes a 'first mover', able to act early and hit hard in sensitive places.

Critics will reasonably ask how Australia can threaten to hurt the CPC and not risk massive economic and cyber-retaliation. Might not the US and the UK wonder why a nation reliant on trading relations with China employs deterrent diplomacy? Might they caution Australia, a junior ally, not to provoke China because CPC retaliation may escalate tensions that lead to miscalculation and hostilities? Yet, to do nothing but complain is naïve. To rely solely on allies insults Australia's nationhood. To make concessions in the hope of more reasonable behaviour from a CPC totalitarian regime is appeasement. It could also be reasonably asked whether critics of this chapter's proposed strategy have one of their own.

Developing and disseminating a de-escalation strategy and establishing a fourth armed service will be politically and ethically challenging for a liberal democracy like Australia. There will be no appetite to build a Response Force until grey-zone escalations are apparent and painful. This realisation may come too late. An analogy would be the metaphorical frog not noticing the rising water temperature. Work on a grey-zone strategy that justifies and guides the development of capabilities should begin soon secretly in anticipation of that realisation. To wait for an electronic Pearl Harbor is to ignore history.

Part VII:
Epilogue

15

Australia's war dead: government policy, military practice and the Vietnam War

Kate Ariotti

I was delighted to be asked to write for this *festschrift*.[1] I have long admired David Horner's contributions to Australian and international scholarship, and I spent several remarkable weeks in 2015 working alongside him on a commemorative journey to Gallipoli. I was also, truth be told, a little surprised. Horner's oeuvre is focused on command, alliances, policy, intelligence and strategy—what is often thought of as traditional military history. My research, which has examined the experiences of prisoners of war, the evolution of war narratives and, most recently, the treatment of the war dead has been situated more in the second 'world' of Australian war history—the sociocultural.[2]

---

1   The research for this chapter was funded by Australian Research Council DECRA Fellowship DE200100099 'Between Death and Commemoration: An Australian History of the War Corpse'.
2   On the two worlds of Australian war history see Joan Beaumont, 'ANZAC Day to VP Day: Arguments and Interpretations', *Journal of the Australian War Memorial* 40 (February 2007), www.awm.gov.au/articles/journal/j40/beaumont. Beaumont's updated and expanded discussion of Australian military historiography can be seen in 'Australian military historiography', *War & Society* 42, no. 1 (2023), doi.org/10.1080/07292473.2023.2150485.

On reflection, however, I realised how instrumental Horner's work—specifically, his explication of the war–politics nexus, and the relationship between political and military leadership—has been in enabling historians like myself to explore Australian responses to war more broadly. His examination of the relationship between Prime Minister John Curtin, US General Douglas MacArthur and General Thomas Blamey during the Second World War, for example, has informed our understanding of the fighting experiences of Australian forces in the Pacific and the influx of American troops into Australian cities,[3] while his studies of the Australian government's negotiation of its military commitment to the conflict in Vietnam, and the effectiveness of Australian command during that war, help explain the increasing social disquiet within Australia over its nature and conduct.[4] Many of the societal effects and cultural legacies of war cannot be fully understood without situating them within the 'big-picture' political, strategic and operational frameworks expounded by scholars like Horner.

This is certainly the case when we consider the history of the treatment of Australia's war dead. Despite the seemingly insatiable appetite of Australians for celebrating their war history, only limited public and scholarly recognition has been given to the fact that corpses are part of the hard reality of the military experience. Death itself has been a key theme in Australian histories of war: the fear of death, the infliction of death upon the enemy, and emotional reactions to death are commonplace in accounts of the battlefield.[5] The intimate effects of death, too, have been explored through studies of grief and mourning,[6] while its broader cultural legacies have been

---

3   David Horner, *High Command: Australia's Struggle for an Independent War Strategy* (Sydney: Allen & Unwin, 1982), doi.org/10.4324/9781003120193; David Horner, 'MacArthur and Curtin: Deciding Australian War Strategy in 1943', in *Australia 1943: The Liberation of New Guinea*, edited by Peter J Dean (Port Melbourne: Cambridge University Press, 2014), 25–44, doi.org/10.1017/CBO9781107445239; David Horner, 'Australia in 1942: A Pivotal Year', in *Australia 1942: In the Shadow of War*, edited by Peter J Dean (Port Melbourne: Cambridge University Press, 2012), 11–29, doi.org/10.1017/CBO9781139540681.
4   David Horner, *The War Game: Australian War Leadership from Gallipoli to Iraq* (Sydney: Allen & Unwin, 2022), 240–325; David Horner, *Strategic Command: General Sir John Wilton and Australia's Asian Wars* (Melbourne: Oxford University Press, 2005).
5   For example, Bill Gammage, *The Broken Years: Australian Soldiers in the Great War* (Canberra: Australian National University Press, 1974); Hank Nelson, *POW Prisoners of War: Australians under Nippon* (Sydney: Australian Broadcasting Corporation, 1985); John Murphy, *Harvest of Fear: A History of Australia's Vietnam War* (Sydney: Allen & Unwin, 1993), doi.org/10.4324/9780429039362.
6   Joy Damousi, *The Labour of Loss: Mourning, Memory and Wartime Bereavement in Australia* (Cambridge: Cambridge University Press, 1999), doi.org/10.1017/CBO9780511552335 and *Living with the Aftermath: Trauma, Nostalgia and Grief in Post-War Australia* (New York: Cambridge University Press, 2001); Pat Jalland, *Changing Ways of Death in Twentieth Century Australia: War, Medicine and the Funeral Business* (Sydney: UNSW Press, 2006); Bart Ziino, *A Distant Grief: Australians, War Graves and the Great War* (Perth: UWA Press, 2007).

assessed through the lenses of commemoration and remembrance.[7] However, this focus on the battlefield, grieving families and memorials has rendered invisible—or at least blurred—much of the political and logistical work performed to facilitate the passage of Australian war dead 'from temporal to eternal'.[8] Most references to the vicissitudes of the dead body are found in studies of Australian war graves units and workers operating on the former battlefields of Gallipoli and the Western Front in the aftermath of the First World War.[9] But the recovery, identification and processing of the remains of Australians who died in other wars has not yet been comprehensively addressed. Nor has there been any sustained study of how and why these processes—and the human responses they provoked—changed over time.[10]

The treatment of war dead has received more attention in Europe and the US than in Australian scholarship. French historians Luc Capdevila and Daniele Voldman have examined the ways in which human remains were handled in modern war and conflicts in North and South America, and Western Europe. They have noted how Western civilisation's obsession with the remains of war dead is something of a paradox in the light of the twentieth-century capacity to completely destroy bodies in war.[11] In North America, meanwhile, historians have paid significant attention to the Civil War, when efforts to treat soldiers as worthy of individual identification, burial and commemoration first developed, and have situated the war corpse

---

7   KS Inglis, *Sacred Places: War Memorials in the Australian Landscape*, 3rd edition (Melbourne: Melbourne University Press, 2008); Carolyn Holbrook, *Anzac: The Unauthorised Biography* (Sydney: NewSouth, 2014).
8   Luc Capdevila and Daniele Voldman, *War Dead: Western Societies and the Casualties of War*, translated by Richard Veasey (Edinburgh: Edinburgh University Press, 2006), 37, doi.org/10.1515/9781474465625.
9   Ziino, *A Distant Grief*; Julia Smart, '"A Sacred Duty": Locating and Creating Australian Graves in the Aftermath of the First World War', Australian War Memorial Summer Scholar Paper, 2016, www.awm.gov.au/sites/default/files/julia_smart_0.pdf; Romain Fathi, '"We refused to work until we had better means for handling the bodies": Discipline at the Australian Graves Detachment', *First World War Studies* 9, no. 1 (2018): 35–56, doi.org/10.1080/19475020.2018.1476171; Fred Cahir et al., *Australian War Graves Workers and World War One* (Singapore: Palgrave Macmillan, 2019).
10   There are some exceptions: Jim Eames, *The Searchers and Their Endless Quest for Lost Aircrew in the Southwest Pacific* (St Lucia, Qld: University of Queensland Press, 1999); Bruce Scates et al., *Anzac Journeys: Returning to the Battlefields of World War Two* (Port Melbourne: Cambridge University Press, 2013), doi.org/10.1017/CBO9781139196420; Ian McPhedran, *Where Soldiers Lie: The Quest To Find Australia's Missing War Dead* (Sydney: HarperCollins Publishers, 2019). More recent scholarship includes Kate Ariotti, 'Between Death and Commemoration: The Treatment of Australian POW Dead on the Thai–Burma Railway, 1942–45', *Australian Historical Studies* 53, no. 2 (2022): 327–47, doi.org/10.1080/1031461x.2021.1981414.
11   Capdevila and Voldman, *War Dead*.

in the longer history of human attitudes towards dead bodies.[12] Scholars of American history have also examined the repatriation of American war dead in more contemporary contexts, including the First World War and the Korean War.[13] As for other nations, Beatrice Trefalt has investigated the work of Japanese community agencies to recover the remains of Japanese soldiers who died in the Pacific during the Second World War, arguing that it represents one way by which younger generations of Japanese remember and reconcile with their country's difficult past.[14] Recovery of Vietnamese war dead, too, has been considered. Van Nguyen-Marshall examines the contemporary efforts of civilians to collect and bury the corpses of those who fled Quảng Trị city during the 1972 Easter Offensive, while Heonik Kwon's study of the 'ghosts' of war in Vietnam reveals how contemporary Vietnamese communities are negotiating the physical and spiritual remains of their war dead, both military and civilian.[15] Australian historian and former platoon commander in 8 RAR in Vietnam, Bob Hall, has also written of his work with 'Operation Wandering Souls' to help the Vietnamese Government locate thousands of missing from the National Liberation Front/the People's Liberation Armed Forces and the Peoples' Army of Vietnam.[16]

This chapter is inspired by the Horner-esque approach of studying the connections between politics and war—and government policy and military practice—to consider the treatment of the bodies of Australian military personnel who died in the Vietnam War. It explains how the more limited nature of the war, the issue of conscription and the impetus to align with the

---

12 See, for example, Drew G Faust, 'Battle Over the Bodies: Burying and Reburying the Civil War Dead, 1865–1871' in *Wars Within a War: Controversy and Conflict over the American Civil War*, edited by Joan Waugh and Gary W Gallagher (Chapel Hill: University of North Carolina Press, 2009), 184–201, doi.org/10.5149/9780807898444_waugh.12. On deep-time history and the war corpse, see Thomas Lacqueur, *The Work of the Dead: A Cultural History of Mortal Remains* (Princeton: Princeton University Press, 2015).

13 Michael Sledge, *Soldier Dead: How We Recover, Identify, Bury and Honour our Military Fallen* (New York: Columbia University Press, 2007); Lisa M Budreau, *Bodies of War: World War I and the Politics of Commemoration in America, 1919–1933* (New York: New York University Press, 2010); Chris Dickon, *The Foreign Burial of American War Dead* (Jefferson: McFarland, 2011); Bradley Lynn Coleman, 'Recovering the Korean War Dead 1950–1958: Graves Registration, Forensic Anthropology and Wartime Memorialisation', *The Journal of Military History* 72, no. 1 (2008): 179–222, doi.org/10.1353/jmh.2008.0013; Judith Keene, 'Bodily Matters Above and Below Ground: The Treatment of American Remains from the Korean War', *The Public Historian* 32, no. 1 (2010): 59–78, doi.org/10.1525/tph.2010.32.1.59.

14 Beatrice Trefalt, 'Collecting Bones: Japanese Missions for the Repatriation of War Remains and the Unfinished Business of the Pacific War', *Australian Humanities Review* 61 (2017): 145–59.

15 Van Nguyen-Marshall, 'Appeasing the Spirits Along the "Highway of Horror": Civic Life in Wartime Republic of Vietnam', *War & Society* 37, no. 2 (2018): 206–22, doi.org/10.1080/07292473.2018.1469107; Heonik Kwon, *Ghosts of War in Vietnam* (Cambridge: Cambridge University Press, 2008).

16 Bob Hall, 'Operation Wandering Souls: Australians are Helping Locate Some of its Thousands of Missing in Action', *Wartime* 55 (July 2011): 25–29.

US ally underpinned significant changes to Australian repatriation policies. The chapter also demonstrates that the adoption of (and integration within) American military mortuary processes facilitated a new way of handling Australian remains that transformed wartime mourning practices. Examining these broader policy and logistical issues enables a clearer picture of the operational framework in which Australian dead were situated and provides the context for understanding the emotional responses to death in the Vietnam War.

The world wars and Korea

For most of the twentieth century, Australian policy regarding the war dead aligned with that of the imperial motherland. The British followed a strict non-repatriation rule; any serviceman (or woman) who died in overseas wars or conflicts was buried in the closest military cemetery to where they fell. Originally instigated in early 1915 to put a stop to the privately funded and often unsanitary return of remains to Britain from France, the British policy of non-repatriation also enshrined the principle of equitable treatment of the dead. This was a particularly important issue across the British Empire and in the US at the turn of the twentieth century, when military service became viewed as an expression of citizenship and armies were comprising citizen (volunteer or conscript) soldiers. The policy of non-repatriation, its proponents argued, also promoted a sense of perpetual fraternity among the dead. They had fought and died together; non-repatriation ensured they would lie together in eternal rest. More pragmatically, at a time when wars were being fought far afield, non-repatriation avoided the expense and logistical challenges of shipping remains across the vast stretch of the British Empire.

In both the First and the Second World War, then, successive Australian governments did not bring home the bodies of those who died overseas. Most of the approximately 102,000 Australians who died during the two world wars were buried or, where no remains could be identified or located, commemorated in cemeteries constructed and maintained by the Imperial (now Commonwealth) War Graves Commission across the world. Australian soldiers seemed to accept that, if they were killed, their bodies would not be returned to their families at home. Non-repatriation was, as Bart Ziino explains, part of their nascent military tradition—no Australians who died in Sudan, South Africa or China had been returned to Australia for burial—and underpinned much of British war history. There was 'a common attitude', Ziino writes, 'that those who marched away gave their bodies to the cause'.[17]

Bereaved families also accepted—if more reluctantly—the overseas burials of their loved ones, even after the Second World War, when the proximity of the Pacific burial grounds to Australia presented a challenge to the logistical argument for non-repatriation.[18] The all-encompassing nature of these two 'total' wars—framed as wars of imperial and national survival—plus the mobilisation of society towards the respective war efforts and, as Pat Jalland writes with reference to the First World War, the scale of loss felt around the country, encouraged stoic acceptance of both death and bodily absence.[19] The 'distant grief' of the bereaved morphed into a commemorative culture framed around the absence of the dead. Thousands of memorials were erected in towns and cities across the country. Both monumental and utilitarian, these memorials functioned as 'surrogate graves', providing a site at which individuals and communities could perform traditional mourning and funeral rituals.

The non-repatriation policy was also extended to Australian personnel who died in Korea between 1950 and 1953.[20] In a reflection of their dominance over the command of the UN Forces in Korea, the US military provided much of the logistics and support services available to British Commonwealth troops. This included the processing of the dead and the management of graves through the American Graves Registration Service.[21] Korea thus marks the first time that the remains of Australians who died in war, and their graves, were managed by military personnel outside of the British Empire.

---

17 Ziino, *A Distant Grief*, 36.
18 Scates et al., *Anzac Journeys*, 59–61.
19 Jalland, *Changing Ways of Death*, 75–105. For First World War as total war, see Bart Ziino, '"Total War" in Australia: Civilian Mobilisation and Commitment, 1914–18' in *Australians and the First World War: Local-Global Connections and Contexts*, edited by Kate Ariotti and James Bennett (Cham: Palgrave Macmillan, 2017), 165–82, doi.org/10.1007/978-3-319-51520-5_10.
20 The Wall of Remembrance at the United Nations Military Cemetery in Korea lists 346 Australian dead. Of these, 281 were buried in the cemetery in Korea and 10 were buried in the postwar plot of the Commonwealth War Graves Commission Cemetery in Yokohama, Japan. Forty-four were (and remain) classified as 'missing in action'; their remains could not be recovered from North Korea after the war. A further 11 Australians died after being returned to Australia during the period of the war and are buried in civilian cemeteries across the country.
21 'Report by Captain A.E. Chinn: British Commonwealth War Graves, Korea', AWM114 135/4/3.

The Americans considerably modified their own corpse management systems in Korea. They introduced new forensic and mortuary techniques, computer-led matching of unidentified remains with 'missing' personnel and, significantly, concurrent repatriation. American policy had traditionally been to repatriate, at next-of-kin's request, military personnel who died in overseas wars after the cessation of hostilities.[22] However, the more limited nature of the war in Korea—military operations intended to restore the pre-war political situation rather than total annihilation of the enemy—ensured that there was sufficient transport, personnel and other resources available to deal with the dead while the conflict was ongoing. War graves operations were thus grafted onto wartime military infrastructure.[23] As a result, the dead could be evacuated from the battlefield (or a temporary cemetery), identified, embalmed and sent on their way to the US within 30 days.[24]

Australian dead were processed through the Americans' new systems, but they continued to be buried in the closest permanent military cemetery: chiefly, the UN Memorial Cemetery in Pusan (Busan), South Korea. Officially opened in April 1951, this cemetery became the official and only war cemetery in Korea for UN forces and the only UN war cemetery in the world. While Australian repatriation policy remained unchanged in Korea, it was clear that the introduction of concurrent repatriation represented a fundamental shift in the treatment of the dead by one of Australia's key allies. These changes to American policy and practice became increasingly important for Australians during the Vietnam War.

Shifts in repatriation policy

Australian involvement in Vietnam was initially limited to the mid-1962 deployment of specialist Army advisers, known as the Australian Army Training Team Vietnam (AATTV). By 1965, the war had escalated. Some

---

22 John D Martz, 'Homeward Bound: Graves Registration and Recovery in the Korean War', *Quartermaster Review* (May/June 1954) qmmuseum.army.mil/research/history-heritage/mortuary-affairs/Homeward-Bound.html.
23 Coleman, 'Recovering the Korean War Dead', 196.
24 Martz, 'Homeward Bound'. Most American personnel who died during the war were returned to the US, where, depending on the wishes of next-of-kin, they were buried either in private or national cemeteries. A small minority of first-generation American personnel were returned to 'home' nations at the request of next-of-kin. See Coleman, 'Recovering the Korean War Dead', 207.

60,000 Australian military personnel served in Vietnam until the end of the Australian commitment in January 1973. Total Australian casualties were approximately 3,600; the number of deaths is contested but exceeds 500.[25]

Australian repatriation policy during the early years of the Vietnam War depended on the location and nature of the military service of the deceased soldier. In 1962, the *Repatriation (Special Overseas Service) Act* defined 'special service' areas in which Australian forces were engaged on 'special duty'—essentially, warlike operations—against an enemy at the request of the host country. This included the Malay Peninsula, South Vietnam and, later, Borneo. Australian military personnel serving on special duty in one of these special areas were eligible for full repatriation benefits, including pensions and medical treatment. It also meant that if they were to die on special duty, their bodies would be disposed of according to Australian wartime tradition—they would be buried at government expense in 'the nearest appropriate locality to the place of death'—that is, the closest military cemetery.[26] For Australians serving in the special service areas defined by the 1962 Act, the 'nearest appropriate locality' was Terendak Military Cemetery in what was then Malaya (in 1963, the Federation of Malaya aligned with the British colonies of North Borneo, Sarawak and Singapore to form Malaysia). This cemetery was situated within Terendak Camp, a military establishment built in Malacca by Great Britain, Australia and New Zealand to accommodate the 28th Commonwealth Infantry Brigade when it moved from North Malaya in the late 1950s. The cemetery held the remains of brigade troops and their dependants who died during their occupation of the camp, as well as Commonwealth casualties from the early fighting against the Indonesians—*Konfrontasi* (Confrontation)—in Borneo.

In 1963, the policy was amended. The government rule allowing the repatriation, at public expense, of the bodies of civilians employed on Commonwealth business overseas at the time of their death, such as public servants, was extended to military personnel. This was only on the provision that their death, and the nature of their service at the time of death, did

---

25 For conflicting totals of Australian military deaths during the Vietnam War, refer Joan Beaumont et al., *Australian Defence: Sources and Statistics*, vol. 6 of The Australian Centenary History of Defence (South Melbourne: Oxford University Press, 2001), 334; Headquarters Company, 1st Australian Task Force website (www.hq1atf.org/), 'Vietnam Casualty List – All Casualties', www.hq1atf.org/ozcas1.htm (site discontinued).
26 Clem Lloyd and Jacqui Rees, *The Last Shilling: A History of Repatriation in Australia* (Melbourne: Melbourne University Press, 1994), 319; Forbes to Menzies, 1 September 1965, NAA A463 65/4015.

not confer eligibility for benefits under the 1962 Act.[27] This change led to anomalies. An Australian serviceman who died while employed on garrison duties in Malaysia, for example, was equated to a public servant; his remains then could be repatriated to Australia at public expense. His counterpart who was allotted for special service, however, was deemed to be on warlike operations and, if killed, would be buried in Terendak. There was one caveat to this policy. Though it was not encouraged, families of military personnel killed on special service were able to request the return of remains at private expense. The next-of-kin or a beneficiary had to cover all costs associated with preparation of the body for travel, transportation, and eventual burial or cremation.[28] These costs typically amounted to between 300 and 400 pounds, the equivalent of up to A$12,000 in 2022.[29] Funding the repatriation of a family member who died as a result of military service overseas was a significant financial impost.

Australians who died early in the Vietnam War—members of the AATTV and 1 RAR killed in accidents, on operations or as a result of illness—were thus flown to Malaysia by the RAAF and buried in Terendak Military Cemetery or returned to Australia at private expense. Philanthropy facilitated many of these early repatriations.[30] Perhaps the most high profile was that of AATTV member Warrant Officer Kevin Wheatley, who was killed alongside Warrant Officer Ronald Swanton on 13 November 1965 while operating with US Special Forces in the mountains north of Saigon. Their bodies were recovered by a patrol the next day; it appeared that Wheatley died trying to save the wounded Swanton. 'Dasher' Wheatley was a well-known soldier, previously of 1 RAR, and the death of this 'indestructible' man 'stunned' his Army friends.[31] His wife, Edna, had little hope of raising the funds necessary to repatriate her husband's body. Just prior to Wheatley's death, she had started work as a barmaid in her local Returned Services League (RSL) for a weekly wage of 20 pounds.[32] The 'hero's widow' soon

---

27 Alan S Hulme, 'Burial of Servicemen Who Die Overseas—Draft Submission for Cabinet', NAA A1209 1965/6472.
28 Forbes to Menzies, 1 September 1965, NAA A463 65/4015; Harrison, Adjutant-General, AHQ Canberra to HQ Australian Army Force, Singapore, 27 May 1965, AWM98 R381/1/1.
29 Monetary conversion from Reserve Bank of Australia's Pre-Decimal Inflation Calculator: www.rba.gov.au/calculator/annualPreDecimal.html.
30 See, for example, 'Fighting Men May be Buried in Malaya', *Canberra Times*, 29 June 1965, 3; '£400 Offer Accepted', *Canberra Times*, 30 June 1965, 4; 'Stoffelijk overschot militair wordt overgebracht near Perth', *Dutch Australian Weekly*, 9 July 1965, 2; 'Adviser Killed in Vietnam', *Canberra Times*, 14 September 1965, 1; 'WO Had Planned Return', *Canberra Times*, 15 September 1965, 12.
31 'Adviser's Death Stunned Mates', *Canberra Times*, 17 November 1965, 28.
32 Michael C Madden, *Dasher: the Kevin Wheatley VC Story* (Sydney: Big Sky Publishing, 2021), 208.

received offers of financial help to return his body. A group of anonymous Sydney businessmen offered to pay for the repatriation and make all necessary arrangements. Although she believed that her husband would not have asked to be returned to Australia, Edna accepted the offer 'for the sake of our four children'.[33] One month after Wheatley's death, the *Canberra Times* reported that he had been recommended for the highest of military honours, the Victoria Cross.[34]

Joint author of the operational volumes of the Official History of the Vietnam War, Ian McNeill, argues that the publicity surrounding the fundraising to return the bodies of Australia's early Vietnam dead—particularly the posthumously honoured Kevin Wheatley—embarrassed the government and caused a drastic change to its stance on repatriation.[35] Indeed, on 21 January 1966, Acting Minister for Defence, Alan S Hulme, outlined that, subject to the practicalities of recovering bodies and any further escalation of operational demands, Australian military personnel who died in Vietnam would be repatriated to Australia at public expense.[36] In fact, this change had been coming for a while. Many of the arguments used to justify non-repatriation during the two world wars and Korea had lost their currency by the mid-1960s. The imperial iconography and sentiment that infused the treatment of the dead during the First and Second World Wars, in particular, was not relevant to the war in Vietnam, which—despite concessions to Australian operational independence—was fought within a strongly American framework.

Traditional concerns over the logistics of returning bodies were also no longer as valid. In a May 1965 sitting of the House of Representatives, Bert James, the Labor MP for Hunter, alluded to the possibilities afforded by improved transport infrastructure when he asked Minister for Air Peter Howson if the RAAF's new 'modern transport aircraft' meant that Australian servicemen killed in Vietnam could be flown home 'for burial in their native soil'.[37] In that same month, American and Australian military representatives signed

---

33 'Help for a Hero's Widow', *Canberra Times*, 20 November 1965, 3.
34 'Vietnam VC Report', *Canberra Times*, 11 December 1965, 1. Wheatley's Victoria Cross was gazetted in December 1966.
35 Ian McNeill, *To Long Tan: The Australian Army and the Vietnam War 1950–1966* (Sydney: Allen & Unwin and Canberra: Australian War Memorial, 1993), 48.
36 Statement by Acting Minister for Defence, the Hon. Alan S Hulme, 21 January 1966, NAA A1209 1965/6472.
37 House of Representatives Official Hansard, no. 18, 1965, 4 May 1965: Bert James, Labor MP for Hunter, question to Peter Howson, Minister for Air, 1095, historichansard.net/hofreps/1965/19650504_reps_25_hor46/.

the 1965 Military Working Arrangement, outlining the responsibilities of each nation to the war effort. As part of the arrangement, the US Military Assistance Command in South Vietnam agreed to provide equivalent logistical, administrative and personnel support to the Australian force as that supplied to the Americans, including 'preparation of remains'.[38] The embalming of bodies by American military mortuary specialists, therefore ensuring their preservation for travel, also invalidated one of the most pressing of the logistical issues that had underpinned Australian non-repatriation policy in the first half of the twentieth century.

The financial implications of overseas burial versus repatriation were also taken into consideration. In November 1965, the same month in which Wheatley and Swanton were killed, Hulme submitted to Federal Cabinet a full report on the issue of the Vietnam dead, outlining the arguments supporting government-funded repatriation or maintaining the status quo.[39] It included recommendations made by the Defence Administration Committee: namely, that repatriation was in line with the policy of Australia's American ally; that it was clearly the course of action favoured by the next-of-kin of those already killed in the war; and that, at that stage, the return of bodies would not be too much of a financial or logistical imposition due to the operational situation. On the latter point, the Committee argued that the costs of returning bodies to Australia for private funerals would probably be, in the long term, less than the costs of maintaining military graves in South-East Asia.[40] Indeed, at the time of Hulme's report, the costs (and other difficulties) of creating and maintaining burial grounds in the region for the dead of the Second World War were still evident; a cemetery for the POWs who had died on the island of Ambon between 1942 and 1945 was still not complete.[41]

Another powerful argument for government-funded repatriation concerned the politics of conscription. In the early years of the Vietnam War, the Menzies government introduced compulsory military service under the *National Service Act 1964*. Twenty-year-old males were obligated, if their date of birth was drawn in a nationwide lottery, to serve for a period in

---

38   'Military Working Arrangement between COMAAFV and COMUSMACV (May 1965), Appendix C, Documents, in McNeill, *To Long Tan*, 457–59.
39   Alan S Hulme, Draft Cabinet Submission: 'Burial of Servicemen Who Die Overseas', NAA A1209 1965/6472.
40   Hulme, 'Burial of Servicemen'. Families who had paid for repatriation prior to the policy change were reimbursed by the government.
41   Scates et al., *Anzac Journeys*, 54.

the Army. Compulsory overseas military service had a fractious history in Australia—it had been rejected in two profoundly divisive referendums during the First World War—and it proved similarly controversial in the 1960s. Opposition to the policy grew when it was proclaimed that national servicemen could be sent to Vietnam.[42] The government acknowledged there would be ramifications for burial practices. 'National servicemen are not volunteers', Hulme wrote in his Cabinet submission:

> [S]hould a national serviceman be killed overseas, either on operations or garrison type duty, his next-of-kin may expect that, if it is permissible to have his body returned to Australia at private expense, it should be returned at public expense.[43]

Hulme recognised families could argue that in transgressing the longstanding voluntarist principle of military service and assuming control of the conscript's body in life, the government had an obligation to return it home in the case of death.

The leading veterans' organisation, the RSL, opposed any potential change to repatriation policy. National Secretary Alexander (Bill) Keys wrote to Prime Minister Menzies to voice the League's commitment to the continued overseas burial of Australian war dead, explaining that those who die in war should be buried in specific war cemeteries that were maintained in perpetuity. The RSL National Executive had resolved that 'the cemeteries abroad under the control of the British War Graves Commission … were the most appropriate resting place for servicemen killed while in action abroad'.[44] Keys also expressed the RSL's concern about the expense of returning remains to Australia, and claimed that the money would be better directed into caring for the bereaved.[45] Other groups, however, had already flagged some of the points raised in Hulme's submission to Cabinet. The Secretary of the Cairns and District Trades and Labour Council sent a scathing letter to Menzies requesting Australian repatriation policy be brought into line with American. 'We would point out that the United States government apparently adopts this policy [repatriation at government expense],' he wrote, 'and as the Federal Government appears

---

42 On Australian protest during Vietnam War, see Greg Langley, *A Decade of Dissent: Vietnam and the Conflict on the Australian Home Front* (Sydney: Allen & Unwin, 1992); for anti-conscription protest specifically, see Carolyn Collins, *Save Our Sons: Women, Dissent and Conscription during the Vietnam War* (Melbourne: Monash University Publishing, 2021).
43 Hulme, 'Burial of Servicemen'.
44 Keys to Menzies, 17 January 1966, NAA A463 1965/4015.
45 'Australia to Pay for Return of Dead', *Canberra Times,* 22 January 1966, 8.

to whole-heartedly support United States foreign policies generally, that your Government accede to this request.'[46] Members of the public noted the inequitable treatment of government officials who died overseas and Australian soldiers, and members of the opposition also made representations in favour of government-funded repatriation. In a November 1965 letter to Menzies referring to the repatriation of an Australian embassy official from Thailand, South Australian Labor MP Clyde Cameron asked 'whether the Government considers that the Third Secretary of the Australian Embassy at Thailand is entitled to preferential treatment over an Australian soldier killed in action in Vietnam'.[47]

Australian forces serving in Vietnam were aware of the potential policy change. In November 1965, Brigadier Owen Jackson, Commander of Australian Army Forces Vietnam, told Army HQ in Canberra that he knew the issue of Vietnam dead was under government consideration and that options were being discussed, including the return of all dead at public expense or the burial of the dead in a military cemetery in Vietnam. Jackson strenuously opposed the latter option. 'I strongly recommend,' he wrote to Army HQ, 'that remains not be buried in Vietnam':

> It is difficult to state concrete reasons but there is in my opinion a strong feeling in my command against local burial. This is a feeling I have not found previously amongst Australian soldiers in other parts of the world.[48]

Jackson attributed this 'strong feeling' to the 'vicious' nature of the war, the instability of the South Vietnamese Government, the 'at least superficial unhygienic poverty of the country', and the need to secure any burial ground against enemy attacks prior to a funeral service.[49] His opposition to the creation of an Australian military cemetery in Vietnam was noted, though Army HQ reminded Jackson that 'we have had to bury in foreign soil before'.[50] They also stated that remains not requested to be returned to Australia by next-of-kin would have to be buried somewhere and that the Malaysian Government was likely, in the near future, to restrict burials in the limited capacity Terendak Cemetery.[51] Cremation was suggested as an

---

46 Craig to Menzies, 22 July 1965, NAA A463 1965/4015.
47 Cameron to Menzies, 22 November 1965, NAA A1209 1965/6472.
48 Jackson to HQ Army Canberra, November 1965, AWM98 R381/1/1.
49 Jackson to HQ Army Canberra, November 1965.
50 HQ Army Canberra to Australian Army Vietnam, 8 December 1965, AWM98 R38/1/1.
51 HQ Army Canberra to Australian Army Vietnam, 8 December 1965.

option but this was quashed upon investigations into the South Vietnamese civilian contractor's method of cremating Korean soldiers, which involved the slow burning of the body over an open fire for approximately 18 hours.[52]

Despite the protests of those opposed to burial in Vietnam, Federal Cabinet requested that the Director of the Commonwealth War Graves Commission, Pacific Region, Brigadier Athol Brown, visit South Vietnam in February 1966 to assess the feasibility of establishing an Australian cemetery in Saigon. Brown reported that it was highly unlikely any cemetery would be desecrated, pointing to French graves in cemeteries of the former colonial power as an example, but acknowledged that it would be challenging to ensure maintenance to the standards expected by Australian servicemen and their families. He also noted the strength of opposition among Australian personnel: 'There is undoubtedly a feeling among the troops,' Brown reported, 'that permanent burial in Vietnam is not desirable ... The only comment from the troops ... was that "the Government sent us here and they should provide us with a return ticket even if the return half is used after we are dead."'[53] A proposal from South Vietnamese officials to incorporate the graves of Australian war dead into their national military cemetery in Saigon was immediately rejected, as was the idea that Australians killed in Vietnam could be consolidated in a national cemetery somewhere in Australia.[54] Ultimately, no Australian cemetery was constructed in Vietnam. Most servicemen who died after the policy change were repatriated to Australia, while those whose next-of-kin did not request return of remains were buried in Terendak.[55]

---

52 AUSTARM Vietnam to Army HQ Canberra, 25 December 1965, AWM98 R38/1/1. The crematorium was in Viet Cong territory, which was another factor against its use. Cremation, moreover, did not solve the problem of where to put remains, as urns still needed to be stored somewhere. In 1967, the US forces brought two crematory units into Saigon to control cremation of the dead.
53 'Report on the Result of Investigations into the Possibility of Establishing a War Cemetery in South Vietnam as Directed by Cabinet during January 1966', AWM98 R161/1/1. My thanks to Dr Robert Hall for drawing my attention to this source.
54 'Report on ... the Possibility of Establishing a War Cemetery'.
55 Warrant Officer Kevin Conway of the AATTV (the first Australian to die in Vietnam) was originally buried in Mac Dinh Cemetery in Saigon and was reinterred at Singapore's Ulu Pandan Cemetery in late 1964. His body was reburied in Kranji War Cemetery, Singapore in the mid-1970s. A total of 24 Australians were interred in Terendak, including 15 after January 1966. The remains of one soldier were transported to his home nation of Ireland, while the ashes of several others were repatriated to Scotland and elsewhere in the United Kingdom.

Processing remains

As in Korea, Australians who died in Vietnam were processed through US military mortuary services. The bodies of those killed in action were removed from the battlefield to a helicopter landing zone as quickly as possible by either armoured personnel carriers or on litters. RAAF or US Army 'dust-off' helicopters then flew them to the nearest American hospital. For Australians operating in Phuoc Tuy, this was usually the 36th Evacuation Hospital (commonly referred to as 36th Evac) on Vung Tau Air Base. American Graves Registration personnel had established a cadaver collection point at 36th Evac; here the dead were formally identified, ideally by two members of their unit or at least one Australian serviceman, and death certificates were issued by either American or, if available, Australian medical officers.[56] Post-mortems were performed if the cause of death was unknown or if it had occurred in suspicious circumstances. (Courts of Inquiry or investigations were also held in the latter case.) Once all relevant paperwork was complete, the body was transported to the American mortuary at Tan Son Nhut Air Base, north of Saigon.

This mortuary was first established in the early 1960s by the USAF. In 1965, in recognition that most deaths in Vietnam were among Army personnel, it was transferred to the US Army.[57] As casualties increased, facilities were expanded. A headquarters and in-processing section (including an identification laboratory and an embalming room) were co-located to form the mortuary complex. A pathology laboratory operated from an annex mounted on the back of a truck parked in the complex. The Tan Son Nhut mortuary could officially hold up to 250 sets of remains at any one time.[58] American personnel, typically servicemen with a civilian background as mortuary technicians or funeral directors, worked in the mortuary complex seven days a week through all hours of the day and night.

First, bodies were stripped of uniform, boots and personal effects. These were inventoried and checked by mortuary or quartermaster personnel; anything that might distress the next-of-kin or cast the deceased in a negative

---

56 Regulations stipulated that death certificates issued to bodies destined for cremation in Australia had to be signed by an Australian medical officer.
57 *Vietnam Studies: Logistic Support* (Department of the Army: CMH Pub 90–15–1, 1974), 204, webdoc.sub.gwdg.de/ebook/p/2005/CMH_2/www.army.mil/cmh-pg/books/vietnam/logistic/.
58 Mortuary Affairs Center, 'Memorial Affairs Activities—Republic of Vietnam', March 2000, web.archive.org/web/20110907033043/http://www.qmmuseum.lee.army.mil/mortuary/MA-Vietnam.htm.

light, such as pictures of nudes or letters containing offensive language, were removed.[59] Fingerprints were taken and dental charts created. As in Korea, civilian anthropologists helped identify badly decomposed, co-mingled or dismembered bodies. The remains were then embalmed—both military and civilian embalmers worked at Tan Son Nhut—dressed in a clean uniform, strapped into an aluminium transport casket and held for a period (usually eight hours) to ensure the effectiveness of the embalming.[60] Remains that were badly decomposed or dismembered were often placed within a layer of plaster so that embalming fluid did not seep out. This also helped to 'impart to remains human and natural appearance' and ensure their safe transit.[61] The entire process, from examination of the body to readiness for repatriation, took just under 12 hours.[62]

The nature of the work at Tan Son Nhut mortuary took its toll on the staff. 'You learned to breathe a certain way,' one former technician told a journalist 50 years after the war.[63] Another remembered the relentlessness of it all, explaining that the mortuary was almost always over capacity. 'There were remains all over the place,' Glen Fruendt explained. 'It almost became a normal way of operation because we were so busy.'[64] Despite the many challenges, the American mortuary personnel recognised the importance of their work as agents for the bereaved. 'We treated the remains of the soldiers that were killed with respect,' another explained. 'You had to do the job right and you had to treat them like a member of the family.'[65]

Certainly, the families of those Australians who died in Vietnam appreciated the efforts of American mortuary personnel. The May 1966 death of Private Errol Noack of 5 RAR—the first conscript killed—generated considerable attention in Australia. Errol's father, Wally Noack, exercised his right to grieve over his serviceman-son's body. 'I told the Army and the Undertaker,' he explained to a friend years after the war, 'that I was determined to see Errol before the Funeral':

---

59   Leamon Smith, quoted in Matthew M Burke, 'Vietnam at 50: For Those Who Prepared Vietnam's Fallen, a Lasting Dread', *Stars and Stripes*, 4 November 2014, 75. stripes.com/index.php/archives/vietnam-50-those-who-prepared-vietnams-fallen-lasting-dread (site discontinued).
60   Wooden and fibreboard caskets were used on Australian courier flights for a short period but their fragility during the transport process necessitated a return to aluminium caskets. AUSTFORCE Vietnam to Army Canberra, 6 December 1967, AWM98 R1/3/7.
61   AUSTFORCE Vietnam to Army Canberra, 10 March 1967, AWM98 R1/3/7.
62   Mortuary Affairs Center, 'Memorial Affairs Activities'.
63   Gary Redlinski, quoted in Burke, 'Vietnam at 50'.
64   Glen Fruendt, quoted in Burke, 'Vietnam at 50'.
65   Glen Fruendt, quoted in Burke, 'Vietnam at 50'.

> The American specialists embalmed Errol, using a new process, soon as Errol died they pumped a special liquid into his blood veins, and they say that in 25 years Errol will be the same as when he died … Errol looked as though he was just sleeping with all his natural colour.[66]

Wally Noack visited his son at the funeral parlour multiple times prior to Errol's burial.[67] Clearly, this was an important aspect of his mourning process.

The Australian force continued to rely on 36th Evac as a collection point for the dead even after the establishment of 1st Australian Field Hospital (1 AFH) at Vung Tau in April 1968, which did not have facilities for the holding of remains. However, after 36th Evac closed in late 1969, 1 AFH opened its own refrigerated collection point or 'deadroom'.[68] Australian dead were transported there directly from the battlefield or, if they died after medical treatment, from the hospital. 1 AFH staff, mainly orderlies and quartermaster personnel, assumed many of the tasks that had been performed at 36th Evac. Bodies brought from the field were checked for grenades and ammunition in their uniforms and webbing before being stripped (uniforms and boots were usually incinerated), cleaned and identified. A medical officer certified death, and personal effects were categorised and prepared for the next-of-kin. The body was then placed in a plastic bag and stored in a refrigerator.

Many of the personnel who worked in the 1 AFH deadroom had not previously seen a corpse. '[I]t was a shock to the system,' Bob Roach recalled years after the war. 'Never having viewed a body in my life before and here was one that was freshly dead':

> We weren't allowed to do too much to these guys, just clean them, dress their wounds and put them in a clean body bag because usually they'd been shoved in, in the mud and God knows where they were out in the scrub. Nine times out of 10 it had been raining because it's always bloody raining over there, so you'd just cut their gear off them, clean them up, dress their wounds. The sergeant would bandage up their wounds or whatever, put them in a fresh body bag, put them in the fridge.[69]

---

66 Wally Noack to Barry, 5 February 1989, Papers of Private Errol Noack, AWM PR03142.
67 Wally Noack to Barry, 5 February 1989, Papers of Private Errol Noack, AWM PR03142.
68 Streeton to 1ALSG & 1AFH, 9 December 1969, AWM98 R506/1/26.
69 Robert 'Bob' Roach, Interview 1201, 27 November 2003, UNSW Canberra Australians at War Film Archive.

The 1AFH deadroom did not have embalming facilities; remains continued to be sent to Tan Son Nhut to be prepared for repatriation. 1AFH mortuary personnel like Roach took it in turns to accompany remains on 'casket runs' from Vung Tau to Saigon.[70]

The logistics of return

While the Army managed the processes of preparing the dead for repatriation, the RAAF was responsible for transporting remains from Vietnam to Australia.[71] Most RAAF squadrons in Vietnam were based at Vung Tau Air Base, close to the Australian logistics support centre and the main Australian medical facilities. From mid-1965, the RAAF flew fortnightly 'courier service' flights between Richmond Air Base in New South Wales and Vung Tau using C-130 Hercules transport aircraft to move cargo, supplies and personnel. These flights initially evacuated wounded personnel to RAAF Butterworth, Malaysia, or to Australia for medical treatment, as well as caskets containing remains. In mid-1966, after public criticism about the conditions on board courier aircraft used for the wounded and sick, special medevac flights using later model C-130s also flew fortnightly between Richmond and Vung Tau.

Complaints arising from the practice of transporting the living with the dead also contributed to changes in the medevac process. On several occasions, wounded patients shared the same flight as the bodies of their friends killed in action.[72] In one instance, the seal of a casket broke open mid-air, causing 'great distress' to passengers and crew.[73] Flight Lieutenant Ian Favilla, RAAF Senior Medical Officer in Vietnam from 1966 until late 1967, argued that living patients should not be transported on the same flights as the dead.[74]

---

70 Robert 'Bob' Roach, Interview 1201.
71 Many of the bodies of Australian personnel repatriated at next-of-kin expense prior to the January 1966 change in repatriation policy were transported from Vietnam to Australia on civilian (commercial) aircraft.
72 Brendan G O'Keefe, *Medicine at War: Medical Aspects of Australia's Involvement in Southeast Asia 1950–1972* (Sydney and Canberra: Allen & Unwin and Australian War Memorial, 1994), 94. See also Gay Halstead, *Story of the RAAF Nursing Service 1940–1990* (Metung: Nungurner Press, 1994), 329.
73 Chris Coulthard-Clark, *The RAAF in Vietnam: Australian Air Involvement in the Vietnam War 1962–1975* (Canberra and Sydney: Australian War Memorial and Allen & Unwin, 1995), 255–56.
74 O'Keefe, *Medicine at War*, 95.

15. AUSTRALIA'S WAR DEAD

By March 1967, RAAF regulations for the movement of caskets stated that 'under no circumstances' were medevac passengers to be loaded on to the same aircraft as corpses.[75]

Caskets were subsequently released from Tan Son Nhut for transportation to Vung Tau Air Base only after inspection by the RAAF Movement Control Officer in Saigon. RAAF 35 Squadron, which flew Caribou transports from Vung Tau, assisted with the movement of caskets between bases. Flight Lieutenant Jeff Pedrina recalled one occasion when he collected seven caskets from Tan Son Nhut and flew them to Vung Tau: 'I walked past the aluminium caskets, stacked either side of the cargo compartment … feeling sorry for the occupants and a little unsettled … I did not even know who they were or how they had died, thousands of miles from home.'[76]

Transportation of remains was governed by the Australian forces' imperative to ensure the dignity of the dead and respect for the bereaved. At Vung Tau, hatless RAAF personnel performed the 'delicate task' of placing the dead onto the C-130. This visible marker of respect for fellow servicemen was written into a staff instruction issued by the Movement Control Officer.[77] Caskets were loaded head-first; they could be stacked on top of one another, but no cargo could be placed either underneath or on top. The RAAF Air Movement Officer at Vung Tau was personally responsible for ensuring that caskets were loaded appropriately and that all necessary paperwork—statement of recognition, death certificate, personal information and an embalmer's certificate—had been handed to the flight crew.[78] The importance of correct loading of caskets was made clear in April 1969 when Military Command Adelaide reported that the last two deceased soldiers returned to Adelaide had arrived upside down, 'resulting in damage to face of soldier' and causing 'problems relating to viewing by NOK [next-of-kin]'.[79] This particular instance of mishandling was traced to confusion over the correct orientation of caskets among civilian airline personnel in Australia (where it was not logistically possible for the RAAF to transport bodies within Australia, the domestic commercial airline, TAA,

---

75 RAAF Movement Control Officer, 'Staff Instruction No 2/67: Handling of Caskets Containing Human Remains—Service Aircraft', 7 March 1967, AWM98 R1/3/7.
76 Jeff Pedrina, *Wallaby Airlines: Twelve Months Caribou Flying in Vietnam* (Canberra: Air Power Development Centre, Royal Australian Air Force, 2006), 118–19.
77 Loading personnel were also expected to be 'quiet and respectful' as they handled the casket. RAAF Movement Control Officer, 'Staff Instruction No 2/67'.
78 'Staff Instruction No 2/67'.
79 Military Command Adelaide to AUSTFORCE Vietnam, 24 April 1969, AWM98 R1/3/7.

was contracted as couriers). To guard against similar errors in the future, each casket was stencilled before leaving Vietnam with yellow arrows and markers indicating the top side.[80]

Depending on the weather, the task and the international situation—during Confrontation, for example, Australian aircraft could not always fly through Indonesian airspace—C-130 couriers departed Vung Tau, refuelled at RAAF Butterworth, Malaysia, and then landed in either Darwin or Perth before continuing to RAAF Richmond, near Sydney. Human remains were considered imports and were subject to Australian quarantine laws. The Movement Control Officer signalled the first Australian port of call 72 hours prior to the departure of a flight carrying caskets to provide the service number, rank and full name of the deceased, and certification in each case that death had not been due to either an infectious or contagious disease.[81] When the C-130 landed, health officers boarded and sprayed it with insecticide.[82] Transit of the dead within Australia was contingent on the destination, including whether there was a military presence near the deceased's hometown. Australian-based RAAF squadrons couriered bodies to either the nearest RAAF station or civil airport; TAA carried them if RAAF transportation was not feasible. Upon arrival at their final destination, caskets were either forwarded by Army transport to funeral directors or were collected by undertakers.[83]

Many families accepted the government's offer of a full service (military) funeral. Families and communities were moved by the ritual of bearer and firing parties, slow march through hometown streets and military bands playing the Last Post and Reveille. Errol Noack's father found great comfort in the military traditions at his son's funeral. 'It was of course a big military funeral,' he wrote to a friend, 'with the military band, with muffled Drums it was very impressive.' [84] Recognising their loved one's commitment to service, some families elected to bury their dead in military portions of their local cemeteries.[85] Others interred them in civil sections along with family and members of their community or opted for cremation. From 1966 on,

---

80 AUSTFORCE Vietnam to Army Canberra, 6 May 1969, AWM98 R1/3/7.
81 RAAF Movement Control Officer Vietnam Movement, Staff Instruction no 1/677, 7 March 1967, Restricted: Funerals, 10 March 1967, AWM98 R1/3/7.
82 Halstead, *Story of the RAAF Nursing Service*, 330.
83 ArmyMov Sydney to AUSTFORCE Vietnam, Movement of Deceased Remains, 1 May 1969, AWM98 R1/3/7; '20 Diggers fly home to recover', *Courier Mail*, 2 September 1966, 1.
84 Wally Noack to Barry, 5 February 1989, Papers of Private Errol Noack, AWM PR03142.
85 'Vietnam Fighters Return. Military Honours for 8 War Dead', *Courier Mail*, 3 September 1966, 7.

families, rather than the state, determined the final resting place of those who died in Vietnam. Regardless of their location, they now had the right to mourn in the presence of their dead.

Conclusion

The Vietnam War heralded significant changes to the treatment of Australian war dead. The evolution of repatriation policy from one of strict non-return to one in which the dead were repatriated at government expense reflected important political and logistical shifts, including recognition of the financial implications of overseas burial, public reaction to the deployment of conscripts and increased transport capability and access to American mortuary specialists. The introduction of government-funded repatriation also represented strategic change. The traditional imperial rhetoric that had underpinned non-repatriation was not relevant in a war fought outside the British framework. Returning the dead brought Australia into closer military and cultural alignment with the US, a key ally in the Cold War era.

Examining the repatriation of Australia's Vietnam dead demonstrates how important histories of strategy, command, policy and logistics are to the sociocultural history of war. As this chapter shows, analysing the practicalities of mortuary affairs provides the important detail necessary for assessing the emotional response to death in Vietnam, and for understanding the development of a new way of mourning Australian losses in war. David Horner and I may have different emphases in our studies of war history, but we are similar in our desire to understand the Australian experience of war. One of his greatest legacies is providing the framework necessary for historians like me to bridge the two 'worlds' of Australian war history and embed our studies of war's social and cultural effects in the important broader context of government policy and military practice.

Appendix 1: David Horner: professional career

Academic qualifications

1980: PhD, The Australian National University (ANU)

1975: MA (1st Class Honours), University of New South Wales (UNSW)

1973: MA (Qualifying), Flinders University

1969: Diploma of Military Studies (Merit), RMC – Duntroon

Current roles

Professor Emeritus, Strategic and Defence Studies Centre (SDSC), Coral Bell School of Asia Pacific Affairs, The Australian National University (ANU)

Official Historian of Australian Peacekeeping, Humanitarian and Post–Cold War Operations since March 2004

Previous appointments

Academic

1999–2014: Professor of Australian Defence History, SDSC, ANU

1996–1999: Senior Fellow, SDSC, ANU

1994–1996: Fellow, SDSC, ANU

1990–1994: Research Officer (Grade 2), SDSC, ANU

Military

2003: Special Project—Australian Strategic Command in the Iraq War—Australian Defence College (Army Reserve appointment)

1998–2002: Head, Land Warfare Studies Centre (Army Reserve appointment)

1990–1998: Inactive Army Reserve

1987–1990: Directing Staff (Research), Joint Services Staff College

1984–1987: Military Visiting Fellow, UNSW at the Australian Defence Force Academy (ADFA)

1984–1985: Head of Chief of the General Staff (CGS) Exercise Staff, Army Headquarters

1984: Staff Officer, CGS Office, Army Headquarters

1983: Course member, Australian Command and Staff College

1981–1982: Staff Officer in Directorate of Combat Development, Army Headquarters

1978–1980: Full-time study, Department of International Relations, ANU

1977: Officer Commanding A Company, 1st Battalion, the Royal Australian Regiment (RAR)

1976: Adjutant, 1 RAR

1974–1975: Full-time study, Faculty of Military Studies, Royal Military College (RMC) of Australia, Duntroon

1972–1973: Adjutant, Adelaide University Regiment

1970–1971: Commander 11 Platoon, 3 RAR

1970: Officer trainee, Infantry Centre

1966–1969: Staff Cadet, RMC of Australia, Duntroon

Awards

2015: Elected Fellow of the Academy of the Social Sciences in Australia (FASSA)

2015: Prime Minister's Literary Award for History (joint winner)

2015: St Ermin's Hotel Intelligence Book of the Year

2009: Member of the Order of Australia (AM) for service to military history

1981: JG Crawford Prize for most outstanding ANU PhD thesis

1977: Churchill Fellowship

1969: CEW Bean Prize for History, RMC – Duntroon

1969: Blamey Prize for first in the Arts class, RMC – Duntroon

Professional memberships

Royal United Services Institute for Defence and Security Studies Australia

The Society for Military History (US)

Other professional activities

Churchill Fellowship recipient (1977) to visit and carry out research at military history institutions in Canada, the US and the UK

Member of the Council of the United Service Institute of the ACT (1981–1982)

Member of the Australian War Memorial committee preparing a proposal for an Atlas of Australia at War (1983)

Foundation treasurer and committee member of the Association for the History of Australian Defence and Foreign Policy (1982–1988)

Associate and, later, member of the International Institute for Strategic Studies (IISS) (1984–2004)

Member of the ACT Consultative Committee for the International Year of Peace (1985–1986)

Member of the Australian Dictionary of Biography armed services working party (1988–2020; Chair 1994–2020)

Member of the RSL National Defence Committee (1990–1998)

Member of the Australian Army's Military History Advisory Committee (1993–present)

Consultant to the Department of Veterans' Affairs (1985–2001)

Consultant to the Commonwealth Superannuation Corporation in a matter concerning eligibility for pensions (1995)

Consultant to the Australian Army, advising on force structure and military history issues (1991–2008)

Historical adviser to the Prime Minister: accompanied Prime Minister Keating to Kokoda in Papua New Guinea in April 1992 for the 50th anniversary celebrations

Lecturer on the cruise ship *Fairstar* to celebrate the 50th anniversary of the Battle of the Coral Sea (1992)

Adviser to various publishers on manuscripts for publication (1981–present)

Referee for articles for professional journals in Australia and overseas

Author of numerous articles for newspapers such as *The Age*, *The Sydney Morning Herald* and *The Australian*

Member of the ACT Accreditation Panel to consider postgraduate qualifications in various Australian Defence Force (ADF) schools and colleges (1993–1995)

Editor of the Australian Army History Series (1994–2012)

Member of the Social Sciences Library Advisory Committee, ANU (1995–2004)

Member of the Joint Services Staff College (JSSC) Academic Advisory Board (1995–1998)

Visiting Fellow in Military History, Australian Army Command and Staff College (1996–2001)

Member of the Editorial Advisory Board of the *Journal of Conflict Studies* (1995–2008)

Member of the Board of the *Australian Dictionary of Biography* (1996–2020)

Historical adviser to the Kokoda Track Memorial Walkaway project at Concord Hospital, Sydney (1997)

Historical consultant to the AWM (1997–1998, 2004, 2012)

Armed forces editor, *Australian Dictionary of Biography* (2001–2020)

Historical adviser to the Battle for Australia Commemoration Committee (1999–2008)

Member of the ACT Government's Veterans' Memorial Reference Group (2004–2006)

Member of the Australian Army Battle Honours Committee (2007–2022)

Member of the Defence Honours and Awards Appeals Tribunal (2008–2015), a statutory government appointment

Member of Australian Army Journal Editorial Board (2008–2012)

Member of the Australian Government's Anzac Centenary Advisory Board (2011–2014)

Interviewee on numerous television and radio programs and in documentaries (1977–present)

Appendix 2: David Horner: publications

Books

Crisis of Command: Australian Generalship and the Japanese Threat, 1941–1943. Canberra: Australian National University Press, 1978.

New Directions in Strategic Thinking (editor, with Robert O'Neill). London: George Allen & Unwin, 1981.

Australian Defence Policy for the 1980s (editor, with Robert O'Neill). St Lucia: University of Queensland Press, 1982.

High Command: Australia and Allied Strategy, 1939–1945. Sydney: George Allen & Unwin, and Canberra: Australian War Memorial, 1982. Republished as *High Command: Australia's Struggle for an Independent War Strategy, 1939–1945*. Sydney: Allen & Unwin, 1992. Republished with the same title by Routledge: Abingdon, 2021. doi.org/10.4324/9781003120193.

The Commanders: Australian Military Leadership in the Twentieth Century (editor and principal contributor). Sydney: George Allen & Unwin, 1984. Republished 1992. Republished 2021 with the same title by Routledge: Abingdon. doi.org/10.4324/9781003119708.

Australian Higher Command in the Vietnam War. Canberra: Strategic and Defence Studies Centre, 1986.

SAS: Phantoms of the Jungle: A History of the Australian Special Air Service. Sydney: Allen & Unwin, 1989. Republished 1991 and 1992.

Duty First: The Royal Australian Regiment in War and Peace (editor and principal contributor). Sydney: Allen & Unwin, 1990.

Reshaping the Australian Army: Challenges for the 1990s (editor). Canberra: Strategic and Defence Studies Centre, 1991.

General Vasey's War. Melbourne: Melbourne University Press, 1992.

Strategic Studies in a Changing World: Global, Regional and Australian Perspectives (editor, with Desmond Ball). Canberra: Strategic and Defence Studies Centre, 1992.

When the War Came to Australia: Memories of the Second World War (with Joanna Penglase). Sydney: Allen & Unwin, 1992.

The Gulf Commitment: The Australian Defence Force's First War. Melbourne: Melbourne University Press, 1992.

The Army and the Future: Land Forces in Australia and South-East Asia (editor). Canberra: Directorate of Departmental Publications, Defence Centre, 1993.

The Battles that Shaped Australia: The Australian's *Anniversary Essays* (editor). Sydney: Allen & Unwin, 1994.

The Gunners: A History of Australian Artillery. Sydney: Allen & Unwin, 1995.

Armies and Nation-Building: Past Experience—Future Prospects (editor). Canberra: Strategic and Defence Studies Centre, 1995.

Inside the War Cabinet: Directing Australia's War Effort, 1939–1945. Sydney: Allen & Unwin, 1996.

Breaking the Codes: Australia's KGB Network (with Desmond Ball). Sydney: Allen & Unwin, 1998.

Blamey: The Commander-in-Chief. Sydney: Allen & Unwin, 1998.

Defence Supremo: Sir Frederick Shedden and the Making of Australian Defence Policy. Sydney: Allen & Unwin, 2000.

Making the Australian Defence Force. Vol. 4 of The Australian Centenary History of Defence. Melbourne: Oxford University Press, 2001.

The Second World War (1): The Pacific. Oxford: Osprey, 2002.

SAS: Phantoms of War: A History of the Australian Special Air Service. Sydney: Allen & Unwin, 2002.

Strategic Command: General Sir John Wilton and Australia's Asian Wars. Melbourne: Oxford University Press, 2005.

Duty First: A History of the Royal Australian Regiment, 2nd ed. (editor, with Jean Bou). Sydney: Allen & Unwin, 2008.

Australian Peacekeeping: 1947–2007 (editor, with Peter Londey and Jean Bou). Melbourne: Cambridge University Press, 2009.

In Action with the SAS (with Neil Thomas). Sydney: Allen & Unwin, 2009.

Australia's Military History for Dummies. Milton: Wiley, 2010.

Australia and the New World Order: From Peacekeeping to Peace Enforcement: 1988–1991. Melbourne: Cambridge University Press, 2011. doi.org/10.1017/cbo9780511779459.

The Good International Citizen: Australian Peacekeeping in Asia, Africa and Europe: 1991–1993 (with John Connor). Melbourne: Cambridge University Press, 2014. doi.org/10.1017/cbo9781139196437.

The Spy Catchers: The Official History of ASIO 1949–1963. Sydney: Allen & Unwin, 2014.

Gallipoli 100 (consultant editor). Sydney: Faircount Media, 2014.

The Limits of Peacekeeping: Australian Missions in Africa and the Americas, 1992–2005 (with Jean Bou, Bob Breen, Garth Pratten and Miesje de Vogel). Melbourne: Cambridge University Press, 2019. doi.org/10.1017/9781316182338.

The Long Search for Peace: Observer Missions and Beyond, 1947–2006 (with Peter Londey and Rhys Crawley). Melbourne: Cambridge University Press, 2019. doi.org/10.1017/9781108628938.

Strategy and Command: Issues in Australia's Twentieth-Century Wars. Melbourne: Cambridge University Press, 2021. doi.org/10.1017/9781009067041.

The War Game: Australian War Leadership from Gallipoli to Iraq. Sydney: Allen & Unwin, 2022.

Monographs

History of the Prince Alfred College Cadet Unit. Adelaide: Gillingham, 1964.

'Australian and Allied Intelligence in the Pacific in the Second World War'. Working Paper 28, Strategic and Defence Studies Centre, Canberra, 1980.

Report to the Winston Churchill Trust on the Study of Military History. 1978.

The Army in the 1980s (compiler). Canberra: Australian Army, 1982.

Land Forces in the Defence of Australia (with Stewart Woodman). Report prepared for the Directorate of Army Studies, February 1991.

Chronicling the Peacekeepers: Report on the Feasibility of an Official History of Australian Peacekeeping Operations. Commissioned by the Australian War Memorial, May 2002.

Australian Strategic Command in the Iraq War 2002–2003 (with Leanne Rees). Report prepared for the Australian Department of Defence, July 2003.

Australia's Strategic Involvement in the Middle East: An Overview. Emirates Lecture Series 56. Abu Dhabi: Emirates Center for Strategic Studies and Research, 2004.

Researching Recent Conflicts: Report on the Feasibility of an Official History of Australian Operations in Iraq and Afghanistan. Commissioned by the Australian War Memorial, March 2012.

The Report of the Inquiry into Unresolved Recognition for Past Acts of Naval and Military Gallantry and Valour (with Gary Bornholt, Don Chalmers, Mark Lax and Alan Rose). Canberra: Defence Honours and Awards Appeals Tribunal, January 2013.

Journal articles and chapters of books, et al.
(does not include chapters in books edited by Professor Horner)

'The Military Lessons of the Seven Weeks War'. *Army Journal* (December 1968): 44–49.

'The Defence of Sydney in 1820' (with GP Walsh). *Army Journal* (May 1969): 13–23.

'The Fall of Atlanta'. *Army Journal* (June 1969): 28–44.

'Maj-Gen George Vasey'. In *Army Diary 1976*, edited by Colonel FP Johnson, 8. Golspie, Scotland: Method Publishing Co, 1975.

'Special Intelligence in the South-West Pacific Area in World War II'. *Australian Outlook* (December 1978): 310–27.

'Crisis of Command: Australian Generalship and the Japanese Threat'. *Journal of the Royal United Services Institute of Australia* (April 1981): 69–78.

'Staff Corps Versus Militia: The Australian Experience in World War II'. *Defence Force Journal* (January/February 1981): 13–26.

'Australia and Allied Strategy in the Pacific, 1941–1945'. *Defence Force Journal* (November/December 1981): 45–53.

'Australian Estimates of the Japanese Threat, 1905–1941'. In *Estimating Foreign Military Power*, edited by Philip Towle, 139–71. London: Croom Helm, 1982. doi.org/10.4324/9781003150916-5.

'High Command: The Australian Experience'. In *Tookarook* (Journal of the Australian Command and Staff College), 1983. Also in *Defence Force Journal* (September/October 1984): 11–18.

'Introduction'. In George Johnston, *War Diary 1942*, 1–6. Sydney: William Collins, 1984.

'The Military Aspects of Curtin's Overseas Visit in 1944'. *Defence Force Journal* (November/December 1984): 17–28.

'John Curtin as a War Leader'. In *Australia in World War II*, edited by R Lewis, 73–80. Melbourne: History Teachers' Association of Victoria, 1985.

'Introduction'. In reprints of Gavin Long, *To Benghazi* and *Greece, Crete and Syria*, xvii–xxi; xv–xxi. Sydney: William Collins, 1986.

'Strategies of Land Warfare'. *Defence Force Journal* (January/February 1987): 45–55.

'Vasey in Greece'. *Journal of the Australian War Memorial* (April 1987): 21–32.

'Military History in Australia'. In *Australians on War and Peace*, edited by Hugh Smith, 9–14. Canberra: Australian Defence Studies Centre, Australian Defence Force Academy, 1987.

'Australia under Threat of Invasion' and 'Strategic Policy-Making 1943–1945'. In *Australia: Two Centuries of War and Peace*, edited by Michael McKernan and Margaret Browne, 245–95. Sydney: Allen and Unwin, 1988.

'MacArthur and Blamey: The Problem of Coalition Warfare'. In *We Shall Return! MacArthur's Commanders and the Defeat of Japan*, edited by William Leary, 23–59. Lexington: University Press of Kentucky, 1988.

'A Complex Command: The Role of the Commander, Australian Force, Vietnam'. *Journal of the Australian War Memorial* (October 1988): 19–30.

'The Australian Army and Indonesia's Confrontation with Malaysia'. *Australian Outlook* (April 1989): 61–76.

'The ADF and the Operational Level of War'. *Defence Force Journal* (September/October 1989): 3–12.

'The Continental School of Strategic Thought'. *Defence Force Journal* (May/June 1990): 35–46.

'Military Biography' and 'Historians in the Australian Defence Force'. *Journal of the Australian War Memorial* (November 1991): 23–26; 31–32.

'The Security Dimension of Australian Foreign Policy'. In *Australia in a Changing World: New Policy Directions*, edited by Fedor Mediansky, 83–101. Sydney: Maxwell Macmillan, 1992.

'The ADF in the Gulf War'. *Journal of the Royal United Services Institute of Australia* (October 1992): 34–43.

'Digger bashing British'. *Pageant: Australia's History Magazine* 3 (April/May 1993): 4–7.

'Defending Australia in 1942'. *War and Society* (May 1993): 1–20.

'Strategy and High Command'. In *The RAAF in the Southwest Pacific Area 1942–1945*, 52–72. Canberra: RAAF Air Power Studies Centre, 1993.

'Writing History in the Australian Army', *Australian Journal of Politics and History* 40, no. 1 (1994): 72–79.

'The Chinese Liaison Officer in Australia, 1942–1945'. *Journal of the Australian War Memorial* 25 (October 1994): 12–22.

'The Military Strategy and Command Aspects of the Australian Army's Amphibious Operations in the South-West Pacific Area'. In *Australian Army Amphibious Operations in the South-West Pacific: 1942–45*, edited by Glenn Wahlert, 27–49 (Sydney: Army Doctrine Centre, 1995).

'Australia and the Pacific War'. *NIRA* [National Institute for Research Advancement, Japan] *Review* (Summer 1995): 36–38.

'Australian Army Strategic Planning Between the Wars'. In *Serving Vital Interests: Australia's Strategic Planning in Peace and War*, edited by P Dennis and J Grey, 75–101. Canberra: School of History, Australian Defence Force Academy, 1996.

Various articles on Defence in the *Australian Encyclopaedia*, 1996.

'The Army's Role in the Maritime Defence of Australia'. In *In Search of a Maritime Strategy: The Maritime Element in Australian Defence Planning since 1901*, edited by David Stevens, 19–42. Canberra: Strategic and Defence Studies Centre, 1997.

'Security Objectives'. In *Australian Foreign Policy: Into the New Millenium*, edited by FA Mediansky, 73–91. Melbourne: Macmillan, 1997.

'From Korea to Pentropic: The Army in the 1950s and Early 1960s'. In *The Second Fifty Years: The Australian Army 1947–1997*, edited by Peter Dennis and Jeffrey Grey, 48–70. Canberra: School of History, Australian Defence Force Academy, 1997.

'Combined Operations in the Southwest Pacific: The Australian Army in MacArthur's Operations'. In *The U.S. Army and World War II: Selected Papers from the Army's Commemorative Conferences*, edited by Judith L Bellafaire, 287–302. Washington, DC: Center of Military History, United States Army, 1998.

'Force Structure: The Hardware Dimension'. In *Australia's Security in the 21st Century*, edited by J Mohan Malik, 168–93. Sydney: Allen & Unwin, 1998.

'Australian Army Leadership: The Historical Background'. In *Preparing Future Leaders: Officer Education and Training for the Twenty-First Century*, edited by Hugh Smith, 83–106. Canberra: Australian Defence Studies Centre, Australian Defence Force Academy, 1998.

'Curtin and MacArthur at War'. *Wartime* 2 (April 1998): 34–40. Canberra: Australian War Memorial.

'Australian Military Biographies'. In *Ranging Shots: New Directions in Australian Military History*, edited by Carl Bridge, 81–92. London: Sir Robert Menzies Centre for Australian Studies, University of London, 1998.

'The Final Campaigns of the Pacific War'. In *1945 War and Peace in the Pacific: Selected Essays*, edited by Peter Dennis, 82–94. Canberra: Australian War Memorial, 1999.

'The Influence of the Boer War on Australian Commanders in the First World War'. In *The Boer War: Army, Nation and Empire*, edited by Peter Dennis and Jeffrey Grey, 173–90. Canberra: Army History Unit, 2000.

'Stress on Higher Commanders in Future War'. In *The Human Face of Warfare*, edited by Michael Evans and Alan Ryan, 134–59. Sydney: Allen & Unwin, 2000.

'MacArthur: An Australian Perspective'. In *MacArthur and the American Century: A Reader*, edited by William M Leary, 109–42. Lincoln: University of Nebraska Press, 2001.

'Field Marshal Sir Thomas Blamey and the Australian Army'. *Australian Defence Force Journal* 18 (May/June 2001): 43–52.

Entries on: 'Australian Military Forces, 1939–45'; 'Armour'; 'Artillery'; 'Special Air Service Regiment'; 'Field Marshal Sir Thomas Blamey'; 'Development of the Australian Defence Force'; 'Intelligence'; and 'Land Warfare Studies Centre'. In *Australian Defence: Sources and Statistics: The Australian Centenary History of Defence*, Volume VI, edited by Joan Beaumont, 118–20, 129, 130–32, 137, 140–41, 239, 244. Melbourne: Oxford University Press, 2001.

'One Hundred Years of Army History'. In *A Centenary of Service: One Hundred Years of the Australian Army*, edited by Peter Dennis and Jeffrey Grey, 61–76. Canberra: Army History Unit, 2001.

'Australia/New Zealand: Armed Forces' and 'World War II: Armed Forces, Australia and New Zealand'. In *Reader's Guide to Military History*, edited by Charles Messenger, 39–40, 726. London: Fitzroy Dearborn Publishers, 2001.

'Field Marshal Sir Thomas Blamey and the Australian Army'. *Journal of the Royal United Service Institute of Australia* 23 (December 2001): 43–52.

'Kokoda Commanders'. In *Wartime* 18 (April 2002): 6–11.

'Towards a Philosophy of Australian Command'. *Command Papers* 2/2002 (June 2002): 24. Weston Creek: Centre for Defence Command Leadership and Management Studies.

'The Evolution of Australian Higher Command Arrangements'. *Command Papers* 3/2002 (July 2002): 30. Weston Creek: Centre for Defence Command Leadership and Management Studies.

'Kokoda Heroes'. *Wartime* 20 (October 2002): 16–19.

'Higher Direction of the Army in the Vietnam War'. In *The Australian Army and the Vietnam War, 1962–1972*, edited by Peter Dennis and Jeffrey Grey, 33–57. Canberra: Army History Unit, 2002.

'Strategy and Generalship: Strategic and Operational Planning in the 1943 Offensives'. In *The Foundations of Victory: The Pacific War 1943–1944*, edited by Peter Dennis and Jeffrey Grey, 24–43. Canberra: Army History Unit, 2004.

'Australia's Strategy and Command in New Guinea'. *Pacific War* 4 (July/August 2004): 3–8.

'General MacArthur's War: The South and Southwest Pacific Campaigns'. In *The Pacific War: From Pearl Harbor to Hiroshima*, edited by Daniel Marston, 119–42. Oxford: Osprey, 2005. doi.org/10.5040/9781472895967.ch-007.

'The ANZAC Contribution: Australia and New Zealand in the Pacific War'. In *The Pacific War: From Pearl Harbor to Hiroshima*, edited by Daniel Marston, 143–58. Oxford: Osprey, 2005. doi.org/10.5040/9781472895967.ch-008.

'Australia and Coalition Warfare in the Second World War'. In *Entangling Alliances: Coalition Warfare in the Twentieth Century*, edited by Peter Dennis and Jeffrey Grey, 105–24. Sydney: Australian Military History Publications, 2005.

'Recent Military Operations and Their Place in Australian History'. *United Service* 57, no. 2 (Winter 2006): 11–16.

'Reflections'. In *Vietnam: Our War—Our Peace*, edited by J Moremon, 132–33. Canberra: Department of Veterans' Affairs, 2006.

'Malaya and Singapore in the Context of the Defence of Australia'. In *Legends and Legacies: Perspectives on Australian Soldiers' Battle and Captivity Experiences in the Far East During the Second World War*, edited by Rosalind Hearder, 8–15. Sydney: 2/15 Field Regiment Association, 2006.

'The Higher Command Structure for Joint ADF Operations'. In *History as Policy: Framing the Debate on the Future of Australia's Defence Policy*, edited by Ron Huisken and Meredith Thatcher, 143–62. Canberra Papers on Strategy and Defence 167. Canberra: ANU ePress, 2007, doi.org/10.22459/hp.12.2007.10.

'Chronicling the Peacekeepers: Problems of Writing the Official History of Australian Peacekeeping, Humanitarian and Post–Cold War Operations'. *History Australia* 5, no. 1 (2008): 10.1–10.11. doi.org/10.2104/ha080010.

'Lieutenant Thomas Currie Derrick VC, Australian Soldier'. In *I Am Soldier: War Stories from the Ancient World to the 20th Century*, edited by Robert O'Neill, 182–85. Oxford: Osprey, 2009.

'Deploying and Sustaining INTERFET in East Timor in 1999'. In *Raise, Train and Sustain: Delivering Land Combat Power*, edited by Peter Dennis and Jeffrey Grey, 204–29. Sydney: Australian Military History Publications, 2010.

'The British Empire in the Pacific War'. In *The Pacific War as Total War. NIDS International Forum on War History: Proceedings*, 103–14. Tokyo: National Institute for Defense Studies, March 2012.

'Australia in 1942—A Pivotal Year. In *Australia 1942: In the Shadow of War*, edited by Peter Dean, 11–29. Melbourne: Cambridge University Press, 2013. doi.org/10.1017/cbo9781139540681.004.

'MacArthur and Curtin: Deciding Australian War Strategy in 1943'. In *Australia 1943: The Liberation of New Guinea*, edited by Peter Dean, 25–44. Melbourne: Cambridge University Press, 2013. doi.org/10.1017/cbo9781107445239.005.

'Britain and the Campaigns in Greece and Crete'. In *Defense of the Wider Realm: The Diplomacy and the Strategy of the Protection of Islands in War.* Proceedings of the National Institute for Defense Studies International Forum on War History, Tokyo, March 2014.

'The Army, the Navy and the Defence of Australia and the Empire 1919–1939'. In *Armies and Maritime Strategy: 2013 Chief of Army History Conference,* edited by Peter Dennis, 119–44. Sydney: Big Sky Publishing, 2014.

'Sir Frederick Shedden: The Forerunner'. In *The Seven Dwarfs and the Age of the Mandarins*, edited by Samuel Furphy, 113–24. Canberra: ANU Press, 2015. doi.org/10.22459/sdam.07.2015.05.

'Advancing National Interests: Deciding Australia's War Strategy, 1944–45'. In *Australia 1944–45: Victory in the Pacific,* edited by Peter Dean, 9–27. Melbourne: Cambridge University Press, 2015. doi.org/10.1017/cbo97813 16015445.004.

'The Emerging Strategic Environment'. In *On Ops: Lessons and Challenges for the Australian Army Since East Timor,* edited by Tom Frame and Albert Palazzo, 33–50. Sydney: UNSW Press, 2016.

'The AIF's Commanders: Learning on the Job'. In *The AIF in Battle: How the Australian Imperial Force Fought, 1914–1918*, edited by Jean Bou, 108–35. Melbourne: Melbourne University Press, 2016.

'The Evolution of Australian Official War Histories'. In *War, Strategy and History: Essays in Honour of Professor Robert O'Neill,* edited by Daniel Martson and Tamara Leahy, 73–90. Canberra: ANU Press, 2016. doi.org/10.22459/wsh.05.2016.07.

'Researching History at SDSC'. In *A National Asset: 50 Years of the Strategic and Defence Studies Centre,* edited by Desmond Ball and Andrew Carr, 121–36. Canberra: ANU Press, 2016. doi.org/10.22459/na.08.2016.07.

'Blamey: The Commander-in-Chief'. *Remembrance: Official Magazine of the Shrine of Remembrance, Melbourne* 1, no. 2 (November 2016): 19–22.

'Preparing for War 1901–1914'. In *1914: Mobilising for the Great War*, edited by Bobbie Oliver, 4–18. Sydney: Big Sky Publishing, 2016.

'Peacekeeping, Humanitarian and Post–Cold War Operations'. In *Charles Bean: Man, Myth, Legacy*, edited by Peter Stanley, 182–98. Sydney: UNSW Press, 2017.

'Kokoda: An Epic in Australian History?'. In *Kokoda: Beyond the Legend*, edited by Karl James, 288–305. Melbourne: Cambridge University Press, 2017. doi.org/10.1017/9781316995617.018.

'Australians as Peacekeepers'. *Wartime* 88 (Spring 2019): 52–58.

'Why was 5 RAR stationed at Nui Dat?'. In *Vietnam Vanguard: The 5th Battalion's Approach to Counter-Insurgency 1966*, edited by Ron Boxall and Robert O'Neill, 21–44. Canberra: ANU Press, 2020. doi.org/10.22459/vv.2019.02.

'Australian Higher Command in the Korean War: The Experience of Brigadier John Wilton'. In *In from the Cold: Reflections on Australia's Korean War*, edited by John Blaxland, Michael Kelly and Liam Brewin Higgins, 165–82. Canberra: ANU Press, 2020. doi.org/10.22459/iftc.2019.08.

'Eighty Years of Regional Engagement'. In *An Army of Influence: the Australian Army's Connection with the Region*, edited by 2019 Chief of Army History Conference, 5–24. Canberra: Australian Army History Unit, 2020.

'The "Fourth Arm" of Australia's Defence: ASIO and the early Cold War'. In *Fighting Australia's Cold War: The Nexus of Strategy and Operations in a Multipolar Asia, 1945–1965*, edited by Peter Dean and Tristan Moss, 63–72. Canberra: ANU Press, 2021. doi.org/10.22459/facw.2021.03.

'Eighty Years of Regional Engagement'. In *An Army of Influence: Eighty Years of Regional Engagement*, edited by Craig Stockings and Peter Dennis, 20–37. Melbourne: Cambridge University Press, 2021. doi.org/10.1017/9781009086929.003.

'War Leadership'. *Wartime* 102 (Autumn 2023): 10–17.

Entries on: Sgt MV Buckley; Maj Gen WL Eames; Lt-Col Howell Price and his brothers; Field Marshal Sir Thomas Blamey; Lt-Gen Sir John Lavarack; Gen Douglas MacArthur; Sir Frederick Shedden; Maj-Gen RA Vasey; Gen Sir John Wilton; Major Susan Felsche; and Sir Charles Spry in the *Australian Dictionary of Biography*. www.adb.online.anu.edu.au.

Book reviews in: *Defence Force Journal, Australian Journal of Politics and History, RMC Historical Journal, Journal of the United Service Institute of Australia, Yolla, Journal of the Australian War Memorial, The Age, The Australian, The Sydney Morning Herald, Conflict Quarterly, Australian Book Review, Australian Journal of Political Science, Australian Journal of International Affairs, The Journal of Military History, Wartime* and *Labour History*.

www.ingramcontent.com/pod-product-compliance
Lightning Source LLC
Chambersburg PA
CBHW050525300426
44113CB00012B/1962